PROBLEMS IN EVIDENCE

Fifth Edition

∎ ∎ ∎

By
Kenneth S. Broun
Henry Brandis Professor of Law, University of North Carolina

Robert P. Mosteller
J. Dickson Phillips Professor of Law, University of North Carolina

Paul C. Giannelli
Albert J. Weatherhead, III & Richard W. Weatherhead Professor of Law, Case Western Reserve University

AMERICAN CASEBOOK SERIES®

WEST®
A Thomson Reuters business

Mat #40769098

American Casebook Series is a trademark registered in the U.S. Patent and Trademark Office.

COPYRIGHT © 1973, 1981, 1988, WEST PUBLISHING CO.
© 2001 West, a Thomson business
© 2011 Thomson Reuters

    610 Opperman Drive
    St. Paul, MN 55123
    1–800–313–9378

Printed in the United States of America

ISBN: 978–0–314–19889–1

PREFACE TO THE FIFTH EDITION

Ken Broun and Bob Mosteller welcome Paul Giannelli to this edition. Paul joins us with excellent contributions very much like those made by past co-authors Dean Lou Bilinois, John Strong, and Robert Meisenholder. As has been our consistent practice, while we have made refinements in a number of the problems in the Fourth Edition, the basic framework remains.

We have added more than forty new problems. Many concern the range of issues create by the Supreme Court's new approach to confrontation in *Crawford v. Washington*. A number have been added for expert testimony and revisions have been made regarding DNA evidence. Others deal with character evidence in criminal cases, including other crimes evidence and prior sexual assaults in both civil and criminal cases. Some examine the challenges presented by new technology when evidence comes from cell phones and computer hard drives. A new problem also raises issues that the new federal rule concerning "inadvertent disclosure" of privileged attorney-client material can help resolve.

Long-time users of this Problem Book will find some of the questions in what we believe are more logical locations. Scientific expert testimony has been moved from Chapter 8, which concerns the relevancy concept, to Chapter 12 with other aspects of expert testimony. Conversely, problems concerning the rape shield principle have been moved from Chapter 12 to Chapter 8 where other aspects of character evidence are examined.

As with earlier editions, the Fifth Edition provides citations to the McCormick hornbook to make it convenient for the two books to be used together. It is also coordinated with Broun, Mosteller, and Giannelli, Cases and Materials in Evidence (7th ed. 2006).

The authors of this edition owe much to the feedback and suggestions of law professors and students who have provided insights for improvements on existing problems and inspiration for new ones. We find great value and vitality in the use of problems in evidence classes. New generations of students see wrinkles to long-used problems and alterations in technology and social understanding work their own revisions to the appropriate approach to how to answer unchanged questions. We hope our explicit additions to and revisions of the solid foundation of previous editions carry continue its vitality as a valuable teaching tool for the foundational course of evidence.

KENNETH S. BROUN
ROBERT P. MOSTELLER
PAUL C. GIANNELLI

October, 2010

Preface to the Fourth Edition

One of the original authors of this problem book, Kenneth S. Broun, is joined in this edition by an author of the third edition, Robert P. Mosteller, and by a new colleague, Louis D. Bilionis. The authors of this edition gratefully acknowledge the excellent contributions made by John William Strong and Robert Meisenholder to the concept of the book and to a great many of the problems.

Virtually all of the problems contained in the third edition remain in this edition. However, many of them have been rewritten. We have edited all problems, in some instances substantially, in order to make sure that they are all readable, easily understood and accessible to today's law students. We have tried to modernize the problems to take into account current technology, especially in dealing with demonstrative evidence and writings.

In addition, we have added more than seventy new problems. In some instances, the problems were added in order to provide alternative situations involving issues raised by existing problems. In others cases, we have added problems that we think raise interesting evidentiary issues that were not covered in the prior editions. For example, the prior editions contained no problems in Chapter 2, Limitations of the Adversary System. This edition contains four problems dealing with the subject matter of that chapter, which can be used instead of or in connection with cases.

Like the third edition in connection with an earlier version of the same casebook, this edition of the problem book is organized so that it can be used easily with Strong, Broun and Mosteller, Cases and Materials in Evidence (5th Ed. 1995). As was the case with all of the earlier editions, the book can also be used with the McCormick hornbook and no casebook. Citations are provided to the appropriate McCormick sections and to the applicable Federal Rule of Evidence.

The authors of this edition thank the several generations of students and their teachers who have used these problems at many law schools. Many of the improvements in this edition have come about as a result of input from students and faculty throughout the lifetime of this book. We hope that they will continue to provide commentary to us on both the old and the new problems in the book.

Kenneth S. Broun
Robert P. Mosteller
Louis D. Bilionis

October, 2000

PREFACE TO THE THIRD EDITION

The original authors of this problem book, Kenneth S. Broun and Robert Meisenholder, are joined in this edition by John William Strong and Robert P. Mosteller. Professor Meisenholder has retired but has graciously permitted his name to be continued on the book and allowed the continuation of his excellent contributions to the first and second editions.

Most of the problems contained in the earlier editions remain in the third edition but many new problems are added both as alternatives and as problems which raise issues not covered in the earlier books.

The most significant change in this edition is organizational. The book is now organized so that it can be used easily with the new edition of Cleary, Strong, Broun and Mosteller, "Cases and Materials in Evidence," (West Publishing Co. 1988). The new organization gives the teacher the choice of using the problems with the McCormick hornbook, as was suggested in the first and second editions, or with the Cleary, Strong, et al. casebook. Other casebooks might also be used in connection with the problems although further organizational changes would almost certainly have to be made.

The authors believe that the use of the problems with the McCormick hornbook alone is a viable way in which to present the course. The students have the opportunity to work with the facts as contained in the problems and to refer to the hornbook for the applicable law. Nevertheless, law teachers are used to working with cases and to providing students with examples of legal analysis through the use of cases. Furthermore, cases provide other fact situations and possible solutions to legal problems which may be valuable in class discussion of the problems. The casebook also provides a good opportunity for coverage in some subject matter areas which do not lend themselves well to the problem area. A good example of this is Chapter 2 of the casebook, "Limitations of the Adversary System." The authors believe that this is an area which can be better covered by the case method. A Chapter 2 is included in the problem book for organizational purposes only. No problems are provided.

As a result of the change to possible use with the casebook, Appendix C to the second edition, which consisted of cases, has been eliminated. Appendices A and B, which are case files, have been continued. Teachers who have used Appendix B in the second edition should be alert to some significant revisions in that file.

The new authors of this problem book join with its original authors in expressing their appreciation to a growing number of students at an expanding number of law schools who have used these problems. This new edition, like its predecessors, would not be possible without the input from students on the problems contained in the book and on the usefulness of the problem method in general. The authors also want to express their appreciation to the many law teachers throughout the country who have used the earlier editions of the book and provided useful comments on various problems.

Kenneth S. Broun
John William Strong
Robert Mosteller

June, 1988

PREFACE TO THE SECOND EDITION

Introduction. The first edition has received much greater use and acceptance in more law schools than we could have expected. Of course we are gratified that "our rather ambitious hope" that the first edition would "furnish impetus for use of the 'problem method' in the teaching of the usual course in evidence" has been realized. Very important was the use of the first edition by various instructors despite a long tradition of teaching evidence by the case method. We are very indebted to those persons for their pioneering efforts in showing that the use of problems as a basic tool for teaching evidence is feasible.

There are a number of reasons for a second edition. After the first edition was published the Federal Rules of Evidence were adopted for the federal courts and were copied in a number of states. Although the first edition was usable and was used in covering the new federal rules, added or substituted problems make this edition more adaptable for use under a case law system, the Federal Rules or other rule systems. A second important reason for a second edition should be mentioned. Some instructors may have been concerned about using a problem book in several successive years. From our own experience in reusing the first edition (and apparently from the experience of others), we believe that in many ways a problem book is more reusable than a casebook; the class discussion is even less predictable. Nevertheless, the addition of new problems and new types of problems furnishes the basis for a greater selection of problems and thus makes continuing use of the same volume more attractive. In preparing this edition we have retained many of the problems in the first edition, but have also added many new problems in order to increase the number of problems from which selection may be made. Finally, a second edition furnishes the opportunity to add to both the practical and theoretical content of this work in the employment of the problem method. To this end, two new features are added. Appendices A and B contain realistic partial case files that furnish the basis for problems which are distributed throughout the volume and which may be used at the instructor's discretion. Appendix C contains a few important cases, primarily cases referring to the Sixth Amendment, which the instructor may use in raising constitutional questions that are closely related to certain evidence rules.

Types of Problems Included in this Book. Some of the new problems are similar in form to those in the first edition. Others deal more specifically with the Federal Rules of Evidence or differ from first edition problems in that they are intended solely for use as a basis for student demonstrations of techniques in introducing evidence. Perhaps the most significant innovation in the second edition is the addition of problems based upon the case files contained in Appendices A and B. The use of a number of problems based upon a case file should add both a greater touch of realism to the discussion and, more importantly, enable the student to appreciate the role of the law of evidence in the entire trial process. The other innovation is the use of the edited cases in Appendix C. The cases concerning the right of confrontation could be covered as a unit in traditional case method fashion. However, we suggest instead that the cases be used as background reading in connection with some of the problems concerning the hearsay rule and exceptions to the hearsay rule.

The McCormick Citations. The first paragraph of the similar heading in the Preface to the first edition is pertinent to this second edition. However, contrary to the explanation in the remainder of this part of the Preface to the first edition, the second edition includes a special chapter of problems relating to the admission and exclusion of evidence (Chapter 11).

The Federal Rules Citations. For coverage of the Federal Rules to the extent that an instructor desires, we have included citations to pertinent federal rules at the beginning of each chapter and after each problem. An instructor may want to require that the student obtain West's Federal Rules of Evidence Pamphlet in addition to the Problem Book and McCormick, 2d. It has been our experience that reference to the contents of this pamphlet furnishes ample basis for discussion of the application of the Federal Rules to the problems. Of course, it is possible for the instructor to add the assignment of a federal case or two for a particular problem. By like token, selected problems are usable for coverage of an individualized local code of evidence or system of evidence rules.

Coverage. The remarks in the Preface to the first edition are particularly relevant here. The instant edition furnishes a larger source of problems for selection in order to cover the course in accordance with the wishes of the instructor.

Conclusion. We acknowledge our appreciation to our students who have contributed to our use of the first edition, and now we can add our expression of appreciation to various instructors who have used the first edition. It is our hope that this second edition will further aid and promote the use of a problem method of teaching, a method which we firmly believe has many advantages.

KENNETH S. BROUN
ROBERT MEISENHOLDER

December, 1980

PREFACE TO THE FIRST EDITION

Introduction. It is our rather ambitious hope that the publication of this volume of evidence problems will furnish impetus for use of the "problem method" in the teaching of the usual course in evidence. In expressing this hope, we recognize that the problem method may take various forms. The authors have used problems as the sole basis for class discussion in 11 different classes in three law schools. For the most part, we have assigned only the problems and the cited McCormick hornbook sections to the student. We have been satisfied with this teaching method and, not surprisingly, this book is designed with such a use in mind. However, we believe that these problems also may be used effectively in other ways. Some source other than the McCormick hornbook, such as a casebook, or a combination of sources, such as a casebook and library references, might also provide an effective basis for discussion of the problems. The problems might also be used as a problem supplement for a course in which a casebook is the primary basis for class discussion.

Types of Problems Included in this Book. The problems in this book are, with only a few exceptions, set in the trial court. Our belief is that it is important for the student to see evidentiary problems in that setting. It is in the trial court that evidence questions are almost always finally decided. In the relatively infrequent instance that an evidentiary question reaches the appellate court, the higher court is not in a good position fully to assess the trial court's ruling. The rules of evidence, which give considerable discretion to the trial judge, reflect the inability of the appellate courts to recreate the flavor of the trial. For such reasons, interesting and significant appellate opinions in evidence cases are extremely rare. Problems have no such limitations. Thus, we have tried to create problems that are designed not only to illustrate evidence doctrine but which also cause the student to consider how he or she, as trial judge, might exercise the discretion allowed by the law of evidence. The student will also often be called upon to plan the presentation of evidence and, frequently, to decide whether, as a trial lawyer, he or she would exercise the option to bring an evidence rule into play by an objection or offer of proof. The professor may ask the student actually to conduct some examinations of witnesses based upon the information set forth in these problems. To the extent that such an exercise duplicates exercises in courses such as Trial Advocacy, such a duplication is simply reflective of the fundamental role which the law of evidence plays in the trial and in trial advocacy.

The sources of the problems contained in this book are varied. Some are based upon appellate court cases with variations of the facts. Some are based, in varying degrees, upon unreported incidents in the trial courts. Some are the products of the authors' imaginations.

The problems vary in type, scope, length and difficulty. Our major goal has been to include problems that will suggest variants, that will raise theoretical questions concerning ideal solutions, and that will foster the relation of the law of evidence to practical trial use.

The McCormick Citations. Almost all of the problems in this volume are followed by a citation to McCormick, Evidence (2d Ed. 1972). The citation is shortened to McCormick, 2d Ed., § 00. The cited sections are those which the authors of this book believe are the most pertinent to the issues raised in the problem. It is not our intention to discourage reference to other sections of the hornbook or to any other source. On the contrary, we would encourage both the student and the teacher to consider all aspects of the problem and their variants without limitation to issues raised in particular hornbook sections.

In one area in particular, the McCormick citations may not be complete. Most of the problems will involve, to some extent, questions which concern the procedure of admitting and excluding evidence (McCormick, Chapter 6). However, no attempt is made to refer to pertinent Chapter 6 sections each time such a question is raised. Citations to Chapter 6 sections are included only after problems in the first part of the book on the theory that the student will read those sections in connection with the problems considered early in the course and refer to those sections on his own as new procedural questions arise later. In the event that the teacher elects to omit the early problems which contain the Chapter 6 references, or changes the order in which the problems are to be considered in class, the teacher and the student should both be careful to note the applicability of material contained in Chapter 6 to the problems.

Coverage. The number of problems that we have included in this book is much greater than the number that could be adequately discussed in the average course in evidence. We have deliberately adopted this course in order to provide a choice of problems for coverage of many particular areas—a choice which will permit a reflection of a particular teacher's viewpoint. In our experience, depending upon the type of problem, the usual class coverage will vary from one to three problems.

The selection of problems to be considered in class is, of course, in the discretion of the individual teacher. One may elect to take selected problems from each of the chapters of this book. One may also elect to exclude from coverage certain chapters. For example, one possible exclusion would be the problems contained in Chapters 27 and 28, Burdens of Proof and Presumptions. The subject matter of those chapters may overlap with that of other courses, such as civil and criminal procedure.

One important area of the law of evidence that is entirely excluded from this volume is constitutional privileges. The matter is treated textually in Chapters 13, 14 and 15 of the McCormick hornbook. Neither of the authors covers this material in his basic evidence course. The primary basis for the omission, both from our class coverage and from this book, is the fact that these subjects are usually reviewed adequately in other courses such as

Criminal Law, Criminal Procedure and Constitutional Law. However, intrinsically there is no reason why these subjects may not be covered by problems and individual teachers may wish to supplement this volume with their own problems on constitutional privileges.

Conclusion. By way of acknowledgment, we express our appreciation to our students at the University of Washington, University of North Carolina and University of Texas, who served as a testing ground for almost all of these problems and whose fertile imaginations contributed substantially, not only to the problems themselves, but also to the notion that the problem method could be used successfully in law teaching.

KENNETH S. BROUN
ROBERT MEISENHOLDER

July, 1973

SUMMARY OF CONTENTS

――――――――

TABLE OF CONTENTS

PROBLEMS IN EVIDENCE

Fifth Edition

TOPIC 1

AN INTRODUCTION TO THE ADVERSARY SYSTEM

■ ■ ■

CHAPTER 1

CHARACTERISTICS OF THE
ADVERSARY SYSTEM

■ ■ ■

1–1. Deep in the jungles of the emerging nation of Sagaluci lives a primitive tribe. The tribal members believe that the spirit of the Supreme Being which they worship is incorporated into the deadly cobras found in their area of the jungle and that the actions of the cobras are therefore controlled by the Being. Given these beliefs, the tribe's criminal procedure has been quite simple. A person charged with a crime is "tried" by spending the night in a ten-by-ten foot enclosure with a cobra. If the accused survives, he or she goes free. If the accused does not, of course, the tribal court is spared the bother of a sentencing hearing.

(A) You are the special advisor to the attorney general of Sagaluci. She and you decide to attempt to convince the "cobra" tribe that a trial more closely resembling a modern world model is preferable to trial by ordeal. What are the fundamental differences between trial by ordeal and a modern trial? What arguments would you use to persuade the tribe to change its system?

(B) Assume that you are able to convince the tribe to change its trial procedure. Many models of modern trials are available to you. For example, who should be the trier of fact? A jury? An independent judge? The chief of the tribe? In addition, who should be responsible for the presentation of evidence? Should there be a judge who acts both as the trier of fact and as the principal investigator? (This is the inquisitorial system, common in many European countries.) Should each side, perhaps through an attorney, present its case in a light most favorable to its position? (This is the adversarial system that prevails in English speaking nations.) What are the benefits and detriments of the inquisitorial system as opposed to the adversarial system?

1–2. (A) Daniel is charged with a theft from his place of employment. At trial, the prosecution seeks to admit against him an adoptive admission under Rule 801(d)(2)(B). Generally, the silence of a party is admissible as an adoptive admission when an accusatory statement is made by another person in the party's presence which, if untrue, the party would naturally be expected to deny under all the circumstances.

The prosecution argues that an adoptive admission occurred on the day of Daniel's arrest. He was asked by the store manager to come into the manager's office and was told to have a seat. The manager brought another employee, Helen, into the office. In a conversation between Helen and the manager, Helen stated that she had seen Daniel remove a $100 bill from the cash register and stick it in his coat pocket. Daniel, who was sitting some ten feet away in the manager's office, made no response.

Daniel's counsel objects to the admission of the evidence. In ruling on the objection, what preliminary questions must be resolved? Are they governed by Federal Rule 104(a) or 104(b)?

(B) Randy is charged with the burglary of a home. Under procedures that you should assume were constitutionally valid, the victim, Victor, who had seen the perpetrator run from his home, picked Randy's photo from a police mug book. Victor previously had described the perpetrator as having a physical description similar to Randy and as wearing a red ski jacket with black trim and red gloves.

To help establish Randy's identity as the perpetrator, the prosecution seeks to introduce at trial the testimony of Vicki, who was the victim of a residential burglary the day before the one involving Victor's house. Vicki's home is one block from Victor's. Vicki also saw the perpetrator, walking in on him while he was ransacking her home. She described the perpetrator to the police as similar in general appearance to Randy and told them that the man was wearing a red parka with black trim and red gloves. She identified Randy from a constitutionally valid lineup conducted after Randy's arrest for Victor's burglary. Also, when Randy's home was searched pursuant to a constitutionally valid warrant, a clock radio similar to one stolen from Vicki, but bearing no unique features, was seized.

Randy is on trial in state court for the burglary of Victor's home. At the time of this trial, Randy has not yet been tried for the burglary of Vicki's home. Randy's counsel objects to the admission of evidence concerning the burglary of Vicki's home. The state has adopted rules of evidence that are closely patterned after the federal rules, and its Rules 104 and 404(b) read identically to the similarly numbered federal rules. No state court precedents, however, have yet been handed down interpreting either rule.

Randy's defense counsel concedes that if Randy had been convicted of Vicki's burglary, the evidence possibly would be admissible under state Rule 404(b) to help prove identity. However, counsel argues that, as an untried crime, the evidence is admissible only if it is shown by clear and convincing evidence that Randy was the perpetrator. Should the ruling on the preliminary question of Randy's involvement in the burglary of Vicki's home be governed by Rule 104(a) or 104(b)? What standard of proof should be employed to determine this preliminary question?

McCormick, 6th Ed., § 53; Federal Rule of Evidence 104.

1–3. Automobiles being driven by Perkins and Edwards collided. Perkins filed suit against Edwards, alleging Edwards' negligence in the driving of his automobile. Edwards answered, denying that he had been the driver, or even a passenger in the automobile, at the time of the collision. At trial, Wilson testified that Edwards had been driving the car at the time of accident. Wilson also authenticated a copy of his diary (not the original diary) in which he had written for the date of the collision that he had been in a car driven by Edwards which had collided with another car. The diary contained other entries related to Wilson's personal affairs as well as to his occupational affairs. Consider the following alternative situations.

(A) Edwards' attorney objected that the copy of the diary was not the best evidence. The judge sustained the objection. Perkins' attorney continued by asking Wilson questions on subjects not related to the diary. On appeal by Perkins after judgment for Edwards, Perkins assigns as error the ruling of the trial judge. Assume that the evidence was admissible under the best evidence rule, but that it was inadmissible hearsay. Will the appellate court consider this error? Before continuing the examination after the judge sustained the objection, should Perkins' attorney first have taken some other action? If so, exactly what should counsel have done or said?

(B) Assume the same situation and question, except that Edwards' attorney objected only in this manner: "We object, your Honor."

(C) Assume that the copy of the diary was admissible under the best evidence rule and the hearsay rule, but that it was inadmissible because it opened up a new issue not within the pleadings. Edwards' attorney said, "We object to the admission of that copy of the diary, your Honor."

(D) Assume Edwards' attorney objected, "The exhibit marked for identification and offered is irrelevant, incompetent, and immaterial." The judge overruled the objection. Perkins obtained judgment. The diary actually is inadmissible under the hearsay rule. Will the appellate court consider error upon assignment of error by Edwards on appeal?

(E) Assume that Edwards' attorney objected to the admission of the copy of the diary because of the best evidence rule, and that the judge overruled the objection. Perkins obtained judgment. Assume that the copy was admissible under the best evidence rule, but was inadmissible under the hearsay rule. On Edwards' assignment of error, will the appellate court consider the error in the judge's ruling?

(F) In Parts (B) and (D) above, suppose the objection was phrased in these terms: "Objection, your Honor. The copy is incompetent, irrelevant, and immaterial, and is inadmissible hearsay." Would you change your answers to the questions in Parts (B) and (D)?

McCormick, 6th Ed., §§ 51–52; Federal Rule of Evidence 103.

1–4. James was prosecuted for the assault of Robert. Robert testified that James jumped him from behind and stabbed him with a knife. James claimed self-defense and testified that Robert grabbed him as he started to leave the tavern where the incident occurred and forced him toward the back of the tavern. James stated that Robert had a knife in his hand and that he (James) raised his arm to ward off a knife blow, receiving a wound to his hand. He testified that he grabbed Robert's hand that held the knife and pressed it against a wall. James then put his hand in his own pocket, pulled out and opened a pocket knife that he was carrying, and stabbed at Robert haphazardly. James further testified that he was in danger, frantic, and did not remember how he removed his knife from his pocket and opened it, except that he had to do it all with one hand while he held Robert against the wall with the other.

The knife referred to below had been introduced as State's Exhibit No. 4, after testimony that it was seized from James at the time and place of the alleged assault on Robert.

On cross-examination of the defendant James, the prosecutor asked questions attempting to show that it would have been impossible for James to hold off Robert with one hand and reach into his pocket and open his knife with the other. The following then occurred:

PROSECUTOR: Will you demonstrate to the jury how you held Robert with one hand and withdrew the knife from your pocket and opened it with your other hand?

DEFENSE ATTORNEY (to the witness): Keep your seat until I find out what she wants.

PROSECUTOR: I would like you to demonstrate how you got this knife to open.

DEFENSE ATTORNEY: I object to it; not proper cross-examination.

THE COURT: Objection overruled.

THE WITNESS: I am willing.

DEFENSE ATTORNEY: I submit further, your Honor, the only way she can make a demonstration is to bring the complaining witness into the demonstration and make it complete.

PROSECUTOR: All right. Step over here. [At this point the witness left the witness box and he and the complaining witness, Robert, stood in front of the jury box.]

PROSECUTOR: Put this knife in your pocket.

DEFENSE ATTORNEY: May I suggest, counsel, that the knife apparently is rusty. It is not in the same condition. I tried to open the blade yesterday and couldn't.

PROSECUTOR: I opened it half a dozen times.

DEFENSE ATTORNEY: You probably opened the blade you wanted to have opened.

THE COURT: Proceed.

PROSECUTOR:

Q.   Assuming you are in a scuffle, we will see how long it takes you to withdraw that knife and open the blade. Go ahead; you are in the scuffle.

A.   My fingernail has been rotted off with trisodium phosphate, cleaning fluid. I don't have any nail (exhibiting hand to the jury).

DEFENSE ATTORNEY: Do the best you can.

A.   Well, I lit into him with my head and shoulders—

DEFENSE ATTORNEY: May I suggest, counsel, you have your witness put his hands where they were.

PROSECUTOR: Did you have your hands on him, Robert?

ROBERT: I had my hands like that (illustrating).

DEFENSE ATTORNEY: Just a minute. He is not testifying.

THE COURT: Let the defendant have Robert put his hands where the defendants says they were.

PROSECUTOR:

Q.   Where were they?

A.   (demonstrating) This hand was straight up like this (illustrating) and my hand was like that (illustrating).

Q.   Go ahead; draw your knife.

A.   I put my head into—

Q.   Where is the knife? Was it open?

A.   I can't open it. My fingernails are too short.

Q.   Try to open it with one hand.

A.   I can't get hold of the blade, my fingernail is off.

Q.   You say for what reason?

A.   I had my hands in trisodium phosphate, cleaning fluid, over at the Ford hatchery and the fingernail is curled.

DEFENSE ATTORNEY: May he please hold up his nail and show it to the members of the jury? (Witness exhibits his hands to the jury.)

THE COURT: Is that all you want?

PROSECUTOR: This is all.

The defendant was convicted and filed notice of appeal.

(A) Can the defendant appeal successfully on the ground that the court abused its discretion in overruling the objection of counsel and permitting the above-described demonstration? Do you believe defense counsel should have proceeded in any other way? If so, exactly what should counsel have done and said?

(B) Assume that at the beginning of the prosecutor's examination, she had stated: "I would like you to demonstrate how you got this knife open with one hand." Suppose that the defense attorney had then objected, "That's not a proper question," and that the judge had sustained the objection. What should the prosecutor do to attempt to have the defendant conduct the demonstration she sought in order to show that the defendant could not open the knife with one hand?

McCormick, 6th Ed., §§ 51–52, 212, 214; Federal Rules of Evidence 103, 403.

1–5. Jenkins is being prosecuted on fourteen counts of armed robbery. During its case-in-chief, the prosecution presented substantial evidence showing that Jenkins went on a twelve-day crime spree during which he robbed fourteen elderly victims at knifepoint. All fourteen victims testified, identifying Jenkins as the perpetrator. The prosecution also introduced into evidence several items of property that had been seized from Jenkins' apartment pursuant to a lawful search; each item of property was identified by a victim as having been stolen by the perpetrator during the robbery.

During his case-in-chief, Jenkins takes the stand to claim that he was out of the state during the twelve-day period during which the robberies occurred. When Jenkins began his testimony, the trial judge clenched his jaw in apparent agitation, folded his arms across his chest, spun his chair, and turned his back to the defendant. The judge remained in that posture as defense counsel's examination of Jenkins proceeded.

(A) Must defense counsel object in order to preserve any claim of error based upon the judge's behavior? If so, when must defense counsel object? Should counsel object in the presence of the jury? What steps, if any, should defense counsel take to ensure that the record will be adequate to raise the claim of error before the appellate court?

(B) Assume that the following occurs during Jenkins' direct testimony:

MS. AUSTIN (Attorney for the defendant): Your Honor, I respectfully object. I have been examining my client for the past ten minutes or so, and throughout, you had your back turned to him. The jurors are noticing, and I am afraid this is prejudicing the jury.

THE COURT: Your objection is overruled. Do you want to move for a mistrial based on that?

MS. AUSTIN: No, Judge. But may the record reflect that you turned your back to the defendant the minute he began his testimony, and that you remained that way for ten minutes with your arms across your chest?

THE COURT: I haven't done anything the entire time. Did I look at other witnesses when they were testifying? Did you keep a record of that?

Has defense counsel succeeded in making a record of the trial judge's behavior? What further steps might counsel take?

McCormick, 6th Ed., §§ 8, 52; Federal Rules of Evidence 103, 614.

1–6. Unile Corporation undertook to store electronic equipment for Paula. When the equipment was returned, Paula claimed it had been damaged by negligent handling and storage. The matter went to trial, where Paula's attorney established that the property had been in the immediate charge of Eddie, an employee of Unile. On cross-examination, Unile's attorney brought out that Eddie had quit his job with Unile Corporation a week after Paula's property was returned.

Paula's counsel then called Will to the stand to testify regarding a conversation in which Will, Paula, and Eddie had engaged several months after the equipment was returned to Paula. The conversation occurred when the three of them met quite by accident in a restaurant. After the preliminary questions concerning the time, place, and subject matter of the conversation, Paula's attorney asked Will, "What if anything did Eddie say to you concerning any negligence on his part in handling Paula's electronic equipment while it was being stored with Unile Corporation?" There was no objection. Will answered, "Eddie said to me, 'I guess, Will, I was negligent in handling and storing Paula's equipment as I did.' "

Later, Paula's attorney called Paula to the stand. After Paula testified to the meeting and the occurrence of the conversation referred to in the paragraph above, Paula's attorney asked, "Did Eddie say anything to you about his handling of your equipment while it was in the possession of the Unile Corporation, that is, concerning any negligence on his part?" Unile's attorney objected that the question called for hearsay. The objection was overruled. Paula answered, "After he said he was wrong to Will, he said to me, 'Paula, I'm sorry I was negligent in that storage matter.' "

(A) Unile lost the suit and judgment was entered for Paula. Assume that Eddie's statements as testified to by both Will and Paula were inadmissible hearsay. On appeal, can Unile successfully urge that the admission of the statements was error?

(B) Assume the facts stated above with the following changes: When counsel asked Will the question, the Unile attorney objected on the ground that the question called for hearsay. The objection was overruled, and Will answered. Paula was then called and questioned but the Unile attorney did not object to the question, and Paula answered it. Again, judgment was entered against Unile and for Paula. Also assume again that Eddie's statements were inadmissible hearsay. On appeal, can Unile successfully urge the admission of the statements was error?

(C) Assume that Unile's attorney objected, on grounds of hearsay, to both Will's and Paul's testimony with regard to Eddie's statement and that the objections were erroneously overruled. During its case-in-chief, Unile's attorney called Eddie to the stand. In answer to appropriate questions, Eddie testified that he recalled the conversation in the restaurant with Paula and Will. Eddie was asked whether he made the statements to Paula and Will as they had testified and, over objections, was permitted to deny that he had made such statements. The Unile attorney then asked, "Well, what did you tell them about this matter?" Over objection, Eddie was permitted to answer, "I told them that in no way was I anything but careful in handling and storing Paula's stuff."

Assume that judgment was entered for Paula and against Unile. On appeal, can Unile raise the admission of Eddie's statements as testified to by Will and Paula as error?

(D) Assume the same facts as in Part (C), except the judgment was entered for Unile and against Paula. Can Paula raise the admission of Eddie's testimony as error on appeal?

McCormick, 6th Ed., §§ 52, 55, 57; Federal Rule of Evidence 103.

1–7. Patricia and Dorothy, each driving her own automobile, collided at a city intersection. Patricia brought suit on a negligence theory against Dorothy, who counterclaimed on a negligence theory.

In her opening statement to the jury, Patricia's attorney said in part, "After the collision, the plaintiff, Patricia, stopped at the curb on the west side of Willow Street, went over to Dorothy, the defendant, and said she would go to call the police. She did call the police from an office about a half block away."

Patricia testified as part of the plaintiff's case and described the accident. In answer to questions by her attorney, she testified that she had called the police (as indicated in her attorney's opening statement), that she waited for the police to arrive, and that an officer finally arrived but she had not learned his name. Patricia's attorney then asked her, "After the officer was there and questioned you, where did you go?" She answered, "The officer told me I was free to leave the scene and I returned to my home." Defendant Dorothy's attorney neither objected to this question nor moved to strike the answer.

(A) In the presentation of her case, the defendant, Dorothy, took the stand. During the course of her examination, her attorney asked her, "You have just testified that the police officer who arrived at the scene interviewed both you and Patricia. Now, did the police officer issue a citation to either of you?" Patricia's attorney objected. Should the objection be sustained or overruled?

(B) Assume the above objection was overruled and that Dorothy answered, "No, he did not." Later, Dorothy's attorney called as a witness the police officer who had come to the scene. After questioning him about the scene of the accident, Dorothy's attorney asked the officer the following:

Q. You didn't make any charge against Dorothy, the defendant?

A. No.

Plaintiff's attorney then cross-examined the officer:

Q. Now, I think the jury deserves an explanation as to why you didn't charge Dorothy.

DEFENSE COUNSEL: Your Honor, I don't think that this is proper.

THE COURT: She may inquire.

PLAINTIFF'S COUNSEL:

Q.   Is there any particular reason why you didn't charge Dorothy?

A.   Yes, there is.

Q.   Please give that reason to us.

A.   The reason is that she is a young driver and I felt that she made a mistake out there by traveling too fast for the conditions, and I knew that it would probably end up in a lawsuit and we'd be here in the courtroom like we are here today.

DEFENSE COUNSEL: Your Honor, I object to that and ask for it to be stricken.

THE COURT: She may inquire.

PLAINTIFF'S COUNSEL:

Q.   Based upon your investigation, did you feel that the law had been violated?

DEFENSE COUNSEL: Now, your Honor, I object. I think his personal feelings * * *.

THE COURT: Counsel approach the bench. [At the bench.] I am getting very uncomfortable. We are now in an area where everything is improper. Now, defense counsel started this by asking about whether or not this officer had issued citations. I will permit you to proceed but I suggest you are doing so at your own peril because most of this is reversible error if objected to by opposing counsel.

DEFENSE COUNSEL: [In open court.] Again, your Honor, I think that we can only go into the matters that are proper. We could have not asked about violations, I admit that. However, now I think that we are going beyond that issue into an improper field.

THE COURT: I am going to sustain the objection. You may inquire as to what he observed.

PLAINTIFF'S COUNSEL:

Q.   Did you, based upon your investigation, feel that Defendant's vehicle at the time of the collision was driving in a reasonable manner under the circumstances?

A.   No.

DEFENSE COUNSEL: Again, your Honor, I renew my objection.

THE WITNESS: [Without waiting for a ruling from the Court.] She is required by law to see the actual and potential dangers ahead.

PLAINTIFF'S COUNSEL: All right.

Q.   Do you, based on your investigation, feel that the—strike that. I am not going to go into this any more.

THE COURT: Will counsel please approach the bench? The jury is recessed for ten minutes. [Jury leaves the courtroom.] Unless there is some area of expertise that supports witnesses giving their conclusions, then they should not be asked the series of questions that have been asked recently. They can testify as to the distance from which the thing could be observed. They can testify to the nature of the weather conditions, the extent of the visibility, and conditions of the highway, and all that sort of thing. By observing debris and that sort of thing, they can establish points of impact. However, you are in an area that is not within the expertise of this city police officer unless you can establish it in some other fashion than through the question you are now asking. Now, if you were the jury, what would you do? And I think you are correct that all this resulted from defense counsel's improper question about the defendant not getting a ticket. I feel very uncomfortable with what is happening here because I think it creates error to be asking these questions, and I do not know that another error is justified by defense counsel's error in asking whether the officer ticketed the defendant—that's my problem.

PLAINTIFF'S COUNSEL: Well, I agree. We all are a little uncomfortable, your Honor, but I think it is opened up.

THE COURT: I think you had a right to ask him why he did not ticket her.

PLAINTIFF'S COUNSEL: Yes.

THE COURT: That was an improper question but you were asking * * *.

PLAINTIFF'S COUNSEL: In the direct examination, defense counsel opened the issue up further, in my judgment, and I think the record will bear that out. I am going to have to live with this record if I get a verdict and that's why I cut it off when I did.

THE COURT: I am toying with the idea of striking all that testimony, but I do not really think I can undo it in that fashion in any event. The jury will have to pick out the pieces that are improper on both sides. So I guess I will just let it stand. It is interesting—one improper question creates a hundred different problems. And, of course, the question was not improper as you did not object to it, so it is certainly not the Court's function to object.

Were the judge's rulings in Part (B) correct?

McCormick, 6th Ed., §§ 11, 52, 55, 57, 246, 250; Federal Rules of Evidence 103, 701, 802, 803(8).

1–8. Cable was a newspaper reporter for a local city newspaper whose "beat" was city hall. He brought a suit in federal court against Alert, a county deputy sheriff, alleging a wrongful arrest in violation of the federal constitution. Cable alleged that he had been arrested on a street in the city by Alert, that Alert had refused to show him any warrant or explain any reason for the arrest, that when he finally was shown the warrant it named an entirely different person, that he had been arrested as the wrong person, and that the erroneous arrest occurred maliciously. Cable was held for four hours, posted bail, and no further action has been taken against him.

Assume that the case is being tried to a jury. In plaintiff's case-in-chief, he showed that the arrest was clearly unlawful. Cable's counsel asked Cable on direct examination whether for a week or so before the arrest he had experienced any difficulties in contacting and getting any information from public officials from whom he usually received information. Defendant's attorney objected that the question asked for irrelevant evidence, whereupon plaintiff's attorney stated to the judge that Cable's answer to the proposed question would be "connected up" by later testimony. Plaintiff's counsel stated that she would show that defendant, some days before the arrest, had spread a rumor that Cable was a fugitive from justice; that the rumor had led his usual news sources, other reporters, and others to regard him with suspicion for a week to ten days before the arrest; and that the rumor was untrue. The judge then said, "I will overrule the objection, but if the testimony is not connected up, the jury will be instructed to disregard the testimony." Cable proceeded to answer the question in the affirmative, whereupon defendant repeated the objection by moving to strike the answer. The judge denied the motion to strike, repeating the statement recounted above.

Over objection by the defendant, a second witness called by Cable's attorney testified that for about ten days before the date of the arrest there were rumors that plaintiff was a fugitive from justice. At no time during the trial did anyone (including the defendant's attorney and the judge) mention the above matter again nor was there any attempt to introduce the further evidence that Cable's attorney had promised.

Cable obtained a substantial verdict and judgment. On appeal by the defendant, should the failure of plaintiff to introduce the foundation or "connecting up" evidence be considered error? Suppose the case had been tried without a jury. Would your answer or the reasons for your answer be affected?

McCormick, 6th Ed., §§ 54–55, 58, 60, 185; Federal Rules of Evidence 103, 104, 401.

1–9. Doug is being prosecuted in state court for knowing possession of stolen property. Doug has a single prior conviction in his criminal record—a conviction nine years ago for knowing possession of stolen property. Prior to trial, Doug's counsel filed a motion *in limine* to prevent use of this prior conviction under Rule 609 of the state rules of evidence. The trial judge denied the motion at a hearing held the week before trial, stating "I will permit use of the conviction for impeachment, if the defendant testifies. Of course, should the time come, I will instruct the jury that the evidence is only admissible for impeachment."

At trial, Doug took the stand on his own behalf, admitting that he possessed the property but strenuously denying that he had any reason to believe that it was stolen. While still on direct examination, the following then occurred:

Q. (By Attorney for the Defendant) Doug, have you ever been convicted of a crime?

A. Yes, once.

Q. Please tell the jury about that conviction.

A. I was convicted of knowing possession of stolen property. It was nine years ago, when I was just 18. I pled guilty and got probation.

Doug is convicted of the current charge. On appeal, will the appellate court consider Doug's claim that it was error to deny his motion *in limine*? Assume that the state rules of evidence are identical in wording to the federal rules, but that no state court precedent controls the question.

McCormick, 6th Ed., §§ 42, 52, 55; Federal Rules of Evidence 103, 609.

CHAPTER 2

LIMITATIONS OF THE ADVERSARY SYSTEM

■ ■ ■

2–1. You have just been elected the district attorney for your state judicial district. Your predecessor maintained a "closed file" policy permitting defendants and their counsel access only to those materials for which disclosure is mandated by state discovery statutes or the state or federal constitutions. Members of the local criminal defense bar are urging you to adopt an "open file" policy permitting the defense pretrial access to the complete prosecutorial and investigative file.

Should you adopt an "open file" policy? What considerations weigh for and against such a policy?

McCormick, 6th Ed., §§ 3, 97.

2–2. Henry was convicted and sentenced to death by a jury for the murder of a store clerk during the robbery of a convenience store. The trial consisted of two phases—the first adjudicating the guilt or innocence of Henry and the second devoted to the question whether Henry should be sentenced to death or to life imprisonment without parole. During the first phase, the prosecution relied heavily on two pieces of evidence: (1) a videotape of the entire incident recorded by the store's surveillance camera that shows a man strongly resembling Henry robbing and shooting the store clerk; and (2) the testimony of Ricky, who shared a jail cell with Henry while the latter awaited trial and who maintained that Henry admitted killing the store clerk in order to "leave no witnesses." Henry was the sole witness called by the defense during the guilt-innocence phase. He testified that he was on the other side of town with his girlfriend, Geena, at the time of the crime. On cross-examination of Henry, the prosecution established that Henry has three prior convictions for armed robbery and that he was released from prison just one week before the convenience store crime. Neither the prosecution nor the defense offered any additional evidence during the sentencing phase.

Henry appealed the conviction and death sentence to the state supreme court, which affirmed. Henry has obtained new counsel who is conducting further investigation of the case in hope of finding grounds for setting aside the conviction or death sentence through a petition for habeas corpus. Consider the following possible grounds. Which are stronger? Weaker? Why? Is there additional information that you would like to know in making your assessments?

1. Ricky was a long-term paid informant who was deliberately placed by police in Henry's cell to elicit the confession, rendering Ricky's testimony constitutionally inadmissible against Henry under the Sixth Amendment. (In general, the government may not deliberately elicit a confession from a defendant without securing a waiver of his right to have counsel present.) Henry's trial counsel failed to preserve the issue at trial because he was unaware of these facts. The prosecutor similarly was unaware.

2. Instead of the facts as stated in the preceding paragraph, assume that Ricky had no relationship with the police and that Ricky ended up in the same jail cell with Henry because Ricky had been arrested on a drug charge carrying a possible sentence of ten years imprisonment. Prior to Henry's trial, Ricky's ex-wife, Mickey, called the detective in charge of the Henry investigation to report that Ricky had told her that he did not want to testify against Henry and that he had made up the story of Henry's confession to gain an edge with the prosecutor in his own case. The detective knew Mickey had a lengthy criminal record and bore a grudge against Ricky and so considered Mickey a very unreliable source. The detective paid Ricky a visit and asked him about Mickey's claim. Ricky denied making any such statement to Mickey. The detective gave no further thought to the matter. Neither the prosecutor nor the defense became aware of the matter until now.

3. Instead of the facts as stated in the preceding paragraphs, assume that Ricky has voluntarily recanted his trial testimony against Henry and is prepared to testify that he made up the story of Henry's confession in the hope of getting a break in his own drug case.

4. Henry's trial counsel repeatedly fell asleep during the guilt-innocence phase of the trial.

5. During his closing argument to the jury during the guilt-innocence phase, Henry's trial counsel stated that even though Henry denied the crime and claimed an alibi, "it is obvious to all of us that Henry did it, and that he should be convicted of a crime here, because a video is worth a thousand words." Counsel went on to stress, however, that the jury should convict Henry only of felony murder, and not premeditated and deliberate murder, because the videotape shows that Henry was intoxicated and flustered and fired the fatal shot impulsively. (Assume that under state law a conviction of premeditated and deliberate murder is necessary to make Henry eligible for the death penalty.) Henry's trial lawyer gave Henry no notice that he would make such an argument to the jury.

6. Geena, Henry's girlfriend, was prepared to testify that Henry was with her on the night of the crime. Henry's trial lawyer did not call her as a witness because he thought the jury would find her incredible.

7. Rev. Jonas Jones, a very well-respected member of the community, can testify that he saw Henry and Geena together miles from the crime

at the time it occurred. When he learned that Henry was charged with the crime, Jones called Henry's trial lawyer to offer his account. No one was in the office at the time, so Jones left a voicemail message stating his name, his phone number, and noting that he had some information that might be helpful in Henry's case. Counsel received the message, jotted down the name and number, but then lost the slip of paper and therefore could not follow up on the call.

McCormick, 6th Ed., §§ 3, 97, 154.

2–3. A bill currently before the state legislature provides:

In all criminal prosecutions, upon the request of the defendant, the judge shall instruct the jury that it has the final authority to decide whether or not to apply the law to the facts before it, that it is appropriate to bring into its deliberations the feelings of the community and its own feelings based on conscience, and that nothing would bar the jury from acquitting the defendant if it feels that the law, as applied to the facts, would produce an inequitable or unjust result.

What effects would this bill have on the conduct of criminal trials? Is it wise or unwise? Why?

2–4. (A) Voters in your state recently approved an amendment to the state constitution providing various rights for the victims of a crime including: (1) the right to be present and to not be excluded from all public proceedings concerning the crime; (2) the right to be heard and to submit a statement at a public proceeding to determine the acceptance of any negotiated plea concerning the crime; and (3) the right to be heard and to submit a statement at a public proceeding to determine the defendant's sentence for the crime. What possible effects will the amendment have on the conduct of criminal trials and the application of the rules of evidence?

(B) Suppose the amendment set forth in Part (A), above, were an amendment to the federal constitution. Would its possible effects be any different?

TOPIC 2

THE FRAMEWORK OF DECISION

∎ ∎ ∎

CHAPTER 3

ALLOCATING THE CASE

■ ■ ■

3–1. Clement, a farmer, consults you as to the possibility of bringing a trespass action against Dokes, who Clement discovered in his south pasture on October 1. Clement does not contend that Dokes did any damage to his property, but Clement does not want anyone on his farm without his permission. He therefore proposes to make an example of Dokes.

Your research reveals the existence of the following statute:

Entry upon private lands of more than one acre by the holder of a valid hunting license for the purpose of taking wildlife thereon shall not be grounds for an action of trespass unless the owner of such lands shall have posted the lands by signs reasonably adequate to afford notice that hunting is prohibited; but nothing herein provided shall afford a defense to an action of trespass against one who shall have entered upon private lands having actual notice that such lands are closed to hunting.

Given this statute, what facts must Clement allege in his pleading to state a cause of action in trespass against Dokes?

Your factual investigation of the case causes you to believe that at trial it is likely to be contested whether, at the time of the alleged trespass:

1. Dokes was on land owned by Clement.

2. Dokes held a valid hunting license.

3. Dokes was hunting.

4. Clement had posted his property, as required by statute.

5. Clement previously had told Dokes personally that he did not allow hunting on his land.

Which party should be assigned the burden of going forward on these various elements of the case? Why?

McCormick, 6th Ed., § 337.

3–2. Indusco, Inc., brings suit against Air Insurance Co. seeking to recover $750,000 for the loss of a twin-engine airplane owned by Indusco and insured by Air Insurance. The plane crashed while on a flight, killing all persons on board. The plane itself was a total loss.

The policy issued by air insurance provided in its declaration section that "[t]he Aircraft will be operated only by the following named pilots: Bird, Ace, and any other properly certified pilot with a minimum of 100 multi-engine hours." The policy further provided that Air Insurance "would pay for all direct physical loss or damage to the Aircraft, whether incurred in flight, while taxying, on the ground, or moored." Under the exclusion section of the policy, however, it was provided that "[t]his policy does not apply * * * (4) while the Aircraft is being operated by any person other than the pilot(s) stated in the declaration section of this policy."

The persons on board at the time of the crash included Bird, properly listed as an authorized pilot in the policy, and Hobby, a pilot of some experience but with less than 100 hours in multi-engine aircraft. Because all persons aboard were killed in the crash, there is no direct evidence available as to who was flying the plane at the time of the crash.

Will Indusco have the burden of producing evidence as to who was flying the plane at the time of the crash? Would Air Insurance? Why?

McCormick, 6th Ed., § 337.

CHAPTER 4

BURDEN OF PROOF

■ ■ ■

4–1. Pratt sues Bakco, Inc., a local bakery, for damages for personal injuries which Pratt alleges were sustained when she was struck by one of Bakco's delivery trucks. Pratt testifies in her own behalf that her injury occurred at approximately 6:00 a.m. one foggy morning while she was crossing a street in a suburban business district, with the light and in a crosswalk. Pratt further testifies that when she was two steps from the curb a panel delivery truck of a dark color emerged from the fog at a high rate of speed, struck Pratt a glancing blow, and proceeded without stopping. Pratt further states that while she did not see the truck distinctly she smelled a strong aroma of freshly baked bread immediately before and after she was struck. Pratt offers additional evidence that Bakco owns and operates three panel delivery trucks which are dark blue in color, and further that Bakco was scheduled to make a delivery to a grocery store two blocks from the scene of Pratt's injury at 5:45 a.m. on the day in question.

Pratt's counsel rests after presenting the foregoing evidence plus proof of damages. Bakco them moves for a directed verdict. Prepare an argument in support of this motion.

McCormick, 6th Ed., § 338.

4–2. While attempting to unlock his front door while carrying several bags of groceries, Peter felt something brush past him into the house. On investigation, he discovered a raccoon in his kitchen. When Peter attempted to "shoo" the raccoon out of the house it bit him on the ankle and then escaped through the open front door. Peter could not produce the animal for examination, so his doctor advised him to take shots for rabies, an extremely painful course of treatment.

Three days following Peter's encounter with the raccoon, Peter's mother notices an item in the classified section of the local newspaper which offered a reward for the return of a pet raccoon named "Rocky," missing for a week. The address of Rocky's owner, Olive, is located less than one-half mile from Peter's home.

Peter now brings suit against Olive who admits the loss of Rocky four days before Peter was bitten. However, Olive denies that Rocky was the offending raccoon. At trial, Peter offers, in addition to his own testimony, the testimony of Dr. Vic, who states that he is the only veterinarian practicing in Peter and Olive's community and that within the last five years he has treated no raccoons. On cross-examination, Dr. Vic testifies that raccoons are common in the area and that they frequently will approach human habitations to rifle garbage receptacles for food. Peter calls two additional witnesses, Barbara, the owner of the only pet store in the community, and Coe, president of the local chapter of the Society for the Prevention of Cruelty to Animals, both of whom testify that they have never heard of a domesticated raccoon in the area other than Rocky.

If Peter produces no further evidence (except on damages) and Olive moves for a directed verdict at the close of the plaintiff's case, how should the court rule? (Assume the jurisdiction imposes strict liability upon the owners of wild animals for damages caused by them.)

McCormick, 6th Ed., § 338.

4–3. Assume that in Problem 3–2 (Chapter 3) Air Insurance is held to have the burden of producing evidence relative to the identity of the pilot at the time of the crash. At trial, Air Insurance offers evidence that the plane could be flown from either the left or right front seats, each of which had a full set of controls. Air Insurance further offers evidence that at the time of the take-off, Hobby occupied the left front seat and that at that time no one occupied the right seat. There was expert testimony that the left front seat is customarily the pilot's seat, and that traffic patterns are designed to facilitate flying from that position.

Has Air Insurance satisfied its burden of producing evidence? If so, how should the jury be instructed?

McCormick, 6th Ed., §§ 338, 339.

4–4. Evelyn Small brought an action against the Hansen Meat Processing Company under the state's Environmental Protection Act. The act provides, *inter alia,* that private citizens have standing to bring actions in the state courts for the protection of the environment. The act further provides, in part:

> Sec. 4. (1) When the plaintiff in the action has made a prima facie showing that the conduct of the defendant has polluted, impaired or destroyed the air, water or other natural resources or the public trust therein, or is likely to do so, the defendant may rebut the prima facie showing by the submission of evidence to the contrary. The defendant also may show, by way of an affirmative defense, that there is no feasible and prudent alternative to defendant's conduct and that such conduct is consistent with the promotion of the public health, safety and welfare in light of the state's paramount concern for the protection of its natural resources from pollution, impairment or destruction. Except as to the affirmative defense, the principles of burden of

proof and weight of the evidence generally applicable in civil actions in the circuit courts shall apply to actions brought under this act.

Small's action seeks to enjoin Hansen from operating a small meat processing plant near a city park. It is undisputed that the plant and the park were built about the same time. The plant is located at the edge of an industrial area that is separated from a residential area by the park. Small testified at the trial that the smell emanating from the plant is intense and destroys her enjoyment of the park. Five other witnesses on behalf of the plaintiff testified that they are regular users of the park and that the smell is intense. In defense, the Hansen company introduced the testimony of four witnesses, none of whom is connected with the company, who testified that they are regular users of the park and "are not bothered by the smell." In addition, Hansen presented the testimony of a witness, conceded by plaintiff to be an expert in meat-processing techniques, who stated that Hansen is using the same odor suppressant techniques as all other meat producers of Hansen's size. The expert added that while other techniques are available, the cost of such procedures would be so costly, considering the size of Hansen's operation, that Hansen would have to go out of business if it were forced to adopt them.

Assuming that, as trial judge, you were satisfied as to the credibility of all of the witnesses, how would you rule on the question of whether to enjoin Hansen's operation? Analyze your decision in terms of the burdens of producing evidence and persuasion as they are allocated under Section 4 of the Environmental Protection Act.

McCormick, 6th Ed., §§ 336, 338–339.

4–5. You are the administrative assistant to a state legislator who is not a lawyer. One of your tasks is to brief your employer on the significance of bills introduced which would effect technical changes in legal practice and procedure.

A bill has been introduced which provides that "punitive or exemplary damages shall not be awarded by any court of this state except where gross negligence or wilful misconduct has been shown by clear and convincing evidence." At present, the jurisdiction allows punitive damages upon showing of gross negligence by a preponderance of the evidence.

Prepare an explanation of the effects this legislation will have if enacted.

McCormick, 6th Ed., § 340.

4–6. You live in a state that has always provided that the prosecution has the burden of proving beyond a reasonable doubt all facts necessary to establish a criminal defendant's guilt and that this burden of persuasion includes proving beyond a reasonable doubt that the defendant was not insane at the time of the crime. (Insanity is a complete defense to criminal liability under state law. A verdict of not guilty by reason of insanity means that the defendant faces no criminal sanction but it remains possible that the defendant thereafter might be involuntarily committed to a mental institution pursuant to civil commitment proce-dures.) State law also has traditionally provided that the defendant is not entitled to have the jury consider the defense of insanity unless he or she has introduced "some" evidence (or can point to "some" evidence intro-duced by the prosecution) from which a juror might find each of the elements of the defense. As such, the defendant bears a burden of going forward with the defense (or, alternatively phrased, a burden of produc-tion) which, once met, triggers the prosecution's burden of persuasion.

A highly publicized homicide case recently ended in a controversial acquittal on the ground of insanity. The acquittal has sparked an intense legislative campaign to reform the insanity law in your state. You are counsel to the legislative subcommittee dealing with the matter. The following proposals have been advanced in the subcommittee:

    1.   Abolition of the defense in its entirety.

    2.   Retention of the defense, but with reallocation of the burden of persuasion to the defendant to prove the existence of every element of the defense beyond a reasonable doubt.

    3.   Retention, but with reallocation of the burden of persuasion to the defendant to prove the existence of every element of the defense by clear and convincing evidence.

    4.   Retention, but with reallocation of the burden of persuasion to the defendant to prove the existence of every element of the defense by a preponderance of the evidence.

    5.   Retention, but with alteration of the defendant's burden of pro-duction to make it more difficult for the defendant to obtain a jury instruction on insanity. The proponents of this idea also are interested in the possibility of increasing the defendant's burden of production in conjunction with proposals 2, 3, and 4, above. However, they are uncertain how to phrase the new standard.

    6.   Retention of the defense and the state's traditional allocation of the burden of persuasion on the prosecution, but with a reduction of the prosecution's burden of persuasion to the standard of clear and convincing evidence, or to the preponderance standard.

The subcommittee needs your advice. Are all these options constitu-tional? Which proposal is most preferable? Least preferable? Why? Might any of the proposals be improved?

McCormick, 6th Ed., §§ 336–341, 346–348.

    4–7.   Nick is charged with bank robbery. The man committing the robbery wore a dark raincoat, a handkerchief covering the lower part of his face, sunglasses, and a hat pulled down as low as possible. Five witnesses testified that the robbery took place, but because of the dress of the robber, none of these witnesses could positively identify Nick as the robber. A sixth witness, John Rogers, who is deaf and unable to speak, was in the bank on business. Rogers testified that, in his opinion, Nick was the man "who committed the robbery." He based his opinion upon his recollection of the "bridge of the nose" and the "wrinkles on the forehead" of the robber. Assume that the identification of Nick was made for the first time in open court and that Rogers' testimony was the only testimony connecting Nick to the robbery. As trial judge, would you grant the defendant's motion for judgment of acquittal (or the equivalent motion in your jurisdiction) at the close of the prosecution's case?

McCormick, 6th Ed., §§ 338, 341.

4–8. A criminal prosecution for leaving the scene of an accident is brought as a result of the occurrence described in Problem 4–1 above. The defendant in the criminal case is Driver, an employee of Bakco. In addition to the evidence offered by the plaintiff in the civil case, the prosecution introduces testimony that Driver was the only driver employed by Bakco who was assigned to make deliveries in the area of the accident on the morning in question, and further that Driver made such a delivery at the only grocery within a 15 block radius of the accident scene at 6:05 a.m. on the morning in question.

At the close of the prosecution's case, should the court grant Driver's motion for judgment of acquittal?

McCormick, 6th Ed., §§ 338, 341.

4–9. You represent a criminal defendant. The trial judge instructs the jury:

A reasonable doubt is one that is founded upon a real tangible substantial basis and not upon mere caprice and conjecture. It must be such doubt as would give rise to a grave uncertainty, raised in your mind by reasons of the unsatisfactory character of the evidence or lack thereof. A reasonable doubt is not a mere possible doubt. It is an actual substantial doubt. It is a doubt that a reasonable man can seriously entertain. What is required is not an absolute or mathematical certainty, but a moral certainty.

Is the instruction objectionable?

McCormick, 6th Ed., § 341.

4–10. David is prosecuted for first degree murder on the theory that he intentionally killed the victim with a specific intent to kill formed after premeditation and deliberation. David does not deny the killing but claims that he was heavily drunk at the time and thus lacked the requisite specific intent, premeditation, and deliberation. State law recognizes that voluntary intoxication might negate those elements.

The jury is instructed:

The defendant contends that he should be excused because he was drunk. You may find there is evidence which tends to show that the defendant was drunk or intoxicated at the time of the acts alleged in this case. Generally, voluntary intoxication is not a legal excuse for crime. The law does not permit a person who commits a crime in the state of intoxication to use his own vice or weakness as a shelter against the normal legal consequences of his conduct. However, if you find that the defendant was intoxicated, you should consider whether this condition affected his ability to formulate the specific intent which is required for conviction of first degree murder. In order to find the defendant guilty of first degree murder, you must find beyond a reasonable doubt that he killed the deceased with malice and in the execution of an actual specific intent to kill formed after premeditation and deliberation. If, as a result of intoxication, the defendant did not have the specific intent to kill the deceased formed after premeditation and deliberation, then he would not be guilty of first degree murder. However, the intoxication must be so great that his mind and reason were so completely overthrown so as to render him utterly incapable to form a premeditated and deliberate purpose to kill. Mere intoxication cannot serve as an excuse for the defendant. It must be intoxication to the extent that the defendant's mental processes were so overcome by excessive use of liquor that he had temporarily, at least, lost the capacity to think and plan.

Is the instruction objectionable?

McCormick, 6th Ed., § 341.

Chapter 5

Presumptions

■ ■ ■

5–1. Robert rented a car from Columbia Rent-a-Car Company's office at the Bigton Airport late one July evening. The next morning, the car was found smashed against a telephone pole on a straight portion of state highway several miles from the airport. Robert was found dead inside the car. The weather had been clear and dry for about a week before the accident. The highway on which the accident occurred was lightly traveled. Based upon an autopsy, a pathologist is of the opinion that Robert died as a result of the impact of the automobile against the telephone pole. An examination of the car when it was towed to a nearby garage indicated that the car's brakes were not functional. Experts who examined the car stated that it was possible, but not likely, that the brakes were rendered nonfunctional by the collision. Robert's heirs brought a wrongful death action against Columbia Rent-a-Car. At the trial, they introduced the above-stated evidence and nothing more. Columbia moves for a directed verdict. As trial judge, what would be your ruling on Columbia's motion?

Would your ruling be affected by the existence of a presumption in the law of the jurisdiction to the effect that "a decedent is presumed to have exercised ordinary care for his own safety in accordance with the natural instinct of human beings to guard against danger?"

McCormick, 6th Ed., §§ 338, 342–344; Federal Rules of Evidence 301–302.

5–2. Herbert piloted his own small plane. One clear day, on a trip from his home to an Atlantic Coast beach resort, Herbert and the plane disappeared. The wreckage of the plane was never found. He carried no passengers. Herbert's flight plan would have taken him across some water and it was assumed by all concerned that the plane crashed at sea. However, no debris was ever located. Seven years and one day after the loss of the plane, Herbert's wife, Susan, as beneficiary of Herbert's life insurance policy, brought suit on that policy. There is a presumption in the law of the jurisdiction that when a person has disappeared from his home and has remained absent for at least seven years without word, the person is presumed dead.

At the trial, Susan introduced evidence of the above facts and rested. The insurance company then introduced the following proof:

(1) Herbert and Susan were having marital difficulties and Herbert had told several of his friends that he would leave Susan if he "had half-a-chance."

(2) One week before the flight, Herbert sold some stock held in his broker's name for $25,000. On the day before the accident, he withdrew a total of $30,000 from two bank accounts.

(3) Stanley, a life-long close friend of Herbert, testifies that while vacationing in Bermuda one year before Susan's action was filed he saw a man who closely resembled Herbert and "could have been" Herbert, sitting in a bar. The man looked in Stanley's direction and then ran out of the bar. Stanley ran after him but lost him when the man ducked into a doorway.

Susan introduced no proof in rebuttal. Both sides moved for directed verdicts. What result?

Assuming that both motions for directed verdicts are denied, how should the jury be instructed with regard to the burden of persuasion and the presumption of death?

McCormick, 6th Ed., §§ 342–344; Federal Rules of Evidence 301–302.

5–3. Firefighter Insurance Company issued a fire insurance policy to Cal providing fire insurance for a business building that Cal owned and in which he conducted a business. A fire destroyed the building. After the filing of a claim by Cal under the policy, the insurance company brought a suit for a declaratory judgment, seeking a judgment declaring that the policy was void and restraining the commencement of any action by Cal against the insurance company on the policy. The complaint charged that the fire was procured by Cal, and that Cal had made proof of loss in which he swore under oath that the cause of the fire was unknown. It sought judgment under two provisions of the policy. The first provision stated the policy would be void "in case of any fraud or false swearing of the insured touching any matter of this insurance or the subject thereof, whether before or after a loss." The second provision provided that the policy would be void and excluded liability as to "fires of incendiary origin, said fires being caused by the policyholder, its agents, servants, or employees."

At the trial, plaintiff insurance company introduced the proof of loss signed by the defendant policyholder, who admitted under oath that the signature was his and that it was sworn to before a notary public as the document indicated. Plaintiff also introduced a short videotape identified by a bystander, and taken by the bystander for other purposes. The tape showed the defendant coming out of his building through a side door while pouring out a trail of liquid from a very large red can marked "Gasoline" in white letters, dropping the can a few feet from the door. Then the videotape showed the defendant lighting a match from a book of matches. (The person in the videotape appeared very clearly to be the defendant as he appeared in the courtroom). The videotape stopped at this point. The bystander explained that he had driven off, having taken a shot of something else in the background that he had desired to film. The bystander also identified the defendant as the person he saw doing the above-described acts when he took the videotape. (He said he took the "shots" from his car and just didn't think anything about what he saw and recorded with respect to the defendant.) Fifteen minutes after the bystander said he took the videotape, a call was made to the fire department reporting a fire in defendant's building. Experts who were sent immediately to the scene while the fire was in progress testified, describing physical evidence of the fire being started outside by a trail of burning gasoline leading into the building through the above-mentioned side door. They testified that no other cause was discovered. They stated their opinion that the fire started about fifteen minutes before the time at which the fire call came to the fire department. Other witnesses testified they saw smoke coming from the building about ten minutes or so before the time it had been established that the call to the fire department had been made.

Defendant's case consisted of witnesses who placed defendant in a city many miles away from the location of the building for many hours before and after the fire occurred. He did not testify. He presented no evidence concerning the videotape or any of the above-mentioned evidence of plaintiff.

An appellate court opinion in this jurisdiction states, "We decide that in this jurisdiction that there is a presumption that in the case of any burning of a building it is presumed that the burning was not from incendiary causes with which the owner of the building or of its contents had any connection."

(A) Plaintiff moves for a directed verdict at the end of all of the evidence. What result?

(B) Assume the judge denied a directed verdict. Should she inform the jury of the presumption? If she does so, what should she say?

McCormick, 6th Ed., §§ 342–344; Federal Rules of Evidence 301–302.

5–4. A statute of State A provides as follows: "Any lessee of lands of State A for the operation of natural gas wells on such state lands who unreasonably wastes gas shall be subject to proceedings in the superior courts of this state for the purpose of enjoining unreasonable waste of gas. [Several actions not pertinent to this problem are listed as an unreasonable waste of gas.] Blowing, releasing, or permitting natural gas to escape from any gas wells on such lands of the state before the removal of gasoline from such natural gas shall constitute unreasonable waste of gas in the absence of evidence to the contrary supplied by the lessee accused of unreasonable waste of gas."

The state commenced a suit for an injunction against the lessee of certain state land, alleging unreasonable waste of gas under the above statute. The state introduced evidence in an attempt to show that the lessee released gas from natural gas wells before removing gasoline from the gas. The lessee introduced contrary evidence. Assume that at the end of the bench trial and after the close of evidence the court was in doubt on the fact issue of whether the lessee had released gas. How should the court decide the case?

McCormick, 6th Ed., §§ 342–344; Federal Rule of Evidence 301.

5–5. (A) Assume that the case in Problem 5–2, above, was brought in a federal district court in State A. Before he disappeared and at the time he disappeared, Herbert lived with Susan in State B. Susan still lives in that state. The corporate defendant is a corporation organized in State A with its principal place of business in State A. Jurisdiction was based upon diversity of citizenship. In State A, under applicable law, the "seven year presumption" is not mentioned to the jury in the courts of State A. In State B the rule is that this presumption is mentioned to the jury, and the jury is instructed that the presumption places the burden of proof upon the opponent. Therefore, under the State B rule, the burden of proof would be placed upon the defendant company to show that the insured is alive. Should the jury be instructed in accordance with the State B rule?

(B) Assume that at the beginning of the trial of the above case, defendant company was permitted to amend its answer to assert that the entire subject of the suit was the subject of a prior settlement agreement entered into the day before trial between the plaintiff and the defendant company. At the trial, defendant introduced the alleged written settlement agreement which was signed by plaintiff's attorney but not by plaintiff. In rebuttal, plaintiff testified plaintiff's attorney did not have any authority from plaintiff to sign the settlement. Plaintiff recited what she had told her attorney prior to the date of the settlement agreement, and the conversation, as she recited it, seemed to indicate quite clearly that plaintiff's attorney had no authority from plaintiff to enter into the settlement agreement. In State A, there is no existing statutory or case law presumption concerning the above matter. In State B, by case law, there is a presumption that an attorney has specific authority to enter into a settlement agreement for his client. State B case law does not indicate how this presumption operates. In both states the rule is that an attorney must have specific authority from the client to enter into a settlement agreement binding the client. The attorney's general authority to act for the client is not sufficient.

Should the judge take into account the "State B presumption" on a motion of defendant to dismiss at the end of the case? If so, what should be its operation?

McCormick, 6th Ed., § 349; Federal Rules of Evidence 301–302.

5–6. Paula, an undergraduate student majoring in chemistry, is charged with the crime of possession of heroin. Under the applicable state statute, in order to be guilty of this crime, the defendant must have had knowledge at the time of possession that what she possessed was a narcotic. However, the statute further provides that "such knowledge may be presumed from the fact of possession." At the trial of the case, the State introduced evidence that Paula was arrested on an unrelated cause. There was a search of her person (assume that the search was valid) and heroin was found in a plastic wrapping in her jacket pocket. She was alone when she was arrested. Paula moves for a directed verdict on the ground that there has been no evidence of her knowledge with regard to the nature of the drug and claims that the statutory presumption is unconstitutional. As prosecutor, what reply to Paula's motion would you make? What result and why?

Assume that Paula's motion for a directed verdict was denied. Paula took the stand in her own defense, admitted possession but denied that she knew that what she had in her possession was heroin. She stated he believed it was powdered sugar to be used in a chemistry experiment. How would you instruct the jurors with regard to the effect of the statutory presumption on their decision?

McCormick, 6th Ed., §§ 346–348.

5–7.   John was charged with credit card theft, a crime created by the following statute.

> A person is guilty of credit card or identification card theft when he acquires, obtains, takes or withholds a credit card or identification card from the person, possession, custody or control of another without the cardholder's or issuer's consent. Possession or control of credit cards or identification cards issued in the name of two or more other persons by a person not an issuer or agent thereof shall constitute prima facie evidence of violation of this statute.

At the trial, the prosecutor's evidence indicated that at the electronics department of a department store John selected a television set and then presented a credit card issued by the department store to pay for the set. Upon demand for further identification by the clerk, and failure of John to produce any, the clerk became suspicious of John and called a store security officer. The security officer concluded that John was using someone else's card and was not authorized to do so, whereupon the police were called. The two police officers who arrived arrested John and took him to the local jail. There it was discovered that he had on his person a second credit card issued by the same department store and issued in still another name not his own. He did not have a credit card in his own name on his person and was charged with credit card theft. One of the persons named on one of the credit cards testified he had missed his credit card after his home had been burglarized, but he had not reported it as missing. The other person named on the second card could not be located.

At the trial, in defense, John's attorney presented clear evidence that John had a credit card issued in his name to him by the same department store. Clear evidence also was presented that John was so near-sighted he could not read the credit cards without glasses, and that he owned glasses to correct his eyesight sufficiently so that he at least could read the names of the holders of credit cards of the type issued by the department store.

John took the stand to testify on his own behalf. He testified that on the day of his arrest he had left his home to go by bus to the downtown district in which the department store was located in order to accomplish several errands and to go to the department store to buy a television set. He had no cash at home except sufficient cash for bus fare, and was out of blank checks for a checking account he maintained. On his way downtown he had to transfer and thus use two different buses. In each bus he found a different credit card issued by the department store (to two other persons). He put them in his wallet. After he got off the bus downtown, he fell and broke his glasses. He left the glasses at an optical shop for repair. He was so disturbed by later events of the day that he could not remember where the optical shop was located. When he attempted to make the purchase at the department store he presented the card that he presented (which he could not read without his glasses) thinking it was his and not one of the cards he had found. He testified that, by mistake, he had left his card at home and had not taken it with him as he thought. He had asked the police to check if it was at home, but the police had never done so as far as he knew. He also testified that he had intended to go to the store's credit department after he bought the television set and turn in the two credit cards he had found, but he was arrested first. He could not produce his own credit card because as soon as he was released from jail he searched his home and could not find it. The store records showed a credit card had been issued to him.

(A) After the presentation of the evidence by both sides, defendant's attorney moved for a direct verdict. Should the motion be granted?

(B) Assume that the judge denied defendant's motion. The judge gave various instructions to the jury. He also gave the following instruction, to which defendant's attorney had previously objected:

> When, beyond a reasonable doubt, a person other than the issuer or the issuer's agent has in his possession or under his control credit cards issued in the names of two or more other persons he is presumed to have violated the above law (the judge had first outlined the statutory law prohibiting credit card theft). This presumption means that the possession of such two other credit cards is strong evidence of violation of the law.

The judge refused requested instructions of the defendant that did not mention the presumption to the jury.

Was the instruction erroneous? If so, should defendant's request have been granted? Or should some other instruction with regard to the statutory presumption have been given? If so, state such instruction.

McCormick, 6th Ed., §§ 346–348.

CHAPTER 6

THE ORDER OF PROOF

■ ■ ■

6-1. John was a dealer in surplus and bankrupt stock of all kinds including second hand cars. He kept the second hand cars in a field in a rural area. Robert was charged with stealing one of these cars. The car involved was specifically described in the information by make, model, year of manufacture, and serial number.

In the presentation of the prosecution's case, the prosecutor called John to the stand and he testified that the car that was allegedly stolen was in the field before the time of the alleged taking, that he missed the car the day after it was allegedly stolen, that he reported to the police that it was gone, and that a car discovered in the possession of Robert was that same car. Cross-examination proceeded as follows.

Q. Did Robert drop by your place in town during April and have a conversation with you? (objection overruled).

A. Yes.

Q. Did you not, at that time, state to him that you had a bunch of second hand cars in a field out in the country and that he could go out there and take his pick in payment of a debt you owed him? (objection sustained)

Q. During April, didn't you tell a Mr. Grant Stinson that you had an arrangement with Robert that in payment of a debt Robert could take his pick of your second hand cars? (objection sustained)

Q. Did you ever tell Robert he could take this Chevy which he is accused of taking? (objection sustained)

Assume that later in the presentation of defendant's case, defendant Robert took the stand and testified that he took the car mentioned in the information pursuant to an agreement between himself and John that he could have his pick of the second hand cars in the above-mentioned field in return for his cancellation of a debt John owed him.

Were the rulings of the judge sustaining the three objections above correct?

McCormick, 6th Ed., §§ 21–27; Federal Rule of Evidence 611.

32

6–2. Bernice sues Dr. Henry Farnsworth, an anesthesiologist, for medical malpractice allegedly committed in connection with a surgical procedure. Dr. Farnsworth performed a procedure on Bernice's spine in order to deaden some of the nerves coming from the spinal cord and thus relieve the chronic pain she had been suffering. The procedure involved the placement of electric needles at the nerve endings. During the procedure, some of the needles were misplaced and entered Bernice's spinal canal, causing permanent paralysis from the waist down. Plaintiff claims that Dr. Farnsworth was negligent in attempting to use this procedure on a patient such as Bernice and in his conduct of the procedure.

One of the witnesses called by the defendant was Dr. Lillian Wolfson, also an anesthesiologist. Dr. Wolfson had been in charge of the anesthetic during the surgical procedure which resulted in Bernice's paralysis. Dr. Wolfson testified to Dr. Farnsworth's conduct of the procedure and that the procedure was conducted in accordance with the standards of anesthesiologists in this and similar communities. She was asked no questions concerning the wisdom of performing the procedure in the first instance.

On cross-examination, counsel for Bernice asks the following question:

> Doctor, do you have an opinion within a reasonable degree of medical certainty as to whether Dr. Farnsworth was acting in accordance with the standards of anesthesiologists in this and similar communities when he attempted to perform this procedure on Ms. Bernice?

Defendant objects to this question as beyond the scope of the direct examination. What ruling by the court?

McCormick, 6th Ed., §§ 21–27; Federal Rule of Evidence 611(b).

6–3. Enrique brought a products liability case against Church Valve Company for the rupture and explosion of a propane cylinder on a ship owned and operated by Enrique. Enrique alleges that Church defectively designed the safety relief valve that was used with the cylinder and that the valve was sold without adequate warnings.

Shortly after the explosion, two engineers retained by Enrique's counsel, Oppenheimer and Fermi, visited the scene and inspected the remains of the ship and, in particular, the cylinder and valve. Fermi performed tests on the valve that showed that while it was supposed to release once pressure in the cylinder reached 375 pounds per square inch, it in fact would not release when as much as 600 pounds per square inch of pressure was applied. Oppenheimer meanwhile concluded that any defect in the valve could not have had a causal effect on the rupture and explosion. In his pretrial report, Oppenheimer concluded instead that the cause was a defective weld in the cylinder. He reached this conclusion because at that time he assumed that the cylinder had not been misused in any way by Enrique and that the pressure in the cylinder therefore never exceeded 375 pounds per square inch. Relying on the same assumption, as well as on Oppenheimer's report, Fermi similarly reported his opinion that a defective valve was not the cause of the incident.

By the time of trial, both parties agree that there is substantial evidence that Enrique overfilled the cylinder with liquid and that the pressure in the cylinder thus could have been considerably higher than Oppenheimer and Fermi had assumed in their pretrial reports. Indeed, Oppenheimer abandoned his initial conclusion about the cause of the incident once he learned of this.

In plaintiff's case-in-chief, Enrique's counsel calls Fermi to testify concerning his examination of the parts of the cylinder which he saw. He identified diagrams and photographs of the scene. He described the tests he performed on the safety relief valve and the results of those tests which determined that the valve would not release under pressure up to 600 pounds per square inch. Enrique's counsel was careful to ask Fermi no questions concerning his opinion about the cause of the rupture and explosion and confined the examination to questions concerning what he observed and did at the site of the explosion.

(A) On cross-examination, Church's counsel asks Fermi for his opinion about what had made the cylinder burst. Fermi responded that he had concluded that the rupture was caused by a defective weld in the cylinder wall and that he relied on Oppenheimer's opinion to the same effect in reaching his own conclusion. Further cross-examination of Fermi reveals to the jury Oppenheimer's role in investigating the incident and the nature of his pretrial report.

Enrique's counsel made timely objection to this line of cross-examination. Did the trial judge err?

(B) Assume that in permitting the line of cross-examination suggested in Part (A), above, the judge remarked: "I think it is beyond the scope but I will allow it in my discretion." Enrique's counsel then asks for a ruling that Church's counsel be prohibited from using leading questions. What ruling by the court?

McCormick, 6th Ed., §§ 21–27; Federal Rule of Evidence 611.

6–4. (A) George is being sued civilly for wrongful death in the shooting of Vincente. During its case-in-chief, the plaintiff called Officer Denise Daniels to describe the scene of the shooting, including the location of Vincente's body and the presence of George at the scene. On cross-examination, George's counsel asked Daniels whether she and another officer, Sam Sorensen, had spoken with George at the scene of the shooting and whether Sorensen, no longer with the police force, took notes. Over the plaintiff's objection, defense counsel was then permitted to have Daniels read Sorensen's notes of what George had said. According to those notes, George said that Vincente had started the fracas and had threatened to kill George.

Assume that George called no witnesses and offered no evidence after the plaintiff rested its case-in-chief. Under the "General Rules of Practice for the Superior Courts" in this jurisdiction, "if no evidence is introduced by the defendant, the right to open and close the argument to the jury shall belong to him." If the defendant does introduce evidence, however, the right to make the last argument to the jury belongs to the plaintiff.

Who is entitled to the final argument before the jury?

(B) Suppose instead that during her direct examination of Officer Daniels, plaintiff's counsel had Daniels read to the jury the following from the first page of Sorensen's notes: "Upon arriving at the scene, Daniels and I spoke to George. He admitted shooting the decedent and said he'd had it coming to him for years." George's counsel then asks the court for a ruling that Officer Daniels read from the sixth page of Sorensen's notes, where it is noted by Sorensen that "George insisted that it wasn't his fault and that Vincente 'deserved it' because he started the fight and threatened to kill George."

Again, assume that George called no witnesses and offered no evidence after the plaintiff rested its case-in-chief. Who is entitled to the final argument before the jury?

McCormick, 6th Ed., §§ 21–27, 56; Federal Rules of Evidence 106, 611.

TOPIC 3

RELEVANCY AND ITS LIMITS

■ ■ ■

CHAPTER 7

THE CONCEPT OF RELEVANCY

■ ■ ■

7–1. In Problem 1–1, you were asked to construct a modern legal system for a tribe that had previously used trial by ordeal—an evening with a deadly cobra. Please review the facts of that problem. Assume that you have been successful in converting the tribe from its former ways. A modified Anglo—American trial system has been decided upon under which the tribal chief will serve as the trier of fact. As special representative of Sagaluci's attorney general, you will decide questions of procedure and evidence at the trials.

The case before the newly constituted court is as follows: A charge of theft has been leveled against a young villager. The youth, Chata, was apprehended by the owner of the property and brought to the hut occupied by the owner and his family. In a spirit of fairness, Chata was offered an opportunity to undergo trial by cobra. He refused. Before he could be forced into the enclosure by the owner and his family, other members of the tribe rushed in and took Chata to the chief's hut. The chief was not told of Chata's refusal to undergo the cobra ordeal.

At the trial, the advocate representing the prosecuting family seeks to introduce evidence of Chata's refusal to undergo the cobra ordeal. Will you permit this evidence to be brought to the chief's attention?

McCormick, 6th Ed., §§ 184–185; Federal Rules of Evidence 401–403.

7–2. Paul wishes to bring an action upon a promissory note for $5,000 against Andrew, and knows that Andrew insists that the note is a "forgery." Paul's attorney knows that both he and Andrew's attorney will call expert witnesses concerning the signature, that their testimony will differ, and that a variety of contradictory evidence is available in favor of both parties. Paul's attorney would like to call Winston to the stand to testify that three days before the alleged execution of the note Andrew came to Winston and attempted to borrow $2,500, and that Winston loaned Andrew the money. Winston does not know the purpose for which Andrew wished to use the loan funds. Is this evidence admissible?

Paul's attorney also wishes to introduce, after Winston's testimony, testimony of other witnesses that Andrew borrowed money from others on three occasions shortly before and after the note in issue was purportedly executed. Is the evidence of the $2,500 loan from Winston more likely to be admitted in light of this additional testimony?

McCormick, 6th Ed., §§ 184–185; Federal Rules of Evidence 401–403.

7–3. Caroline brought a wrongful death and survival action against Aerial Surveys, Inc., on behalf of herself and her five children. Seeking compensatory and punitive damages, Caroline's complaint alleges that her husband Carl died in a plane crash due to the negligence of the defendant. The trial judge has ordered that the question of punitive damages be reserved for a second phase of the trial that will be reached only if the jury first finds Aerial Surveys negligent and awards compensatory damages for the plaintiff.

(A) At trial, the plaintiffs offer evidence that Carl and Caroline's fifteen-year-old son Samuel committed suicide approximately twelve months after Carl's death, leaving a suicide note stating: "I'm going to be with Dad now." Is the evidence admissible?

(B) A television news crew took videotape of the crash site showing that Carl's body had been badly burned and that he had been decapitated. Counsel for Aerial Surveys objects to the admission of the videotape, offering to stipulate that Carl had been badly burned and decapitated. Should the objection be sustained? What effect if any should be given to the defense offer to stipulate? Suppose the videotape had been broadcast and observed by Carl and Caroline's daughter Gretchen, who occasionally suffers nightmares in which she sees the sights depicted in the videotape?

McCormick, 6th Ed., §§ 184–185; Federal Rules of Evidence 401–403.

7–4. Would testimony of Sally Water with regard to any or all of the matters contained in Appendix B, *State v. Well*, Document 9, be relevant?

McCormick, 6th Ed., §§ 184–185; Federal Rules of Evidence 401–403.

7–5. Daniel, a police officer, is charged with the murder of Louis Herbert, a self-proclaimed militant radical. The prosecution contends that Daniel purposely shot to kill Herbert without provocation because of Herbert's radical views. The defendant claims that the shooting occurred during an attempt to interrogate Herbert on a police matter and that the shooting was in self-defense. As part of the defense case, the defendant calls Mark Trowbridge as a witness. After Trowbridge states his name, address and occupation (unemployed), the examination continues:

Q. Mr. Trowbridge, please tell the court and the jury whether or not you have been a member of an organization known as the Sons of Freedom?

A. Yes, I have. I was a member of the Sons organization for three years.

Q. Did you attend meetings of that organization?

A. Yes, all the time.

Q. At those meetings, did you ever see a man by the name of Louis Herbert?

A. Yes, he was an active participant in the meetings.

Q. How many meetings did you see Herbert at?

A. We would meet several times a month over the three year period. Herbert was always there. I could see him because he sat at the front table with the other officers.

Q. Do you know what his position was in Sons of Freedom?

A. Yes, I believe he was in charge of recruiting new members.

Q. What are the goals and objections of Sons of Freedom?

A. The organization is dedicated to resistance against all forms of police tyranny.

Q. How does the organization tell its members to resist the police?

A. Shoot to kill whenever you can.

Q. Did Sons of Freedom have that policy when you were a member?

A. Yes, the announced policy was "Kill the pigs wherever and whenever you can."

Q. Do you know to whom the term "pigs" was intended to refer?

A. Yeah, the cops, the police.

Q. Did you ever hear Herbert articulate that policy?

A. No, but he was there when others were shouting it.

For the prosecution, would you object to any portion of this testimony? At what point in the testimony would you object? What would your objection be? For the defense, how would you respond to the objection? What ruling would you expect the court to make? Are there any additional facts not presented in this problem which, if established, might increase the likelihood of admissibility of this evidence?

McCormick, 6th Ed., §§ 184–185; Federal Rules of Evidence 401–403.

7–6. Jack was found dead of a gunshot wound to his head, at the temple (the flattened space on the side of the forehead). Jack had taken out a life insurance policy six months before he died, but the life insurance company refused to pay the beneficiary, his wife Priscilla. In Priscilla's suit against the life insurance company to recover on the policy, the defendant life insurance company alleged as a defense that Jack had died "as the result of a suicidal, self-inflicted gunshot wound." Plaintiff's evidence indicated the following facts. Jack died from the firing of a revolver, a .44 caliber Magnum handgun, purchased by him two weeks before his death. The wound at his temple was not a contact wound but was caused by a shot fired a short distance from his head. He was found dead in the front seat of his automobile, the back seat of which was packed with camping gear. The gun causing his death was beside his body in the front seat. Also found in the front seat was a .22 caliber pistol in a holster. A small cellophane bag was in the front seat. The firing pin of the revolver that caused Jack's death was defective in that it was loose, permitting the gun to fire in a partially cocked position. The gun also had a very "light trigger." About 36 hours after Jack was found and his body had been handled and removed, a test for gunfire residue was made on his hands. The test was negative. (Assume that the results of a test under such circumstances are ambiguous.) At the time Jack was found, his automobile was in the middle of a narrow side road about 50 feet from a state highway. The road went to Clear Lake Resort, about 250 feet beyond where Jack was found dead in his automobile. Priscilla testified that she and Jack had a happy home life with their three-year-old daughter, that Jack had been happy at his work, that he had never mentioned taking his own life, that he loved camping and the outdoors and guns, that he had several handguns, that Clear Lake Resort was his favorite camping spot, and that he was going to Clear Lake to camp on the weekend. Jack's best friend testified to observations that were similar to Priscilla's testimony.

Defendant's case consisted primarily of the testimony of Jack's brother, Bob. Bob testified that Jack became despondent when he had been drinking and during several drinking episodes had told Bob that he (Jack) "ought to end it all." Just a week before Jack was found dead, he had talked to Bob about his drinking and despondent moods and stated that a solution to his problems would be to take his life at Clear Lake Resort, the place he was always happy.

(A) During the presentation of plaintiff's case, plaintiff's attorney attempted to introduce (after proper authentication) a check in the amount of $15.00 made out to Clear Lake Resort Store (there was such a store at Clear Lake Resort), signed by Jack and dated the day of Jack's death. The check was found in the cellophane bag in the front seat of the automobile. (The bag also contained some dried food and the postcard mentioned below.) Should defendant's objection to the admission of the check be sustained?

(B) Plaintiff's attorney also attempted to introduce evidence that two days before Jack headed for Clear Lake Resort, he wrote the bank with which he had a loan on his automobile that he would pay an installment a week overdue during the next week. Should this evidence be admitted over defendant's objection?

(C) When defendant's attorney presented defendant's case, she attempted to introduce (after proper authentication) a stamped addressed postcard found in the cellophane bag mentioned above. The postcard was addressed to a cousin of Jack in another state and on it was written, "I am going to have a good time here at Clear Lake Resort." Defendant's attorney had previously established that there was no post office, no post box, nor any mailing facility at Clear Lake Resort, nor any on the route from Jack's house to Clear Lake Resort. There were no such facilities within 20 miles of the resort in all directions. Should plaintiff's attorney's objection to the admission of this postcard be sustained?

(D) Defendant's attorney also attempted to introduce evidence that two days before Jack headed for Clear Lake Resort he wrote a letter to the bank which held the mortgage on his house (jointly owned by Jack and Priscilla) and paid the monthly installment on the mortgage three months in advance. Should this evidence be admitted over plaintiff's objection?

McCormick, 6th Ed., §§ 184–185; Federal Rules of Evidence 401–403.

7–7. (A) Davis is prosecuted for the murder of his wife. Davis denies the killing. Stevens, a prosecution witness, would testify that he had a conversation with Davis a few days after the killing in which Davis noted that he had been interviewed by the detectives who were investigating his wife's death and was asked to take a lie detector test. (Davis was under some suspicion at the time but had not been charged.) Stevens asked Davis what his response to the detectives' request had been. Davis laughed and said, "I've had lots of dreams about killing her. I really don't know about taking a lie detector test."

Davis' counsel objects. What ruling?

(B) When Davis learned that a warrant had been issued for his arrest, he did not turn himself in immediately but instead asked a friend to drive him to his wife's burial site. Once en route to the cemetery, however, a deeply distraught Davis told his friend that he just didn't know what to do and ordered his friend to continue driving past the cemetery. Davis had a handgun in his possession and his friend heeded the command, continuing in the same direction on the highway (and thereby heading north toward the United States–Canada border about ninety miles away). Police learned of Davis' whereabouts and followed him by car and helicopter, making contact with him by cell phone. Davis made several comments to police over the cell phone that, while not explicit, suggested that he might be contemplating suicide. Police eventually succeeded in persuading Davis to turn himself in. A lawful search revealed $10,000 in cash in the vehicle. The cash belonged to Davis, as did the vehicle.

Is this evidence admissible against Davis?

McCormick, 6th Ed., §§ 184–185; Federal Rules of Evidence 401–403.

7–8. (A) Richard brings an action against Harold, age eleven, for damages resulting from Harold batting a baseball through Richard's window and striking Richard on the side of the face. You represent Harold. Your defense is that, considering Harold's age and experience, he was not negligent under the circumstances.

Neither Harold nor his parents have insurance that would provide liability coverage under these facts. Obviously, the most effective way to introduce this fact into evidence is by direct means such as through the testimony of Harold's mother that she had no applicable policy of insurance. Which of the following theories is your best argument for the introduction of such proof? What objection and argument might you anticipate with regard to each of the theories?

(1) The evidence should be admitted because it tends to show that a verdict against Harold would be an undue burden upon him or upon his parents.

(2) The evidence should be admitted because it tends to negate Harold's negligence; persons who are not insured are less likely to be careless than those who have insurance.

(3) The evidence should be admitted to rebut the jury's natural assumption that the defendant is insured and therefore a judgment against him would not be a burden on him.

If none of these theories is accepted by the court and Harold's mother's testimony is excluded, in what other ways might the lack of insurance come to the jury's attention? Would it be ethical for an attorney to pursue them?

(B) Assume that Harold's parents in fact carried an insurance policy that covered Harold's action. At the trial, the plaintiff's counsel attempts to call an insurance agent to the witness stand to testify to the existence of the policy. Would such testimony be admissible?

Assume that the evidence of insurance is not admitted. During the defendant's case, David testifies that he observed the plaintiff standing before the mirror in the courthouse men's room shortly before the beginning of the trial. David testifies that he saw the plaintiff apply a red dye to his face, making a scar appear more visible. During cross-examination, plaintiff's counsel attempts to bring out the fact that David is an investigator for the insurance company insuring Harold's parent against liability in this case. Is that evidence admissible?

McCormick, 6th Ed., §§ 184–185, 201; Federal Rules of Evidence 401–403, 411.

7–9. Refer to Appendix A, *Hines v. National Motor Co.* The case is a wrongful death action brought by the widow of a man, Chester Hines, killed in a single car automobile accident. The action is brought against the manufacturer of the car, National Motor Company. The complaint alleges that the steering mechanism on the car, a 2010 Cheetah, was defective. The defect allegedly caused the steering to malfunction and the car to crash. National Motor is fully covered under a liability insurance policy issued by All–Farm Insurance Company.

1. At trial, plaintiff seeks to introduce evidence that defendant is fully insured by All–Farm. Defendant objects. The judge inquires as to why the evidence was being offered. Plaintiff responds that the evidence is relevant to defendant's ability to pay any judgment entered against it. How should the trial judge rule on the objection? If inadmissible, why?

2. Assume that the trial judge sustained the objection based upon the purpose of plaintiff's explanation of why the proof was offered. Plaintiff then offers an alternative theory. The evidence is offered to show that, given the existence of an insurance policy fully covering liability, the defendant was more likely to have been careless in the design of its cars

than without that evidence. Defendant again objects. How should the trial judge rule? Why?

3. Assume that the trial judge again sustains the objection to the evidence. Plaintiff temporarily withdraws its offer of proof of insurance. However, during the defense case, the defendant calls Francine Davis as a witness. Ms. Davis testifies to marital strife between the Hines and to Chester Hines' frequent drunkenness. (See Appendix A, Document 9). Assume that the court overrules an objection to this evidence (See Problem 8–9.) On cross-examination, plaintiff seeks to bring out the fact that Davis was originally contacted by Ronald Watson and that Watson is an investigator for All–Farm Insurance Company. He is also Davis' brother. The plaintiff indicates that it would introduce proof that the defendant was insured by All–Farm. Defendant objects both to the cross-examination of Davis and to the introduction of evidence of the insurance policy. What ruling by the court? Why?

McCormick, 6th Ed., §§ 184–185, 201; Federal Rules of Evidence 401–403, 411.

CHAPTER 8

FORMALIZED APPLICATIONS OF THE RELEVANCY CONCEPT

■ ■ ■

SECTION A. OTHER HAPPENINGS

8–1. Refer to Appendix A, *Hines v. National Motor Co.* The case is a wrongful death action brought by the widow of a man, Chester Hines, killed in a single car automobile accident. The action is brought against the manufacturer of the car, National Motor Company. The complaint alleges that the steering mechanism on the car, a 2010 Cheetah, was defective. The defect allegedly caused the steering to malfunction and the car to crash. Counsel for both parties ask for pretrial rulings on the admissibility of the following items of proof:

(A) Plaintiff's counsel would like to offer evidence of other incidents of steering "locks." The details of the other incidents are set out in Document 11, Answer to Interrogatory 26.

(B) Defendant would like to offer proof that no instances of a steering lock on a 2010 model Cheetah have ever been reported to National. In response to this offer, plaintiff calls the court's attention to defendant's answer to Interrogatory 16 (Document 11), indicating that the steering system and mechanism remained the same for the 1998, 1999 and 2000 model Cheetahs.

As trial judge, would you rule on the evidentiary questions raised prior to trial? If so, what would be your ruling?

McCormick 6th Ed., §§ 200; Federal Rules of Evidence 401–403.

8–2. Paul was severely injured when the vehicle he was driving—a 2009 Vortex—stalled on an interstate highway late one night and was struck from behind by another vehicle. After settling with the driver of the other automobile, Paul proceeded to trial against the manufacturer of the Vortex on a strict liability design defect claim. Paul's complaint alleges that as he traveled on the interstate, his headlights flickered and began to gradually dim. He intended to take the next exit off the interstate, but his headlights became so dim that he was unable to see and was forced to slow down and pull toward the side of the road, when the engine stalled. Only then did a warning light on the instrument panel activate to inform Paul of an electrical problem. Before Paul could push his car into a safe location, he was struck by the other vehicle. Paul alleges that the charge warning light system was defectively designed and unreasonably danger- ous because the charge light would not illuminate until the alternator was almost completely disabled and the battery lacked enough charge to operate the vehicle, thereby failing to warn the driver of an imminent dangerous situation.

During the defendant's case-in-chief, an expert in automotive safety and design testifies that she did not think the Vortex's warning system was defectively designed because all of the automobiles manufactured by the defendant from 2000 to 2009—some 1.9 million cars—used the same warning system and she had heard of no similar complaints. Paul's counsel objects. What ruling?

McCormick, 6th Ed., §§ 15, 200; Federal Rules of Evidence 401–403, 703, 705.

8–3. Genevieve was the executor of the estate of deceased. Gene- vieve was empowered under the terms of Theodore's will to sell personal and real property belonging to the estate without prior court approval. Sales of real and personal property were made by Genevieve and those sales were duly listed by her in her final accounting. However, that accounting is being challenged by some of the beneficiaries on the ground that the sales prices were too low. Specifically, the beneficiaries charge that Genevieve failed to exercise due care in the sale of the property.

You will represent the beneficiaries at the hearing on the objections to the accounting. Your objective is to show that fair market value was not received in each instance. Consider the evidence of value you would be able to use with regard to each of the following items of property involved in the objections:

(A) A Residence Used by Theodore as His Home. The house was 45 years old at the time of the sale and contained 11 rooms, including an indoor swimming pool. The lot was one-half acre. The house was the Theodore family residence since the time of its construction and is located in a neighborhood that was once one of the finest in the city. However, particularly within the 10 months preceding the sale, property values have declined sharply. Some of the local landowners attribute the decline to an economic downturn in the community brought about by the closing of three important employers. The property was appraised for $680,000 three years before the sale. It was sold for $570,000. You have evidence of the following sales (except where noted, assume that the condition of the house and the lot is roughly comparable to that of the Theodore resi- dence).

(1) A 20–year–old house, two blocks from the Theodore residence, containing 8 rooms on a one-half acre lot. The house sold three months before the Theodore sale for $584,000.

(2) A 50–year–old house containing 10 rooms and an outdoor swimming pool on a lot just over a quarter-acre in size. The house, which is located four and one-half blocks from the Theodore residence, sold for $710,000 one year before the Theodore sale.

(3) A 5–year–old house containing 12 rooms and an indoor swimming pool on a one-half acre lot one block from the Theodore residence. The house sold for $660,000 one month before the Theodore sale.

(4) A 45–year–old house, containing 12 rooms and an outdoor swimming pool on a three-quarter acre lot, located two blocks from the Theodore house. The house was described as being in "superb condition for its age." It sold for $770,000 eight months before the Theodore house.

(5) A 30–year–old house, containing 10 rooms and an indoor swimming pool, on a one-half acre lot located one mile from the Theodore house. It sold for $650,000 three weeks after the Theodore sale.

(B) Genevieve sold a Rembrandt drawing belonging to the estate for $35,000. Evidence is available that other Rembrandt drawings, from a later stage in Rembrandt's career, recently sold at prices ranging from $50,000 to $100,000.

(C) Genevieve sold the annual corn crop from a farm owned by the estate to another farmer for resale at market. The price at which the crop was sold was considerably under the market price of corn at the Chicago Board of Trade on the day of the sale.

McCormick, 6th Ed., § 199; Federal Rules of Evidence 401–403.

8–4. Ron Connally was a star 6'4", 218 lb. first baseman on a major college baseball team. A switch-hitter who throws lefthanded, Connally led his team in all three major offensive categories during his junior year, finishing with a .376 batting average, 34 home runs and 98 runs batted in. At the end of his junior season, Connally was named to the first string of several major All–American teams. Just before his senior year, he was struck by an automobile driven by Philip Schaeffer. Because of injuries suffered in the accident, Connally's right leg was amputated just below the knee. In an action brought by Connally against Schaeffer for damages based upon his injury, Connally's attorney introduced evidence showing that, prior to the accident, Connally had been contacted by several Major League Baseball teams concerning the possibility of playing professional baseball. Connally testified that he had a strong desire to play professional ball prior to the accident. Connally's attorney then sought to introduce evidence of various contractual arrangements between rookie baseball players and their Major League Baseball franchises. All of these players had played for college teams that played schedules roughly comparable to that of Connally's team. Following is the evidence that Connally sought to have introduced:

Lester Stern, 6'3" 212 lb. first baseman; bats and throws left handed: $2,000,000 contract over three years. Stern was All–American as a junior and senior. In his junior year (his best season), Stern batted .410 with 22 home runs and 72 runs batted in. His statistics dipped to .340–18–64 in his senior season.

Mike Lambert, 6'4", 201 lb. first baseman; bats and throws right handed: $1,900,000 contract over three years. Lambert was very promising as a sophomore (posting numbers of .336–5–18 in limited play), but he sat out almost all of his junior year with a shoulder injury. He returned healthy after successful surgery and was named All–Conference as a senior after a .320–31–101 season.

Louis Grant, 6'2", 188 lb. right fielder; switch-hits and throws left handed: $1,450,000 contract over two years. Grant was All–Conference as a junior, batting .389 with 8 homers and 42 runs batted in. Grant also led the conference with 34 stolen bases. He left college after his junior year to enter professional baseball.

John Jones, 6'5", 217 lb. right fielder; bats and throws right handed: $2,000,000 contract over three years. Jones was second-team All–American as a senior and had been All–Conference as a junior. He had his best offensive year as a senior at .350–29–104.

Dave Anderson, 6'3", 200 lb. third baseman; bats and throws right handed: $2,500,000 contract over three years. Anderson was All–Conference as a senior and third-team All–American. His statistics were .348–30–89.

Is all or any of this evidence admissible? What additional facts might affect your ruling as trial judge?

McCormick, 6th Ed., §§ 198–199; Federal Rules of Evidence 401–403.

8–5. On August 6, 2009, five armed masked thieves sprinted into the Nice, France Museum of Fine Arts and made off with four masterpieces, including Claude Monet's *"Cliffs Near Dieppe."* Assume that the Monet painting has never been found. Assume that a law suit is brought in a United States District Court that includes, among its issues, the value of the painting. You have available to you as expert witnesses some of the leading Monet experts in the world. You also have the records of sales of Monet paintings at auctions and private transactions over the past several years. How would you go about proving the value of the painting? Could you, independent of the expert testimony, introduce the prices paid for Monets at these auctions and private transactions? What evidentiary foundation would you have to lay for the introduction of such evidence?

McCormick, 6th Ed., § 199; Federal Rules of Evidence 401–403.

8–6. Richard, a law student, commenced a suit against the owner of his rooming house. Richard claimed that he suffered a heart condition, an unusual lung condition, headaches, cramps, and nausea, all caused by a gas emanating from a chemical placed in the attic of the house to repel bats and rodents. The chemical, chloropicrin, was a liquid in a bottle with a "wick" attached to and extending through a cap on the bottle. Allegedly, gas emanated from the chloropicrin and seeped into Richard's room while he was sleeping, causing his condition.

Plaintiff introduced testimony of an expert who had been in the house two days after the above-mentioned gas emanation occurred and who testified—on the basis of tests in the house with the actual bottle of chloropicrin that had been in the attic—that in her opinion the chloropicrin in the attic had produced gas and was producing gas, that the gas could have seeped into plaintiff's room, and that such gas could affect human beings. Her experiments were conducted with the windows of plaintiff's room closed, whereas plaintiff had testified he had usually kept one window partly open when he lived in the room. Defendant's attorney's objections to the testimony of plaintiff's expert were overruled.

Defendant offered the testimony of an expert on chloropicrin. The expert described experiments, undertaken at the request of defendant's counsel, with chloropicrin in a laboratory to determine the rate of evaporation of gas from chloropicrin under various described conditions of humidity, air currents, and temperatures. The expert then stated his conclusion that the chemical produced gas in such minute quantities that it could not produce gas sufficient to affect a human being. He also described tests in the laboratory with bats and rodents and concluded that the chemical did not repel those animals. Upon cross-examination, it was made clear that the witness did not know the conditions in the attic or the rooming house. Thereupon, on motion of the plaintiff's attorney, the testimony of the expert was stricken and the jury was told to disregard it.

(A) Were the judge's rulings correct?

(B) Do you see any objections to the judge appointing an expert of his choice to conduct experiments in the above case?

McCormick, 6th Ed., § 202; Federal Rules of Evidence 401–403, 706.

SECTION B. PERSONALITY TRAITS AND BEHAVIOR PATTERNS—CIVIL CASES

8–7. Peter brings a derivative action on behalf of the shareholders of XYZ, Inc., an industrial diamond manufacturing company, against the corporate president, Gerald. The suit charges that Gerald used inside information about a possible merger of XYZ with another company to his own profit. Although the acts in question, if proven, would constitute federal criminal offenses, no criminal action against Gerald has been taken or is contemplated. Peter contends that the profits from such transactions belong to XYZ.

As part of his defense case, Gerald calls the president of the National Association of Industrial Diamond Manufacturers, Mary. Mary seeks to testify that:

(A) Gerald has a reputation in the business as a business person of high integrity;

(B) in her opinion, Gerald is a business person of high integrity who would not improperly use inside information for his own personal gain; (3)

Gerald has donated large sums of money to the Association's fund to investigate improper corporate practices; and (4) Gerald is a regular churchgoer and a Sunday school teacher.

Plaintiff objects. What ruling by the court?

McCormick, 6th Ed., §§ 187–188, 192; Federal Rules of Evidence 404–405.

8–8. Richard brought suit against the weekly news magazine *Tempo* for defamation. To establish damages, Richard called several witnesses who testified to his sterling reputation in the city in which he lives prior to the allegedly defamatory publication and to his sullied reputation after the publication. In its case-in-chief, *Tempo* called Becky, Richard's sister and business partner. Over Richard's objections, Becky testified that Richard knowingly understated his income in his tax returns for the past three years, is delinquent in child support payments he owes, and was convicted three years ago of misdemeanor shoplifting in the small and remote mountain community where Richard maintains a summer home.

(A) Assume that the defamation alleged in Richard's complaint is that the magazine referred to him as a thief. Was the judge correct to overrule Richard's objections?

(B) Assume that the defamation alleged in Richard's complaint is that the magazine referred to him as an agent of international terrorism. Was the judge correct to overrule Richard's objections? What additional proof might the defendant introduce in this circumstance to better insure the admissibility of the evidence?

McCormick, 6th Ed., §§ 186–187; Federal Rules of Evidence 401–405.

8–9. Refer to Appendix A, *Hines v. National Motor Co.,* Document 9. Defendant calls Francine Davis to the stand and seeks to elicit her testimony with regard to the matters contained in her statement. Plaintiff objects. What ruling by the court?

McCormick, 6th Ed., §§ 184–185, 188–190; Federal Rules of Evidence 401–405.

8–10. Refer to Appendix A, *Hines v. National Motor Co.* Defendant calls Thomas Edmonds to the witness stand. Defendant seeks to establish that the car Edmonds was driving was passed by Hines' Cheetah about two miles before the accident. Edmonds was also driving north on Highway 86. Edmonds will testify that Hines' car was traveling at approximately 75 miles per hour in a zone for which the posted speed limit was 55 miles per hour. Plaintiff objects. What ruling?

McCormick, 6th Ed., §§ 184–185, 189, 195, 200; Federal Rules of Evidence 401–406.

8–11. Refer to Appendix A, *Hines v. National Motor Co.* Defendant has several neighbors of the Hineses ready to testify that Chester Hines had a reputation in the community in which he lived as a careless driver. It also has evidence of at least five other accidents in which Hines was involved as well as evidence of several traffic offense convictions, including three speeding violations within the last three years. Plaintiff moves *in limine* for the exclusion of this evidence. What ruling by the court?

McCormick, 6th Ed., §§ 189, 195, 200; Federal Rules of Evidence 404–406.

8–12. A car driven by Donna was involved in an intersection collision with a pick-up truck driven by Gus and owned by Owens Construction Company. The accident occurred about 7:15 on a Thursday evening. The intersection at which the accident occurred was a four-way stop. The only witnesses to the accident were the two drivers. Both drivers were seriously injured in the wreck. There is no dispute about the fact that the front of the truck collided with the left front of Donna's car. Donna claims that she was out into the intersection when the truck went through its stop sign and ran into her car. Gus claims that he was out into the intersection when Donna "peeled" away from her stop sign directly into the path of the truck. Donna files suit against both Gus and Owens Construction charging that Gus was negligent and that Owens is vicariously liable. Owens' defense is both lack of negligence on Gus' part and the absence of agency. With regard to Owens' defense of no agency, Gus states that he was on his way to visit his mother at the time of the accident. Both Gus and Owens counterclaim against Donna for damages suffered as a result of the wreck.

The following are some of the items of proof offered by the parties at the trial. Which, if any, are admissible?

(1) Donna offers proof that, in the past six years, Gus has received six citations for going through stop signs or red lights. Four of those citations were given after a vehicle driven by Gus had been involved in a collision with another vehicle.

(2) Gus and Owens offer the testimony of several of Donna's neighbors that Donna "frequently peeled away" from stop signs and stop lights and that her car was specially equipped to reach high speeds quickly.

(3) Donna offers the testimony of Jack, the owner of Jack's Bar and Grill, that Gus has been in his bar almost every weekday for the past year, has generally stayed from 5 to 7 p.m., and has generally consumed four or five double bourbons during that time. Jack can't remember whether Gus was in the bar on the night in question. There is no evidence in the record with regard to Gus' sobriety or intoxication on the night of the accident.

(4) Donna offers the testimony of an employee of Owens, called as an adverse witness, to the effect that Owens often calls on its employees—including Gus—to run after-hours errands. The witness would testify that the employees are given general use of the company's vehicles so that they will be able to run those errands.

(5) Owens offers the testimony of one of its executives that all of Owens' trucks are given a weekly safety check every Thursday morning.

(6) Owens offers the testimony of the same executive that all of Owens' truck drivers are given extensive driving tests before entering Owens' employment.

McCormick, 6th Ed., §§ 186, 188–189, 195; Federal Rules of Evidence 401–406.

8–13. Sterling Sales Company brings suit against the Tyson Supply Company for breach of contract. Tyson offered to sell 50,000 figrans to Sterling for $100,000 and provided under the terms of the offer that it could be accepted "by mail before October 15." Sterling's vice-president for purchasing, Godwin, remembers dictating a letter to Tyson stating her acceptance on October 10. A photocopy of such a letter, dated October 10, is contained in the files. Godwin remembers signing the letter and placing it in her "Out–Mail" box. Her secretary does not specifically remember the acceptance letter. However, the secretary can state that it is his regular practice to type a letter dictated to him within a few hours after dictation, place the typed letter on his boss' desk, wait for her to sign the letter and then take it from her. He would then photocopy the letter for filing in the appropriate file, place the original signed letter in its addressed envelope, seal it, and then place the envelope in a box on his desk marked "Out–Mail", where it would be picked up by a member of the office's mailroom staff. The mailroom staff thereafter would apply the appropriate postage to the letter (using a postal meter) and deposit the letter in the U.S. Postal Service mail box in the lobby of the building.

Tyson's defense is that the offer was never accepted. Of course, it denies ever receiving the acceptance letter.

Assume that in the jurisdiction there is a presumption providing that a letter properly addressed, stamped and mailed was duly delivered to the person to whom it was addressed.

As attorney for Sterling, can you prove enough to take advantage of the presumption? If you think you can, what witnesses would you call and what would be the substance of their testimony?

McCormick, 6th Ed., § 195; Federal Rule of Evidence 406.

SECTION C.   PERSONALITY TRAITS AND BEHAVIOR PATTERNS— CRIMINAL CASES

8–14. Your client, Jonathan Day, an attorney, is charged with subornation of perjury. The prosecution alleges that he caused a witness, a motel operator, to falsify a motel registration card and to testify in court that the record was a true and accurate record of his motel. The card, if it had been a valid record, would have established an alibi for Jonathan's client, Michael, in a robbery prosecution. Jonathan admits putting the motel operator on the witness stand and causing him to testify as to the validity of the card, but he denies that he knew that the card was false.

Knowledge that the testimony was false is an essential element of subornation of perjury.

You believe that a former client of Jonathan's, Linda, will testify for the prosecution that Jonathan had offered to provide her with an airtight alibi in the extortion case in which he represented her. She will state that Jonathan told her that he was friendly with a motel owner in another city and that the owner would testify that she was at the motel at the time of the crime and would prepare a registration card to that effect. Linda will state that she refused to accept Jonathan's offer because she was afraid that the plan would not work. Assume that Jonathan has not testified and that the state offers Linda's testimony. Will you object? On what grounds? What will be the court's ruling?

McCormick, 6th Ed., §§ 188, 190; Federal Rule of Evidence 404.

8–15. Over objections, could the testimony of Cal Coleman to the matters he related in Appendix B, *State v. Well*, Document 13, be introduced by the prosecutor at the forthcoming trial in *State v. Well*?

McCormick, 6th Ed., §§ 188, 190; Federal Rules of Evidence 401–405.

8–16. Refer to Appendix B, *State v. Well*. Assume that in addition to the evidence set forth in the file, the state also has available to it information concerning the circumstances of the death of Well's first wife, Glenda. Glenda was killed while she and Arnold were picking blueberries along a country road. She died as a result of a bullet wound in her head. The bullet was of a type commonly used in hunting rifles. Arnold claimed that Glenda had simply fallen as she was walking along side of him. There were no other witnesses to the event. Several hunters were known to have been in the area. However, no hunter carrying the kind of rifle that would have fired the bullet that killed Glenda was ever located. Arnold was not prosecuted as a result of Glenda's death. The state now seeks to introduce evidence of this prior incident. What ruling by the court?

McCormick, 6th Ed., § 190; Federal Rules of Evidence 404–405.

8–17. Peter is charged with the murder of his wife, Karen. Karen's body was found at the bottom of a narrow staircase in the couple's home early on Christmas morning. Peter had called the police to tell them that he had found the body and that she had "fallen down the staircase." There was considerable blood splattered on the staircase from top to bottom. An autopsy revealed multiple lacerations of the victim's head. The autopsy report concluded that the cause of death was blunt force trauma of the head caused by multiple blows. There were also contusions and abrasions on Karen's arms, legs and feet. Although he still maintained that his wife's death was the result of a fall, Peter was indicted for her murder. Unless convicted of her murder, Peter stands to inherit his wife's substantial estate.

Among the items of proof to be offered by the prosecution at the trial is evidence of the death of a family friend, Eleanor, seventeen years earlier. Eleanor's husband had been killed in an accident. Peter and his then wife, Paula, befriended her and her two small children. Although Eleanor and Karen were not related, they were very similar in appearance. On the evening before her death, Eleanor and her family had had Thanksgiving dinner with Peter and Paula. Peter had then gone back to Eleanor's home to help put the children to bed. Peter returned to his own home after about an hour. The next morning, Eleanor's body was found at the bottom of a staircase at her home. Peter had apparently been the last person to see her alive. There was considerable blood at the bottom of the staircase, as well as a few drops at the top, above a light switch. After the body was removed, the defendant helped clean the area. An autopsy determined the death to be the result of a fall down the stairs. The autopsy report stated that there was "no indication of foul play." No charges were ever brought against any person as a result of Eleanor's death.

Peter became the legal guardian of Eleanor's children, and they lived with him until the time of Karen's death. Peter received no money as a result of becoming their guardian, but did receive some household goods such as silverware and children's furniture.

After Karen's death, Eleanor's body was exhumed and a second autopsy performed, this time by the same forensic pathologist who had performed the autopsy on Karen. The pathologist found multiple lacerations to the head. She determined the cause of Eleanor's death to be blunt force trauma to the head. She also found distinct lacerations on one hand, on a forearm, and on the back of the victim.

Before his trial on first degree murder charges in connection with Karen's death, defendant moves *in limine* for the exclusion of evidence of Eleanor's death. What ruling by the court and why?

McCormick, 6th Ed., §§ 188, 190; Federal Rule of Evidence 404.

8–18. Adams was a nurse at a Veterans Administration hospital. Vincent, a patient under Adams' care suffering from a debilitating illness, died under suspicious circumstances. State and federal prosecutors declined to press charges but Vincent's wife brought a wrongful death action against Adams claiming that Adams surreptitiously administered a fatal drug overdose to her husband and that Adams did so deliberately. The case went to trial where Adams did not dispute the cause of Vincent's death but defended on the ground that he was not the person who administered the fatal drug. A jury returned a verdict for Adams.

Two years later another seriously ill patient under Adams' care died under circumstances very similar to Vincent's and Adams has been indicted for murder. At Adams' trial the prosecution seeks to introduce evidence showing the circumstances surrounding Vincent's death together with evidence, unavailable in the earlier wrongful death action against Adams, that Adams admitted to a friend that he killed Vincent to spare him from suffering.

As Adams' defense counsel, on what grounds will you object? How should the court rule?

McCormick, 6th Ed., §§ 188, 190; Federal Rule of Evidence 404.

8–19. X is charged with robbery and attempted rape. The victim, V, lived in a large apartment complex. X allegedly broke into her apartment late one night and attempted to rape her. He left when she began to scream, but took with him her wallet containing some cash and a credit card. The assailant wore a ski mask. However, V identified X's voice at a police lineup. In addition, when X was arrested, V's credit card was found in his possession.

At the trial, the prosecution seeks to introduce evidence of six other incidents at the same apartment complex within the past six months. The evidence is as follows:

(1) X used a credit card belonging to A. A had been attacked in her apartment by a man with a ski mask. She was raped and her wallet containing the credit card was stolen.

(2) B was raped in her apartment by a man wearing a ski mask. B described the man as being the same height, weight, build and race as X. X was arrested on suspicion of B's rape approximately one block from the apartment complex on the night of the assault but was later released.

(3) C can identify X as a man she saw "lurking" in the entrance to the apartment complex in which V lived, three weeks before the alleged attack on V.

(4) D can identify X's voice as belonging to the man who raped her in her apartment.

(5) E states that she was assaulted in her apartment by a man wearing a ski mask. The man fled after someone knocked on the door. She and her friend followed him down the stairs and out across the lawn. As he was fleeing, the man took off his mask. Although it was dark, she believes that the man was X.

(6) A roll of wide adhesive tape was found in X's home. The roll matched, both in texture and in the way it was torn, tape placed over the mouth of another rape victim in the same apartment complex.

(A) Assume the state's rules of evidence contain a Rule 404 that tracks the similarly numbered federal rule verbatim but that the state has not adopted counterparts to Federal Rules 413–415. Should any or all of this evidence be admissible?

(B) Assume the state has adopted a verbatim counterpart to Federal Rule 413. Has your opinion on the admissibility of any of this evidence changed? Why?

McCormick 6th Ed., §§ 185, 190; Federal Rules of Evidence 403–404, 413.

8–20. Henry is charged with sexual assault on his twelve-year-old stepson, S. The prosecution was initiated based upon information supplied to the police by Henry's estranged wife, Wendy. Wendy alleges that, before the couple split up, Henry attacked S while Wendy was away from the home and forced him to perform a sexual act. S will testify to the event, although his story contains several inconsistencies. Henry denies that any such act occurred and that the charges were trumped up by Wendy and S because of marital and family disharmony.

The statute under which Henry is charged provides:

If a defendant who has assumed the position of a parent in the home of a minor victim engages in vaginal intercourse or a sexual act with a victim who is a minor residing in the home, the defendant is guilty of a Class E felony. Consent is not a defense to a charge under this section.

During its case-in-chief, the prosecution seeks to introduce the record of Henry's conviction for statutory rape nineteen years earlier. The events giving rise to the conviction occurred twenty years before the events charged in this case. Henry was twenty years old at the time. He was charged and pled guilty to having consensual sexual intercourse with a fifteen-year-old female. The victim had been a junior counselor at a summer camp at which Henry was one of the supervisors. He served two years in the state penitentiary.

The statute under which Henry was convicted in the earlier case provides:

A defendant is guilty of a Class C felony if the defendant engages in vaginal intercourse or a sexual act with another person who is 13, 14, or 15 years old and the defendant is more than four but less than six years older than the person, except when the defendant is lawfully married to the person.

Defendant objects. What ruling by the court and why?

McCormick, 6th Ed., §§ 188, 190; Federal Rule of Evidence 404, 413–15.

8–21.   Blair is charged with aggravated sexual assault upon a child who lives in his neighborhood. The defense at trial was that the incident never occurred and that the child fabricated the charge. During its case-in-chief the prosecution introduced, over objection, three pornographic pictures involving children and two stories portraying a fictional adult engaging in criminal and perverted sex with a child. All of the foregoing were found stored on the hard drive of Blair's computer during a lawful search. The items had been downloaded by Blair from the Internet.

Did the trial judge rule correctly in admitting the evidence? What if Blair's counsel had offered to stipulate that if the child in fact had been assaulted, the assault occurred with the perpetrator's knowledge and the requisite intent?

McCormick 6th Ed., §§ 185, 190; Federal Rules of Evidence 403–404, 413–15.

8–22.   Paula sues her employer, Dundee Miffle Paper Company, and her office manager, Bill, for sexual harassment. Paula is a secretary/receptionist at the company's local office. In her complaint, she alleges that Bill made unwanted advances toward her and that he, on several occasions, touched her inappropriately. Paula's action against the company is based on her allegations that the company knew of Bill's improper conduct with several other female employees, but nevertheless permitted him to continue to act improperly. Paula claims damages in lost wages and lost promotion opportunities at Dundee Miffle. She also claims that her reputation was damaged by Bill's open shows of "familiarity" with her.

As part of her case in chief, Paula seeks to introduce evidence from three other employees, past or present, of Dundee Miffle, that Bill had touched each of them inappropriately on several occasions under circumstances similar to those alleged in Paula's complaint. She also seeks to introduce evidence from an employee at the firm at which Bill had worked prior to his employment at Dundee Miffle. This witness, Mary, would testify that Bill had grabbed her and, without her consent, touched her breasts at an office Christmas party. The evidence is offered against both Dundee Miffle and Bill.

What is the likely ruling by the court on the admissibility of either of the items of proof? Should Paula's counsel follow any special procedure to make the admission of this evidence possible?

McCormick 6th Ed., §§ 185, 190; Federal Rules of Evidence 403–405, 415.

8–23. (A) In Problem 8–14, Jonathan has told you of several prominent persons who are willing to testify as character witnesses in his behalf. Included in the list is Joseph J. Lundquist, a local attorney and president of the local bar association. Lundquist has known Jonathan as a practicing attorney since they were both admitted to the bar twenty-two years ago. Although the two lawyers do not travel in the same social circles, Lundquist tells you that he knows and respects Jonathan's ability and integrity. Assuming Jonathan does not testify, will Lundquist's testimony in this regard be admissible? If so, what form should it take? Be prepared to conduct a direct examination of Lundquist.

(B) Twenty years ago, Jonathan was suspended from the practice of law for one year on charges that he had improperly dealt with a client's funds. Assuming neither Lundquist nor Jonathan testifies, may the prosecution bring out this fact at the trial? Assuming Lundquist testifies, may the prosecution bring out this fact? How might the prosecution do it? If the defense knew that this evidence would be brought out, how might it affect its preparation and examination of Lundquist?

McCormick 6th Ed., §§ 187, 191; Federal Rules of Evidence 404–405.

8–24. Edna is being prosecuted for embezzlement of funds from a charitable organization she directs. Edna called Alice to the stand to testify to her opinion that Edna is honest and a person of integrity. On cross-examination, and over the defense's objection, Alice acknowledged that she was aware that Edna had been embroiled in controversy six years earlier when, as a high-ranking state government official, Edna was accused of using a state helicopter on multiple occasions for personal trips. Only after the matter was publicized did Edna reimburse the state for the trips, claiming that her failure to do so earlier was an oversight.

In her final argument to the jury, the prosecutor argued as follows:

People rarely change, ladies and gentlemen. Six years ago, Edna misappropriated the property of the taxpayers of your state. Yes, she reimbursed the state, but only after she was caught. Would it surprise you to learn she'd do it again—this time misappropriating funds from a charity? People rarely change, ladies and gentlemen.

As counsel for Edna, do you have an objection?

McCormick 6th Ed., § 191; Federal Rules of Evidence 404–405.

8–25. Doris is charged with the murder of her infant child. The state alleges that the murder was committed in a fit of rage after she was unable to stop the infant from crying.

As part of its case, the defense calls Rev. Smith to the stand. Smith seeks to testify that he has been a minister for thirty-five years. During that time, he has observed thousands of mothers with their infants. He has also taken the opportunity to observe how they act in times of stress. In particular, Rev. Smith observed Doris with her child. He will state that, in his opinion, Doris was a loving mother who was incapable of harming her child. The state objects to this evidence. What ruling and why?

Assume that Rev. Smith was permitted to testify. The state then calls a psychologist, Dr. Brown, to the witness stand. Brown seeks to testify that he had a one hour psychological interview with Doris. Based on that interview, he can state that in his opinion Doris is ordinarily a nonviolent person, but is capable of falling into fits of uncontrollable rage in certain instances. Brown will state that the difficulties of child-rearing might produce such a rage. He will add that extreme action, such as the killing of a child, might be possible during such a rage. The defense objects. What ruling and why?

McCormick 6th Ed., § 191; Federal Rules of Evidence 404–405.

8–26. Thomas is being prosecuted for possession of methamphetamine with intent to distribute. Thomas acquired the drug from an undercover government agent at a so-called controlled buy. His defense is entrapment and the prosecution therefore bears the burden to prove beyond a reasonable doubt that the defendant was disposed to commit the criminal act prior to first being approached by the government agent. To prove Thomas' predisposition, the prosecution offered evidence that Thomas was a sporadic user of methamphetamine and that he once sold a small amount of the drug to a friend. In his case-in-chief Thomas seeks to present testimony concerning his lack of a criminal or arrest record as evidence that he was not predisposed to commit the crime charged. The prosecution objects. What ruling?

McCormick 6th Ed., §§ 187, 191; Federal Rules of Evidence 404–405.

8–27. Hector is charged with the murder of Elliott. He admits stabbing Elliott with a switch-blade knife, but states that he did so in self-defense after Elliott attacked him with an ice pick. Although the fight occurred in a tavern in front of many people, the testimony of the eyewitnesses is conflicting.

(A) During the defense case, the defendant seeks to offer evidence of fights in which Elliott had been involved and in which he started the fight by attacking another person with an ice pick. Is the defendant's evidence admissible?

(B) Assume that the evidence in Part (A) is not admitted, but that several witnesses testify on behalf of the defendant that Elliott has a bad reputation in the community as a violent man. In rebuttal, the prosecution offers the testimony of a witness who will testify that Hector also has a bad reputation in the community as a violent man. Is the prosecution's evidence admissible? Could these same witnesses testify with regard to Hector's "honesty?"

(C) Assume that the prosecution proof with regard to Hector's reputation for violence is admitted. Hector's lawyer seeks to cross-examine the prosecution witnesses testifying to Hector's bad reputation about instances in which Hector had been confronted with potential violence and yet had walked away from the fight. Is the cross-examination proper?

McCormick, 6th Ed., §§ 188, 190, 193; Federal Rules of Evidence 404–405.

8–28. A is charged with the first degree rape of B—forcing her to have sex with him against her will, using a deadly weapon. B will testify that she and A met in a local bar about a month before the alleged rape. On the evening they met, after a few drinks, the two went back to B's apartment where they had consensual sex. The two dated for about a month, having several dates during that time—each one ending in consensual sex. After a month of dating, B sought to break off her relationship with A. On the evening of the alleged rape, B met A at the same bar at which they had first met and told him that the relationship was over. B will testify that A became very angry and stormed out of the bar. She says that when she left the bar, A followed her to her apartment. He grabbed her just as she was about to enter the building, took her into the apartment, and raped her at knife point. He then left the apartment. B called the police. A rape kit analysis showed that B had recently had sexual relations, but there was no evidence of injury. A also plans to testify at the trial. He will say that his sexual relations with B were always consensual. He will also say that, after their last date—the evening that B reported to the police that she had been raped—he told her that he was breaking up with her because he had entered into another relationship. He says B became extremely angry and began to throw things at him. He left the apartment in a hurry. He was arrested later that night.

(A) A's counsel wants to cross-examine B about the times that A and B had consensual sex. What procedure should A's counsel follow in order to have the court permit this cross-examination? Is the court likely to admit this evidence? Is there any basis to exclude it?

(B) A's counsel wants to introduce evidence that B frequently met men at the bar and took them to her apartment for consensual sex. He can introduce six witnesses who will testify that they had sex with B under these circumstances. Two of the men will also testify that B became violent when they broke off their relationships with her. What procedure should the lawyer follow in order to make the admission of the evidence possible? Is the court likely to admit it?

(C) A's counsel also wants to introduce evidence that, one year before the alleged rape, B was convicted of prostitution. Is the court likely to admit this evidence?

(D) A's counsel further wants to introduce evidence of the rape kit analysis. The analysis showed the presence of recently deposited semen from someone other than A. Is the court likely to admit this evidence? Is there any basis to exclude it?

McCormick, 6th Ed., § 193; Federal Rule of Evidence 412.

8–29. John is charged with the rape of Jane. The defense has available to it evidence that Jane has, on four prior occasions, accused four different men of rape. All of the charges were dismissed when Jane declined to testify at trial. A psychiatric evaluation of Jane exists which concludes that she imagines sexual assaults that have not in fact occurred.

Jane testifies to the rape. May the defense cross-examine Jane about her prior accusations? May an expert testify with regard to the psychiatric evaluation?

McCormick, 6th Ed., §§ 44, 193; Federal Rules of Evidence 412, 608.

8–30. Paula sues her employer, Dundee Miffle Paper Company, and her office manager, Bill, for sexual harassment. The allegations of Paula's complaint are set out in Problem 8–22.

At the trial, the defendants want to introduce evidence (1) that Paula dated the office's assistant manager, Ted, for several months and was seen embracing him at several office events as well as at an after-work pub and (2) that Paula has a reputation in the office as a flirt and a willing participant in casual sex.

What do the defendants have to do to make the admission of this evidence possible? What is the likely ruling by the court on the admissibility of either of the items of proof?

McCormick, 6th Ed., § 193; Federal Rule of Evidence 412.

SECTION D. THE INTERSECTION OF RELEVANCY AND ANCILLARY POLICY CONSIDERATIONS

8–31. Seneca Company operates the mountain bike concession at Granite Mountain State Park in South Dakota. In the aftermath of a biking accident on the cliff trail, the state park authority put up signs indicating that riding bikes on the cliff trail was prohibited because of narrow trails and unstable rock formations.

Wendy has sued Seneca and wants to introduce evidence about the sign to help prove the nature of the danger on the trail at the time of her accident. Seneca objects on the ground that this is a subsequent remedial measure and should therefore be excluded. Wendy responds that it was not Seneca's subsequent remedial measure but rather that of a third party. What should be the result?

McCormick, 6th Ed., § 267; Federal Rule of Evidence 407.

8–32. Watts Company manufactures grain harvesting machinery. It is being sued by Glenn in the aftermath of a fire that destroyed one of his machines and burned a substantial acreage of Glenn's wheat land on his Kansas farm. Watts conducted an internal examination of its design and determined that the fire was likely caused by wear between a cable on the machine and the electrical system. Glenn obtained that document during discovery and seeks to introduce it. Watts also sent out a letter to all its customers warning of the possible defect and then voluntarily recalled the equipment. Glenn seeks to introduce those two actions as well. Watts objects to the introduction of any of the evidence on the ground that it is barred by the rule prohibiting the admission of subsequent remedial measures. What result? Would it matter to the result if Watts had taken any of these actions after Glenn's machine was manufactured?

McCormick, 6th ed., § 267; Federal Rule of Evidence 407.

8–33. Cam was driving his own tractor-trailer truck on the inside lane of two one-way west lanes of a divided freeway. Suddenly the truck stopped. Cam started it again and headed for the outside shoulder of the two lanes. The truck stopped again in the outside lane with the back end of the truck about two feet into the inside lane. It was about 7:30 p.m. and dark but with a faint glow on the western horizon. The highway was level for several miles in each direction. About five minutes after this second stop of the truck, Jane, driving her automobile at about 45 miles per hour, ran into the back end of the truck while swerving toward the inside lane in an attempt to avoid the truck. She did not see the truck until it came within the headlight beams of her automobile, allegedly because there were no lighted red or other lights on the back end of the truck and no warning lights of any kind placed upon the highway.

The complaint of Jane's subsequent suit against Cam, insofar as charges of negligence were concerned, merely alleged that Cam had negligently permitted his truck to be stopped on the highway without warning lights of any kind on the back end of his truck or on the highway. Defendant's answer denied the allegations of the complaint.

At the trial of Jane's suit she testified to the above matters which were within her personal knowledge, including the fact that there were no lights of any kind upon the back end of the truck or upon the highway.

After Jane testified, her attorney called Mary, who came upon the scene almost at the time of the accident. She testified that there were no lights on the back end of the truck or on the highway when she came upon the scene. Then the following questions of Mary occurred.

MS. CORRELL (Attorney for Plaintiff):

Q.   Were you present at the time any flares were put out?

A.   Yes.

Q.   What were they?

A.   Those regular red flares that they use.

Q.   For what purpose?

MR. NORDAN (Attorney for Defendant): I object to this as being immaterial, what was done after the accident happened. She can inquire what was done before the accident happened, what they did to prevent other people being hurt.

MS. CORRELL: If he realized he had a stalled truck, it would be the duty of the truck driver to use due diligence to warn people of danger.

THE COURT: I think she may answer the question.

A.   To warn people of danger.

Q.   Do you know where the flares were?

A.   The first two flares that came out I furnished the flares. I do not remember the person that put them out.

MR. NORDAN: I move to strike out "that she furnished the flares," or flares were put out after the accident happened, as being wholly immaterial and having a tendency to mislead the jury.

MS. CORRELL: I will consent that this may be stricken out, about her furnishing the flares.

THE COURT: All right, it may be stricken.

Q.   Do you recall whether or not any flares were taken from the truck or trailer?

A.   Yes, there were.

Q.   What was done with those flares that were taken from the truck or trailer?

MR. NORDAN: I move to strike that out as immaterial, irrelevant, and highly prejudicial.

MS. CORRELL: It seems to me that is entirely proper.

THE COURT: I agree.

Q.   It happened how soon after the accident?

A.   I should judge about five to ten minutes after the accident before there was a flare stuck out on the highway.

A state highway officer happened upon the scene of the accident about the same time as Mary did. He testified that when he came upon the scene the truck had no lights of any kind on the back end of the truck and that there were no flares or other warning lights on the highway. Then the following questioning occurred in his examination by Jane's attorney.

MS. CORRELL:

Q.   What was done after your arrival?

A.   The driver, I think it was the driver of the truck that was struck, had some fuses there, and I had some fuses, and he went down and lit his fuses.

MR. NORDAN: I object and move to strike the answer. What they did at that time was immaterial, irrelevant, and very prejudicial.

MS. CORRELL: It shows what he had and what was available for him to put out.

MR. NORDAN: Now, after counsel has stated the reason for it I renew my objection that it should be stricken on the ground stated.

THE COURT: Objection overruled.

(A) In the above examinations of the two witnesses, were the rulings of the judge correct?

(B) Suppose that a pretrial conference was held four weeks before the trial. At the pretrial conference, the attorney for the defendant stated that before the accident no flares were set out on the highway but there were flares in the truck. This matter was recited as an admitted fact in the pretrial conference order. Would the above questioning of the above two witnesses have been permissible over objections?

McCormick, 6th Ed., § 267; Federal Rule of Evidence 407.

8–34.   Refer to Appendix A, *Hines v. National Motor Co.*, Document 11. Plaintiff's counsel seeks to offer evidence of the recall of the Cheetahs as set forth in defendant's answer to Interrogatory 30. Defendant objects. What ruling?

McCormick, 6th Ed., § 267; Federal Rule of Evidence 407.

8–35.   Mary was seriously injured when the car she was driving was hit by Union Pacific's freight train at a crossing in a rural section of eastern Washington. At this point, the road crosses two sets of railroad tracks. It has crossbuck signs indicating that a railroad crossing is ahead but no flashing lights or bars that would lower upon a train's approach. Mary was familiar with the crossing since she lives ten miles away and had used it numerous times. The area along the tracks contained trees and other vegetation at the time of the accident that helped obscure a motorist's vision. On the day of the accident, vision was also obscured by a freight car parked up the track in the direction from which the Union Pacific train approached, approximately one hundred yards from the crossing.

Mary seeks to introduce the fact that a year after the accident the tracks were cleared of all vegetation for thirty feet on each side pursuant to a company policy in effect at the time of the accident. While the policy was in effect at the time of the accident, clearing at specific crossings is determined under the policy by review of a set of factors listed in the policy. The specific review that triggered this clearing occurred after the accident. In addition, the State of Washington has a statute that requires the periodic cutting of all trees more than four inches in diameter within sixty feet of any public road that crosses railroad tracks. The clearing the company did under its policy also satisfied that statute, which is enforced by five year inspections by the state and would have forced some clearing shortly after the accident as well.

In addition to questioning whether the policy falls within the definition of a subsequent remedial measure, the plaintiff questions whether it is subsequent to the accident since the policy was in effect before the accident and whether protection should be provided because the clearing activity was not voluntary since it was required by the statute. Is admission of the clearing barred as a subsequent remedial measure?

McCormick, 6th Ed., § 267; Federal Rule of Evidence 407.

8–36. Link Company and Duffy Manufacturing entered into an agreement for Link to repair and upgrade the fencing around Duffy's plant. Duffy managers became concerned after they received bills that the work was too extensive and expensive and scheduled a meeting with Link officials to settle the differences between the parties. At the meeting, no agreement was reached.

After the meeting, Duffy wrote a letter to Link stating that the communication was a follow up to the conversation at the meeting. The letter contained an itemized breakdown of invoices, including those for the work that Duffy contended went beyond the agreement. It recited the amount of work completed that Duffy said it authorized and the amount of additional fencing for which bills were submitted that Duffy contended was beyond the agreement. It contained Duffy's records about the amount of time its gate records indicated Link's employees had been on the site, and its calculation of the value of the materials used. The letter argued that the total amount billed constituted a windfall to Link and was unreasonable. It asked Link to explain and justify its bills.

Link seeks to introduce the letter. Duffy seeks to have it excluded under Rule 408. Link argues it is simply a demand to reduce the bill and because it contains no indication it is an effort to settle the dispute. Is the letter protected by Rule 408? Are there other purposes for which the letter might be admitted other than showing liability?

McCormick, 6th Ed., § 266; Federal Rule of Evidence 408.

8–37. Transport Care Company (TCC) operates a shipping business with a fleet of delivery trucks. Bonnie, Clare, Dianne, and Frank were drivers of separate cars that collided with a TCC truck. Each alleged that the TCC truck ran a stop sign and caused a collision. TCC entered into settlement negotiations, settling two of the suits. Frank seeks to introduce evidence of the terms of the two settlements reached and the offers made in the third case. TCC objects in each case that these negotiations and the results reached are inadmissible under rules that encourage negotiated settlements. Should the evidence be admissible?

(A) TCC settled with Bonnie for more than 50% of the amount of her claim. She had alleged the TCC driver ran the stop sign, a position that TCC denies at trial. Bonnie is not expected to be a witness at trial.

(B) TCC also settled with Clare, who made a similar allegation, for a similar amount to that given to Bonnie. She is expected to testify as a witness at trial against Frank stating that he was speeding and that caused Frank's car to collide with the others.

(C) TCC negotiated with, but did not reach a settlement with, Dianne. She made allegations similar to those of Bonnie and Clare, and is also expected to testify that Frank was speeding.

McCormick, 6th Ed., § 266; Federal Rule of Evidence 408.

8–38. Block Corporation provides equipment to Cube Company under an agreement that specifies that upon final shipment of the equipment, payment in the amount of $400,000 shall be due. Some time before the final equipment was shipped, Cube wrote to Block and said it no longer needed the equipment and would not pay for any further shipments. Block wrote back and demanded payment of $250,000. It indicated that it had retained the services of attorneys in Cube's home city in case payment was not made, and ended its letter with the words "we want to get this handled without having to involve the attorneys."

Cube does not make the payment. Suit results. Cube wants to introduce the letter as evidence that the equipment provided was valued at no more than $250,000. Block argues that the letter is barred as part of a settlement negotiation.

McCormick, 6th Ed., § 266; Federal Rule of Evidence 408.

8–39. Dr. Phil Stark sued the medical practice, Forrest Medical Services, where he had been employed for wrongful dismissal. Phil and Forrest officials then entered into a settlement negotiation. After some period of discussion, Forrest sent a letter to Phil offering reinstatement on the same terms that had been in effect before his dismissal without any back pay. Phil responded with a letter indicating he will accept the reinstatement immediately but believes he should be paid in part at least for the lost wages. Forrest correctly viewed Phil's letter as a rejection of its offer and counteroffer, and it withdrew its offer.

The parties agree that the letters come within the protection of Rule 408. However, at trial, Forrest cross-examined Phil about job offers he received and rejected while out of work in the months after his termination to show his failure to mitigate damages. Phil seeks to introduce the letters regarding the settlement negotiation as relevant to the claim that he failed to mitigate damages as "another purpose" not barred under Rule 408. Forrest contends that it goes to the prohibited purpose of damages under the Rule. How should the court rule?

8–40. Your law firm represents a small restaurant. The owner of the restaurant, Phillipe, has complained that the only two local milk processors, Dairyland and Wholesome, have been fixing the prices of milk products and thus substantially increasing his cost of doing business. A decision is made to institute a civil action under the state antitrust laws, charging price-fixing. You are assigned the job of factual investigation. Although you recognize that much of your detailed investigation will have to await the discovery process, you are able to uncover some basic facts prior to trial. Be ready to report to the senior partner on how in-court benefit may be derived, if any can be derived, from the following items of proof:

(A) Six months ago, Dairyland and Wholesome were indicted under the state antitrust laws for fixing the prices of milk products. Wholesome pleaded nolo contendere and was fined $10,000. Dairyland pleaded not guilty, but the charges were dropped against it. The trial judge approved the dismissal of the charges against Dairyland after he was told by Dairyland's attorney that "the company agrees to engage in no further price fixing." There is no special statute permitting the introduction of evidence of criminal antitrust proceedings in a civil case.

(B) Shortly before contacting your office, Phillipe was approached by David, the owner of Wholesome, who apparently had received information that Phillipe was considering the antitrust action. David told Phillipe at that time that while there had been some price fixing in the past, "that kind of conduct is over." He offered to pay Phillipe $500 and to lower the price of milk to Phillipe $.03 a gallon in the future if Phillipe would not institute the antitrust action and would not testify against Wholesome in any other antitrust action. Phillipe refused the offer. Might your view of this evidence be affected by the knowledge that an agreement to lower the price to one customer and not to others may itself constitute an antitrust violation under these circumstances?

McCormick, 6th Ed., § 266; Federal Rules of Evidence 408, 410.

8–41. Paul was injured when he slipped and fell on the floor of a supermarket. As he was seated in the store awaiting medical attention, he had a conversation with the store manager. Paul complained to the manager about his ankle and back and stated that he could not stand up. He also added that his clothes were ruined. The manager responded to these statements: "Don't worry, we'll pay your bills. This was really careless on our part." Is Paul's testimony about the manager's statements admissible? (Assume there is no hearsay problem).

McCormick, 6th Ed., §§ 266, 267; Federal Rules of Evidence 408–409.

TOPIC 4

COMMUNICATING DATA TO THE TRIER OF FACT

■ ■ ■

CHAPTER 9

JUDICIAL NOTICE

■ ■ ■

9–1. Daniel is accused of robbing a bank in Columbus, Ohio. The robbery took place during January just before closing on a Friday, when the bank stayed open until 6 p.m. A witness who was outside the bank believes he can identify Daniel even though it was dusk at the time. Daniel claims he was at a trade association meeting in Cincinnati at the time of the robbery and has a good friend who spoke to him around 4 p.m. at that meeting.

(A) In order to challenge the eyewitness identification, Daniel's attorney requests the court take judicial notice that there was no light from the sun at the time of the crime. He provides the court with a copy of the local newspaper, the Columbus Dispatch, which contains the times of sunrise and sunset on the day of the robbery. Should the court grant the request?

(B) Daniel's attorney also requests the court take judicial notice that it is dark a half hour after sunset, arguing that everyone knows this. Should the court grant the request?

McCormick, 6th Ed., §§ 328–330, 332–334; Federal Rule of Evidence 201.

9–2. In Problem 9–1 above, (A) assume that Daniel's attorney provides the court with the website of the Naval Observatory, a division of the U.S. Navy, which contains the dates and times of sunrise and sunset in various cities. Should the court grant the request?

(B) Daniel's attorney also wants the court to take judicial notice of the term "civil twilight"—the time at which there is no light from the sun (approximately 30 minutes after sunset). He provides the court with the website to Wikipedia, which defines the term. Should the court grant the request?

(C) In order to strengthen the alibi defense, Daniel's attorney requests the court take judicial notice that the trade association was meeting in Cincinnati on the date of the crime. He provides the court with the website of the trade association, which lists all its meeting dates and locations. Should the court grant the request?

(D) Daniel's attorney further requests the court take judicial notice that the distance between Columbus and Cincinnati is 101 miles and the estimated travel time is 1 hour and 42 minutes. He provides the court with the MapQuest website. Should the court grant the request?

(E) Assume the case is tried in federal court and the prosecutor requests the court take judicial notice that the bank is insured by the Federal Deposit Insurance Corporation (FDIC), a jurisdictional element of the offense. She provides the court with a website for the FDIC. Should the court grant the request?

McCormick, 6th Ed., §§ 328–330, 332–334; Federal Rule of Evidence 201.

9–3. Refer to Appendix A, *Hines v. National Motor Co.* As part of its case-in-chief plaintiff presents the trial judge with a copy of the March 17, 2010, *Island Morning Times*, the daily newspaper for the community where the accident occurred. The paper contains a standard weather report stating that there had been no precipitation on March 16, 2010. In addition, the paper also contains an article indicating that the area is suffering from a drought and that there had been no substantial rainfall for twenty days. Based on this newspaper, plaintiff asks the judge to instruct the jury that the jury should take as established the fact that the weather conditions were dry at the time of the accident. Defendant objects. What ruling by the court?

McCormick, 6th Ed., §§ 328–330, 332–334; Federal Rule of Evidence 201.

9–4. Refer to Appendix B, *State v. Well.* In the trial of the case, the state asks the judge to take judicial notice that blackberries were not in season on June 30, 2010, in Clay County, Callice. In support of its request, the State hands the judge a copy of a report of the State Department of Agriculture. The report states that, because of weather conditions, blackberries were not ripe for picking in Clay County until the last week in July. Should the court take judicial notice of this fact?

McCormick, 6th Ed., §§ 328–330, 332–334; Federal Rule of Evidence 201.

9–5. Bill Black and Albert Sanga, each driving his own automobile, collided on a public highway. Bill was injured and subsequently died. In a wrongful death suit brought by Bill's wife for Bill's death, Albert is alleged to have been negligent in two respects: (1) driving while intoxicated, and (2) driving at a negligent speed and also in excess of speed limits. In addition, the complaint alleges that Bill died from leukemia that was caused by his physical injuries suffered in the accident.

At the trial, plaintiff introduced evidence that Albert was seen drinking three Margarita cocktails in a public bar from about 120 minutes to 60 minutes before the accident. Results of a blood test administered by the police four hours after the accident were introduced, after a necessary foundation for the introduction of the test (relating only to the taking of the test at the time it was administered) was laid. The test registered less than .10 percent alcohol in the blood. (Assume there is a state statute which specifies that a reading of .10 percent or more is prima facie evidence of intoxication for the purpose of a criminal charge. Assume also that other evidence in plaintiff's case would not support her case sufficiently to avoid taking the issue of driving while intoxicated from the jury.)

The only substantial evidence of defendant's alleged excessive speed submitted in plaintiff's case was evidence that the accident occurred on dry, new concrete, and that defendant's auto created skid marks in a straight line of 150 feet.

Finally, on the issue concerning leukemia, in addition to various evidential facts concerning plaintiff's injuries resulting from the accident and the subsequent appearance or discovery of leukemia, plaintiff's attorney elicited the testimony of an M.D., who was a general practitioner, that leukemia could be caused by physical trauma, and that in his opinion Bill's leukemia had been occasioned by the physical injuries suffered by Bill in the instant accident. On cross-examination, it was brought out by questions to the witness and reading excerpts that this opinion was contrary to statements in recent medical textbooks. At the time, no instruction concerning the textbooks was given the jury, although immediate instruction was requested. The law of the jurisdiction was that they could not be admitted as evidence, but could be used for impeachment purposes.

At the end of plaintiff's case, defendant moved for a directed verdict on the ground that plaintiff's proof of intoxication and speeding was insufficient to take the case to the jury. During the argument on the motion in the absence of the jury, plaintiff submitted to the judge, and requested that she take into account, the following materials in deciding the motion.

(1) A book, *Defense of Drunken Driving Cases*, by Richard E. Erwin, J.D., 1971, and a slide calculator, "Alco–Calculator", published by the Center of Alcoholic Studies, Rutgers University, New Brunswick, N.J. These materials contained equations and a slide rule calculator, which, if applied by the judge, would indicate that defendant's blood *at the time of the accident* had at least .10 percent alcoholic content, assuming the defendant weighed 150 pounds or less. The materials were based upon a blood clearance factor of .015 percent per hour to the time of the test. Nevertheless, the materials also indicated that the blood clearance factor could vary in individuals from .006 percent an hour to .04 percent an hour. Plaintiff's attorney argued it was manifest that defendant weighed less than 150 pounds. Plaintiff cited cases in which expert testimony based upon the above calculations was held admissible. Plaintiff's attorney also argued that the judge should take into account common knowledge that drinking of three cocktails of three ounces in size within an hour would make one intoxicated so as to affect his driving one hour after the end of such drinking. He argued that everyone knows that Margarita cocktails at public bars are about three ounces and contain two ounces of alcoholic beverages of at least 80 proof.

(2) Plaintiff's attorney also argued that the application of a Skidmark Speed Calculator contained in *Traffic Accident Investigator's Manual*,

published by the Traffic Institute of Northwestern University, which he had at hand and offered to the judge for her examination, would indicate that the defendant was traveling at a minimum speed (on dry new concrete) which would exceed the speed limits and would in any event constitute negligent driving (or could do so) under the other circumstances indicated by plaintiff's evidence.

(A) Defendant's attorney objected to any consideration of the above-mentioned volumes, although he admitted they were standard authoritative works. Must the judge take the above matters into account in ruling upon the motion for a directed verdict? May she do so over objections of defendant? Would your answers be changed if authoritative treatises were admissible evidence in the particular jurisdiction?

(B) Assume the judge indicated she would take the above matters into account and on that basis she would decide against the motion for a directed verdict. Defense counsel thereupon requested a continuance of the trial for one week, during which time she stated she would gather evidence to present to the judge on a continued hearing of her motion to rebut the matters submitted by plaintiff to the judge. Defense counsel contended that she could show the plaintiff's materials did not apply in the circumstances of this case. How should the judge rule?

(C) Assume that the judge denied defendant's motions and trial proceeded with defense counsel presenting the defendant's case.

Defendant's evidence consisted in part of defendant's testimony that he had not drunk any alcoholic beverage whatsoever within at least 24 hours before the accident, and thus there must have been some error in the test of his blood. In making an alternate defense, defendant's attorney also introduced an expert's testimony concerning the meaning of the disappearance rate of alcohol in the blood (which he explained in detail) in this case, in connection with the test actually taken by defendant. He testified to experiments with defendant under conditions similar to those indicated by plaintiff's evidence and to the resulting conclusion that, because of the alcoholic disappearance factor peculiar to defendant and assuming the accuracy of the actual test of defendant, defendant would not have had a test score equal to the statutory minimum for a presumption of intoxication even if the test had been taken immediately after the accident in this case. Finally, defendant presented two experts who testified that at the present there was absolutely no scientific knowledge or proof that traumatic injury could cause leukemia, and that the injuries suffered by plaintiff in their opinion could not have caused plaintiff's leukemia. (Other evidence presented by defendant is immaterial to this problem.)

Defendant renewed his prior motion for a directed verdict. The judge (taking into account the materials presented by plaintiff on the prior motion) denied the motion. Again, was the judge's action correct?

(D) At a conference concerning the instructions to be given the jury, plaintiff requested that the instructions include the textbook statements and the tables that were submitted to the judge on the first motion and the conclusions which would follow from the application of these materials. Should the judge include these matters in her instructions to the jury?

(E) Assume that the jury verdict was for the plaintiff. Defendant's attorney on a motion for new trial submitted an affidavit of a juror who claims that he had said to his fellow jurors in the jury room that he drank Margaritas every so often and that three Margarita cocktails affected his driving—and would affect anyone's driving. In two other jurors' affidavits, the affiants said they had made similar remarks about the drinking of three cocktails—but not Margarita cocktails. A fourth juror's affidavit stated she had read a magazine article in *Reader's Digest* which said that three drinks would render a person intoxicated for purposes of driving and that she told the jurors about the article. Two other jurors' affidavits stated that the affiants did not drink liquor and that their decision to reach a verdict for the plaintiff was affected by the statements of the four above-mentioned jurors. (Local law required a unanimous verdict). Assume that in the particular jurisdiction in which the case was tried, matters involving allegedly prejudicial misconduct of jurors may be examined on motions for new trials and that if such conduct is established, such a motion may be granted. Could the judge validly take into account the statements of the four jurors mentioned above?

McCormick, 6th Ed., §§ 68, 328–333; Federal Rules of Evidence 201, 606.

9–6. John was arrested and charged with riding as a passenger on a motorcycle without a helmet, glasses, goggles, or a face shield as required by applicable state law. John was riding on the motorcycle, sitting immediately behind the driver of the cycle. He was not wearing a helmet, glasses, goggles, or face shield.

The applicable statute provided: "It shall be unlawful (1) for any person to operate or ride upon a motorcycle or motor-driven cycle unless he wears glasses, goggles, or a face shield of a type approved by the state equipment commission, or (2) for any person to operate or ride upon a motorcycle unless he wears upon his head a protective helmet approved by the state equipment commission. Such a helmet must be equipped with either a neck or chin strap which shall be fastened securely while the motorcycle or motor-driven cycle is in motion." The statute provided a criminal penalty for violation of its terms. Pursuant to the statute the state equipment commission promulgated regulations approving certain types of glasses, goggles, face shields, and helmets.

At the conclusion of the prosecution's case against John, defense counsel moved to dismiss the prosecution on the ground that the statute was unconstitutional under the due process clauses of the state and federal constitutions and was violative of the equal protection clauses of the state and federal constitutions. In her argument and a brief on the motion, defendant's attorney argued that the statute was unconstitutional as an attempt to safeguard the passenger, and that it did not safeguard any person other than the passenger. In the course of making her arguments, the defendant's attorney argued that the court should notice that in the area in which the accident occurred there was an average rainfall of 34 inches, that the temperature was often at, near, or below the freezing level in certain months of the year, that motorcycle driving was particularly hazardous on wet or snow-covered streets and roads, that goggles, glasses, or face shields would substantially obscure vision of the drivers and the passengers in rainy or snowy weather, and that under many weather circumstances eyeglasses, goggles, or face shields would tend to "fog up" and thereby obscure vision. She also urged that helmets, goggles, glasses, and face shields interfered with the peripheral vision of drivers and passengers. From this she concluded that far from protecting drivers and passengers, but more particularly persons other than drivers or passengers, the legislative requirement established a definite menace to drivers, passengers, and others. In due course, the prosecuting attorney objected to the consideration of any of these matters on the ground that there was no proof of them in the record.

In his turn, the prosecutor in the course of his arguments mentioned the following matters. He stated that it is well known that the number of motorcycles on the highways and streets is substantial. He mentioned the current number of state licenses issued for motorcycles and the percentage of such licenses to the current number of licenses for automobiles and trucks. He mentioned that stones are "kicked up" by tires of all types of motor vehicles, that motorcycle drivers and passengers have less protection from stones kicked up by tires of motorcycles or passing autos and trucks than do occupants of autos and trucks, that motorcycle drivers and passengers are particularly subject to being struck on the head by such stones, and that if a passenger were so struck the incident could so injure the passenger or somehow affect the passenger that the driver would be distracted. This distraction might cause him to drive so as to injure others on the street or highway. One result of this situation generally might well be the increase in the rates of all motorcycle liability insurance (or under a no-fault statute, the increase of rates for all motorcycle drivers), if the helmets, etc., were not required. In this connection, he also urged that motorcycles have less stability, and are less subject to control than four-wheeled vehicles, and that motorcycles cannot be stopped in as short a distance as a four-wheeled vehicle under the same circumstances. He also argued that motorcycle passengers are particularly subject to head injuries, as compared to passengers of four-wheeled vehicles. In this connection, he urged that motorcyclists are more prone to weave in and out in traffic, and also disobey the traffic laws. Further, he argued that motorcycles cannot be seen as easily on the highway by drivers of four-wheeled vehicles as other four-wheeled vehicles. And for these reasons as well as others, helmets are required for the protection of motorcycle drivers and passengers and for the protection of others on the highway. Defendant's counsel objected that the judge could not consider any of the above matters since there was no proof in the record of any of them.

(A) Which, if any, of the above matters may the judge take into account in reaching a decision on the motion?

(B) In the particular state in which this case was tried, discussions on the floor of the legislature were not preserved in any official documents. At the hearing before the judge on the motion to dismiss, however, the prosecuting attorney presented to the judge a quotation in an issue of a newspaper published in the state capital the day after the bill for the statute requiring helmets was reported to the Senate of the legislature by a committee of the Senate. The newspaper quoted the statement of the chairman of that committee to the Senate in the presentation of the bill to the Senate. His statement, as reported in the newspaper, pointed out hazards to others on streets and roads when motorcyclists and their passengers ride without helmets. The prosecutor also offered the judge two articles from a national magazine, *Motorcycling*, in which the authors urged the reasons that motorcyclists and their passengers should wear helmets and eye protectors. The biographies of the authors as race champion motorcyclists were shortly reviewed at the head of each article.

May the judge take these matters into account?

(C) The judge remarked at the hearing on the motion to dismiss that he had ridden a motorcycle for years, that several years before the hearing he had been riding a cycle without any head protection when a stone hit him in the face, causing him to lose control of the cycle, and thereby involving him in a collision with an automobile, and that he thus knew that riding without helmet or eye protection involved hazards to others on streets and roads. Was this a proper matter for the judge to take into account on the motion?

McCormick, 6th Ed., §§ 329, 331, 333–334; Federal Rule of Evidence 201.

9–7. John and Joe were tried in a federal district court for conspiring to import and actually importing cocaine into the United States from a foreign country. The matter which they were actually charged with importing is described in the controlling statute as follows: " * * * any of the following substances whether produced directly or indirectly by extraction from substances of a vegetable origin, or independently by means of chemical synthesis, or by combination of extraction and chemical synthesis * * * [the statute then listed the following substances] coca leaves, and any salt, compound, derivative, or preparation thereof which is chemically equivalent or identical with any of these substances, except that the substances shall not include decocainized coca leaves or extraction of coca leaves, which extractions do not contain cocaine or ecgonine."

At the trial, an expert called by the government testified to the chemical content of the substance seized from the defendants. She testified that the substance consisted of approximately 60 percent cocaine hydrochloride. The government did not introduce any evidence or testimony that cocaine hydrochloride is a derivative of coca leaves. [The fact is that it is such a derivative.]

At the end of the case the trial judge instructed the jury as follows: "If you find the substance [which the defendants were accused of importing] was cocaine hydrochloride, you are instructed that cocaine hydrochloride is a substance within the statute [the above statute which the judge had just previously read to the jury]."

At a prior conference of counsel and the judge concerning the instructions to be given the jury, defendant's counsel objected to the above instructions, and upon his objection the government's attorney merely stated that cocaine hydrochloride was derived from coca leaves.

(A) Assume that Federal Rule of Evidence 201 is controlling. Was the court's instruction proper?

(B) Could (and should) the prosecutor have done anything more to secure judicial notice of the nature of cocaine hydrochloride prior to the conference on instructions? Assume that the matter came to the prosecutor's attention after he could no longer call the expert or another expert to testify that cocaine hydrochloride was a derivative of coca leaves.

(C) Could (and should) defendant's attorney have raised any question concerning the taking of judicial notice of the nature of cocaine hydrochloride prior to the conference on instructions?

McCormick, 6th Ed., §§ 329–334; Federal Rule of Evidence 201.

9–8. In Problem 4–2, above, Peter alleges that he was bitten by a raccoon owned by Olive and that Olive is liable for his damages under the common law rule which makes the owner strictly liable for damages caused by such an animal.

At the trial, Peter does not offer any evidence as to whether a raccoon is a wild animal. However, before resting his case, Peter's attorney requests the judge to take judicial notice of that fact. Olive's attorney objects and offers the judge a book entitled *Pets of the World* in which the author states that raccoons have frequently been domesticated as pets. The judge refuses to read the book tendered by Olive, stating that she considers the question one of substantive law, not of fact, and that she will instruct the jury on the wild animal rule. Is this ruling erroneous? Prepare an argument appropriate for presentation to an appellate court that the ruling is error.

McCormick, 6th Ed., §§ 329–334; Federal Rule of Evidence 201.

9–9. Duff and Szach were engaged in a political campaign, each seeking the office of governor of the state of Irk. Duff was a businessman and during the campaign he flew to Tokyo, Japan, on private business. While there he met with a group of Japanese and American businessmen in an attempt to raise money for his campaign. In talking to the group he mentioned that Szach, although he was married, was "keeping a mistress." (Not all those present were friends of Duff.) The rumor of Szach's extramarital affair spread over Irk and Szach began a suit for slander against Duff, alleging in his complaint the remark made, the publication in Japan of the remark, persons to whom it was made, the time and place of the remark, the fact that the remark was not in the public interest, the fact that the remark was made maliciously, and a basis for damages, which were recited, together with a prayer for relief. It was not alleged that the remark was false or untrue. Before the answer was served and filed, plaintiff's attorney took the deposition of defendant, whose attorney was present, and among other questions, asked him this, "You didn't think you could get by with this in Japan, did you?"

Defendant then answered the complaint. In his answer, defendant pleaded that the remark attributed to him was true, and denied all the allegations of the complaint mentioned above.

The case came to trial. Plaintiff called an expert on Japanese law who, over objections, was permitted to testify that under the law of Japan there can be recovery in defamation for truthful remarks if the remarks were made intentionally to harm the defendant and were not made to promote the public interest. The expert also testified, again over objections, that in this case on the facts given to her in a hypothetical question, the remarks under Japanese law were not in the public interest.

Was the court correct to overrule the objections to this testimony?

McCormick, 6th Ed., § 335.

9–10. In State A, Rider rented a motorcycle from Motorents, Inc., a company incorporated in State A. The motorcycle was manufactured by Caron Co., Inc., in State B. Rider then drove the motorcycle to various communities in State A, State B, and State C, and while in State C had an accident allegedly resulting from defective brakes of the motorcycle. He then commenced suit against Caron Co. in a State A court on the theory of strict product liability. In State A, contributory negligence is a defense, whereas it is not a defense in State B and State C. Plaintiff's complaint was in the usual form of a complaint for strict product liability. In its answer Caron Co. denied the allegations of the complaint and alleged events and circumstances constituting the affirmative defense of contributory negligence. Plaintiff presented evidence supporting his complaint, but his evidence did not negate any alleged contributory negligence. Defendant presented evidence which, if believed, supported the defense of contributory negligence. Both parties then rested. In the conference concerning instructions to be given the jury, plaintiff's attorney stated to the judge that under the law of State B and under the law of State C contributory negligence was not a defense to a claim based upon strict product liability. He requested the judge take judicial notice of the laws of State B or State C and instruct the jury that contributory negligence was not a defense in the case, that defendant could be liable regardless of any contributory negligence on the part of plaintiff in connection with the accident that was the subject of the suit, and that the jury disregard defendant's evidence which indicated contributory negligence.

(A) Assuming that the judge was satisfied that under State A conflict of laws case law, State C law would control the substantive case, should she give the instruction requested by the plaintiff? (Assume that the following State A statute is controlling upon the judge: "Every court shall take judicial notice without request of the common law, constitutions and public statutes of the United States, and of every state, territory and jurisdiction of the United States, and of the official compilation of codes, rules, and regulations of the state except those that relate solely to the organization or internal management of an agency of the state and of all local and county acts.")

(B) Is this statute more desirable than the Uniform Judicial Notice of Foreign Law Act?

McCormick, 6th Ed., § 335.

CHAPTER 10

REAL AND DEMONSTRATIVE EVIDENCE

■ ■ ■

10–1. You are the attorney for the police department in a small town. There have been several arrests for narcotics violations in the town recently and the police fear a significant increase in drug traffic in the town. The chief of police is particularly concerned about securing convictions based upon arrests for narcotics violations, particularly in light of cases of which he has heard where a seized narcotic has been excluded from evidence because of a break in the "chain of possession." The chief asks you to devise a procedure whereby the substance seized from the defendant can be sent to the state police laboratory (located 150 miles away), analyzed by the chemist, and transferred to the county prosecutor's office (located in the county seat, 22 miles away) for use at the trial in a manner that will enable (1) the arresting officer to state positively that the substance identified at trial is the same as that seized from the defendant and (2) the chemist to testify that the substance identified at trial is the same substance analyzed in the laboratory. In devising the procedure, you should consider not only the distances involved but also the size and nature of the local police operation. There is no separate evidence room in the local police station. There is a common safe in the station in which valuables of all descriptions are kept. All police officers as well as the department's four secretary-clerks have the combination to the safe. The police force is sufficiently small that an officer often cannot be spared from duty for any significant length of time.

What procedure would you devise under these circumstances?

McCormick, 6th Ed., § 212–213; Federal Rules of Evidence 401–403.

10–2. Early one morning, you receive a telephone call from a client, John. John is calling from his cell phone while driving to the hospital emergency room. He says that he, his wife and their two teenage children have all become violently sick to their stomachs. The previous evening, the family had ordered a bucket of chicken from a local take-out restaurant. All of the family members had tasted the chicken, but it had tasted peculiar and none were able to finish their pieces. Being a diligent, not to mention somewhat litigious, fellow, John thought that he would check on his legal rights before even determining his and his family's medical condition. You wisely ask him whether he still had the remnants of the dinner. John, consistent with his cautious nature, had saved the contents in a bag on his kitchen counter.

In order to have any cause of action against the restaurant, you know that the chicken will have to be tested for the presence of nasty bacteria or the like. What should be done with the bag of chicken in order to preserve its evidentiary value? How can you get the chicken to a laboratory for testing?

McCormick, 6th Ed., §§ 212–213; Federal Rules of Evidence 401–403.

10–3. Plaintiffs, Peter and Eleanor Houston, bring an action for the wrongful death of their teenage son, Joseph, against Burgers R Us and its local franchise. The action is based upon Joseph's death after eating a hamburger purchased at defendant's franchise. The Houston's claim that the hamburger contained a lethal form of E coli bacteria causing the illness resulting in Joseph's death.

Joseph became ill shortly after eating a portion of a hamburger purchased from Burgers. Joseph had been with several of his friends, eating food purchased from Burgers, while the group "hung out" in the Houston's family room. Joseph stopped eating the sandwich because "it tasted funny." The four other teenagers present had eaten sandwiches other than hamburgers. After Joseph was taken to the hospital, his father, Peter, found about half of a hamburger sandwich in the garbage can in the Houston family room. He kept the hamburger in the refrigerator until the next day when Joseph died. Peter and Eleanor, as well as the other five Houston children, had access to the refrigerator. Shortly after returning home from the hospital, about two hours after Joseph's death, Peter called his lawyer and told her what had happened. The lawyer, Jane, told Peter to keep the remains of the sandwich and she would be come over to get it immediately. Jane arrived about fifteen minutes later, talked to Peter for a few minutes and then put the sandwich in her briefcase. She went home for the evening, where she placed the hamburger in her refrigerator. Jane lives with her husband and three children, ages 12, 10 and 7. The entire family opened the refrigerator at some point during that evening, but, in accordance with Jane's instructions, they did not touch the package containing the hamburger.

The next day, Jane returned the hamburger to her briefcase and brought it to a laboratory. The laboratory technician, Milton, immediately took possession of it and placed it in a sealed envelope. The envelope was placed in a refrigerated unit. Milton took the hamburger in the sealed package from the unit later that day. He broke the seal of the envelope and tested its contents. He discovered the presence of the E coli bacteria that allegedly caused Joseph's death.

During the wrongful death case, plaintiffs seek to introduce the results of Milton's test. Before doing so, they call Peter and Jane to testify to their actions with regard to the hamburger. They then call Milton who testifies to his handling of the hamburger and his tests. Milton, testifying as an expert, also states that the hamburger contained E coli bacteria and, in his opinion, contained those bacteria at the time that a portion of it was consumed by Joseph, two days earlier.

Defendants object to Milton's testimony based upon a failure to properly authenticate the substance tested by him. What ruling by the court and why?

McCormick, 6th Ed., §§ 212–213; Federal Rules of Evidence 401–403.

10–4. Refer to Appendix A, *Hines v. National Motor Co.*, Document 7. Defense counsel would like to call Officer Schwartz to testify to the facts contained in his supplemental report. Counsel also would like to introduce the unbroken bottle. Plan the direct examination of Schwartz on this question. Will the bottle be admissible?

McCormick, 6th Ed., §§ 184–185, 212–213; Federal Rules of Evidence 401–403.

10–5. At 7 a.m. one morning, the owner of a three-story retail store building discovered Ron on the roof of the building, stuck in an air ventilator shaft on the top of the building with his head and shoulders at the level of the roof. When the police arrived they found that the metal housing above the shaft, which normally rose three feet above the roof and was affixed to the roof by screws, was lying on the roof next to the shaft. They found screws scattered about but no screwdriver. However, they did find a "jimmy" (a short crowbar) on the roof next to the shaft. Ron was charged with burglary. Ron's defense is that late at night, while he was drunk, he fell off the roof of the hotel building next door onto the roof of the store building, and in an attempt to get off the roof of the store building, he decided to try to leave by going down the air ventilator shaft.

Before trial, for some reason, the police lost the "jimmy" which was found near the shaft. The prosecutor would like to introduce a second, similar "jimmy" into evidence. Can he do so successfully over anticipated objections? How should he attempt to do so?

McCormick, 6th Ed., §§ 212–213; Federal Rules of Evidence 401–403.

10–6. Refer to Appendix A, *Hines v. National Motor Co.*

(A) Plaintiff would like to introduce a diagram of the scene of the crash of Mr. Hines' car. Plaintiff intends to use the diagram in connection with the testimony of several witnesses, including Officer Robert Schwartz. The exhibit was prepared by Officer Schwartz. The basis for preparation of the diagram was a county map of roads, drawn to scale and showing the exact alignment and curvature of roads. Officer Schwartz carefully measured the distances from the road to the tree, which was the Hines' vehicle's final resting place. The car itself is shown to scale. Decide what witness you would use to lay the foundation for the introduction of the chart and plan the testimony necessary for its introduction into evidence. Could you simply have any witness familiar with the scene testify that the exhibit is a fair and accurate depiction of the scene immediately after the accident?

(B) Assume that plaintiff, rather than introducing a blow-up of the document, would like to have Officer Schwartz draw the same diagram on a blackboard in the courtroom. Plan the testimony necessary for the witness to draw the diagram. What problems exist in connection with such a drawing? Would it make any difference if Officer Schwartz, instead of using the blackboard, began to draw the diagram on a chart showing the configuration of the actual road on which the accident took place and simply added the position of the Hines' car and the tree it hit?

(C) Assume that instead of a diagram and a blackboard drawing, plaintiff seeks to introduce a computer generated video presentation of the accident scene, with graphics showing the road and a picture of the Hines' car smashed against the tree. Would such a presentation be admission? If so, what foundational testimony would be necessary to support its admission.

McCormick, 6th Ed., §§ 212, 214, 218; Federal Rules of Evidence 401–403, 901.

10–7. Refer to Appendix A, *Hines v. National Motor Co.* Plaintiff's counsel calls plaintiff, Livia Hines, to the witness stand. Counsel would like to introduce, through her, a photograph of her husband taken two years before his death. The photograph shows Chester smiling broadly and carrying the Hines' two-year-old niece on his shoulders. It was taken at a family picnic by Hines' brother, the father of the little girl. Plan the testimony necessary to introduce the photograph. Assuming defendant objects, will the photograph be admissible?

McCormick, 6th Ed., §§ 212, 214–215; Federal Rules of Evidence 401–403.

10–8. Refer to Appendix B, *State v. Well.* Assume that, in addition to the other evidence set forth in the file, the state has the following photographs available to it:

(A) A photograph showing the place where Mary was found in the ditch. The photograph was taken by a county surveyor two years before the date of the accident. There were no significant changes in the scene from the time of the picture to the time of the incident.

(B) A photograph showing Mary's lifeless body at the accident scene. She is lying on a stretcher alongside the police ambulance. The photograph was taken by one of the two police officers who arrived on the scene. No bruises are discernible.

(C) A photograph taken by the medical examiner's photographer showing Mary's nude body just before the autopsy was to begin. The photograph clearly shows the abrasions on her head and abdomen.

What foundation should be laid for the introduction of these photographs? Is each of them admissible over objection?

McCormick, 6th Ed., §§ 212, 214–215; Federal Rules of Evidence, 401–403, 901.

10–9. The Women's Clinic Building was badly damaged by a bomb that went off early one morning. Fortunately, there was no one in the building at the time. The guard, Louis, who had been stationed in the lobby of the building had taken an unauthorized coffee break at a local diner. Before leaving the building, Louis made sure that the surveillance television camera was operating. After the explosion, the police checked the camera and found it intact. They also were able to salvage the video tape showing the front entrance to the building for the preceding three hours. The latter part of the tape shows one person entering the building. Although the individual is masked and wears a hood, he also wears a distinctive black tee shirt, seemingly hand printed, with the words "Save the Babies." The tape shows the individual dropping a package in the lobby and then running from the building. The ensuing explosion also appears on the tape just seconds later.

Various evidence leads the police to arrest Damon for the bombing. A tee shirt identical to the one shown in the video tape is among the items found in Damon's room in a legal search after his arrest.

The prosecution seeks to introduce the video tape at Damon's trial. What evidentiary foundation should the prosecution lay for its introduction?

McCormick, 6th Ed., §§ 184–185, 212, 216; Federal Rules of Evidence 401–403, 901.

10–10. Defendant, Harry Hart, is charged with hit and run. The prosecution alleges that his car struck a pedestrian, John Davis, causing him serious injuries. Davis was crossing a downtown street in the crosswalk when a car, turning right on a red light, struck him. Witnesses will testify that the driver of the car stopped for a moment, looked back out of the window of the car and then sped off at a high rate of speed. No witness can identify Hart as the driver of the car. Furthermore, no witness can remember the license plate number of the car that struck Davis. However, Joseph Watkins, who was standing close to the site of the accident, took a cell phone photograph of the rear of the car striking Davis. The photograph clearly shows the license number of the car—a number registered to Hart. Hart's car meets the description of the car that hit Davis. The prosecution calls Watkins as a witness. He testifies that he was at the accident scene and describes the car hitting Davis. He also identifies a digitally reproduced slide of the photograph as the one he took of the accident. However, he has no independent recollection of the license plate number. Defendant objects to the introduction of the photograph. What ruling by the court?

McCormick, 6th Ed., §§ 215–216; Federal Rules of Evidence 401–403, 901.

10–11. Margaret is the owner of a motel situated on property adjacent to an animal hospital owned and operated by Don, a veterinarian. Margaret brings suit to enjoin Don from maintaining a nuisance by allowing the dogs under his care to bark and howl loudly throughout the night to the great disturbance of Margaret's motel guests. At the trial

Margaret testifies that in anticipation of the trial she prevailed upon Fred, a friend owning a tape recorder, to occupy one of the motel rooms for a night and record the various animal noises audible therein. Margaret identifies a tape shown her by her attorney as the tape Fred had delivered to Margaret the morning after Fred's stay in the motel. Margaret's attorney then offers the tape in evidence and proposes to play it for the court. Has Don any valid basis for objection? Should the tape be admitted only if additional foundation is supplied? What foundation?

McCormick, 6th Ed., §§ 212, 216; Federal Rules of Evidence 401–403, 901.

10–12. Susan is charged with the murder of her husband, Mark. The prosecution claims that she shot Mark in the head while the two of them were lying in bed. The motive for the murder was allegedly a large insurance policy that had been taken out on Mark's life. Susan claims that Mark was killed when the pistol he kept under his pillow for protection against intruders accidentally discharged.

Shortly after Mark's death, his sister, Nancy, gave the police an audiotape that she said had been given to her by Mark two days before his death. Mark told her not to listen to the tape, but to give it to the police in the event that anything happened to him. Although Nancy was understandably upset by her brother's request, she heeded his instructions. When the police played the tape, they heard a male voice stating:

> My wife, Susan, and I are having serious troubles in our marriage. I know that she has been seeing someone. She is also violent at times and has threatened to kill me. There is a large insurance policy on me, payable to her. I fear that she is going to try to kill me in order to collect on the insurance.

Nancy identifies the voice on the tape as that of her brother, Mark.

Assume for purposes of this problem that the statements on the tape are admissible as exceptions to the hearsay rule. Assume also that the state has no other information available to it to authenticate the tape other than the circumstances under which Nancy says she received it and her identification of her brother's voice. Should the tape be admitted?

McCormick, 6th Ed., §§ 212, 216; Federal Rules of Evidence 401–403, 901.

10–13. In the trial of Ken for armed robbery, three eyewitnesses testified for the state that the person whom they had testified was at the scene of the crime and whom they identified as Ken had not been wearing eyeglasses. The defense attorney introduced testimony that Ken's vision was very poor, that he had had glasses of a certain power prescribed, and that he always wore these glasses except when he was at his home. Defense counsel then placed a lens maker upon the stand who testified that, with the defendant's prescription, he had made a set of lenses which he had placed in frames. The lenses he made, if worn by a person with normal eyesight, would enable such a person to see with Ken's uncorrected natural vision. Ken's attorney then attempted to introduce the described lenses into evidence as an exhibit, planning to ask each juror to put on the frames and look through these lenses. Should the exhibit be admitted for this purpose over objection?

McCormick, 6th Ed., §§ 212, 217; Federal Rules of Evidence 401–403.

10–14. Nelson was on a guided tour for visitors conducted through the manufacturing plant of Glen Corp. While on the tour, he fell from a steel walkway and sustained severe injuries. Nelson sues Glen Corp., charging negligence in the construction and maintenance of the walkway. The Glen Corp. takes the position that the railings on the walkway were sufficiently high and were safely constructed.

At the time of the trial, the particular walkway and railings are no longer in existence. They have been replaced by a differently designed walkway.

(A) Counsel for Glen Corp. wants to use in court a model of a part of the walkway and railings as they existed at the time of Nelson's fall. The model is four feet deep, three feet wide, and four feet high. Assuming all the necessary information would be available to counsel, what evidentiary foundation should be laid for an introduction of the model? Assuming the model is admitted into evidence, defendant's attorney would like to have it examined by the jurors in the jury room. It is very heavy but can be lifted and carried by four strong people. Can the model properly be sent to the jury room?

(B) Instead of using the model in question, counsel for the defendant creates a computer simulation of the accident scene. The simulation, using animation, shows the scene of the accident and illustrates that Nelson could not have fallen from the walkway unless, contrary to express instructions, he had climbed onto the walkway railing. Assuming again that all the necessary information would be available to counsel, what evidentiary foundation should be laid for the introduction of the model? Will the simulation be admissible? Should the jury be permitted to use the simulation during its deliberations?

McCormick, 6th Ed., §§ 212,214, 217–218; Federal Rules of Evidence 401–403.

10–15. Helen sues William for child support, claiming that William is the father of her now six-month-old child. As part of her case-in-chief, Helen testifies and identifies a six-month-old baby as her child. The baby bears a striking resemblance to William. Her counsel asks that she be permitted to walk past the jury box holding the baby. Defendant objects. What ruling by the court?

McCormick, 6th Ed., §§ 212, 217; Federal Rules of Evidence 401–403.

10–16. Malcolm purchased a 25 pound sack of flour, milled by the Miller Corp. He placed the sack on a kitchen shelf, closed by doors. The bottom of the shelf was at floor level. He opened the sack and left it open. Four weeks later, after he had used about one-third of the flour, he delved into the sack with a cup to obtain a cup of flour and a shriveled object, covered with flour, was in the cup. He determined the object to be a dried mouse and promptly fainted and fell to the kitchen floor. In an action brought against the Miller Corp., Malcolm alleges damages for physical injuries occurring when he fainted and fell, as well as damages for mental suffering by reason of resulting nervousness, etc. While Malcolm's attorney was examining him at the trial, during questioning concerning his aversion to mice, the attorney's left hand was partly closed. Without warning she stretched out her left arm, opened her hand and revealed to Malcolm what was actually a toy mouse. Malcolm fainted, and the trial was thereby interrupted. During the interruption, defendant moved for a mistrial. Should the motion be granted?

McCormick, 6th Ed., § 217; Federal Rules of Evidence 401–403.

10–17. In the incident involving Ron's sojourn in the air ventilator shaft (*see* Problem 10–5, above), the hotel building from which Ron claimed he fell was the only building adjacent to the store. No windows faced the roof of the store building. From the top of the hotel roof to the top of the retail building the distance was 18 feet and from the top of the retail store to the ground was 36 feet. At the back of the retail store building were two piping systems to the roof, made of tile pipe, which could possibly be used (with care) as though the pipes were ladders.

In the presentation of the state's case, the prosecuting attorney introduced several photographs of the roof of the retail store with respect to the adjoining hotel building, and photographs of the piping on the back side of the store building. They were all taken by a police photographer shortly after Ron was found on the roof. After the photographs were introduced, the prosecuting attorney moved that the trial be recessed for a view by the jury of the back of the retail building and the roof of the building. Over objection of defendant's attorney, the judge so ordered. Although the defendant's attorney requested that Ron be permitted to accompany the jury, that request was refused, the judge stating that Ron's attorney could accompany the jury. Over objections, the judge appointed an attorney (who had nothing to do with the case otherwise) to take the jury to the scene, rather than any court official. The judge himself did not accompany the jury. Means of getting upon the roof had been arranged. By the time of the view, the roof had been recovered with asphalt, the ventilation housing shaft had been removed and the shaft had been covered up by the new roofing material. While the jury was on the roof on the side where the piping ran from the ground to the roof, a police officer, without apparent direction from anybody, climbed up the pipe from the ground to the roof while the jury watched. The attorney for defendant objected to the attorney in charge of the jury when he saw that this incident was about to happen but to no avail. When the trial resumed the next morning, a defense motion for mistrial was denied.

Assume that there is no statute specifically covering views in this jurisdiction.

(A) Should any of the defense attorney's objections have been upheld? Assuming you were the prosecuting attorney, how would you have planned in advance for the view to be conducted?

(B) At the end of the case, the judge included a very short instruction, along with his other instructions to the jury, to the effect that they could consider anything they had learned on the described view as evidence in the case. Was the instruction proper?

McCormick, 6th Ed., § 219; Federal Rules of Evidence 401–403.

10–18. Emma sues the Metro Transit Authority for damages for personal injuries, alleging that while she was attempting to alight from the Authority's bus number 108 through the rear door, and while the door was still open, the driver placed the bus in motion causing Emma to fall to the street. Emma alleges that the action of the driver constituted negligence which was the proximate cause of Emma's injuries. Defendant denies the allegations of the complaint, contending at trial that the accident could not have happened as alleged by Emma since the bus was equipped with an interlock device which prevents it from moving while the rear door is open.

During the trial, Metro's counsel moves that the jury be allowed to view the bus in Metro's garage, and the court grants the motion. The jury is then taken to the garage where it boards a bus which is stipulated by the parties to be of the same model as the one from which Emma fell. Over plaintiff's objections the jury is seated in the bus while counsel for the defendant takes the wheel and one juror stands on the treadle which opens the rear door. Counsel then announces that he is attempting to put the bus in motion, but the bus does not move. On the return to the courthouse, plaintiff moves for a mistrial based on the above events. What arguments should be advanced in support of this motion?

McCormick, 6th Ed., § 219; Federal Rules of Evidence 401–403.

10–19. In the trial of Malcolm's claim against the Miller Corp. (*see* Problem 10–16, above), the object found in the flour was introduced into evidence and was passed from juror to juror on a tray. When the jury retired, the plaintiff's attorney requested that the jury be permitted to take the object to the jury room but the request was refused by the trial judge.

After the jury had been deliberating for some time, a bailiff brought word that the jury would like to examine the mouse. Over objection of defendant's attorney, the judge then ordered that it be taken into the jury room. Shortly thereafter, the jury announced it had reached a verdict, and the verdict was for the defendant. Two days later the plaintiff's attorney moved for a new trial on the ground that affidavits of two jurors indicated that when the mouse was brought into the jury room, a juror had immersed it in a glass of water, washing off all of the encrusted flour on it, and the jury had determined that it was a piece of dried liver which plaintiff had probably dropped into the flour by accident or otherwise, and that it had already dried out by the time his attorney saw it. Plaintiff's counsel also presented affidavits of two experts indicating the object was really a dried mouse, and the excuse that such expert evidence had not been presented at the trial because (1) plaintiff had testified it was a dried mouse, (2) it clearly appeared to be a dried mouse covered with flour, and (3) defendant had not introduced any evidence at the trial even remotely contrary to plaintiff's evidence at the trial. Should a new trial be granted?

McCormick, 6th Ed., § 220; Federal Rule of Evidence 606(b).

10–20. David was tried for armed robbery. The presentation of the prosecutor's case occupied the first day. On the first morning, the prosecutor brought out by relevant testimony of eyewitnesses to the robbery that the accused had in his possession a sawed-off shotgun with which he threatened his victims. At the beginning of the afternoon session on the first day, the prosecutor brought to counsel table a shotgun (not a sawed-off shotgun) and some other physical objects. All these things could be seen by the jury. He introduced into evidence the other objects as things allegedly obtained by the defendant in the robbery. The shotgun was never referred to in any way during the entire afternoon. No weapon allegedly used by the defendant in the robbery was introduced in evidence. The prosecution rested and the jury was dismissed for the day. The defense moved for mistrial on the ground of the presence of the shotgun. Should the mistrial be granted?

McCormick, 6th Ed., §§ 184–185, 212–213. Federal Rules of Evidence 401–403.

CHAPTER 11

WRITINGS AND RELATED MATTERS

■ ■ ■

SECTION A. AUTHENTICATION

11–1. The Westville School District, pursuant to statutory authority, seeks to condemn a parcel of land owned by Jean Carmichael. The sole issue in the case is the value of the land. The School District's appraisers place the value of the land at $75,000. Carmichael would like to show that the district, two months prior to the commencement of these proceedings, offered to buy the land from her for $85,000. In support of this claim, Carmichael's lawyer presents a document to the court containing the following:

October 18, 2010

The Westville School District hereby offers to purchase the following land [the land in question is described] for the sum of $85,000.

> *A.P. Garfinkle* [signature]
> President of the Board
> Westville School District
>
> *George Prendergast* [signature]
> Secretary of the Board
> Westville School District

State of Doubt   )
)
County of West   )

Before me, Kathleen Curry, notary public, on this day personally appeared A.P. Garfinkle, President of the Board of the Westville School District, and George Prendergast, Secretary of the Board of the Westville School District, personally known to me to be the persons whose names are subscribed to the above instrument, and acknowledged that they executed the above instrument as the act of the Westville School District.

Given under my hand and seal, this 18th day of October, 2010.

[Seal]

Kathleen Curry [Signature]
Notary Public

Would this document be admissible over objection without further authentication? What evidentiary foundation would you lay to introduce the document into evidence? What if the document contained the official seal of the school board?

If this document were issued by the president and secretary of a private corporation rather than a school district, would the court's ruling be different? What if the private corporation document contained a corporate seal?

McCormick, 6th Ed., §§ 221, 224, 229, 229.1; Federal Rules of Evidence 901–902.

11–2. Theresa Rankin, a prominent business person, opened her mail one morning and found the following printed correspondence:

"Fifty of the city's business people support George Klaklo for Mayor. How about you?"

This statement was followed by the names of fifty of the town's prominent business people. Included in the list was the name, "Theresa Rankin." Rankin is the only business person in the town with that name. The correspondence bore the letterhead: Citizens for Klaklo, 83 Main Street (the address of Klaklo's campaign headquarters).

Rankin not only had never indicated support for Klaklo but in fact supported Klaklo's opponent in the mayoral race. Calls to other persons verified that the correspondence had been widely mailed. Rankin became enraged and filed suit against Klaklo alleging that the letter invaded her right of privacy. Klaklo answered the complaint by denying all of its allegations.

At the trial, Rankin's attorney called Rankin to the witness stand and Rankin identified the letter as the one she had received. The attorney then offered the letter in evidence. Defendant objected. What ruling by the trial judge? Consider what additional evidentiary foundation might better insure the introduction of the letter.

McCormick, 6th Ed., §§ 221, 224, 229; Federal Rules of Evidence 901–902.

11–3. Fuller, who owns a small appliance repair shop, brought a libel action against McCray. The action is based upon a letter which appeared in the neighborhood newspaper, *The Weekly Chronicle*. The letter, which bore McCray's signature, accused Fuller of stealing a toaster left at his shop for repair. McCray had been in Fuller's shop several days before the letter appeared asking for return of a toaster. Fuller swears that the toaster was never left at his shop. McCray now denies ever writing the letter to the *Chronicle*.

Fuller has copies of the newspaper in which the letter appeared. The editor of the newspaper has turned over to Fuller the original of the letter he says he received in the mail. The letter bears the subscription, "Martha McCray."

As attorney for Fuller, how might you go about obtaining the admission in evidence of:

(1) the letter as printed in the newspaper;

(2) the letter received by the newspaper bearing McCray's signature.

McCormick, 6th Ed., §§ 221–224, 229; Federal Rules of Evidence 901–902.

11–4. (A) Phillip was charged with the murder of James, who was killed while in his room at a hotel. The State seeks to show that Phillip was registered under the name John Clastoniksic at the same hotel on the night of the murder. In an effort to introduce a page of the hotel register to prove Phillip's registration, the state first called a hotel clerk who testified to the genuineness of the hotel register page for the date in question. The state then called Melissa, a handwriting expert, who testified that she had examined Phillip's signature on a property receipt given by Phillip to jail authorities. The receipt had previously been admitted into evidence. The expert was then handed the hotel register and asked whether there was a signature on it in Phillip's handwriting. Over objection, Melissa identified the signature "John Clastoniksic" as having been written by Phillip. When the state then offered the hotel register in evidence, the defendant's attorney objected and requested a hearing in the absence of the jury. Defendant's attorney offered to call a second expert who would give his opinion that the signature on the register was not Phillip's signature and also offered to call Phillip to testify that he had never signed the hotel register under the particular name, his own name, or any other name. Should the judge hear the evidence? Should the judge admit the register?

(B) Suppose that when the prosecutor was questioning Melissa as related above, the judge interrupted and said, "Counsel, let me look at that hotel register, I know the writing of the defendant of my own personal knowledge." The judge looked at the register, and said, "That is Phillip's signature there, the one written 'John Clastoniksic.' Counsel, on this basis alone I will overrule any objection to authentication and admit the register into evidence." Would the judge's action be correct?

McCormick, 6th Ed., §§ 68, 207, 221–223, 229; Federal Rules of Evidence 605, 901.

11–5. Tot Toters, Inc., is commercially engaged in the business of transporting children between their homes and private schools. Paula, mother of Tim, age 7, engaged Tot Toters to convey her son to and from his elementary school. On November 15, 1999, Tot Toters' van left the school without Tim and the latter, apparently attempting to walk home, was struck and severely injured by a car. Paula brings suit against Tot Toters. In its defense, Tot Toters wishes to introduce in evidence a tape made by the automatic phone answering device maintained to take messages at its office. The recording is of a woman's voice which is clearly audible and says, "Don't pick up Tim at school today, November 14. His father will get him." None of Tot Toters' employees can remember ever speaking with Paula personally, and the employee playing back the messages on November 15 did not recognize Paula's voice.

As Tot Toters' counsel, what foundation would you consider sufficient for admission of the tape?

McCormick, 6th Ed., § 228; Federal Rules of Evidence 901–902.

11–6. Dorothy is charged with larceny. The State has evidence that a call was made to Henningsen's Boutique and answered by Jane, an employee. The caller identified herself as Mrs. Jem, a woman who was known to Jane as a good customer of the store, although Jane had never spoken to her in person or by telephone. The caller stated she wished to purchase certain merchandise as a Christmas present for an employee in her husband's business and she wanted the present sent to a neighboring suburban community. Jane said the store had no delivery service to that community, whereupon the caller said she would try to make some arrangement and would call back. She did call Jane back and said that a Miss Jornel would be at the bus station at four o'clock and had agreed to wait for delivery of the package to her at the bus station, and would take it out to the suburban community and deliver it to the house of the intended donee. Jane agreed the merchandise would be so delivered at the bus station. Thereafter, acting on a suspicion, Jane called the home of Mrs. Jem. A woman identifying herself as Mrs. Jem stated she had never called the store in the calls related above. The store notified the police. The package was taken by a delivery messenger to the bus station, and after some inquiring around, Dorothy came up to the delivery messenger and said she was Miss Jornel, and he delivered the package to her. Whereupon Dorothy was arrested by a detective in plain clothes.

Can Jane simply testify to the telephone calls as related above without further identification of the voices?

McCormick, 6th Ed., § 228; Federal Rule of Evidence 901.

11–7. The law firm of which you are an associate has received the following letter from a client, the local office of Bear, Bull & Co., stockbrokers:

We would like to have your legal opinion upon the following problem which has come to the attention of our office.

As you no doubt realize, a substantial portion of the business of Bear, Bull & Co. conducted here in our local office consists of brokering purchases and sales of securities for our clients, on a commission basis, on the New York and other major exchanges.

Most of the transactions handled by us are on behalf of clients with whom we have enjoyed a continuing relationship and who have established accounts with us. At the same time, however, we frequently receive "call-in" orders (generally by phone, fax or e-mail, but occasionally by regular mail) from persons with whom we have not previously dealt and who are not known to anyone in our office. These persons request that we buy or sell designated securities, sometimes rather large blocks of such securities, for them. Since such "call-ins" frequently prove to be valuable, continuing customers it has always been our practice to execute transactions requested in the above fashion.

It has, however, occurred to some of our salesmen that by adopting the above practice we may be placing Bear, Bull in an unfortunate legal position. We would therefore like your opinion on this question and your suggestions as to possible practices which we might adopt which would serve to afford us adequate legal protection without unduly alienating potential clients of the firm. In the latter connection, I might add that we would be extremely reluctant to go to the length of requiring a person unknown to us to come to our office before executing a transaction on his behalf.

> Sincerely,
> Bear, Bull & Co.
> by s/ Harriet Hornblower

How would you respond to the above inquiry?

McCormick, 6th Ed., §§ 221–228; Federal Rules of Evidence 901–902.

11–8. Apple entered into a contract with Cargon, Inc., under which Cargon was to manufacture and deliver to Apple a quantity of tools and dies. A complicated dispute arose concerning the whole matter and a suit by Apple for damages for breach of contract and for damages for misrepresentation resulted. As to one identifiable part of the tools and dies ordered, Apple took the position that there had been a complete failure of delivery. Cargon claimed that the order for that part had been canceled by agreement and in the alternative that such part of the order had been delivered. Apple's counsel has a typed letter bearing the signature, Alice Dirk. Dirk is a former Vice President of Sales of Cargon. Through oversight, Apple's counsel had not included the letter in a list of documents which the attorneys had stipulated prior to trial were genuine. Apple's counsel wishes to introduce the letter at the trial. The letter contains the printed letterhead of Cargon, Inc., and the printed name at the top right, "Alice Dirk, Vice President of Sales, Tel. (110) 782–3333." The body of the letter reads as follows (after the proper address, date and salutation to Apple):

> I have checked with Lester Quail, the manager of our tool and die sales division, and he told me that of this date the tools and dies, items 9 through 105, have not been delivered to you as per your order. I will investigate this matter further, and communicate with you shortly.

Very truly yours,
(a signature reading Alice Dirk)
Vice President of Sales

The letter is to be introduced as relevant to the point that the items mentioned were not delivered on the date of the letter. If admissible for this purpose, assume the letter is relevant to the issue of failure of delivery of the items.

Assume you are Apple's counsel. What questions would you ask under the alternative circumstances set forth below in order to have the letter admitted into evidence?

(A) Alice Dirk no longer is employed by Cargon, Inc. She is in the city in which the trial will be held and has indicated she would testify she wrote the letter. She remembers nothing of the actual transaction which occurred more than four years before the trial nor does she remember the letter. Assume you wish to attempt to use her as a witness to introduce the letter.

(B) Alice Dirk is unavailable as a witness. Her former secretary, George Secretary, who no longer works for Cargon but is employed in the city in which the trial is held, has indicated he would be cooperative and willing to testify concerning the letter. He has stated he can remember the signing because he happened to know Mr. Apple personally. He indicates he would say that he saw the letter signed and that he knows Dirk's signature. He has personal knowledge of Dirk's former position in the company.

(C) Assume that George Secretary is available as a witness but that he remembers nothing about the letter in question. He can only say that he knows Dirk's signature and her former position in the company and that the signature on the letter is in fact Dirk's.

(D) Neither Dirk nor her secretary is available as a witness. The only witness available is your client, Apple. He tells you he dealt with Dirk only once in all of his difficulties with Cargon. He tells you that several days before the date of the letter, he telephoned a Lester Quail, whom he knew to be the manager of tools and dies sales division, to complain about the lack of delivery of the items in question. Quail pleaded ignorance as to whether there had been delivery or not. Apple then telephoned the Cargon office and asked for the vice-president in charge of sales. The answerer said, "Just a minute" and then a second person answered, and upon Apple's inquiry to him he identified himself as George Secretary, Ms. Dirk's secretary. He asked him to identify himself. He said he was "Mr. Apple" and that he wanted to talk about Cargon's failure to deliver part of an order to him. He said, "Just a minute." A female voice then answered and said, "This is Alice Dirk, Vice President of Sales, what can I do for you?" Apple briefly explained his contract with Cargon, the lack of delivery of the items mentioned in the letter and the failure of Quail on the same day to give him any satisfactory answer to his complaint. The voice on the line said that she would look into the matter and get back to him by telephone or letter. He had never seen the signature of Dirk before he saw the above letter, and he has not seen the signature since.

Assuming, instead, that you are counsel for Cargon, consider what objections you might make to the introduction of the letter under any of the circumstances listed above. Should the letter be admitted?

McCormick, 6th Ed., §§ 221–224, 227–228; Federal Rules of Evidence 901–902.

11–9. (A) Assume that under the facts of Problem 11–8, as set out in Paragraph (D), the letter quoted in the problem arrived via fax. What evidentiary foundation should be laid for its admission? What if it arrived via e-mail?

(B) Assume that in the controversy described in Problem 11–8, Cargon seeks to show that sometime after Dirk's correspondence with Apple, Lester Quail, the manager of the tool and dies division, received the following e-mail:

> To: quail@cargon.com
> From: apple@appinc.com
> Date: October 8, 2009
> Subject: New business

> It has been a pleasure doing business with you and Alice. We have a large project coming up on which we know we will want Cargon to do the tools and dies. We'll be in touch. Many thanks for your diligence. Marvin Apple

Quail will testify that he replied to the e-mail as follows.

> To: apple@appinc.com
> From: quail@cargon.com
> Date: October 8, 2009
> Subject: Continuing our business relationship

> We are pleased that you have found our business relationship satisfactory and that there were no problems with the last order. We look forward to your future contact. Many thanks for your business. Lester Quail

Quail says there was no indication of any problem in the sending of his reply but that he received no further reply from Apple.

Apple denies sending the e-mail bearing his signature. He also will testify that he has never received e-mail correspondence from Quail. He does admit that the mailbox listing for him is in fact his e-mail address.

Assuming the relevance of both e-mails, what evidentiary foundation does Cargon have to lay in order to have both Apple and Quail's e-mails admitted? Assuming the best foundation under the circumstances, will the e-mails be admitted?

McCormick, 6th Ed., § 227; Federal Rules of Evidence 901–902.

11–10. Walter is charged with mail fraud. The indictment alleges that he created a Ponzi scheme—an illegal scheme in which persons were encouraged to invest in a marketing company and then get others to invest in the same company. The company in fact neither manufactured nor sold any product. Each investor could be made whole by selling the product to other people. The last investors would be the ones taking the loss. Walter's desktop computer was seized by the government agents pursuant to a valid warrant. However, the computer's memory had been wiped clean. No incriminating documents or e-mail correspondence was found on it. However, the legal seizure of the computer of one of the mid-level investors, George, was more successful. The government charged that George had sold shares of the company to others as part of the Ponzi scheme.

George's hard-drive contained his e-mail inbox. The inbox contained an email reading as follows:

From: walter@marketing.web
To: george@sub.net
Date: July 26, 2010
Subject: keep selling those shares

Hi George: we will have to dump those shares quickly. The feds are starting an investigation and I am getting worried. Call me. Walt

No other e-mails in George's hard-drive appear to be from or to Walter. However, several other emails in both his inbox and sent-mail files deal with attempts to sell shares in the enterprise in question. If called as a witness in Walter's case, George would claim his Fifth Amendment right not to incriminate himself.

Based on the above facts, does the government have enough evidence to authenticate the e-mail in question as coming from Walter? If not, what additional information might it obtain to establish authenticity.

McCormick, 6th Ed. §§ 224, 227; Federal Rule of Evidence 901.

11–11. Dan is charged with vehicular hit-and-run. His car allegedly hit and badly injured Vernon at about 7:30 p.m. on June, 10, 2010. Dan denies that either he or his car were anywhere near the location at which Vernon was injured—near the North Town Mall—at the date and time in question. He will testify that he was on the other side of town, at a Starbuck's Coffee shop at 7:30 p.m., having coffee with his friend, Joe. The Starbucks he claims he was at is located at the South Side Mall— which is located at least a half-hour from the site of the accident. There is also a Starbucks at the North Town Mall. Unfortunately for Dan, Joe died shortly before the trial and there was no opportunity to preserve his testimony that would have corroborated Dan's alibi. Dan seeks to introduce cell-phone records of text messages that he maintains corroborate the date, time and place of his coffee with Joe. There are three entries in the phone company records for June 10, 2010. The first is a call made from the phone number assigned to Joe to the number assigned to Dan. The phone company will verify both phone numbers. The text message reads: "Meet me at SBs at 7." The second is from Dan to Joe and reads: "Can't do 7, but will be SSM 7:30. Can you do SBs then?" The third is from Joe to Dan: "7:30 at SB works for me." Dan will testify that he sent the second text message and that he understood SSM to refer to the South Side Mall and SB to refer to Starbucks. Does Dan have enough information to authenticate the text messages in question?

McCormick, 6th Ed., §§ 224, 227, Federal Rule of Evidence 901.

11–12. Moe and Jem are owners in fee of adjacent farms. Each inherited his respective property from his father. For the last 40 years, Jem and his predecessor in title have openly and continuously used a road and bridge located on Moe's property to gain access to their own farm. In 2010, Moe wishes to destroy the bridge and close the road because by doing so he will make it difficult for unauthorized hunters to reach his land. Jem objects to the destruction of the bridge and closure of the road, and brings suit contending that he has by his long use obtained a prescriptive easement. The jurisdiction recognizes a presumption that use of the property of another is adverse.

Moe has retained you to resist Jem's claim. He has informed you that the bridge and road were built by his father and that he, Moe, has always assumed Jem's use was purely permissive. To support his claim, Moe has given you a letter which he says he found recently among his father's old income tax returns. The letter is dated October 28, 1964, is addressed to Moe's father, and bears the signature, "Jed." Jedidiah was Jem's father's name. The letter states, "I appreciate the permission you have offered to use your new bridge and road." Do you anticipate you will be able to introduce the letter into evidence? Would your estimate change if you learn on discovery that Jem will testify that his father hated the name Jed and insisted throughout his life that he be called "Jedidiah."

McCormick, 6th Ed., §§ 225, 229; Federal Rules of Evidence 901–902.

SECTION B.   ORIGINAL DOCUMENT RULE

11–13. John was charged with setting off a charge of dynamite which destroyed a building. The prosecutor has convincing evidence that John, prior to the bombing, had acquired dynamite caps marked "Boom Brand." A dynamite cap marked "Boom Brand" was found at the scene of the bombing by the first police officer to arrive on the scene. Should the prosecutor anticipate that the police officer will be permitted to testify over objection that the cap was marked "Boom Brand?"

McCormick, 6th Ed., § 233; Federal Rules of Evidence 1001–1002.

11–14. Gary is being prosecuted for selling a pornographic photograph to a minor. Can the prosecutor elicit a description of the photograph from the minor on the witness stand? (The minor was 17 years old at the time he purchased the photograph.) The prosecutor also has at hand the photograph allegedly sold by Gary.

McCormick, 6th Ed., §§ 230–234; Federal Rules of Evidence 1001–1002.

11–15. Michael was at the scene of a collision between automobiles driven by Joan and Barry and happened to record the entire accident on movie film. Both Joan and Barry know that Michael has the film and their attorneys have viewed it. In a subsequent suit between Joan and Barry, Joan's attorney objects to Barry relating the circumstances of the accident. What ruling by the court?

McCormick, 6th Ed., §§ 230–234; Federal Rules of Evidence 1001–1002.

11–16. Continental Flange Co. sued B & K Manufacturing Company claiming that it delivered $25,000 worth of specially manufactured flanges to B & K. B & K claims that no delivery was ever made.

Malcolm, president of Continental, seeks to testify that, several weeks after the contract for the manufacture of the flanges was entered into, Brooke, president of B & K, visited Malcolm's office. Brooke indicated that she wanted to be relieved of her contractual obligation. Before there was any further conversation between the two individuals, Malcolm asked for Brooke's permission to record their conversation on tape so that there would be no later question as to what was said. Brooke agreed. Brooke then stated that the contract had become burdensome to B & K because of a change in B & K's production schedule. A large order requiring a different kind of flange had been obtained and had to be completed prior to the order requiring the Continental flange. Malcolm stated that, although he would like to accommodate Brooke, he could not do so because of the fact that the flange ordered by B & K was being specially manufactured. Brooke then stated that B & K would do no further business with Continental and terminated the conversation. B & K's attorney objects to Malcolm's testimony with regard to this conversation, contending that Malcolm's testimony is inadmissible in view of the availability of the tape recording. What ruling by the trial judge? Assume that instead of Malcolm's testimony, Continental's attorney sought to introduce, over B & K's objection, a secretary's transcription of the tape recording of this conversation. What ruling by the trial judge?

McCormick, 6th Ed., §§ 230–234; Federal Rules of Evidence 1001–1002.

11–17. Brown is charged in federal court with illegal possession of firearms transported in interstate commerce. As part of its case, the government has the burden of proving that the firearms were in fact transported in interstate commerce. The weapons were seized from the defendant in North Carolina. The government called an ATF agent to the witness stand. The agent testifies that he reviewed documents kept in the regular course of the weapon manufacturers' businesses that showed that the firearms involved were manufactured in Arizona, Connecticut and Montana. Based upon this evidence, the government argues that the firearms must have been shipped in interstate commerce to North Carolina. The defense objects on the grounds that the agent is testifying to the contents of documents that have not been introduced into evidence. The government argues that the testimony is admissible because the places of manufacture were facts that existed independently of the documents. The court overrules the objection.

Was the court's ruling correct?

McCormick, 6th Ed., §§ 230–234; Federal Rules of Evidence 1001–1002.

11–18. Dailey is prosecuted for murder. The prosecutor has his signed confession. The confession was given orally by Dailey, taken down and transcribed by a secretary. The transcribed statement was read by Dailey and then signed by him. The secretary and Oliver, a police officer, could also testify to the substance of the confession as they heard it when it was made orally. Could there be a successful objection to testimony of the secretary and Oliver stating the substance of the confession? Suppose that after the confession was transcribed it was never again shown to the defendant and thus never signed by him?

McCormick, 6th Ed., §§ 230–234; Federal Rules of Evidence 1001–1002.

11–19. After long negotiations, Marcus and Davis reduced an agreement to an unsigned writing. Marcus lived in Kansas and Davis lived in Minnesota. They agreed that Marcus would finalize the unsigned writing in formal form, sign it, and send it on to Davis for signing. Thereupon Marcus had an original produced on his word processor and made three photocopies from the original. He signed the original (refer to this copy as C_1) and of two of the photocopies in ink (refer to these copies as C_2 and C_3). The signature lines on the third photocopy were kept blank (refer to this copy as C_4). He then made a photocopy of C_1 containing his signature (refer to this copy as C_5).

Marcus merely kept C_4 and C_5 in his files. He mailed C_1, C_2 and C_3 to Davis. Upon receipt of these copies, Davis signed C_1 and C_2 in ink. He also made a photocopy of C_1 containing both his and Marcus's signatures (refer to this copy as C_6). He placed C_1, C_3, and C_6 in his files and mailed C_2 back to Marcus.

For purposes of introduction by Marcus' attorney at the trial of a subsequent suit brought by Marcus in Kansas for breach of such contract, which of the copies (C_1, C_2, C_3, C_4, C_5, C_6) may be introduced successfully over an objection under the rules governing the contents of documents, assuming there is no showing that any of the copies is unavailable? Does it make any difference that no one claims that there was any alteration of the terms of the agreement on any of the copies?

McCormick, 6th Ed., §§ 235–236; Federal Rules of Evidence 1001–1003.

11–20. In the case considered in Problem 11–16, B & K sought to support its contention that no delivery of the flanges was ever made by offering the testimony of an employee, Jenkins, who had reviewed the original records of the company and who would testify that he found no record of the delivery of the flanges. Assume that the records, if produced, would be regularly kept business records within the meaning of Federal Rule of Evidence 803(6), providing an exception to the hearsay rule. Would Jenkins' testimony be admissible?

Would it make any difference if Jenkins testifies that the original records were destroyed on August 13 (two weeks after the law suit was filed) pursuant to the company's annual record destruction policy? He can state that the records were due for destruction on July 1, but that he was behind schedule due to the press of other business.

Assume that Jenkins testifies that, at the time of the destruction of the original records, the originals were copied onto microfilm. Jenkins can fully set forth the procedure he uses for microfilming and further state the microfilm is a true and complete copy of the original records. Would the microfilm be admissible? Would the admissibility of the microfilm depend on whether the court finds the destruction of the originals to have been in good faith? Assuming it is admissible, would the microfilm have to be produced in lieu of Jenkins' testimony? If Jenkins based his testimony on his review of the microfilm, rather than the original records, would the microfilm have to be produced in lieu of his testimony?

McCormick, 6th Ed., §§ 235–239, 241; Federal Rules of Evidence 1001–1004, 1006.

11–21. Martin was on trial for violation of income tax law by willful and deliberate failure to report income for certain years from certain transactions. Internal Revenue Service agents had been granted permission to examine the defendant's books and records, and had examined them in defendant's office. At the trial, the government wishes to have these agents testify to the transactions shown in the books. Before the trial, the government had not attempted to subpoena the books for production at the trial. Should it be anticipated that the agents can so testify over objection?

Assuming that the defendant had no personal knowledge as of the time of the trial concerning the transactions involved, would his testimony, based upon an examination of his books before trial with regard to the transactions as allegedly shown in his books be admissible over objection?

McCormick, 6th Ed., §§ 234, 237, 241; Federal Rules of Evidence 1001–1004, 1006.

11–22. Harry brings suit against Doris and others to quiet title to a valuable tract of subdivision land. Doris' claim to the land rests upon a deed allegedly executed, delivered, and recorded in 1945 by Omar who at that time owned the property in fee simple. Doris contends that Omar's deed created a life estate in his nephew Jeff, now deceased, followed by a fee simple remainder in Doris' mother, Ivy, contingent upon Ivy's surviving her husband Joe. Doris claims that Ivy, who it is stipulated died in 1984, did survive Joe, took the property in fee simple, and on her death devised it to Doris. Harry contends that Ivy did not survive Joe, that accordingly her contingent remainder failed, and that Harry is entitled to the property as the sole heir of Omar who died intestate in 1960.

You are counsel for Doris. She has told you that she has never seen the original deed from Omar. She assumes it was delivered to Jeff, the former life tenant. She knows that Jeff has only one living relative, Ingrid. Doris has also checked in the county Recorder's office where she found Omar's deed recorded. She obtained a photocopy of the deed from a clerk. Doris knows nothing personally about the date or circumstances of Joe's death, but when Doris was a child her mother took her to a local cemetery and pointed to a grave saying, "Your step-father is buried there." Doris has given you a photo which she recently took of the headstone of the grave, showing the legend, "Joe, 1922–1980." Doris will testify to any of the foregoing facts.

You would like to introduce a copy of the recorded deed and the photo into evidence. Plan how you would attempt to do so. Would any steps you might take before trial (other than discovery) increase your chances of success?

McCormick, 6th Ed., §§ 233, 237, 240; Federal Rules of Evidence 1004–1005.

11–23. Murphy has been charged with bribery of a police officer, conspiracy to bribe a police officer (involving other persons), and attempt to bribe a police officer. The bribe was allegedly for the purpose of avoiding arrest for a continuous operation of an illegal gambling house.

The police officer by his story was approached by Murphy with an offer of a bribe and in effect responded he would have to think it over, but arranged to meet Murphy in a booth at a particular tavern in two days at a certain time and talk it over again. The officer reported the matter to the Organized Crime Unit of his police department, and it was arranged that the officer would carry in his pocket a miniature microphone and transmitter which would receive and send his conversation with Murphy at the tavern to a nearby receiver hooked up to a tape recorder. The arrangement was carried out and a tape recording of the conversation between Murphy and the police officer at the tavern was so reported. Later the amount offered as a bribe was given and received (actually in the presence of plain clothes police officers so they could see the transaction).

Under unexplained circumstances, the original tape was deliberately destroyed by an assistant prosecuting attorney, but fortunately not before a second tape recording had been made from the original recording by the police. The prosecutor has available testimony indicating the circumstances of the transcription to the second tape, identifying the first tape and the second tape as made from the first tape and containing its exact contents, and all other testimony necessary to demonstrate the accuracy of reproduction by the first tape, and by the second tape from the first tape.

It is important that the prosecutor introduce into evidence and play the second tape in presenting his evidence at the trial of Murphy. On these facts can he do so successfully over objections?

McCormick, 6th Ed., §§ 233–234, 237; Federal Rules of Evidence 1001–1004.

11–24. In the case considered in Problem 11–19, above, suppose that by different accidental fires, all of the copies referred to (C_1–C_6) were destroyed before the subsequent suit for breach of contract. However, before they were destroyed, Marcus had made 20 photocopies of C_2 (a photocopy of the original actually signed by both parties) and had sent all 20 copies to Davis. He also generated another copy of the contract, C_7, on his word processor.

In presenting Marcus' case at the trial, and to prove the contract, Marcus' attorney first proved that C_1–C_6 had been accidentally destroyed by fires. Then, to prove the contract, Marcus' attorney attempted to introduce C_7, which Marcus testified was an exact copy of the contract. Could this be done over objection, and if it were shown that Davis had twenty photocopies of C_2 back in his office in East Grand Forks, Minnesota?

McCormick, 6th Ed., §§ 236–238; Federal Rules of Evidence 1001–1004.

11–25. The Henning Company sued Underwood Bros. Distributing Company for breach of a contract to deliver machinery parts. Henning claims that the contract between the parties called for delivery on or before June 17. Delivery was not made until July 15. At the trial, Henning seeks to introduce what purports to be an unsigned photocopy of a contract to this effect dated March 1 as well as testimony that the original of the contract was destroyed in a fire. Underwood objects to this evidence and produces a document, also dated March 1, bearing what appear to be the signatures of the presidents of both companies and calling for delivery before *July* 17. As trial judge, you are convinced that Underwood's document is in fact the contract signed by the parties. Would you permit the unsigned carbon copy offered by Henning to be introduced into evidence?

McCormick, 6th Ed., §§ 53, 231, 237, 243; Federal Rules of Evidence 1001–1004, 1008.

11–26. Tom, a tenant from month to month in a large apartment complex, has had an eviction proceeding instituted against him by Bud, his landlord. Tom consults you and shows you a written notice of termination bearing the signature "Bud" which Tom says was served on him personally by the apartment manager. The notice appears to you to be in proper form and to have been served on Tom in a timely fashion. Tom also states, however, that he believes that Bud's motive for the eviction is Tom's attempt to form a tenant's organization to resist certain of Bud's practices. An eviction so motivated is prohibited by state statute and this would constitute a defense to Bud's eviction proceeding. As evidence of Bud's motive, Tom tells you that two weeks before he received his notice of termination a letter arrived in the mail while Tom was shaving. Tom's significant other, Sara, read Tom the letter which Tom recalls said: "Dear Tom: Stop leading an illicit union or you are out. I am so advising the apartment manager by copy of this letter. s/Bud." Tom was so enraged by this letter that he tore it into small pieces and flushed it down the toilet without looking at it. Both Tom and Sara had seen Bud's signature previously on the rental agreement for the apartment. Sara's recollection of the content of the letter is the same as Tom's except that she believes the letter said: "Stop living in illicit union or you are out."

(A) Consider whether you will be able successfully to object if Bud's attorney attempts to introduce a photocopy of the termination notice served on Tom.

(B) Consider whether Tom's testimony concerning the letter will be admissible. What objections do you anticipate? Can any of these objections be eliminated by action which might be taken before trial?

McCormick, 6th Ed., §§ 236–238; Federal Rule of Evidence 1003–1004.

CHAPTER 12

TESTIMONIAL EVIDENCE

■ ■ ■

SECTION A. COMPETENCY OF WITNESSES

12–1. Larry is charged with the robbery of a convenience store. The only people in the store at the time of the robbery were a clerk and a customer, Otto. The robber entered the store and pointed a gun at the clerk and Otto, who was standing at the cash register, and demanded all of the money in the register. The money was turned over and the gunman fled.

Larry was later arrested and charged with the robbery. The clerk failed to identify Larry at a lineup, claiming he was just too nervous at the time of the robbery to remember what the robber looked like. Otto, however, immediately picked him out of the lineup as the man who had robbed the store.

Defense counsel asked for a psychiatric evaluation of Otto, basing their request on an affidavit from the store clerk who stated that Otto was a guy who hung around the store who "wasn't too bright" and "probably wasn't right in the head." Should the court grant the psychiatric evaluation?

Assume that the psychiatric evaluation took place and that the psychiatrist testified that Otto has a "severe cognitive disability." According to the report, although Otto's chronological age was thirty-five, he had the mental and emotional age of a six-year-old. The psychiatrist further states that in her opinion Otto is capable of understanding what it means to tell the truth and that he is able to communicate his thoughts, at least on a juvenile level. Should the court conduct any further procedures before permitting Otto to testify? Assuming that all procedures verify the psychiatrist's opinion, should Otto be permitted to testify?

McCormick, 6th Ed., §§ 61–62; Federal Rules of Evidence 601, 603.

12–2. Defendant, Mark, was charged with the sexual abuse of his three-year-old step-daughter, Joan. Joan was four years old at the time of trial. Before any attempt was made to swear her in as a witness, defendant's attorney objected that she was incompetent to testify. The judge overruled that objection, stating there had been no showing to that effect.

Defendant's attorney then requested that the jury be removed temporarily from the courtroom and that he then be permitted to question the witness. The judge stated that was unnecessary and, without waiting for any further statement by the defendant's attorney, the judge immediately interrogated the witness in the presence of the jury as follows:

Q.   Is your name Joan?

A.   Uh-huh.

Q.   Where do you live?

A.   I don't know.

Q.   Do you live in Central City?

A.   I live on 8th Street, I don't know.

Q.   But do you live in Central City?

A.   Uh-huh, I been there.

Q.   Do you go to school?

A.   No.

Q.   Do you go to Sunday School?

A.   What's that?

Q.   You don't go to day school? (no answer)

Q.   How old are you?

A.   I had a birthday party a little while back.

Q.   How old were you then? (no answer)

Q.   Can you count it on your fingers?

A.   One, two, three, four.

Q.   Do you know what it is to tell a lie?

A.   Yes.

Q.   What is a lie?

A.   I don't tell something to my mother.

Q.   What will happen if you tell a lie?

A.   I will get a spanking.

Q.   O.K., Joan. Now we will go ahead, Joan. Ms. Smith and then Ms. Able will ask you some questions now. You just tell them the truth.

At this point the judge's questioning ended, and without more he stated that the prosecutor could begin her examination. Defendant objected, but her objection was overruled. The prosecutor began her examination. On direct examination, Joan testified convincingly to specific acts of abuse committed by the defendant. However, after cross-examination it appeared just as likely that Joan imagined the events based upon suggestions from her mother, Mark's estranged wife. At the end of this cross-examination, defendant's attorney moved to strike all the testimony of the witness.

Did the trial court follow the correct procedure in this case? Should Joan have been permitted to testify? Should the defense motion to strike be allowed?

McCormick, 6th Ed., §§ 62, 70; Federal Rules of Evidence 601, 603.

12–3. (A) Bill and Gene are charged with conspiracy to bomb a public building. You are their attorney. The chief prosecution witness is Dan who claims to have been a participant in the alleged conspiracy. You know that Dan has a record of convictions of robbery, sale of heroin, living on the proceeds of a prostitute, and other unsavory criminal acts. You also know that he seems to be an unwilling witness. Furthermore, you know that, after the alleged conspiracy, Dan was held in jail for quite some time on a narcotics charge because he was unable to post bond, but that the charges were dismissed. On these facts, you are convinced that Dan has been offered some sort of a "deal" by the government, but you are not particularly optimistic that you will be able to elicit any testimony from Dan with regard to the "deal" or with regard to any pressure that was exerted upon him with respect to his testimony. Could you call to the witness stand the deputy prosecutor who will try the case for the government and question him concerning his possible contact or dealings with Dan to try to obtain some sort of favorable testimony? Would you do so?

(B) You also know that the trial judge assigned to the case lives in a house next door to a house which was rented and occupied by Bill and Gene during the time the alleged conspiracy was in progress. Bill and Gene say that Dan never came to the house. Could you call the judge as a witness and ask him if he ever saw Dan in the neighborhood in which he lived?

McCormick, 6th Ed., § 68; Federal Rules of Evidence 601, 605.

12–4. During his lifetime, Edgar Prescott was the owner of a retail shoe store. His brother, Ivan, worked in the store as a clerk. Shortly after Edgar's death, Ivan announced that he and Edgar had an agreement under which Ivan was to be a 20 percent owner of the store as partial payment for his services to the business over the years. Ivan's story is corroborated by Ivan's wife, Mary, who claims that the agreement was entered into at a meeting at Edgar's home approximately ten years prior to Edgar's death. In addition to Ivan, Mary, and Edgar, Fay and Charles Steele, Edgar's daughter and son-in-law, also were allegedly present at the meeting. The Steeles remember a meeting at which Ivan raised the question of his right to a part-ownership of the business, but recall only that Edgar said that he "would consider" such an arrangement.

Barbara Prescott, Edgar's widow and executrix of his estate, refused to honor Ivan's claim. Ivan brought an action against Barbara, as executrix, to establish his interest in the business. Shortly after the action was brought, Ivan died and Mary Prescott, as executrix of his estate, was substituted as plaintiff. The attorneys for Ivan's estate would like to have Mary Prescott testify to the alleged agreement and to the generally affectionate relationship that existed between Edgar and Ivan through the years. The attorney for Edgar's estate would like to have Fay and Charles Steele testify to their version of the meeting at Edgar's house. Fay is named in her father's will, Charles is not. The attorney for Edgar's estate would also like to have Barbara Prescott testify that the relationship between the brothers was extremely strained at the time of the alleged agreement.

(A) Consult the statutes or rules of court of your state. Under those statutes or rules of court, which, if any, of the witnesses mentioned above may testify? If they may testify, will their testimony be limited in any way? How would the statutes quoted below apply?

(B) Assume that prior to Ivan's death, his deposition had been taken by Barbara's attorney. What effect would the taking of this deposition have on your answers to the questions raised in Part (A)?

State 1:

In civil suits and proceedings, * * * no person having a pecuniary interest in the result of the suit or proceeding shall be allowed to testify against the party to whom his interest is opposed, as to any transaction with, or statement by the deceased person whose estate is interested in the result of the suit or proceeding, or when such deceased person, at the time of such transaction or statement, acted in any representative or fiduciary relation whatsoever to the party against whom such testimony is sought to be introduced, unless called to testify thereto by the party to whom such interest is opposed, or unless the testimony of such deceased person in relation to such transaction or statement is introduced in evidence by the party whose interest is opposed to that of the witness, or has been taken and is on file in the cause. No person who is an incompetent witness under this section shall make himself competent by transferring his interest to another.

State 2:

Who may not testify.—The following persons cannot be witnesses:

Parties or assignors of parties to an action or proceeding, or persons in whose behalf an action or proceeding is prosecuted against an executor or administrator, upon a claim or demand against the estate of a deceased person, as to any communication or agreement, not in writing, occurring before the death of such deceased person.

State 3:

In actions by or against executors, administrators, or guardians, in which judgment may be rendered for or against them as such, neither party shall be allowed to testify against the others as to any transaction with, or statement by, the testator, intestate or ward, unless called to testify thereto by the opposite party; and the provisions of this article shall extend to and include all actions by or against the heirs or legal representatives of a decedent arising out of any transaction with such decedent.

State 4:

No party to any action, suit or proceeding, nor any person interested in the event thereof, nor any person from, through or under whom any such party or interested person derives any interest or title by assignment or otherwise, shall be examined as a witness in regard to any personal transaction or communication between such witness and a person at the time of such examination, deceased, insane or lunatic, against the executor, administrator, heir-in-law, next of kin, assignee, legatee, devisee or survivor of such person, or the assignee or committee of such insane person or lunatic. But this prohibition shall not extend to any transaction or communication as to which any such executor, administrator, heir-at-law, next of kin, assignee, legatee, devisee, survivor or committee shall be examined on his own behalf, nor as to which the testimony of such deceased person or lunatic shall be given in evidence: Provided, however, that where an action is brought for causing the death of any person by any wrongful act, neglect or default under article seven, chapter fifty-five of this Code, the person sued, or the servant, agent or employee of any firm or corporation sued, shall have the right to give evidence in any case in which he or it is sued, but he may not give evidence of any conversation with the deceased.

McCormick, 6th Ed., § 65; Federal Rule of Evidence 601.

12–5. In Problem 12–4 above, assume that Ivan did not die, but rather that he remained the plaintiff in the suit. Also assume that the alleged agreement of sale of twenty percent ownership to Ivan included a provision that Ivan would work in the store without wages or salary on a specified part time basis after the date of the agreement and until Edgar's death. Ivan's attorney has inspected the records of the store business. These records indicate the part-time work hours of Ivan in the store after the alleged agreement was made and do not indicate that Ivan received any wages or salary for such work. Can Ivan's attorney introduce (over objection) the testimony of Ivan that Ivan worked in the store without wages or salary from the date of the alleged agreement until Edgar's death, and also introduce the pertinent books of the store business under the statutes or courts rules of your state? How do the statutes quoted in Problem 12–4 above apply?

McCormick, 6th Ed., § 65; Federal Rule of Evidence 601.

12–6. Paul, a proper party to bring a wrongful death suit for the death of Axel in an automobile accident, brings a wrongful death suit against Dell, alleging Dell's negligence caused the accident. This claim is combined with a claim for damages incurred prior to Axel's death. Paul is also a proper party to assert this claim. Over objection, can Dell testify to the circumstances of the accident? Refer to the statutes or court rules of your state. How do the statutes quoted in Problem 12–4 above apply?

McCormick, 6th Ed., § 65; Federal Rule of Evidence 601.

12–7. Suppose Duncan dies with a purported will in being. Able and Baker take his property under the will. If Duncan died without a will, Carter and Davis take his property, by the statute of descent. Carter and Davis bring a suit to contest the will. Should Able, Baker, Carter and Davis all be considered interested parties under the Dead Man's Statute, so that over objection none of them can testify concerning the circumstances surrounding the creation of the supposed will? Refer to the statutes or court rules of your state. How do the statutes quoted in Problem 12–4 above apply?

McCormick, 6th Ed., § 65; Federal Rule of Evidence 601.

SECTION B. ELICITATION AND FORM OF TESTIMONY

12–8. Dennis was charged with income tax fraud. The investigation was conducted by two Internal Revenue Service agents who spent six months investigating Dan's complex business holdings. At the trial, Dan's counsel moved that all witnesses be excluded from the courtroom. The court granted the motion, except that it permitted both IRS agents to remain as designated representatives of the government. The government contended and the judge agreed that assistance from both agents was essential to the prosecution's conduct of the case. The defendant objected, arguing that only one person could be designated a representative under Federal Rule of Evidence 615. The court stated that it had the discretion to expand the number of designated representatives if necessary under the circumstances. Both agents testified at the trial. Each agent's testimony was consistent with the other's. Dan was convicted and appealed. One of his grounds for appeal is the failure to sequester at least one of the agents. What result?

McCormick, 6th Ed., § 50; Federal Rule of Evidence 615.

12–9. Peter brings a law suit against Dan for personal injuries suffered when he was hit by a car driven by Dan. Peter was crossing the street at an intersection. There is no dispute that the accident took place. Peter claims he was walking in the crosswalk and that Dan was speeding up to the intersection, ran a red light, and hit him. Dan claims both that the light was green and that Peter ran into the street outside of the crosswalk. Walt was standing on the corner talking to a friend at the time of the accident. He is called as a witness by Peter. The following examination takes place:

Q. Your name is Walter Smith, and you live at 1212 White Road in this city, is that correct?

A. Yes.

Q. And you sell office furniture for a living, isn't that true?

A. Yes.

Q. And you work for Utility Office Furniture?

A. Yes.

Q. Turning your attention to June 13 of last year, you were at the intersection of First and Main at about 11 a.m. on that date, is that so?

A. Yes.

Q. And you were looking south on First Street, were you not?

Counsel for defendant: Objection, leading.

The Court: Sustained.

Counsel for plaintiff: I will ask another question. Please tell us everything that happened that morning?

Counsel for defendant: Objection to the narrative form of the question.

The Court: Overruled. Please answer the question.

A. I was standing on the corner talking to my friend Bill Jones. Bill's wife had just had a baby, a little girl. Bill had been married before and things hadn't worked out you know. I was real happy for him. Just as I was standing there, this guy comes along like a bat out of hell. I mean he was going super fast. I saw him later and he really looked like some junkie, so I wasn't surprised about his driving. I'd seen the guy around town and thought I sure wouldn't like to meet him on the road. So he comes through and barrels through the red light. No concern for human life, I tell you.

Counsel for defendant: Your honor, I object to the entire answer of the witness as containing information which is irrelevant. Furthermore, the answer is full of unhelpful opinions. I ask that the answer be stricken from the record and that the jury be instructed to disregard.

The Court: Objection sustained. Motion to strike granted. Members of the jury, you will disregard the witness's last answer. Proceed, counsel.

Counsel for defendant: Your honor, I renew my objection to the narrative form of the question.

The Court: Objection sustained. Proceed with your questioning, counsel.

(A) Were the first four questions asked by plaintiff's counsel leading? Why didn't counsel for the defendant object?

(B) Was the court correct in its ruling on the objection to the leading question? If so, how should the question have been worded?

(C) Was the court correct in at first permitting the question calling for the narrative? Why did the judge change her mind? Was she correct in prohibiting further questions calling for a narrative?

(D) What is your assessment of the performance of counsel for defendant? Is she at least in part to blame for the interjection of inadmissible material into the trial? Has the matter been corrected by the court's rulings and instructions to the jury?

(E) How should counsel for plaintiff now proceed? Be ready to continue the direct examination.

McCormick, 6th Ed., §§ 5–6; Federal Rule of Evidence 611.

12–10. (A) Four defendants were arrested for possession of heroin. Allegedly, they and a fifth person, Richard, were engaged in "cutting" a large amount of heroin when officers with a search warrant entered the house in which this activity was being conducted. Defendants contend, among other things, that the substance seized in the raid was not heroin. At the trial, Richard was being examined as a witness for the state. The prosecuting attorney asked the following question to show attempted disposal of the alleged heroin being cut before officers entered the house:

> When someone said that men were approaching the house (a fact Richard had just stated in his testimony), did you then see John (one of the defendants) take some of the stuff and run into the bathroom?

Objected to as leading. What ruling? Suppose this objection were sustained, what should the prosecutor ask the witness in order to bring out the above-mentioned matter?

(B) Assume the direct examiner did manage to elicit testimony from Richard that John attempted to flush the alleged heroin down the toilet. On cross-examination, the defendants' attorney asks the following question:

> Now you have testified that when some men were coming to the house, John took some of the stuff to the bathroom, but you were really upstairs laying on the bed sick as a dog, weren't you? So you couldn't have seen a thing?

Objection? Ruling?

McCormick, 6th Ed., §§ 5–7; Federal Rule of Evidence 611.

12–11. Paul sues David for personal injuries arising out of an automobile accident at the intersection of Pine and Grove Streets. Paul was driving a blue Ford pickup truck; David was driving a blue Honda. Paul calls as his first witness Wally Walters, who testifies that he was standing at the intersection at the time of the accident. The following examination occurs:

Q. Where were you standing?

A. I was a few feet south of the intersection, on the east side of Pine Street.

Q. Were you looking at the intersection at that time?

A. Yes.

Q. Did you see a blue Honda Civic driving at a high rate of speed approach the intersection on Pine Street?

A. Yes

Q. What happened then?

A. The Honda went through a red light and collided with a blue Ford pickup.

Thank you, I have no further questions.

(A) Were any of the questions asked objectionable? Whether or not the questions were improper, help Paul's counsel formulate a more effective direct examination.

(B) Assume that after the examination set forth above, David's counsel began cross-examination with the following questions:

Q. Mr. Walters, on the morning in question you were hurrying to a meeting in connection with your work?

A. Well, I was on my way to a meeting, yes.

Q. You were preoccupied with your business?

A. I am a busy person and I was thinking about some business matters.

Q. Is that a yes or a no?

A. It was a yes.

Q. Part of your business had to do with a letter you had received earlier that day, did it not?

A. Yes

Q. And you were walking down the street reading the letter, weren't you?

A. Well, I was glancing at the letter.

Cross-examiner: I ask that the witness be directed to answer the question.

The Court: He did.

Q. Well, Mr. Walters, you were so engrossed in that letter that you weren't really paying any attention to what was going on and you therefore didn't really see the collision in question?

A. Not so. I looked up from the letter and saw everything clearly. Indeed, the Honda had its muffler out and the sound made me look in that direction.

Were any of these cross-examination questions improper? Whether or not they were improper, help the examiner formulate more effective questions.

McCormick, 6th Ed., §§ 5–7; Federal Rule of Evidence 611.

12–12. In the same trial as Problem 12–9 above, Dan calls Chuckie, a six-year-old boy who was also at the street corner. Chuckie has given a statement to Dan to the effect that he saw Peter run out into the street between two parked cars. The judge has found Chuckie to be a competent witness. The examination proceeds as follows:

Q. Tell us your name, please?

A. Chuckie Brown.

Q. How old are you?

A. Six and a half.

Q. Where do you live?

A. 205 W. Elm Street.

Q. Do you remember June 13 last year?

A. I don't know.

Q. Do you remember seeing someone hit by a car?

A. Yes.

Q. Do you remember where you were when you saw the man get hit?

A. I was on the corner with my Mom.

Q. Can you tell us what you saw?

A. I saw the man get hit by a car.

Q. Where was the man when he got hit?

A. In the street.

Q. Where in the street?

A. I don't know.

Counsel for defendant: Your honor, I ask for leave to lead this witness.

Counsel for plaintiff: I object. I am concerned that the child is too susceptible to suggestion. It is really worse than leading an adult.

The Court: I will permit the leading.

Q. Chuckie, don't you remember seeing the man run out in the street between two cars?

Counsel for plaintiff: Objection, leading.

Was the court correct in its initial decision to permit leading? How should the court rule on the objection now before it? If the objection is sustained, how should counsel for defendant phrase the next question?

McCormick, 6th Ed., § 6; Federal Rule of Evidence 611.

12–13. Ophelia brings an action against the Fountainrock Hotel for the loss of her jewelry box and its contents. She claims that the box was locked and left with a hotel clerk to be deposited in the hotel safe. When Ophelia returned that same evening to get some jewelry from the box, neither the box nor its contents could be located. The hotel admits the loss of the box, but denies that it was locked or that it contained all of the items claimed by Ophelia.

The hotel desk clerk who received the box was Gregory. Gregory is still employed by the Fountainrock. As attorney for Ophelia, you have interviewed him. He stated that he remembered receiving the box from Ophelia and that he placed it in the hotel safe. He told you that the box was locked when he received it. He told you that he would not lie about these things if called to the stand, but because he would like to keep his job at the hotel, he would volunteer nothing. You do not believe that the Fountainrock's lawyers will call Gregory and that you will have to do so. Will you be able to lead him? If so, what foundation will be necessary in order for you to ask leading questions?

Assume, alternatively, that Gregory is no longer employed by the Fountainrock. However, he is employed by another member of the city hotel association. His reluctance to testify is the same. Will you be able to lead him? If so, what foundation will be necessary in order for you to ask leading questions?

McCormick, 6th Ed., § 6; Federal Rule of Evidence 611.

12–14. Assume that in the trial involved in Problem 12–13, Gregory is an employee of the defendant hotel. Assume further that plaintiff's counsel has been permitted to lead Gregory on direct examination. On cross-examination by counsel for the hotel, the following takes place:

Q. Gregory, you see a lot of guests in the course of a day at the hotel, don't you?

Counsel for plaintiff: Objection, leading. This is really his witness.

The Court: Overruled, this is cross-examination.

A. Yes, sir.

Q. And you receive many things for deposit in the safe deposit box?

A. Yes, sir.

Q. So many things that it is difficult for you to remember any particular item?

A. Yes.

Q. So you really aren't sure about whether any particular jewelry box was locked or unlocked, are you?

Counsel for plaintiff: I object again to the leading.

How would you rule as trial judge? Why?

McCormick, 6th Ed., § 6; Federal Rule of Evidence 611.

12–15. Bill, who engaged in stamp speculation and investment as a hobby, bid $15.00 per set for a lot (a large quantity) of Luxembourg stamp sets (the set is numbered by Scott's catalog as B55–59) at a stamp auction on August 6, 2010, but the seller refused to deliver the stamps. To show damages for such failure to deliver in a subsequent suit, it was necessary for Bill to prove the market value of the set. On this issue, on direct examination Bill testified that he had attended 25 stamp auctions during the period between July 1, 2009, and September 1, 2010, at which auctions, sets of Luxembourg B55–59 were sold. His attorney asked him to relate the dates of each auction and the price for which the above-mentioned set was sold at each auction. Bill related the dates of two auctions in July, 1999, and the price at which the above set was sold at each auction, and then stated he was having trouble remembering the dates of the remaining auctions at which the sets were sold and the prices realized for the set. His attorney then asked him whether he could state the dates and the prices for the set realized in such auctions. He answered, "I just can't remember right now." Whereupon his attorney handed him a paper and asked him to look at it. At that point, defendant's counsel requested of the judge that he be permitted to see the paper, and the judge stated, "Counsel, you don't have to see it now." Defendant's counsel objected to this ruling.

Bill looked at the paper and handed it back to his attorney. The attorney then asked the witness to state the dates of the above mentioned auctions at which the set in question had been sold and the prices realized for the set at such auctions, whereupon defendant's attorney objected to the question on the ground that the witness must be testifying from the paper. The objection was overruled. Bill then related the auction dates and prices for eight more auctions, and although he was asked leading questions he could not recite or confirm any more dates and prices. Bill's attorney thereupon handed him the above-mentioned paper again to peruse; Bill did so; and then he testified to ten more dates and auctions. Again the objection of defendant's attorney was overruled. Bill was then unable to continue to testify to the remaining five auctions, and the procedure mentioned just above occurred again. Thereupon Bill testified to the dates and prices at five more auctions.

Later upon cross-examination of Bill the following transpired. (At this time, defendant's attorney had again requested to see the paper handed the witness, as related above, and had looked at it.)

Q. Now you testified to the dates of 25 auctions which you attended and the prices realized for the Luxembourg set at such auctions. How do you know those were the dates and the actual prices at each auction?

A. Well, I know those were the dates and the prices from my auction attendance record which I have here at the trial.

Q. Have you any independent knowledge of the dates of the auctions you attended and the prices realized at those auctions on this set, independent of those records?

A. I have. The only way you give your knowledge of anything like this when you attend as many auctions as I do in one year, you have to go by your records, if you keep any, which I did. I gained my knowledge from my memorandum I made from notations in a little book I always take to the auctions with me. I know the different dates and the prices to which my attention was called and to which I have testified. Obviously, the prices varied. If it was not for the record I kept pertaining to the dates and prices, that I have testified to, if I did not have that record, I would not have any independent knowledge of these prices, except just as I would know what happened to come to my memory.

Q. (by the court) You did attend the auctions you mentioned and hear the sale prices you mentioned?

A. Yes.

Q. (by the court) And at each auction you jotted down the date and the price of this set in a notebook?

A. Yes.

Q. (by the court) In order to testify as to those prices you looked up in the notebook the dates and prices and refreshed your memory?

A. Yes.

Q. But, this paper your attorney handed you, that isn't the little notebook is it?

A. No.

Q. When and how did you prepare this paper your attorney handed to you?

A. About three weeks ago, I copied the dates and prices from the notebook to this paper.

Q. But, now you don't know these auction dates and prices except as they are stated in your notebook and this paper, do you?

A. I do know those different dates and prices without those records in regard to these questions which have been asked me. I know what the dates and prices were after going back to the notebook and that memorandum handed to me here. If I had not got these records, I might not have, just exactly, but I would have been able to tell within a couple of days and several cents of so—maybe within a dollar or so.

Q. But if you knew that much about these dates and prices, why did you have to look at this paper three times?

Q. Well, I can only say what I just said.

(A) Was the judge correct in refusing defendant's attorney's request to see the paper when it was handed to Bill?

(B) Defendant's attorney moved to strike the testimony of Bill on direct, concerning all 25 auctions. How should the judge rule?

(C) Suppose defendant's attorney had objected to the questions of the judge as leading. Should such objections have been sustained?

(D) Suppose defendant's attorney had requested that the judge order Bill to produce his notebook for inspection by defendant's attorney (during cross-examination). Should the judge have granted such a request?

McCormick, 6th Ed., §§ 8–9; Federal Rules of Evidence 611–612, 614.

12–16. Dan was tried for the murder of Myra in a hospital ward. Walter was an attendant in the ward in which the alleged murder occurred. At the trial of Dan, the prosecuting attorney called Walter to the witness stand. First the prosecutor asked Walter several preliminary questions, the answers to which established that the attendant was not present when Myra was killed. The prosecutor intended to establish by Walter that Walter came into the ward that was the scene of the alleged murder immediately after Myra was killed, and to elicit from him a description of the scene he found in the ward. After establishing that Walter was not in the ward when the event occurred, the prosecutor asked Walter whether he went into the ward after the event occurred, and Walter answered in the affirmative. Thereupon the following occurred.

(Direct examination of Walter by Prosecutor Martin):

Q.   Do you recall the exact time?

A.   Yes, ma'am.

Q.   You have some notes on it?

A.   Yes, ma'am.

MS. MARTIN: If the Court please, I would like to have the witness refresh his memory from his notes.

Q.   Did you make these notes yourself?

A.   Yes, ma'am.

MS. EGGERS (Attorney for defendant): Before he uses these notes to refresh his memory, I would like to find out when they were made.

THE COURT: Very well. Just a moment, Walter don't look at your notes until we finish this. She is going to ask some preliminary questions.

BY MS. EGGERS:

Q.   When did you make these notes?

A.   Well, I made these notes just before they said the defendant was coming to trial. I made one or two notes that night.

Q.   These notes—you knew you had to testify?

A.   I didn't know, but I thought probably we would have to testify.

Q.   So in fact you made some notes—?

A.   (interposing) Yes, ma'am.

MS. EGGERS: Your Honor, I think I would object to his using them because they are not actually used to refresh his memory. He can testify from his memory just as well.

THE COURT: Walter, you made these notes—you, yourself, made them to refresh your recollection?

A. Yes, sir; yes.

THE COURT: You may refer to them. Objection overruled.

Walter read his notes, and then testified to the exact time he entered the ward after the event in question, and to all of the circumstances that existed as he saw them upon entering the ward. Assume that the notes not only mentioned the exact time of his entry but also the various details of the scene he saw just after he entered.

Was the judge's ruling correct?

In any event, do you approve of the technique used by the prosecutor to refresh memory here? What questions might have been added by her?

McCormick, 6th Ed., § 9; Federal Rules of Evidence 611–612.

12–17. Assume the facts of Problem 12–13. Ophelia claims that she checked the box just as she left her hotel room to bring it to the desk. At that time, all of the jewelry normally kept in the box was in it. After looking in the box, she immediately locked it and brought it downstairs to the desk. She handed the box to the desk clerk and obtained a receipt for it.

At the time that she first contacted her attorney, one week after the loss of the box, she could remember a few of the items in the box, but had difficulty remembering all of its contents. Her attorney then arranged for Ophelia to be hypnotized by a psychologist experienced in refreshing the recollection of witnesses in court matters. The psychologist, Dr. Seymour, hypnotized her. Dr. Seymour is a professor at the local university. She is an acknowledged expert on the subject of hypnosis and has an excellent national reputation in both legal and academic circles. Only Dr. Seymour and Ophelia were present during the session, although the session was videotaped. A review of the videotape will show that no suggestion of any item was made by Dr. Seymour. After the session, however, Ophelia is able to remember all 35 items that were in the box.

Ophelia seeks to testify to the items at the trial. Defendant objects. What ruling by the court and why?

McCormick, 6th Ed., § 206.

SECTION C. LAY TESTIMONY

12–18. Richard is charged with robbery of a tavern. The prosecutor calls Jake to identify Richard as the robber. Much to her surprise, when she asks Jake on the stand if he can identify anyone in the courtroom as the robber, Jake answers, "Well, gee—I think it was, er, I guess it was, that man over there [pointing to Richard]." Prior to the above testimony, Jake had testified that he had seen the robbery as well as the robber, although the lights in the tavern were not bright.

Defense counsel moves to strike Richard's answer. What ruling by the court? Is further testimony required before a ruling can be made on this issue? If so, whose responsibility is it to present such evidence?

McCormick, 6th Ed., §§ 10–11; Federal Rules of Evidence 602, 701.

12–19. Nick is charged with bank robbery. The man committing the robbery wore a dark raincoat, a handkerchief covering the lower part of his face, sunglasses and a hat pulled down as low as possible. Five witnesses testify that the robbery took place but, because of the dress of the robber, none of these witnesses can positively identify Nick as the robber. A sixth witness, John, who is deaf and unable to speak, was in the bank on business. He testifies that, in his opinion, Nick was the man "who committed the robbery." He bases his opinion upon his recollection of the "bridge of the nose" and the "wrinkles on the forehead" of the robber.

As defense counsel, would you object to John's testimony? If you did object, would your objection be successful?

McCormick, 6th Ed., §§ 10–11; Federal Rules of Evidence 602, 701.

12–20. Diane heard a loud crashing noise while she was standing in front of her house. The noise was created by an automobile collision just around the block out of her sight. At a trial concerning the collision, can she testify over objection that from the noise of the collision one car or the other was exceeding the speed limit of 20 miles per hour? Can she testify over objection that one car sounded like it had a muffler "cut out", and that prior to the collision it sounded as though it was traveling at 50 m.p.h. or at a great speed?

McCormick, 6th Ed., §§ 10–11; Federal Rules of Evidence 602, 701.

12–21. Over objection could Trooper Sten Borne testify to the matter in the last paragraph of Document 3, Appendix B, *State v. Well*?

McCormick, 6th Ed., §§ 10–11; Federal Rule of Evidence 701.

12–22. (A) Paula sued David for causing injuries to Paula in an automobile accident. Paula charged that David crossed a five inch high divider on a four-lane highway and struck Paula's car—the first car in the oncoming traffic. At the trial Paula testified that David's car slid along the top of the divider and then turned into the oncoming traffic lanes smashing into a guard rail at the edge of the oncoming lanes. Paula turned to her inner lane but could not avoid David's car, which occupied part of the inner lane as well as all of the outer lane. Paula could not describe exactly the distances involved and the exact sequence of events. It was important to do so, because David took the position that Paula should have seen David's car in time to continue at her same speed, and pass the point at which David's car crossed the divider, thus avoiding David's car, and that Paula instead stepped on her brakes and thereby smashed into David's car. Paula's attorney then asked her, whether she had applied her brakes when she saw defendant's car and Paula answered, "Yes". Then her attorney asked her, "Now let me ask you this, if you had gone right ahead at that time, if you had not applied your brakes at all and gone right ahead, and the defendant's car would have taken the same course it did, would you have struck defendant's car?" Objection. Ruling?

(B) Suppose that in the above situation, a passenger, Winifred, was riding with defendant. Winifred was injured and brought suit, charging defendant with willful and wanton negligence by reason of defendant's driving at an excessive speed, which caused defendant to lose control of his car and cross the divider. In a subsequent suit on this charge, defendant took the position that contributory negligence was a defense and that Winifred was contributorily negligent by riding with defendant and failing to warn him of defendant's excessive speed. David is on the witness stand and is asked by his attorney: "If Winifred had warned you concerning your allegedly excessive speed, would you have paid any attention to the warning?" Objection. Ruling?

McCormick, 6th Ed., §§ 11–12; Federal Rules of Evidence 602, 701.

12–23. Natalie is charged with running an illegal off-track betting establishment—better known as a bookie joint. Matt Ironhead, the arresting officer, is on the witness stand, testifying for the state. Following are excerpts from his direct testimony. Be ready both to object on behalf of the defense where appropriate and to support the questions and answers on behalf of the prosecution.

Q. State your name and occupation.

A. Matthew Ironhead. I am a detective on the city police force.

Q. How long have you been on the force, Detective Ironhead?

A. I have been on the force for 15 years.

Q. To what unit are you assigned?

A. Gambling.

Q. How long have you been so assigned?

A. Five years.

Q. Turning to the date of June 13 of this year, detective, were you on duty that date?

A. Yes. I came on at three in the afternoon.

Q. Can you tell us what you did on that date?

A. Well, after some routine paperwork, I placed a call to 937–1698. [Previous testimony has established that this was the number of Natalie's dry-cleaning establishment.]

Q. Was there a response at the other end of the line?

A. Yes, I heard Natalie's voice saying "Hello."

Q. What was said then?

A. I said "This is Manny 2, I want number 3 in the sixth in Arlington, across the board." Natalie responded: "How much mister, come on." I said "A saw-buck." She said, "Gotcha," and hung up.

Q. Would you describe Natalie's tone of voice?

A. She appeared to be in a big hurry, she wasn't about to chat, if you know what I mean.

* * *

Q. When you broke into the cleaners as you have described, can you tell us what you found?

A. Well, we didn't find any people. They had obviously blown as quickly as possible out the back door. We knew they had been in there because we had heard talking but they were gone.

Q. What did you find?

A. We found your typical bookie joint set up, three or four phones, pad of paper, blackboards with race results on them, racing forms, that kind of stuff.

Q. Was there any money around?

A. No, you wouldn't expect to find cash around a bookie joint.

* * *

Q. Now after you got in, did the telephone ring?

A. Yes, it did.

Q. Did you answer?

A. Yes.

Q. What did you say?

A. I just said, "Yeah."

Q. What did the person on the other end of the line say?

A. He said, "This is Steve. Put me down for a hundred on Peacelock in the 4th at Shortacres." I said, "Ok," and he hung up.

Q. What did that mean?

A. The caller was attempting to place a bet on a horse named Peacelock in the 4th race to be held later in the day at a racetrack called Shortacres in Honolulu, Hawaii.

McCormick, 6th Ed., §§ 10–13; Federal Rules of Evidence 602, 701–705.

12–24. Gill is a narcotics investigator for the local police department. While working undercover, she arrested the accused, Mark, for possession of crack cocaine with intent to sell. Mark is now on trial and Gill is called as a witness for the State. Gill states that she has been a police officer assigned to the narcotics unit for eight years. The following questions and answers then occur. What objections might be raised to any of the questions or answers and what likely ruling by the court?

Q. Please describe your duties as an officer in the narcotics unit.

A. My job is to investigate possible violations of the laws concerning narcotic drugs, including marijuana, cocaine, heroin and various other substances prohibited or controlled by state law. I sometimes work with informers and find myself observing what we call controlled buys where an informer will arrange to have a sale made at a time and place where the transaction can be observed by police officers. On some occasions, I work undercover where I may pretend to participate with the suspected drug dealers in various activities connected with their operations.

Q. In the course of your undercover work, have you acquired information about the operation of illegal drug deals?

A. I have worked closely in the "business" for eight years. I believe I know the trade as well as the criminals.

Q. Turning your attention to July 20 of last year, where were you working?

A. I was working undercover in the Hay Avenue area.

Q. What were you doing?

A. I had arranged to have a meeting with two other people about the possibility of a drug deal involving crack cocaine. The meeting was to take place at Harry's Bar & Grill on Hay.

Q. How was the meeting arranged?

A. I had had telephone conversations with each of the persons involved.

Q. Who was to be involved in the meeting?

A. Myself, Mark, and another individual named Sheila.

Q. What time was the meeting to take place?

A. About 11 o'clock in the evening.

Q. What happened at about 11 p.m. that evening?

A. I arrived at bar a little early and was waiting outside. Shortly after 11, a car drove up with Sheila behind the wheel. The car was being driven erratically, like the person driving was high on alcohol or drugs. The car pulled up to the curb, slamming into a parking meter as well as a parked car. Sheila staggered out of the driver's side and Mark walked calmly out of the passenger side. However, I could tell that he was angry. If looks could kill, Sheila would have been a dead woman.

Q. What happened then?

A. We all walked into the bar and sat in a booth.

Q. What did you observe when you sat down?

A. Sheila had that glassy eyed stare of someone who had just smoked crack.

Q. Was anything said?

A. Mark said that she had been getting off too much. He told me they had been cooking powder into a slab and Sheila had taken some stuff for herself that was meant for customers.

Q. What did he mean by that?

A. He meant that she had smoked too much crack and was too high. They had been creating crack by heating it into a large unit to be broken off for sales of smaller quantities, called rocks. Dealers do not like their associates using the stuff meant for customers.

Gill's testimony goes on to describe the sale of crack cocaine rock to the informer and the subsequent arrest of Mark and Sheila. Sheila pled guilty and is awaiting sentence.

McCormick, 6th Ed., §§ 10–13; Federal Rules of Evidence 602, 701–705.

SECTION D.   EXPERT TESTIMONY

12–25. David is charged with the murder of his wife. The State alleges that the defendant, an anesthesiologist, caused his wife's death by injecting her with a lethal dose of succinylcholine chloride. At first, the medical examiner could not find traces of poison in the deceased's blood. However, he turned over a sample of that blood to a toxicologist, Martha Smith. Ms. Smith applied a chemical test for the presence of succinylcholine chloride and found substantial quantities of it in the deceased's blood.

The test was developed by Ms. Smith in connection with another investigation, three years earlier. She will testify that she proved the reliability of the test in her own laboratory. She has given lectures about it to the faculty and student body at the local community college. She has also published articles about the test in unrefereed police journals. In the lectures and articles, she gave an articulate statement of the chemical validity of the test, illustrated by charts that were easy for a layperson to follow. She would be able to do the same thing on the witness stand.

Ms. Smith has a masters in chemistry from Ohio State University. She has taken advanced courses in toxicology offered by various police institutes. She has worked as a toxicologist for the State Medical Examiner for fourteen years. The high quality of her work has been recognized both by her superiors and by national groups. Last year, she was recognized as "Toxicologist of the Year" by the state toxicology society.

(A) Defendant moves *in limine* for the exclusion of the evidence concerning the presence of succinylcholine chloride. What result should be expected under prevailing federal and state laws governing the subject matter of expert testimony?

(B) Assume that the court denies the motion *in limine*. Outline a direct examination of Ms. Smith setting forth her qualifications and opinion. Assume also that in reaching her opinion with regard to the presence of succinylcholine chloride, she relied not only on her chemical tests but on conversations with police officers at the scene concerning the contents of the apartment in which the body was found. The information she received from these police officers enabled her to confirm her opinion that nothing else present at the scene could have caused death.

(C) Consider what objections the defense may make to the direct examination as outlined.

(D) As part of her opinion, would Ms. Smith be permitted to say that in her opinion the deceased's death was caused by the deliberate injection of succinylcholine chloride into her body by her anesthesiologist husband?

McCormick, 6th Ed., § 203; Federal Rules of Evidence 401–403, 702–705.

12–26. Jeffrey is on trial for the murder of his wife, Joyce. The state's evidence has established that Joyce disappeared unexpectedly three years ago. She has not been seen since. A human rib was recently discovered in the woods twenty miles from their home. The rib has an artifact that looks like a knife wound. A farmer living near the site where the rib was found has testified that he remembers seeing a man driving a silver luxury sedan on his remote country road heading in the direction of the place where the rib was found. Evidence from the state further established that Jeffrey owns a silver luxury sedan meeting the description given by the farmer. The state also has evidence that Joyce was seeking a divorce at the time she disappeared and that Jeffrey was the beneficiary of her $500,000 life insurance policy.

At this point in the trial, Dr. Paul R. Cabot, a Ph.D. molecular biologist, takes the witness stand. Defense counsel knows that Dr. Cabot will testify that he tested the rib using mitochondrial DNA (mtDNA) analysis. The statistical evidence will show that, at most, less than 3% of the population would be expected to have this mtDNA profile, and Joyce's profile falls into this category.

Generally speaking, every cell contains two types of DNA: nuclear DNA, which is found in the nucleus of the cell, and mitochondrial DNA, which is found outside of the nucleus in the mitochondrion. The use of nuclear DNA analysis as a forensic tool has been found to be scientifically reliable by the scientific community for more than a decade. The use of mtDNA analysis is fairly new. Mitochondrial DNA has some advantages over nuclear DNA analysis. First, while any given cell contains only one nucleus, there are a vast number of mitochondria. As a result, there is a significantly greater amount of mtDNA in a cell from which a sample can be extracted by a lab technician, as compared to nuclear DNA. Thus, this technique is very useful for minute samples or ancient and degraded samples. Second, mitochondrial DNA can be obtained from some sources that nuclear DNA cannot. For example, mtDNA can be found in the cells of skeletonized bones. In contrast, nuclear DNA can be retrieved only from bone marrow which decomposes quickly after death.

On the other hand, mtDNA is not as precise an identifier as nuclear DNA. In the case of nuclear DNA, half is inherited from the mother and half from the father, and each individual, with the exception of identical twins, almost certainly has a unique profile. Although the entire profile is not tested in nuclear DNA analysis, a random match probability in the order of one in several billion is not uncommon. In contrast, mtDNA is inherited only from the mother and thus all maternal relatives will share the same mtDNA profile, unless a mutation has occurred. Because it is not possible to achieve the extremely high level of certainty of identity provided by nuclear DNA, some scientists have argued that mtDNA typing should be a test of exclusion, rather than one of identification.

(A) Jeffrey's attorney argues that the evidence should be inadmissible. How should the court rule?

(B) Assume at a pretrial hearing Dr. Cabot admitted that his lab has never been accredited by an external agency. Although there is no legal requirement that Dr. Cabot's lab be accredited, many laboratories doing DNA forensic work are accredited through the American Society of Crime Laboratory Directors. Jeffrey's attorney argues this fact makes the evidence inadmissible. How should the court rule?

(C) At the same hearing, Dr. Cabot acknowledged that mtDNA procedures sometimes yield results that are contaminated but that no evidence of contamination appeared in this case. Does this concession make the evidence inadmissible?

(D) In addition, Jeffrey's attorney argues that the probative value of this evidence is outweighed by the risk of unfair prejudice and the risk of misleading the jury—in particular, the jury would associate mitochondrial DNA analysis with nuclear DNA analysis and give it the same value, in terms of its ability to "fingerprint" a suspect.

(E) In the alternative, Jeffrey's attorney argues that Dr. Cabot should only be allowed to testify that Jeffrey's wife could not be excluded as the source of the rib. How should the court rule?

McCormick, 6th Ed., §§ 203, 205; Federal Rules of Evidence 401–403, 702–705.

12–27. Armel was arrested for driving while intoxicated. She took a breathalyzer test, which would be admissible at her trial on the above charge. The test showed an alcohol level sufficient to raise a statutory presumption of intoxication. The test has been described in the following terms. "The test is based on a predictable reaction between alcohol in the subject's breath and a chemical solution contained in a small glass ampoule. A sample of the subject's breath is forced into the ampoule and the resulting chemical reaction is measured by comparing the reacted chemical solution to a nonreacted sample by means of a photoelectric device. The results are calibrated in terms of a percentage of alcohol in the blood.''

Contrary to a usual practice in many jurisdictions, the police officers who gave the test to Armel saved and appropriately labeled the ampoules used in such tests. The attorney for the defendant secured the ampoule used in the testing of Armel. She consulted with experts who told her that the ampoules can be retested and the ampoule contents on retesting can yield reliable results which can be compared to the original test results. She engaged an expert chemist who holds this view and the retesting by this expert as described above indicated that the alcohol in the defendant's blood at the time of the original test was not as high as indicated in the original test and in fact was below the statutory standard which would raise a presumption of intoxication. The expert also would testify to reasons why the original test was inaccurate. Several other experts could be called by Armel's attorney to reinforce the above expert's testimony. It could be shown that all of the above experts have impeccable qualifications for their testimony. However, Armel's attorney also knows that the state can find and call expert analytical chemists and toxicologists who would testify that the retesting procedure (of the ampoule) is not scientifically reliable and not generally accepted in the scientific community of chemists familiar with such retesting. Over the objection of the prosecuting attorney should Armel's attorney anticipate that she can introduce the testimony of the experts she has recruited, as indicated above?

McCormick, 6th Ed., §§ 203, 205; Federal Rules of Evidence 401–403, 702–705.

12–28. Frank was charged with molestation of his step-daughter over a two-year period when the child was twelve to fourteen years old. Frank denied he abused the child but did not dispute the possibility that she might have been abused by someone else. During its case-in-chief the state offered the testimony of Dr. Jane Johnson, a child psychologist with an expertise in child sexual abuse. If permitted, Johnson would testify that in her expert opinion the child was telling the truth about being a victim of sexual abuse.

Johnson bases her opinion on her conclusion that the child evidences signs of Child Sexual Abuse Accommodation Syndrome (CSAAS)—a psychological phenomenon prevalent among victims of child sexual abuse. CSAAS first was identified in the psychological literature in the late 1970s. Those works, drawing on clinical consulting experience, identified several factors (or "dynamics") that are frequently present in the cases of children who have suffered sexual abuse. The primary dynamics include secrecy, helplessness, delayed (or conflicted, or unconvincing) disclosure of the abuse, and retraction of accusations. After reviewing Frank's step-daughter's case history and interviewing the child on three occasions, Johnson concluded that all of the foregoing dynamics were present in the child's case.

CSAAS initially was advanced as an aid to treatment; its proponents hoped that it would provide a "common language" for treaters of abused children. Over the years, however, it has come to be used by some psychologists to determine whether or not abuse has occurred—in short, as a diagnostic tool. Its use for such purposes has become popular among some forensic psychologists and, unsurprisingly, prosecutors as well. Its proponents admit that using CSAAS in this fashion is "partly science and partly art form," but they insist that it is a useful and valid predictor of abuse, relying on the only published study on the diagnostic accuracy of CSAAS. That study examined more than 100 cases of known child sexual abuse. The dynamics relied upon by Dr. Johnson and other clinicians as indicative of CSAAS were prevalent in 68 percent of the cases under study.

The psychological literature has approved of CSAAS for treatment purposes but no peer reviewed article has endorsed its use for diagnosis purposes. While Dr. Johnson and a number of other psychologists are on record favoring the use of CSAAS, others—including the authors who first identified the syndrome—have spoken out against its diagnostic use in court, arguing that it partakes too much of clinical experience and not enough of science.

Defense counsel objects. Is Dr. Johnson's proposed testimony admissible? If the court rules that Dr. Johnson's testimony that the child was a victim of abuse is inadmissible, might the prosecution still find some permissible use for Dr. Johnson's knowledge of CSAAS?

McCormick, 6th Ed., §§ 203, 206; Federal Rules of Evidence 401–403, 702–705.

12–29. Steven is charged by federal prosecutors with interstate transportation of a large quantity of marijuana. Five hundred pounds of the substance were found in a light airplane owned by Steven. The plane had crashed into a swampy area. Although authorities arrived shortly after local residents saw the plane go down, no one was found at the scene. The airplane was lying in shallow water at the edge of the swamp. Bare footprints of two individuals were found in the mud at the edge of the water. Steven was charged after an investigation showed his ownership of the airplane and narcotics agents identified him through an analysis of his footprint.

During its case-in-chief, the prosecution called Alex Marx to the witness stand. Following is Marx's testimony on direct examination:

Q. State your name and address.

A. Alex Marx, 111 First Street, Greenville.

Q. What is your occupation?

A. I'm a sculptor.

Q. Please give us your educational background.

A. I have a B.A. in studio art from the University of North Carolina in Chapel Hill. I have also taken some post-graduate work in anatomy and anthropology.

Q. In the course of your work, have you had occasion to study the human foot?

A. Yes, I have. I do a lot of sculpture of the foot. You might say it's my specialty.

Q. Have your studies had any applications other than artistic ones?

A. Yes. Identifying individuals through foot shape has become a hobby of mine. Some people can identify footprints by identifying ridges, as is the case in fingerprints. However, I have found that each person has an absolutely unique foot shape. I can match, without doubt, the footprint with the person making it, provided I see the actual foot.

Q. Is this a common technique?

A. To my knowledge, I am the only person in the world who does it.

Q. How long have you been matching footprints in this manner?

A. Five years. I've looked at hundreds of prints. I've never missed one.

Q. Did you have an opportunity to see Mr. Smith's bare right foot and to compare his foot with the footprints found at the plane crash involved in this case?

A. Yes I did. One of the footprints found at the scene was made by Mr. Smith.

No further questions on direct examination.

Should defense counsel have objected to this testimony? What ruling by the court and why?

McCormick, 6th Ed., §§ 203, 207; Federal Rules of Evidence 401–403, 701–705.

12–30. Drew Insurance Company brought a declaratory judgment action against Michele and James Barfield, its insureds, seeking a judgment that it was not liable under a homeowners policy for a fire in the Barfield home. The company alleges that the fire was started by James in a fit of rage and thus falls within the policy's exclusions for intentional loss.

The parties agree that the fire began on the top of the dining room table in the dining area just inside the front door of the house. Various items had been on the table before the fire, including a plastic bottle of lamp oil that was half-full and sealed. Also on the table prior to the blaze was a note that Michele left for James, criticizing him for his drinking and threatening to leave him if he did not seek help. Testimony at trial also shows that there was a chandelier hung directly over the table and that it had been known to flicker often. After the fire was extinguished, a fire investigator found the plastic oil-lamp bottle. It had melted and was empty, and it appeared that its cap was still attached.

The company wishes to call Ellis as a fire causation expert. An engineer by training, Ellis has worked as an arson investigator for twelve years, seven of those with a municipal fire department and the last five years as an independent expert. He professes familiarity with the scientific literature on fire and its causes and tendencies. If permitted to testify, Ellis would state his opinion that the fire had been intentionally set. Ellis reached this conclusion, he explains, by "following a scientific method—developing hypotheses and testing them. First, I eliminated all accidental causes. Then, given that the fire began on the table, I concluded that there were no other possible sources of ignition of the fire. It follows that the fire must have been intentionally set." Ellis visited the scene a few days after the fire, but he performed no tests and took no samples.

As counsel for Drew Insurance Company, how would you argue the admissibility of Ellis' testimony? As attorney for the Barfields, how would you argue against its admissibility? How should the trial judge rule? On appeal, what is the likelihood of a holding that the trial judge erred?

McCormick, 6th Ed., §§ 203, 207; Federal Rules of Evidence 401–403, 701–705.

12–31.   Refer to Appendix A, *Hines v. National Motor Co.*, Document 8. During the trial of the case, the plaintiff calls Edward Johnson to the witness stand and seeks to have him testify to his opinion as set forth in his statement. Defendant objects. What ruling by the court?

McCormick, 6th Ed., § 210; Federal Rules of Evidence 701–705.

12–32.   Assume that in Problem 12–26 above, blood found in the trunk of Jeffrey's sedan was submitted to older, more traditional typing analysis and was determined to be human blood, type AB, N and Rh negative. So testifies Dr. Mary F. Jenkins, a professor of biochemistry at the state university. Called by the prosecution, Jenkins also testifies that she analyzed a sample of Jeffrey's blood and determined that it was type AB, N and Rh positive—inconsistent with the blood in the trunk. Jenkins' analysis of a sample of Joyce's blood determined that it was type AB, N and Rh negative—consistent with the blood in the trunk. Jenkins further testifies that approximately 3 percent of the world's population is in the blood group AB, approximately 22 percent of the population is in the blood group N, and approximately 15 percent of the population has a negative Rh factor. She further states that by the application of the theory of compound probabilities, the frequency of the occurrence of each of these three factors may be multiplied together in order to obtain a figure which represents the percentage of the population having a concurrence of all three of these factors in their blood. By the operation of that rule, that percentage would be just under .10 percent. She adds that such a percentage would mean that this combination of blood factors would be expected to occur less than once in every 1,000 persons. As defense counsel, to what parts of Jenkins' testimony would you object? On what grounds? What ruling would you expect the court to make?

McCormick, 6th Ed., §§ 203, 205, 210–211; Federal Rules of Evidence 401–403, 702–705.

12–33. The organizers of a rodeo sue Donald for the price of admission. Donald's answer to the complaint admits that he was present but denies that he did not pay. Admission was for cash; no tickets were issued. Plaintiffs offer evidence that 499 persons paid the admission charge and that 1,000 were counted in the stands. Is the evidence admissible? Is it sufficient to withstand a motion for directed verdict? (This problem is from David Kaye, *The Paradox of the Gatecrasher and Other Stories*, 1979 Ariz. St. L.J. 101, giving credit to Dr. L. Jonathan Cohen, a philosopher of science.)

McCormick, 6th Ed., § 210.

12–34. Douglas was charged with the murder of his ex-boss Vincent, who had fired Douglas four months earlier. The crime scene indicated that a violent struggle had occurred and that Vincent was shot during this struggle. Wendy told detectives that she saw someone who fit Douglas's description run from Vincent's house, where the body was found. During an interview, Douglas informed the police that he was home working on his car at the time of the crime. Crime scene technicians found several hairs clutched in Vincent's fingers. An examiner at the state crime laboratory analyzed the hairs using a microscope and concluded that the samples matched. In particular, she explained that many of the approximately twenty-five characteristics (e.g., color, shaft form, hair diameter, pigment size, and shaft diameter) that are used in the analysis were consistent with Douglas's hair but not Vincent's hair. She also stated that, although her conclusion was subjective, she had ten years experience at the lab and had testified in court over forty times. Defense counsel's legal research shows that hair analysis has been admitted in evidence for over a hundred years.

(A) If Douglas's attorney wants to object to the hair examiner's testimony, what arguments should he make? How should the court rule?

(B) On cross-examination, the defense counsel asks whether the hairs of a person other than Douglas could have matched the crime scene hair samples. The expert concedes that microscopic hair analysis is not a positive identification and that someone else in the world could have the same hair characteristics. If Douglas's attorney wants to object to this testimony, what arguments should he make? How should the court rule?

McCormick, 6th Ed., § 207; Federal Rule of Evidence 702.

12–35. In problem 12–34 above, another expert, a firearms and toolmark ("ballistics") examiner, also testified. This examiner used a comparison microscope to compare a bullet retrieved from Vincent's body during the autopsy and a bullet test fired from a .38 caliber revolver found at Douglas's house.

During direct examination, the expert testified that firearms identification involves class and individual characteristics. The class characteristics of a firearm result from design factors and are determined prior to manufacture. They include the caliber and rifling specifications: (1) the land and groove diameters, (2) the direction of rifling (left or right twist), (3) the number of lands and grooves, (4) the width of the lands and grooves, and (5) the degree of the rifling twist. Generally, a .38 caliber bullet with six land and groove impressions and with a right twist could have been fired only from a firearm with those same characteristics. Such a bullet could not have been fired from a .32 caliber firearm, or from a .38 caliber firearm with a different number of lands and grooves or a left twist. In sum, if the class characteristics do not match, the firearm could not have fired the bullet and is excluded as the source.

Individual characteristics differ. When a bullet is fired, microscopic striations are imprinted on the bullet surface as it passes through the bore of the barrel. These bullet markings are randomly produced by imperfections in the bore. The expert further testified that each examiner must decide for herself whether sufficient striae are present to make an identification, that this judgment is subjective, and that there is never a perfect match—i.e., there will always be some differences. The expert concluded that, based on her examination, she believed—to a reasonable scientific certainty—that the striations on both bullets matched and therefore this revolver fired the autopsy bullet to the exclusion of all other weapons in the world.

(A) If Douglas's attorney wants to object to this testimony, what arguments should he make? How should the court rule?

(B) Assume that the expert testified merely that the class characteristics matched and therefore Douglas's weapon could have fired the murder bullet. Is this testimony admissible?

McCormick, 6th Ed., § 207; Federal Rule of Evidence 702.

12–36. In Problem 12–19 above, John's testimony was given through a duly qualified interpreter, Nancy, a teacher of the deaf for some 30 years. After John testified, the state offered Nancy's testimony to the effect that, based upon her years of experience with the deaf, she can positively state that the powers of observation of deaf persons are more keen than those of persons who have normal hearing. She did not know John and could not testify specifically with regard to his powers of observation. As defense counsel, would you object to Nancy's testimony? As prosecutor, how would you respond to the objection? What ruling?

McCormick, 6th Ed., §§ 11–13; Federal Rules of Evidence 701–705.

12–37. Jim owned and operated a model agency, furnishing models to department stores and retail stores selling apparel for women. Every year, Jim sent a calendar to several hundred of his customers. Jim had a contract with Pat, a printer, to print the calendar and to mail it to Jim's customers. Jim furnished Pat with a list of customers for that purpose.

Each year Pat made available to Jim photographs of models dressed in current fashions, from which photographs Jim would choose one for each page of the calendar. For the 2010 calendar, as usual, Jim chose photographs of models dressed in dresses currently fashionable. But through some error, Pat printed Jim's calendars with photographs of female nudes on each page of the calendar, and before the error was discovered, mailed the calendars to the list of Jim's customers. Jim brought suit against Pat for alleged damages on account of lost business and profits allegedly resulting from this error.

(A) Jim's attorney calls Professor Market and begins to ask questions calculated to establish her as a marketing expert. Just as the first question is asked, opposing counsel interrupts and states: "Your honor, we stipulate that Professor Market is an expert on marketing. It is unnecessary for further questions to be asked in order to qualify her as an expert." Should Jim's attorney be permitted to continue to ask questions going to the witness's qualifications as a marketing expert?

(B) Assume that Market is found to be a marketing expert. Jim's attorney then asks Market whether she has heard the plaintiff's evidence to this point, establishing the mailing of the "nudes," a lesser amount of business and profits in 2010 than in previous years, and the testimony of one former customer that he was so offended by the calendar he did not employ Jim's models as in past years. Counsel then asks: "Dr. Market, based upon the evidence you have seen and heard what would be the effect, in your opinion of the mailing of the 'nudes' calendar to Jim's customers, upon Jim's business?" Objection. What ruling?

McCormick, 6th Ed., §§ 12–13; Federal Rules of Evidence 702–705.

12–38. Kathy owned a large building in an older section of the city of Eastown. Late at night the city water main under the street burst and the bursting was not immediately discovered. Water seeped or flowed in the area of the basement of her building. Three hours after the burst, the corner part of her building collapsed. The building was heavily damaged. City employees and Kathy's agents inspected the damaged building and basement shortly after the collapse occurred. Kathy claimed that the collapse was caused by the water from the broken main. However, the city claimed the collapse occurred because the building only had two supporting piers at each corner, two of such supports had collapsed from deterioration independently of the water present, and the basement walls were unable to furnish support independently of the piers. Kathy brought suit for damages charging various acts of negligence in connection with the water main.

As Kathy's attorney, you are preparing for the forthcoming trial of the suit. You plan to call various witnesses who will show the many and detailed facts relating to the incident. After this evidence you are planning to call Mary Mann, an expert on building support. She inspected the building and its environment at various times, including the day of the collapse. She will explain pertinent matters and will relate all the facts she has at hand from personal knowledge. Then a question will be put asking her for her opinion concerning the cause of the collapse of the building. That question will be asked by putting hypothetical facts to her (those facts to which previous witnesses testified) and asking for her opinion on such facts plus the facts that she has stated in her testimony. She will state that the action of the water from the main, and nothing else, caused the collapse.

You have also engaged Dr. Phil More, who is an outstanding expert on the subject matter involved in the suit and who is also known to be an excellent witness on the stand. He has studied all the matters submitted to him and will be a favorable witness, but he had no opportunity to see the situation as it existed originally. You would like to present his opinion as simply and forcefully as possible. And, for this purpose, after he explains various general matters that have indirect bearing on the collapse, you would like to ask him the following questions.

Q. Dr. More, have you listened to the testimony of Ms. Mary Mann who preceded you to the stand?

A. Yes.

Q. You heard all of her testimony?

A. Yes.

Q. Do you remember all of the details of her examination on the stand clearly?

A. Yes, I remember them very well.

Q. Now, Dr. More, based upon all of Ms. Mann's testimony, what is your opinion concerning the cause of the collapse of the building which is the subject matter of the suit?

A. The collapse of the building was caused by the action of the water from the main. . . .

Should you anticipate possible objections to this method of examining Dr. More? Upon analysis of possible objections, if any, would you try to conduct Dr. More's examination in the way described above?

McCormick, 6th Ed., §§ 14–15; Federal Rules of Evidence 703, 705.

12–39. Refer to Problem 12–29 above. Assume that the trial judge rules that an expert with Marx's qualifications may give an opinion with regard to the identity of the person making the footprint at the scene of the crash.

Although Marx actually viewed Steven's right foot, he never actually saw the footprint. He saw photographs of it taken from several angles. He also discussed the depth and shape of the footprint with a police officer who had carefully measured it and he had read a police report containing actual measurements. Should Marx be permitted to give an opinion based upon this information? Contrast the Federal Rules and general law approach to the problem.

McCormick, 6th Ed., §§ 14–15; Federal Rules of Evidence 703–705.

12–40. Plaintiff, Jane Jones, age eight at the time of trial, is suing to recover from injuries allegedly caused by the malpractice of Dr. Marvin O. Smith, a general practitioner. On September 30, she received an injection of penicillin for the treatment of stomach flu. Shortly after the injection she developed a rash over a large percentage of her body. The rash lasted almost two weeks and part of her body (legs, neck and face) remain scarred at the time of the trial.

Jane's mother had accompanied her to the doctor's office where the shot was given. Her mother testified that the doctor had not informed her of the nature of the drug he was administering. She stated that if he had done so she would have told him that the girl had had a slight reaction to penicillin the last time she had it. The defendant doctor, who has not yet taken the stand, stated at a deposition that he in fact had asked the mother whether the child was allergic to penicillin, and the mother had answered that she had never had it before.

Dr. Louise Johnson, a general practitioner practicing in the same city as Dr. Smith, is called as a witness for the plaintiff. She has examined the plaintiff and has told plaintiff's attorney that in her opinion the scarring is permanent. Skin grafting may help but it cannot possibly avoid all of the scars.

Plaintiff's attorney wants Dr. Johnson to testify to the permanent scarring and in addition, to testify that: (1) good medical practice in the community requires that the doctor inquire as to possible penicillin allergy before administering an injection; and (2) penicillin is not accepted treatment for the stomach flu.

Defendant's counsel is generally aware of the nature of Dr. Johnson's proposed testimony. On cross-examination, he would like to elicit the other side of the testimony given by Dr. Johnson on direct, i.e., that if Dr. Smith had asked about penicillin allergy (as he said he did), this is all that was required. No tests for the allergy are presently in use.

Defense counsel also believes that on one occasion plaintiff's mother stated to Dr. Johnson that she really couldn't remember whether or not Dr. Smith had inquired as to the child's past penicillin history.

Prepare both a direct examination of Dr. Johnson on behalf of plaintiff and a cross-examination on behalf of defendant. Consider the form of the testimony under both the Federal Rules of Evidence and the general law.

McCormick, 6th Ed., §§ 13–17; Federal Rules of Evidence 702–705.

12–41. Refer to Appendix B, *State v. Well*, Document 5. At the trial of this case, the state calls Dr. James Tarner, the medical examiner who prepared the autopsy report. The state would like Dr. Tarner to testify with regard to his opinion that the deceased had not been struck by an automobile prior to her death. This opinion is based solely upon his observations during the autopsy. He will state that none of the marks on her body were consistent with her having been hit or grazed by an automobile.

In addition, the state would like Dr. Tarner to testify that, in his opinion, the drowning was caused by someone holding the deceased down in the water. This opinion is based upon the marks found on her body in the autopsy and upon the circumstances of the incident as related to Dr. Tarner by the investigating police officer, Trooper Sten Borne. Dr. Tarner will state that this opinion is based in part upon the absence of other explanations for Mary drowning in water as shallow as the ditch from which she was pulled.

(A) Prepare a direct examination of Dr. Tarner with regard to these opinions.

(B) Assume that Dr. James Tarner testified for the state with regard to the opinions referred to above. Assume further that the autopsy report, Document 5, has not been introduced into evidence. During its case, the defense would like to call Dr. Wilma Martin. Dr. Martin is a forensic pathologist in private practice. She did not participate in the autopsy nor has she spoken to any of the witnesses about the case. However, she was present in the courtroom during Dr. Tarner's testimony and has read the autopsy report. The defense would like Dr. Martin to testify that a person with the blood alcohol and barbiturate count of the deceased could have been in an intoxicated or doped state and that such a person might have fallen into a ditch and drowned without any external force being applied.

Prepare a direct examination of Dr. Martin with regard to this opinion.

McCormick, 6th Ed., §§ 12–17; Federal Rules of Evidence 702–705.

12–42. Edward, a wealthy, 87–year–old widower, died. The terms of his will, executed five years before his death, left his entire estate to three of his children, Mary, Louis and Anne. Elliott, his oldest son, is not mentioned in the will. Elliott files an action contesting the will, claiming that his father was mentally incompetent at the time it was executed. At the time of trial, one of the legatees, Anne, has also died.

As their first witness at the trial, the surviving proponents of the will call a psychiatrist, Dr. Hilda Strauss, to the witness stand. She states her qualifications, which include impressive educational credentials as well as 20 years of private practice specializing in the mental health of the elderly. Dr. Strauss testifies that she had met Edward once, two days before his death, when she had spent approximately five minutes with him. She also testifies that, after Edward's death, she conducted extensive interviews with Edward's children, other than Elliott, all of whom had lived in the same house as Edward all of their lives. She also tells of her interviews with other individuals caring for Edward during his last illness, which had lasted approximately six months. She also reviewed Edward's hospital and other medical records concerning that illness, including nurses' and physicians' comments on his mental state. She further states that interviewing an individual, talking to relatives and care givers and reviewing medical records are all things that she and other psychiatrists regularly do in order to form an opinion with regard to the mental condition of an individual. She adds that her training and experience permits her to render an opinion on an individual's mental condition at an earlier time based upon information received several years later.

The proponents now would like to have Dr. Strauss testify that, in her opinion to a reasonable degree of psychiatric certainty and based upon all of the matters learned in her investigation, Edward had no mental illness at the time of the execution of his will. She further would state that Edward understood the nature of his estate and could make rational decisions with regard to the disposition of his estate. She would conclude that Edward had the capacity to make a will. Assume that this testimony, if believed by the jury, would be sufficient to establish Edward's competence.

In addition to eliciting Dr. Strauss's opinion, the proponents also would like her to detail the basis of the opinion. Among the things to which she would refer in stating her basis are the following: Mary and Louis's statements that their father had stated that he hated Elliott; Anne's statements that six years before Edward's death, Elliott had struck Edward after a heated argument; the opinions of both doctors and nurses treating Edward that he was of sound mind; and Edward's own statements that he wanted to die peacefully and to see his children other than Elliott benefit from his wealth. Assume that Mary, but not Louis, plans to testify at the trial.

Anticipating the material to be covered in Chapters 13 and 14, assume that Dr. Strauss's account of Edward's statements concerning his state of mind would be admissible under an exception to the hearsay rule. Similarly, when Mary testifies, her recollection of her father's statements concerning his hatred of Elliott will be admissible. In addition, if they testify, the treating nurses and physicians would be permitted to give their opinion of Edward's mental condition. However, Dr. Strauss's accounts of Louis's statements concerning his father's attitude and Anne's recollection of the incident in which Elliott struck Edward would be inadmissible hearsay.

Should the trial judge permit Dr. Strauss to give the opinion sought by the proponents? If the opinion is permitted, should Dr. Strauss be permitted to testify on direct examination about all of the aspects of the basis of her opinion set forth above?

McCormick, 6th Ed., §§ 12–17; Federal Rules of Evidence 702–705.

12–43. Dennis is charged with murder of a police officer. The officer was shot as he and orderlies from a mental hospital sought to enforce a commitment order which had been issued against Dennis. Dennis' defense is insanity. Dr. Theresa Malloy is a psychiatrist who worked with Dennis for six months prior to the shooting and for the six months between the shooting and the trial. Dr. Malloy believes that Dennis is a paranoid schizophrenic. His psychosis causes him to believe that he is being persecuted. In particular, he believes that the police and representatives of the mental hospital are trying to kill him. When such individuals arrived to take him to the hospital, Dennis believed he was under attack and that he needed to shoot to protect himself from bodily harm. The nature of the disease is such that it so distorts reality as to prevent the person from understanding his true situation. Under the circumstances, Dennis did not know he was doing wrong.

The jurisdiction in which this case is being tried excuses otherwise criminal acts if, at the time of the act, as a result of a mental disease or defect, the person did not know the difference between right and wrong or have the power to choose between them. The jurisdiction also has a provision identical to Federal Rule 704(a) but has not adopted Rule 704(b). As Dennis's counsel, plan an examination of Dr. Malloy. In the alternative, plan an examination of Dr. Malloy in a jurisdiction which has adopted Rule 704(b).

McCormick, 6th Ed., § 12; Federal Rule of Evidence 704.

12–44. Judith was charged with forgery of a check. She is an indigent and asked the court for the appointment of a questioned document examiner. Judith sought the expert's opinion in order to compare her handwriting with the handwriting on the allegedly forged check. The state did not employ its own expert witness. No funds are provided by the state to enable an accused to hire an expert in a noncapital case. The trial judge denied Judith's request for the appointment of the expert. Judith was convicted and appeals, alleging, among other things, that her rights under the Sixth and Fourteenth Amendments to the United States Constitution were denied by the court's rejection of her request for the appointment of an expert. What result on appeal?

12–45. Paul brought suit for damages to his land by pollution. Paul's attorney, Al, was retained on a contingent fee basis (Al would receive 35% of the recovery, if any; Paul would pay the expenses of the suit in any event). Paul and Al agreed that they would have to obtain an expert witness on a contingent fee basis, or no expert could be obtained. Otherwise, Al assured Paul he had no chances of winning the suit.

Dr. Henry Jamison, an expert in soil analysis, erosion, drainage, etc., had appeared as an expert for Al in other cases. In these cases, Al and Dr. Jamison had never discussed a fee, but upon engaging Dr. Jamison orally, Al had informed Dr. Jamison that he had taken the cases on a contingent fee basis. When some of the cases were lost, Dr. Jamison rendered a bill, but such bills have never been paid. After the last case Dr. Jamison said, "I took my chances, too."

In this case, Al called Dr. Jamison, told him briefly about the instant case and asked him if he would appear on the basis of their previous experience. Dr. Jamison said he would act as the expert witness. At the subsequent trial, Dr. Jamison was called and testified at length, explaining pertinent general matters and stating opinions in answer to lengthy hypothetical questions. It was obvious he was prepared.

On cross-examination, much to Al's surprise, the opponent's attorney managed to obtain testimony from Dr. Jamison that Jamison understood he had been engaged upon a contingent fee basis. The opposing attorney moved to strike the direct examination of Dr. Jamison. Should the motion be granted?

SECTION E.   ATTACKING AND SUSTAINING CREDIBILITY; IMPEACHMENT AND REHABILITATION

12–46.   David was charged with the rape of Vicki. According to Vicki, the attack occurred when she returned to her apartment after celebrating a friend's birthday at a local bar. She went to the emergency room where she was interviewed by a sexual assault nurse examiner (SANE). She identified David, an ex-boyfriend, as her attacker. He was at the bar at the same time as Vicki and her friends but was not part of the birthday celebration. The next day Vicki told her boss about the attack. David claims that everything was consensual until Vicki passed out drunk, at which time he left the apartment. The prosecution calls Vicki as its first witness.

(A) Would the prosecutor be allowed to call Vicki's boss as its next witness to testify that Vicki is a truthful person?

(B) Would the prosecutor be allowed to have the boss relate his conversation with Vicki about the alleged assault—i.e., that she had been raped by David?

(C) Would the prosecutor be allowed to ask Vicki what she had told the nurse at the hospital—i.e., that she had been raped by David?

McCormick, 6th ed., §§ 33, 47; Federal Rule of Evidence 608(a).

12–47.   Daniel is on trial for robbery of a supermarket. One of the state witnesses is John Madison, one of the supermarket clerks. John had identified Daniel at a police lineup as one of the two men who had robbed the store. John is called by the prosecution at the trial. Just as the examination begins, the prosecutor is handed a note by one of her assistants which gives her the following information: John's real name is John Marks. He is presently on parole after serving nine months of a two year sentence for forging checks. A few nights ago, John was seen at a local bar with Susan, the sister of the accused. The prosecutor elects to proceed with the testimony. When John is asked whether one of the persons who committed the robbery is present in the courtroom, he replies, "I don't know, I can't be sure. The man sitting over there (indicating the defendant) looks something like one of the guys, but the handkerchief was pretty well covering the guy's face." What courses of action are available to the prosecution at this point?

McCormick, 6th Ed., § 38; Federal Rules of Evidence 607, 801(d)(1)(A).

12–48. Adam was prosecuted for larceny (obtaining money under false pretenses). The state charges that Adam ran a "flim-flam" operation. At the trial Calvin, a police officer, gave damaging testimony on behalf of the state, but Adam's attorney did not cross-examine Calvin.

(A) Should Adam's attorney anticipate that over objection he will be able to bring out the testimony of Nell, that she was an eyewitness to an altercation between Calvin and Adam in a tavern in which Calvin "took a real beating from Adam"?

(B) Should Adam's attorney anticipate that over objection he can bring out evidence that Calvin has a bias against Adam based upon an incident in which Adam beat up a friend of Calvin's, a man named Mac? The evidence would be in the form of testimony from another witness, Nell, that Calvin and Mac were friends and that she witnessed the fight between Adam and Mac. She would also testify that Calvin was present at the time of the fight.

(C) Should Adam's attorney anticipate that he can bring out evidence, over objection, that Calvin had arrested Adam on two previous occasions, but that charges were not pressed by the prosecutor's office?

(D) Should Adam's attorney anticipate that he can bring out evidence that Calvin had purchased shares of stock in a corporation almost completely owned and controlled by Adam, and that the corporation had become insolvent (all before Adam's arrest on the unrelated instant criminal charge)?

McCormick, 6th Ed., § 39; Federal Rules of Evidence 401–403.

12–49. In the prosecution of Daniel discussed in Problem 12–47 above, one of the key defense witnesses is George, who operated a small hotel in the city of Patlo. George testified on direct examination that Daniel was registered at this hotel on the day on which the robbery took place and that he saw Daniel several times during that day. On cross-examination, the prosecutor first established that George has recently sold his hotel and moved out of state. She now seeks to bring out that George now lives in another state, more than 1,000 miles away from the place of trial, and that he has been brought to the trial from his present home at the expense of the defense. The prosecution also seeks to show that George is being paid $400 a day for every day that he remains in town for the trial.

The defense objects to the prosecution's cross-examination on these points. As trial judge, what ruling would you make on the defense objection? Assuming that you permit cross-examination and assuming that George's answers were evasive, would you permit the prosecution to bring in other witnesses to support its allegations with regard to George? Would you permit the prosecution to bring in other witnesses on this question if George fully admits the prosecution's point? Would you permit the prosecution to bring in other witnesses on this question if George is never asked about these points on cross-examination?

McCormick, 6th Ed., § 39; Federal Rules of Evidence 401–403.

12–50. (A) Under the appropriate federal hijacking statute, Judy and Dan were charged with hijacking an aircraft while it was flying in interstate commerce and with a conspiracy to hijack the aircraft. Bill was named as a member of the conspiracy, but he was not made a defendant.

At the trial of the hijacking and the conspiracy charges, Bill was called as a government witness and gave damaging testimony tending to establish the conspiracy charges. Included in his testimony was testimony that at a certain tavern at a certain time and place he had a conversation with Judy and Dan. He related the conversation, the gist of which was a discussion in furtherance of the alleged conspiracy.

On cross-examination, Bill was asked whether or not he had told his friend, Ed, shortly after the above-mentioned conversation, that he had conversed in the tavern with Judy and Dan as mentioned above and that they had only discussed another criminal venture having nothing to do with the hijacking. Bill refused to answer the question, claiming his privilege against self-incrimination. Defendant thereupon moved for a mistrial. Should the motion be granted? If the motion is denied, what other relief might be available?

(B) Assume that all requests of defendant's attorney were denied. Then still on cross-examination, defendant's attorney asked Bill whether he had hijacked another and different aircraft. Bill refused to answer this question on the ground of self-incrimination. Again, defendant moved for a mistrial. Should the motion be granted? If the motion is denied, what other relief might be available?

McCormick, 6th Ed., §§ 19, 134, 135.

12–51. Assume that in Problem 12–49 above, the prosecution seeks to impeach George on points other than the expense money he received from the defense. Specifically, on cross-examination, the following facts are the subject of questions:

1. That George is an alcoholic and that he retired from business because he could no longer effectively run the hotel due to his alcoholism.

2. That George had been drinking heavily on the day on which he claims to have seen Daniel.

The defense objects to the prosecution's cross-examination on these points. As trial judge, what ruling would you make? Assuming George's answers were evasive, would you permit the prosecution to bring in other witnesses to support its charges against George? If George admitted the prosecution's points? If George was not asked the questions on cross-examination?

Answer the above questions again, assuming that George's problem was not alcoholism, but rather addiction to amphetamines.

McCormick, 6th Ed., § 44; Federal Rules of Evidence 401–403, 608.

12–52. William Wander, the only alleged eyewitness to a homicide for which Jake Brown was being tried, testified at great length to events leading up to the alleged homicide and to the details of the homicide. William was also cross-examined at great length by Jake's attorney. Jake's attorney employed Dr. Henry Cable, a recognized psychiatrist with proper credentials, to attend the trial and observe William while he was testifying. When Jake's case was later presented, Jake's attorney called Dr. Cable to the stand and by questioning qualified him as an expert in psychiatry. By questions, all of which were objected to, Jake's attorney brought out that Dr. Cable had observed William giving his testimony and had heard all of his testimony and that in the opinion of Dr. Cable, William was a "pathological liar" and stated that, in his opinion, such a person could not be believed although he testified under oath. Dr. Cable also set forth the facts noted by him which supported his opinion that William was a "pathological liar."

The following is an excerpt from the direct examination of Dr. Cable:

Q. What is your opinion, Dr. Cable, of the mental condition of Mr. Wander?

A. I think Mr. Wander is suffering from a condition known as psychopathic personality, which is a disorder of character, of which the outstanding features are behavior of what we call an amoral or an asocial and delinquent nature.

Q. Will you define for us, Doctor, what you mean by amoral and asocial?

A. I mean that amoral behavior is behavior that does not take into account the ordinary accepted conventions of morality; and asocial behavior is behavior which has no regard for the good of society and of individuals, and is therefore frequently destructive of both. May I say that in addition to what is commonly recognized by the layman as lying, there is a peculiar kind of lying known as pathological lying, and a peculiar kind of tendency to make false accusations known as pathological accusations, which are frequently found in the psychopathic personality.

Q. Are there treatises on the matter of pathological lying and pathological false accusing?

A. Yes. One of the best books in this country was written by William Healy, who was for many years the head of the Judge Baker Foundation in Boston, whose interest was in delinquency.

Q. What would you say, Dr. Cable, as to the nature of the acts of a psychopathic personality, one having a psychopathic personality?

A. Well, I should say, first of all—

Q. In addition to what you have already said; I don't want you to repeat.

A. Yes, I understand that. First of all, a psychopath is quite aware of what he is doing but he does not always know why he does it; and to characterize the acts in a qualitative way; they are frequently impulsive and very often bizarre, so that they do not make much sense to the casual observer who does not understand what the particular fantasy or imagination there is behind these acts; because the acts actually represent something private to the patient, but from a point of view of common sense and understanding apparently making no sense.

Q. Would it be proper, Dr. Cable, to refer to an individual who has a psychopathic personality as a psychopath? Is that the recognized term that is used?

A. Well, that is an abbreviation, yes sir, and is to be distinguished from a psychotic or insane person. It has nothing to do with conventional judgment of sanity.

Q. Is psychopathic personality a recognized mental disease?

A. It is.

Q. Will you tell us what you mean when you say that psychopathic personality is a recognized mental disease?

A. I mean that it is listed as a standard diagnosis among the standard diagnoses accepted by the American Psychiatric Association, and can be found I think on page 601—I am not certain of the page— of the American Hygiene Laws and General Orders of the Department of Mental Hygiene of this state. You will find there the diagnoses of psychopathic personality among the diagnoses of mental illness.

Q. Is that a classification that has been put out by the State Department of Mental Hygiene?

A. It is, yes, sir.

Q. And, that Order has been effective for how long?

A. That I can't precisely say but I would guess at least 15 years.

Q. Aside from it being included in the classification under the State Mental Hygiene Laws and its Orders, is it recognized in the standard text books or texts on psychiatry?

A. Oh, yes, there has been a great deal written about it both here and abroad, and there are many standard books that cover this subject.

Q. Will you tell us, Dr. Cable, what some of the symptoms of a psychopathic personality are?

A. Well, they are quite variegated. They include chronic, persistent and repetitive lying; they include stealing; they include acts of deception and misrepresentation; they include alcoholism and drug addiction; abnormal sexuality; vagabondage; panhandling; inability to form stable attachments; and a tendency to make false accusations.

Q. How about neurotic classifications? Would it be distinguished from that?

A. I think I should emphasize that these are not hard and fast distinctions; that many psychopaths have certain characteristics which we see in more seriously mentally disturbed psychotic individuals. For example, they very frequently, in fact almost always, exhibit what we call paranoid thinking, about which I will talk later; and they also, on the other hand, exhibit some of the characteristics seen in neurotic individuals in the form of anxiety or over concern about their bodies, or hypochondriasis, or something of that sort; but it is a kind of middle ground between the psychotic and neurotic.

Q. Have you any suggestion for the cause of the disease which you have here described as psychopathic personality?

A. I do not know the cause of it; nobody knows the cause of it. It is a disorder of personality beginning in early youth and almost always—in fact, one can say always—lasting throughout life. But I know some of the apparent causes. These unfortunate people have a conviction of the truth and validity of their own imaginations, of their own fantasies without respect to outer reality; so that they play a part in life, play a role. They may be a hero at one moment and a gangster at the next. They act as if a situation were true which, in fact, is true only in their imaginations; and on the basis of such imaginations they will claim friendships where none exist, just as they have a constant need to make their imaginations come true by behaving as if the outer world were actually in accord with their imagination.

Q. By that, Dr. Cable, do you mean that a psychopath is insensible to the feelings of others?

A. Well, he is amazingly isolated and egocentric. He does not really establish a rapport with other people, and he never knows how other people feel because he is always playing a part as if what he thought to be true was true of others.

Q. Would it be consistent of the behavior of a psychopath in describing his relation with another to tell about trips, visits, exchange of gifts and other acts of association which, in fact, never occurred?

A. Anything is consistent because he will simply tell what he believes at the moment or what needs to be true, and, of course, that would be quite consistent.*

Dr. Cable also testified on direct that his diagnosis was based on various concrete matters observed while William was testifying, including the facts that William had been caught stealing two inexpensive objects

---

* Copyright 1961 by William J. Curran, Frances Glassner Lee, Professor of Legal Medicine, Harvard Medical School and Harvard School of Public Health, in Law and Medicine, Little Brown & Co. Reproduced by permission.

from a retail store, that William had never looked directly at the attorneys questioning him, but looked at the ceiling often when testifying, that he occasionally looked slyly at the jury, that he contradicted himself several times on unimportant details, that his life history had been a rags to riches story involving some unethical occupational conduct, that he had been abandoned as a grade school youth and had been raised in foster homes, etc.

(A) Should the testimony of Dr. Cable be admissible?

(B) Consider the possibilities of cross-examination of Dr. Cable, merely based upon the matters related in this problem. Do any fruitful lines of questioning occur to you?

McCormick, 6th Ed., §§ 43–44; Federal Rules of Evidence 401–403, 608.

12–53. Edward is charged with embezzling money from the supermarket of which he was the manager. One of the principal state witnesses is Gerald, one of the clerks at the market. Gerald will testify that he frequently turned in more money from his cash register than was recorded by Edward on the store's books. Edward's attorney has possession of the results of an I.Q. test which Gerald had taken two years before the trial. Gerald's test score was 65. A psychologist tells counsel that a "normal" I.Q. would range from 90 to 110. The person who administered the test, which was taken in the course of Gerald's school experience, is not available to testify concerning the test score or its administration. However, school administration personnel can authenticate the record of the test. Edward would like to introduce the test at trial. Is it admissible?

McCormick, 6th Ed., § 44; Federal Rules of Evidence 401–403, 608.

12–54. In Problem 12–53 above, Edward's attorney was reasonably satisfied that the factual case of the government against Edward was not true, and he decided to ask Edward to take a lie detector test, administered by a recognized expert in such tests. Edward took the test. The results show that Edward's version of pertinent facts (under which he would clearly be innocent) is true. Should Edward's attorney anticipate that he can introduce the results of this test at the trial in making Edward's defense? Assume Edward will also take the stand as a witness in his own behalf and testify as to his version of the facts.

McCormick, 6th Ed., §§ 47, 206; Federal Rules of Evidence 401–403, 801(d)(1)(B).

12–55. Lawrence, a clerk in a drug store, is charged with dispensing morphine without a valid prescription, a felony. His defense is that he was entrapped. The person to whom he dispensed the drug was a police officer. The officer, Rizzo, will testify that he came into the drug store when Lawrence was the only person present, that he asked Lawrence to sell him morphine, that Lawrence said it would cost him $200 for what he wanted and that Rizzo made the purchase. Lawrence's story is that he was alone at work, that Rizzo came into the store feigning withdrawal symptoms, that he pleaded with Lawrence to give him some morphine and that he gave Rizzo a small amount at the regular price. The principal defense problem is whether to put Lawrence on the witness stand. Lawrence was at one time a licensed pharmacist. Twenty years ago, he was charged with being part of a conspiracy to distribute prescription drugs illegally. He was about to plead guilty to the charge when a deal was worked out with the prosecutor's office whereby the charges would be dropped against him if he would agree to give up his pharmacist's license and to testify for the state. He carried through his part of the bargain. Within six months after this incident, Lawrence was again in trouble with the law, this time for income tax evasion. The tax evasion charges arose out of his failure to report income received in connection with the illegal sale of prescription drugs. He was convicted on this charge and spent nine months in prison.

(A) If Lawrence takes the witness stand, how much of his prior troubles can be brought into evidence? How will this be done? What can the defense do to avoid the introduction of this evidence?

(B) Assume that Lawrence is not a defendant in the action, but rather that the owner of the drug store in which Lawrence had worked is being prosecuted. The state charges that the store owner violated a drug registration law. Lawrence gave testimony favorable to his employer. How much of his prior troubles can be brought into evidence under these circumstances? Is your answer different from your answer in Part (A)?

(C) Assume that the action is not a criminal action, but rather a civil action brought against the drug store by a drug company to collect on an open account. Assume that Lawrence was the witness and that his testimony on behalf of the drug store dealt with the receipt of drugs from the plaintiff company. Would any of your answers with respect to the impeachment of Lawrence change?

McCormick, 6th Ed., §§ 41–42; Federal Rules of Evidence 608–609.

12–56. Donald Smith is being prosecuted in United States District Court for interstate transportation of a large quantity of marijuana for sale in violation of federal law. Smith was the owner of an airplane which was seized by the authorities and found to contain 500 pounds of marijuana. If called to testify, he would state that the airplane had been loaned to his brother-in-law and that he knew nothing of its use to transport marijuana.

Defense counsel knows that the prosecution has available to it, the following items of proof:

1. Smith was convicted three years ago of the assault and battery of his estranged wife. He received a one-year suspended sentence.

2. Smith was convicted of income tax evasion 15 years ago, spent 18 months in a federal prison, and was released on parole nine years ago.

3. Smith was convicted two years ago of transporting cigarettes across state lines by airplane in order to avoid the cigarette tax. He received a 60–day sentence for that offense which carried a maximum six-month jail term.

4. The prosecutor has reliable information that Smith has severely beaten several people in bar fights within the past three months.

5. The prosecutor also learns that when Smith applied for his most recent extension of his pilot's license in North Carolina, he wrote "no" in response to the question that asked whether he had any previous criminal convictions.

6. The prosecutor has been told by one of the persons arrested in connection with the seizure of the airplane that Smith had been involved in the transportation of marijuana and cocaine by airplane on six specific other occasions.

Defendant moves *in limine* to exclude all of the above proof in the event that Smith elects to testify. Must the trial judge rule on this motion? If she rules on the motion, how should she rule? If she grants the motion with regard to the admissibility of these items of proof for impeachment purposes, would any of these items of proof be admissible for other purposes? If she denies the motion, must defendant take the witness stand and suffer the admission of the prior convictions and bad acts into evidence in order to preserve any potential error for appeal?

McCormick, 6th Ed., §§ 41–42; Federal Rules of Evidence 608–609.

12–57. Assume that Arnold Well takes the witness stand in his own behalf and testifies consistently with the statements contained in Document 4, Appendix B, *State v. Well.* Can the state introduce Document 15 during cross-examination of Well?

McCormick, 6th Ed., § 42; Federal Rule of Evidence 609.

12–58. (A) Ted is prosecuted in federal court for bank robbery. The key witness against him is a fifteen-year-old boy, Barry, who says that he saw Ted running from the bank. Barry had been adjudicated a delinquent in proceedings resulting from the theft of money from his employer (the local newspaper). The crime, if Barry had been an adult, would have been embezzlement and would have been punishable by up to five years in the penitentiary. However, at the time of Ted's trial, his probationary status had been terminated.

On cross-examination, Ted's counsel would like to confront Barry with the adjudication of delinquency. May she do so?

(B) Susan is charged with burglary in state court. The key witness against her is fifteen-year-old boy, Harry, who will testify that Susan was near the scene of the burglary shortly before it occurred. Harry has been adjudicated a delinquent in proceedings resulting from an assault on a neighbor boy. Harry's act would have been punishable by six-months in jail had he been an adult. Harry is on probation at the time of Susan's trial and must report weekly to his probation officer. He is subject to incarceration in a juvenile facility if he violates the terms of his probation.

Assume that there is a statute of the jurisdiction in which the case is tried which provides:

"No adjudication, order, or disposition of a juvenile case shall be admissible in a court not acting in the exercise of juvenile jurisdiction except for use in a presentencing procedure * * *."

May the defense cross-examine Harry about his delinquency adjudication?

McCormick, 6th Ed., §§ 39, 42; Federal Rule of Evidence 609.

12–59. William was being tried for armed robbery. The prosecution charges that William held up a filling station, aided and abetted by a woman, Louise. In presenting his case, William's attorney called Louise to the stand. On direct Louise testified that she and William were in another state at the time the robbery occurred. Actually, Louise, in a separate proceeding, had already been convicted of the same robbery and was out on bond, pending appeal. On cross-examination, the following occurred:

Q. Have you been convicted on a criminal charge that you committed the robbery charged in this case? (objection overruled)

A. Yes.

Q. And, didn't you plead "not guilty" in that very case? (objection overruled)

A. Yes.

Were the court's rulings correct?

In the alternative, make the assumption that before William's trial Louise had been pardoned based upon acts of heroism in a prison fire. Would that affect your answers?

McCormick, 6th Ed., § 42; Federal Rule of Evidence 609.

12–60. (A) In Problem 12–55 above, the prosecutor has spoken to two persons who knew Lawrence twenty years ago, at the time when he was first charged with conspiracy to distribute prescription drugs illegally. They genuinely believe that Lawrence is a bad person who would lie, cheat and steal at any opportunity if it served his interest. Assume that Lawrence testifies in his own behalf. May these two witnesses express their opinion of Lawrence's character? What form should this testimony take?

(B) Assume that the testimony referred to in Part (A) is admitted. The defense then seeks to introduce the testimony of Lawrence's present employer that Lawrence is a good person with high moral values. What form should this testimony take? What will the jury be instructed with regard to both this testimony and the testimony involved in Part (A)? Assuming the employer is permitted to testify, may the witness be cross-examined about Lawrence's prior involvement in illegal sale of prescription drugs or his income tax evasion conviction?

McCormick, 6th Ed., § 43; Federal Rules of Evidence 405, 608.

12–61. Arthur was charged with burglary of the Ballard home. Allegedly the burglary occurred in the middle of the afternoon while no one was home. Arthur supposedly drove a pick-up truck into the driveway of the Ballard home, broke open the front door, took out several articles, placed them in his truck and drove off. The house was screened on each side by trees and shrubs, but the driveway and front door were in plain view from the street and one neighboring house across the street. At the trial which occurred three years after the burglary, the prosecuting attorney called Wilma who was an Avon salesperson. She testified that on the afternoon in question she emerged from the house across the street after having visited there to sell Avon products and saw a man take a television set out of the front door of the Ballard home and place it in a truck which was sitting in the driveway. She identified the defendant as the man involved in that incident. At the time she assumed nothing unusual was happening.

On cross-examination, defendant's attorney was permitted to ask if she remembered what she had sold the lady across the street on the day in question. She said she did, and when questioned as to the sale she answered she remembered very well because she had sold the lady (a Mrs. Brick) an Avon Golden Doll Bath Oil, and remembered that well because it was contained in an unusually beautiful bottle, the only such bottle of oil she had ever sold. In answer to further questioning, she stated that Mrs. Brick was a regular customer.

(A) Should objections to questions which called for the above answers have been overruled?

(B) Can Arthur's attorney later bring out successfully by questioning Mrs. Brick the following alternative facts? (1) Testimony of Mrs. Brick that she had never purchased Golden Doll Bath Oil from Wilma or any other Avon salesperson? (2) Testimony that she had never purchased any Avon products from Wilma or anyone else? (3) Testimony that for a month before and a month after the alleged robbery she had been continuously in the Bahamas and no one had occupied her house during that time?

(C) Would testimony of an Avon area manager that the company had never produced a product labeled Golden Doll Bath Oil be admissible?

McCormick, 6th Ed., §§ 29, 45, 49; Federal Rules of Evidence 401–403.

12–62. Refer to Appendix A. *Hines v. National Motor Co.*, Documents 6 and 7. Defendant calls Officer Robert Schwartz to the witness stand to testify with regard to the unbroken bottle. Assume that on direct examination, Schwartz testifies consistently with his statements in Document 7. On cross-examination, plaintiff would like to confront Schwartz with his statement concerning the bottles made in his original report, Document 6. Plan the testimony necessary to introduce this statement. Will the statement be admissible? If Schwartz denies making the earlier report (Document 6), will the report be admissible?

McCormick, 6th Ed., §§ 34, 36–37; Federal Rule of Evidence 613.

12–63. Jerry was injured in a collision between his car and one driven by Laura on July 4. At the scene of the collision, Call Telephone

Company employees were working in a manhole in the street on underground cables and had placed traffic cones for guidance of traffic. Jerry sued both Laura, alleging that Laura's negligence caused or contributed to the accident, and the telephone company, alleging that its placement of the cones was negligent. The traffic cones formed an island in the street and traffic could pass on either side of the island. Jerry's suit was based on the theory that Laura passed the island on the wrong side of the street (Laura's left-hand side of the street) and that the misplaced cones caused her to do so. Laura and the phone company denied the allegations of the complaint.

To establish its version of the placement of the traffic cones, the telephone company attorney called Nancy, a telephone company construction supervisor, to the stand. She stated that she last saw the cone arrangement on the day before the accident and stated, without objection, "There was nothing unusual about the arrangement of the cones nor about the flow of traffic. Traffic was clearly directed." According to her testimony, the traffic cones were arranged differently from the arrangement that had been indicated in Jerry's evidence.

Assume that Jerry's attorney can call to the stand a Mr. Camera, the city superintendent of streets, who would testify that he was also at the scene the day before the accident. At that time, he told Nancy that the placement of traffic cones was completely inadequate and would result in an accident. He would also testify that Nancy responded they would be rearranged before the end of the day but that they were not rearranged before the accident occurred the next day.

The following occurs on cross-examination of Nancy concerning the conversation with Camera on July 3:

By Ms. Teron (Attorney for plaintiff):

Q. Ms. Zamo (Attorney for defendant) asked you what you did while you were there. Did you talk to Mr. Camera, the superintendent of streets?

A. On the third? I can't recall whether I did or not.

Q. Do you recall whether you talked to him or not on the 4th, the day of the accident?

A. I did not.

Q. You did not talk to him the 4th?

A. No, ma'am.

Q. You don't recall whether you did or did not have any conversation with Mr. Camera on the third?

A. No.

Q. Your memory is blank on that subject, is that right?

A. As far as conversation with Mr. Camera it is, yes.

Q. If Mr. Camera were to state on oath that you talked to him on the third, would you deny that you talked to him?

A. No, I wouldn't.

Q. However, you have at this time no personal present recollection of having discussed this system of traffic control with Mr. Camera?

A. I have discussed the traffic with Mr. Camera, but whether it was on the third or not, I don't know.

Q. Do you recall that you discussed these cones with him?

A. No, I don't, not at that time.

Q. You couldn't say when you had your discussion with Mr. Camera?

A. Yes.

Q. When did you have it?

A. I had one on the fifth.

Q. As to before the accident, though?

A. I couldn't say when I had any discussion.

Q. Isn't it a fact that the day before the accident Mr. Camera told you that your system of placement of traffic cones was completely inadequate and would result in an accident?

Ms. Zamo: Just a moment. If the court please, there is no such testimony in the record by Mr. Camera. Therefore the question is improper and should be stricken. There is no such statement.

Ms. Teron: I think I have the time and the place and the persons present and I am entitled to ask this question as an impeaching question, to lay the foundation.

Ms. Zamo: I don't agree you are entitled to ask this question. There is no testimony of words spoken by Camera to him along the lines you have just stated.

Ms. Teron: There doesn't have to be.

Ms. Zamo: You are asking about words spoken—

The Court: Objection sustained.

(A) Did the court rule correctly?

(B) Could Jerry's attorney have taken any different course of action to bring in the conversation of Nancy with Mr. Camera?

McCormick, 6th Ed., §§ 34, 36–37; Federal Rule of Evidence 613.

12–64. Donald is on trial for the robbery of a convenience store. Jack, the clerk at the store, has testified for the prosecution. On direct examination, he fully described the robbery and identified Donald as one of the two robbers. In describing the men's escape from the store, Jack testified that he saw them enter a white, 2000 Ford and drive away from the scene. (Evidence had previously been introduced that Donald owns a white, 2000 Ford.)

Although defense counsel extensively cross-examined Jack, he was not asked about the get-away car. He has now left the town in which the trial is taking place and has gone to his home city, approximately 30 miles away. One of the two defense lawyers is now called to the stand. If permitted, the lawyer will testify that a month before the trial, in an interview with both lawyers representing Donald, Jack stated that he saw the robbers leave the store and enter a car, but that he could not remember the make or year of the car. The prosecution objects to this testimony. What ruling?

McCormick, 6th Ed., §§ 34, 36–37; Federal Rule of Evidence 613.

12–65. In Problem 12–40 above, defendant's counsel has been referred to a medical text, Mark and Hill, Allergic Reactions, 2005, W.W. Norton & Co., New York, which his medical advisors tell him is an accepted treatise in the field. Following is an excerpt from page 687 of that text:

> Skin rashes resulting from penicillin reactions are not likely to be long lasting. The longest lasting rash which has been reported to these authors has been four days. No instance of a penicillin reaction skin rash causing permanent scarring has ever been reported.

Counsel would, of course, like to have this portion of the book introduced in evidence. One possibility that occurs to counsel is to confront Dr. Johnson with the text when cross-examining her about the permanency of the rash. Prepare such a cross-examination. Consider the propriety of confronting Dr. Johnson with the pertinent section of the text if: (1) Dr. Johnson admits relying upon the text in forming the opinion given on direct examination; (2) Dr. Johnson states that although she did not rely upon the text in giving his opinion on direct examination, she would recognize Mark and Hill as an accepted treatise on the problem of allergic reactions; and (3) Dr. Johnson states that she is unfamiliar with the Mark and Hill text.

May the Mark and Hill text excerpt be admitted in any way other than through cross-examination of Dr. Johnson? If so, how?

McCormick, 6th Ed., §§ 15, 321; Federal Rules of Evidence 702–705, 803(18).

12–66. Lewis, a police officer, is charged with attempting to extort money from Richard. Allegedly, Lewis told Richard that he would be harassed in the conduct of his tavern business if he did not agree to pay Lewis $200 a week. Lewis denies ever making such a proposition. Richard was the only state witness at the trial.

On cross-examination, it was brought out by defendant's attorney that Richard had not mentioned the matter to any government authority until three months after the alleged threat. Defendant's attorney also brought out an admission from Richard that, three months after his first complaint to the police, Richard had told one of his bartenders, Alice, that his charges against Lewis were false.

The prosecutor has at hand several items of proof in rebuttal. First is evidence that Richard, prior to his first complaint to the police, had made a statement to a friend, Charles, which was consistent with his testimony on direct examination. Secondly, the prosecutor can prove a similar statement to another friend, Jean, shortly after the report to the police. Thirdly, the state can show through various witnesses that Richard had said to several people, between the time of the alleged threat and his report to the police: "I'm scared to death of the cops. I don't want nothing to do with any of them." Lastly, the state has several witnesses who can testify that Richard has an excellent reputation in the community for truthfulness.

Is any of the prosecution's rebuttal evidence admissible?

McCormick, 6th Ed., § 47; Federal Rules of Evidence 401–403, 801(d)(1)(B).

12–67. Jill sues the Behr Manufacturing Company for product liability based on injuries she suffered when the chain on the Behr chain saw she was operating slipped off its mountings and cut her severely. At the trial, one of her witnesses is Amy, a design engineer formerly employed by Behr. Amy testifies that the chain on the saw in question had a tendency to slip off its mountings and that Behr was aware of this defect at the time that the saw was put on the market. On cross-examination, it is established that Amy was laid off from Behr shortly after the saw was put on the market and that she has been unable to find other, comparable employment. She says, however, that she has no bitterness against Behr and recognizes that the layoff was simply part of a general cutback at the company's manufacturing plant.

On redirect examination, Jill's attorney seeks to bring out the following:

(A) A letter written by Jill to Behr's management before she was laid off expressing concern about the safety of the model chain saw in question.

(B) A letter written by Jill to the editor of a trade publication, dated one week after Jill was laid off, expressing concern about the chain saw.

(C) The transcript of an exit interview between Jill and her supervisor at Behr, conducted on the day that Jill was packing up her office after she was laid off. The transcript, produced in discovery, contains statements by Jill in which she expresses concern about the safety of the chain saw.

Will any or all of these items be admissible?

McCormick, 6th Ed., § 47; Federal Rules of Evidence 401–403; 801(d)(1)(B).

12–68. Toby is charged with espionage—selling classified information to a foreign power. The principal witness for the government is an F.B.I. agent, Margaret. Margaret testifies that she had observed Toby meet with two men she identified as employees of the embassy of the nation involved. On cross-examination, Margaret is confronted with her official report of the incident, dated September 9. The report contains the statement that, on that day, she observed Toby meet with two men. One of them was an employee of the embassy. The other was a co-worker of Toby's at the nuclear research laboratory, Marvin Smith.

The prosecutor and Margaret were both aware of this inconsistency in Margaret's testimony. Margaret's explanation is that she mistakenly identified Smith at the time she filed her report. After interviewing Smith that same day and after reviewing pictures of embassy personnel, she recognized her mistake. On the next day, September 10, she filed a supplemental report correcting her error. The supplemental report is totally consistent with her trial testimony in that it states that both of the individuals with whom Toby met were employees of the embassy.

May the government introduce the supplemental report on redirect examination of Margaret?

McCormick, 6th Ed., § 47; Federal Rules of Evidence 401–403, 801(d)(1)(B).

TOPIC 5

THE HEARSAY RULE

■ ■ ■

CHAPTER 13

THE FOUNDATION OF THE RULE
AND CONFRONTATION

■ ■ ■

SECTION A. DEFINITION AND RATIONALE: STATEMENTS FOR THE TRUTH OF THE MATTER ASSERTED

Using the definition of hearsay in Federal Rule of Evidence 801(a)–(c), consider whether the proof offered in the following questions is hearsay. *See* McCormick, 6th ed., §§ 244–250. Do not at this point be concerned with admissions and prior statements under 801(d).

13–1. Peter is suing Donald for injuries occurring when Donald allegedly drove through a red light at the intersection of Franklin and Columbia Streets. When the accident occurred Donald was driving west on Franklin Street and Peter was crossing Franklin in the crosswalk. At trial, Peter's attorney offers the testimony of the following witnesses:

(A) Alan testifies that he was near the intersection of Franklin and Columbia when he heard an unidentified man say in an excited voice, "That car just ran the red light and hit Peter."

(B) Peter's attorney also offers the written and notarized statement from Alan. It states, "Donald ran a red light."

(C) Beth testifies that Donald ran a red light. Beth knows this because just a moment before she had looked up at the light facing Donald's direction and had seen that it was red. Beth admits that she was looking away at the time of the accident but is quite certain the light did not have time to change to green.

(D) Cathy testifies that she heard a man standing at the intersection yell at Donald: "Stop man, stop! The light's red, man!"

(E) Dianne heard two others standing near the intersection ask questions. She heard a man standing on her right ask, "Did you see that car run the light?" A woman on her left asked someone nearby her, "Could you see the color of the car that ran the light?"

(F) Ed testifies that he heard another woman whom he had seen standing at the intersection say after the accident, "That driver must be color blind."

(G) George, who was crossing Franklin in the same crosswalk as Peter from the opposite side of the street, testifies that he is blind and gets around with the aid of his seeing eye dog Rex. He testified that Rex stood up and started forward across Franklin Street just a couple seconds before he heard the impact. George testifies that Rex communicates that the light for traffic has changed to red and that it is O.K. to cross the street by standing up and starting forward as he did on this occasion.

(H) Helen testifies that she could not see the traffic light but that shortly before Peter was struck she saw drivers heading west on Franklin Street come to a stop at the intersection with Columbia.

(I) Peter claims that he suffered permanent loss of certain mental functions as a result of oxygen deprivation to his brain caused by cardiac arrest after the accident. He offers as evidence the testimony of Ellen, a bystander at the scene of the accident, that a medic pounded upon Peter's chest and injected some substance into Peter's chest in the vicinity of the heart. The medic made no record of his observations and was rendered mentally incompetent by an accident involving his ambulance immediately after he delivered Peter to the Emergency Room. Peter was conscious and breathing freely at the time of his admission to the Emergency Room and was treated there only for leg injuries. Peter offers other evidence that the procedures observed by the bystander would be the standard ones utilized in an attempt to treat cardiac arrest.

(J) Peter offers the testimony of the hospital cashier that Donald's wife came to the hospital on the day of Peter's discharge, asked what the charges for Peter's treatment were, and wrote out a check for that amount.

(K) Ilene testifies that immediately after the accident, Donald jumped into his car and sped away from the scene.

(L) Ilene also testifies that two hours after the accident she saw Donald sitting in a sidewalk cafe across town from the accident. She approached Donald and said to him, "How can you sit there and enjoy yourself when just hours ago you ran that stoplight and hurt that man?" She testifies that Donald made no response to her statement.

(M) Officer Jones testifies that he arrived at the intersection shortly after the accident and had a conversation with witnesses on the scene. Counsel for Peter asks, "Now without telling us what those individuals told you, what if any actions did you take based on their statements to you?" Jones responds, "I issued a ticket to Donald for running a red light."

(N) Alternatively, Officer Jones testifies that he was standing at the intersection and, without talking to anyone, issued a ticket to Donald for running the stop light. Peter's counsel also offers the citation for running a stop light in evidence.

13–2. In his suit against Donald for injuries occurring when Donald allegedly drove through a red light and hit Peter as he walked across Franklin Street, Peter joined Donald's father as a defendant. According to Peter's claim, Donald was driving his father's car, and Peter sued under a theory of negligent entrustment.

(A) One of the issues is the authority of Donald to use his father's car. Peter's attorney offers the testimony of William that, shortly before the accident, he heard Donald, Sr. say to Donald: "Take the car and pick up your mother. I have to do some shopping."

(B) Plaintiff also offers Wanda's testimony that after the accident, Donald, Sr. told her "I let Junior use the car to pick up my wife."

(C) Plaintiff offers the testimony of Walter that two days before the accident Walter's son stated that Donald was a reckless driver. Walter also testifies that the day before the accident, he told Donald's father about the report he had received concerning Donald's driving.

(D) Assume that the testimony in Part (C) has been received. Donald offers the testimony of James that Walter stated the day after the accident that he had not had a chance to tell Donald's father about Donald's poor driving.

13–3. Peter is suing Donald for injuries sustained when Donald's car hit him as he crossed the street (*see* Problem 13–1). Assume that liability has been established, and the only real issue is damages. Peter's leg was broken as a result of the accident.

(A) In support of his claim for damages, Peter offers a silent film of the impact of the injury on his daily activities. The "day in the life" film depicts his difficulties in dressing himself, moving around, etc. Donald objects as hearsay.

(B) Donald offers a film he made of Peter playing tennis to demonstrate that Peter's injuries have in fact not inhibited his activities. Donald made the film while hiding in the bushes near the tennis court. Peter objects on hearsay grounds.

13–4. Matt is prosecuted for drug smuggling. Found in his belongings at the time of his arrest were an airline flight stub indicating that he took a flight from Mexico City to Dallas on June 30 and an electronic bank deposit receipt showing that a withdrawal of $500 was made from an account number in Miami, Florida, on the next day. The account number was independently linked to Matt.

Assume the documents have been properly authenticated. Matt's lawyer argues they are hearsay and have not been shown admissible as business records. The prosecution argues that these are not hearsay because they are computer generated records.

13–5. In his personal injury action against Donald for running over him with a car, Peter also alleges negligence against defendant in that he was driving an automobile with defective brakes, that he knew them to be defective, and that the defective brakes were a cause of the accident.

(A) Donald testifies that, on the day *before* the accident, he took his automobile into a garage to have various matters checked including the brakes. He testifies that at the end of the day he called the service manager of the garage and the manager said: "Everything's OK. Brakes, lights, horn, everything." Suppose that the service manager had also written a signed note which he had delivered to defendant. The note said, "Your car is ready. The brakes are OK." Consider both Donald's testimony and the service manager's note (assuming that the note was properly authenticated).

(B) In the same action, suppose instead that Donald's car was repaired *after* the accident and the repair order called for replacement of the brake anchor, brake cylinder, brake push rod, brake shoes, and brake fluid. These parts of the car were not damaged in the accident. The repair bill also showed these items were repaired. Peter offers the order and bill in evidence after proper authentication.

13–6. Joan and Wanda were partners in a furniture store. Wanda had supplied the capital for the store and Joan ran it. Each owned a half-interest in the operation.

(A) One day, when Wanda was visiting the store, Joan said: "The television business of the store constitutes about one-half of the store's business. Why don't we simply consider that business mine and the rest of the store yours?" Wanda answered: "That's okay with me. From now on, I will pay expenses simply on the non-television business and just get profits from that." Several months later, having gone deeply in debt, Joan left town for parts unknown. Her creditors sought to satisfy her debts to them by seizing the property in the store. Wanda seeks to stop them from seizing anything other than objects connected with the store's television business. The creditors claim that half of everything in the store was Joan's. During the trial of this matter, Wanda's attorney desires to have Wanda testify to Joan's statement set forth above.

(B) In the same action, Wanda's attorney also offers the statement of Sam, who says that, just before leaving town, Joan told him that "the television business of the store is now all mine."

13–7. Electrical power workers Will and Pete, while inspecting the lines, located a damaged electrical transformer. Will went to a nearby house to call the company to have the power shut off before they began work. Just as Will exited the house he called to Pete that the dispatcher had given the "all clear" and that the power had been shut off. Pete and Will then climbed the pole and began work. The power was still on. Will was killed and Pete badly injured as a result of the electrical shock.

In a suit by Pete against the Electric Company is the statement of Will that the dispatcher had given the "all clear" hearsay? If Will had lived and could recite the statement of the dispatcher, would that statement be hearsay?

13–8. (A) In a criminal prosecution of Harvey for operating a house of prostitution, the prosecution offers the testimony of Young that he lived in the same neighborhood as Harvey and that Harvey's house had a reputation as a house of prostitution. Is Young's testimony hearsay?

(B) After being acquitted of criminal charges in his criminal prosecution, Harvey sues Laurel for slandering him in public by saying Harvey ran a house of prostitution. Laurel offers the testimony of Young. What result this time?

13–9. Thomas sued Angelo, who owns Angelo's Italian Restaurant. Thomas claims that he became seriously ill after eating spaghetti and meat sauce, the restaurant's specialty. Angelo's attorney offers to prove that no other guest eating at the restaurant on the night in question complained of illness. Is the testimony hearsay?

13–10. In a personal injury action, Dr. Williams is called to testify that she and four other doctors (who were not called to the stand) met and agreed that plaintiff's injury would permanently prevent him from doing strenuous physical work. Is Dr. Williams' testimony regarding her opinion or the statements made by the other doctors hearsay?

13–11. Polo Watches, a manufacturer of very expensive and ornate watches, brought suit against Knockoffs for trademark infringement and unfair competition for Knockoffs' manufacture of a line of watches that Polo alleges resembles in basic design its more expensive models. In support of its suit, Polo offers a consumer survey conducted by a reputable public opinion survey organization. The survey shows that a majority of consumers when shown a Knockoffs watch identify it as a Polo. Is the survey hearsay?

13–12. In an action in which a material issue is the mental competency of Smith, the attorney for the party seeking to establish incompetency offers Smith's statement allegedly made over the back fence to a neighbor: "Look Marshal, as your superior and as your emperor, I order you to begin preparations for the invasion of England. I am going to have Leon executed because he is treasonably plotting to thwart the invasion." Is it hearsay?

13–13. James, who worked as George's assistant for the last fifteen years of George's life, challenges a will of George that is presented for probate. James contends that the will presented for probate, which does not mention him at all, was superseded by one which contains a substantial bequest to him.

(A) At the trial, James seeks to introduce the testimony of a witness who heard George say just a few days before his death: "I intend to leave James a substantial part of my estate."

(B) Assume that the statement to which the witness would testify is: "James is responsible for my financial success. He deserves to share in the wealth he helped me create."

13–14. In a prosecution for distribution of an illegal drug, PCP, David admitted he sold drugs to undercover drug agents. His defense was that his drug transactions were part of his effort to aid the agents in locating drug dealers. In support of his defense, he called his mother to testify that shortly after he met the agents and some weeks before his arrest he received a telephone call from Bob, one of the agents. His mother inquired who had called. David responded that Bob was a drug agent that he (David) was assisting and that she should not worry. Are the statements of the mother hearsay?

13–15. Dianne is charged with the murder of her husband, Frank. The shooting took place in the living room of the couple's home. Frank was wounded but lived for several days.

(A) After the shooting, just as the ambulance arrived, the ambulance driver heard Frank say: "Dianne, help me out because there is a bullet in my body." The defense offers the ambulance driver's testimony to this effect.

(B) In the same action, the defense also offers the testimony of a hospital nurse who states that just before Frank went into surgery, she saw Dianne bend down to Frank, and he threw his arms around Diane and kissed her tenderly.

(C) In the same action, the prosecution offers the testimony of Lew who states that he had entered into a wager with Fast Eddie in which he had bet $10 that Dianne would shoot Frank within the next year. Lew would testify that shortly after Frank's death, Eddie paid him the ten dollars. Would the treatment of the payment of the bet differ if it was for ten thousand dollars?

13–16. Dennis and Donald are charged with the homicide of Vargas. The afternoon before the killing, Vargas told his friend William that he had recently had a fight with Dennis over some guns; that he, Dennis, and Donald had been involved in the robbery of a sporting goods store; that Dennis and Donald "were out to get him;" and that he was afraid of Dennis and Donald. Vargas then gave William a slip of paper with "Donald, Dennis, 684–2834" written on it. Vargas said that if anything happened to him in the next day William should go to the police, tell them what he had said, and give them the slip of paper. Vargas was shot and killed less than an hour later.

The government seeks to introduce: (1) the slip of paper; (2) Vargas' instruction to William to turn over the note if Vargas was killed; (3) the facts that Vargas gave the slip of paper to William before the killing and that after the killing William contacted the police and turned over the paper; and (4) Vargas' statement that he was afraid of Dennis and Donald.

13–17. Sam and David are under suspicion of drug smuggling. The police intercepted a package containing cocaine that had been addressed to a business owned and operated by Sam. The police replaced the cocaine with a look-alike white powder and hid a transmitter in the package. The package was picked up by Sam who drove away with it. Sam then picked up David and drove to Sam's home, where the two men were observed entering the garage. Shortly thereafter, the transmitter went dead. When the police entered the garage, they found the white powder strewn around the floor and the transmitter smashed.

A short time later, David was seen walking down the street that runs in front of Sam's home. When questioned by the police he stated that he did not know who lived in Sam's home, that he had never been in that residence, and that instead he had just returned from making a phone call at a nearby store. Since the police had been observing Sam's home from that nearby store, the prosecution could establish that his statements were false.

The prosecution seeks to introduce David's statements in his joint trial with Sam on charges of conspiracy to traffic cocaine. Are the statements hearsay?

13–18. Tom was charged along with three other men with bank robbery and conspiracy to commit bank robbery. He was arrested in a car with Sam by police officers who stopped his car and the car that was traveling just in front of him. The car in front contained proceeds from the bank robbery. No physical evidence linking Tom to those men or to the robbery were found in his car. Tom's case was tried separately from the others. The other three men asserted their Fifth Amendment privilege against self-incrimination and were not witnesses for Tom or the government.

Sam was a passenger in Tom's car. When Tom's car was stopped, a police officer ordered Tom and Sam to exit the vehicle. Sam remarked to the officer as he got out, "How did you catch us so quickly?"

Tom objects to the admission of Sam's statement as hearsay.

13–19. Matt is on trial for the murder of Louis. The state charges that Matt and Jerry, who will be tried separately, slashed and beat Louis to death. Various items of circumstantial evidence connect both Matt and Jerry to the killing, including cuts and bruises consistent with being in a serious fight. In addition, the prosecutor has evidence of a statement made by Matt to the police and of a statement of Jerry to the police at a different time and place. Assume the absence of constitutional objection to either statement. In each of these statements Matt and Jerry stated that they were at Flick's Tavern at the time they were accused of killing Louis and that they had a terrible fight on that occasion. They explained the injuries as caused by this fight. The prosecutor also has at hand excellent witnesses who were in Flick's all evening on the date in question and will testify that neither Matt nor Jerry was in the tavern at anytime during that evening. The prosecutor seeks to introduce both Matt and Jerry's statements in evidence.

13–20. Dwayne is charged with the kidnapping and murder of his wife, Victoria. The prosecution offers the testimony of a friend of the wife who testified that Victoria told her an hour before she was seen entering her husband's car that she had a telephone conversation with Dwayne that morning in which she (Victoria) told him that she intended to get a divorce and he responded that he would kill her if she left him. Is the statement hearsay and is it admissible?

13–21. Oliver is charged with the murder of Moore. The prosecution alleges that Oliver shot Moore and then transported his body to Queen Avenue where he reported the crime. Oliver upon reporting the shooting stated that an unknown assailant had killed Moore and wounded Oliver and then fled the scene. Queen Avenue is a street in a business section with small stores and much pedestrian traffic. After Oliver has testified to his version of the shooting, the prosecution asks Detective Jones, who was in charge of the investigation, whether he had sought to find anyone in the vicinity who heard the alleged shots. Jones answered that he had made the attempt. He is then asked whether he had found anyone who had heard the shots allegedly fired by Oliver. Is the answer hearsay?

13–22. John is on trial for kidnapping a child and holding her in his apartment for ransom. After the ransom was paid, the child was released unharmed. The prosecution wants to introduce the testimony of a detective about statements the child made.

(A) The child stated—immediately after her release and before John was identified as a suspect—that she had been held in a room with a multicolored window with two broken panes. Another witness would testify that after John was arrested passing the ransom money, his apartment was searched and it contained an attic room with a multicolored window that had two broken panes. Is the child's statement to the detective hearsay?

(B) What is the hearsay answer if the story related by the child to the detective was that the room described is one she is familiar with from prior experience—that of her uncle's house where she has occasionally visited? She saw the window once when the blindfold slipped.

13–23. Two homicide cases are tried in a city. In both, the perpetrator was described as fleeing the scene wearing a coat with a white fur collar. In the first, the prosecution offers against the defendant testimony of an officer that when he went to the man's house and asked the defendant's wife if he had a coat with a white fur collar, she walked into another room and returned with such a coat. In the other, when the officer asked a similar question, the defendant's wife fainted. Is the testimony of either officer regarding the conduct of the defendants' wives hearsay?

13–24. Susan is being prosecuted for subornation of perjury in connection with allegedly securing a false alibi for her client. The prosecution, after authenticating the transcript through the court reporter, offers two segments of the trial testimony. The first is the part where the motel owner, Sam, testifies that Susan's client had checked into the hotel in the city 300 miles from the crime scene during the time of the bank robbery. The second is later testimony from the same trial where Sam gets back on the stand and admits that his records were false and states that they were produced at Susan's request and in response to payment of $5,000. The defense objects to both segments of testimony as hearsay.

13–25. Bill is being prosecuted for an armed robbery committed against two residents of the city as they left a downtown restaurant. The robbery was witnessed by a passerby, who called 9–1–1 and gave a description of the robber but did not leave his name or otherwise make contact with the police. On two occasions during the criminal proceedings, the prosecution offers the description—male, six feet, wearing a blue and yellow T-shirt—through an officer who heard it broadcast over the police radio while he was on patrol. First, it was offered at a pretrial hearing to determine the lawfulness of the police stopping and frisking Bill, in the course of which they found a handgun roughly matching one that the victims say was used in the robbery. Second, it was offered at trial to show "the effect on the hearer," here the officer, and to explain to the jury why he stopped and patted down Bill, who was walking along the street, apparently window shopping, several blocks from the robbery scene.

13–26. A passenger cruise line, FunCruises, had been cited for a number of safety violations that were widely publicized in the local press after a fatal accident on one of its cruises. FunCruises interrupted operations for a period of time under pressure from regulators and amid fanfare that it was correcting all problems. It resumed operations, and tragically its first cruise met with a disaster when a violent storm arose and sank the vessel. The cause of the sinking is disputed as to whether it was an unavoidable "act of God," or whether it involved negligent maintenance of seals where water ultimately entered which in light of FunCruises' prior safety history should result in punitive damages.

To rebut the claim of knowing negligence, FunCruises wants to introduce evidence that two passengers on that ill-fated cruise were the President of FunCruises and his wife.

13–27. Elizabeth is suing the driver of a car that ran a stop light and collided with his vehicle, causing injuries to Elizabeth's back. The issue is the extent and continuing nature of those injuries. Elizabeth's attorney calls Elizabeth's husband who proposes to testify that when Elizabeth got out of bed that morning, two years after the crash, she gasped and clutched her side and then moaned as she straightened up. He also would testify that on an earlier occasion, she said with a grimace on her face, "You know that feels like daggers are being stabbed into my back when I straighten up."

13–28. Ralph is suing the city bus company in a wrongful death action for the death of his wife, which was caused by the negligent driving of the bus driver. The issue is how much damages he is entitled to as the result of the economic loss to him from the death of his wife. The bus company, which does not dispute liability, seeks to introduce three pieces of evidence. The first is a will executed by Ralph's wife several months before her death in which she willed to her husband $1, stating that she had been faithful, dutiful, and loving to him to which he responded with cruelty and indifference and failure of support. The second is that testimony of a friend of both Ralph and the deceased that at a recent public dinner to honor a victorious local sports team a month before the fatal injury, Ralph's wife stood and in a mock toast said to the ten people at her table, "You know, Ralph, to call you a pig would be to slander a perfectly decent animal." The third is a statement Ralph's wife made to the same friend a week before the fatal injury that she detested her husband and planned to leave him.

13–29. Dave is charged with trafficking cocaine. When the police raided Dave's home in the search of cocaine, which they believe he was selling from his home, they found only a small amount of drugs. The amount itself would not indicate sale. However, the prosecution seeks to introduce evidence that while the police were in Dave's home they answered three phone calls. The phone calls were from unidentified individuals. One asked, "Has the shipment of 'snow' arrived yet?" One stated, "I'll be by in an hour to make a score, if you'll be there." The third directed, "Give my stuff to Jimmy, when he stops by." Is this testimony hearsay? Would it matter if only one call was received and it stated, "Dave, I assume you are still selling cocaine, and wanted to make sure before I came over. Are you still in the business?"

13–30. (A) One of your fellow law students tells you he has attended several civil trials, and on more than one occasion when a witness was asked to relate a remark someone else made out of court, the opposing attorney objected on the ground "the question calls for a self-serving statement to be repeated by this witness," or he moved to strike some repetition of an out-of-court statement on the ground that it was "self-serving." Each time the judge sustained the objection or granted the motion, so the student says there is a rule that a witness cannot repeat out-of-court self-serving statements. He tells you he asked an attorney whether there was such a rule, and the attorney said, "Yes."

(B) The above student also tells you that, in several criminal trials he has seen, the witness was asked to relate what someone other than the defendant said out of court. The prosecutor objected that "the statement was not made in the presence of the defendant." The student then says, "I saw this happen enough so that there must be a rule in a criminal case that a witness cannot relate an out-of-court statement of someone else if the defendant was not present when the statement was made. The same attorney told me this was true, too."

How would you respond to your fellow student?

SECTION B. OTHER STATEMENTS THAT ARE NOT HEARSAY

1. PRIOR STATEMENTS OF A WITNESS

Using the concepts applicable to prior statements of a witness that are not considered hearsay under Federal Rule 801(d)(1), determine whether the following statements are hearsay. *See* McCormick, 6th ed., § 251.

In several problems under Section A the fact pattern involves Peter crossing the street and being struck by a car which may have been driven by Donald (*see* Problem 13–1). Donald is alleged to have sped away from the scene shortly after the accident. In addition to the civil suit, which will be examined in some of the problems in this section, Donald is being prosecuted criminally for the offense of hit and run.

13–31. Alice was at the intersection, and according to information provided by the police to the prosecution, she has made a prior identification of Donald as the driver who struck Peter and fled the scene.

Alice is called to the stand and asked whether she witnessed the accident and responds that she did. She is then asked if she sees in the courtroom the person who hit Peter and fled the scene of the accident and states that she does not recall who that person was. Alice is then asked if she has ever made an identification of the person who was driving the car. She responds that she does not remember if she ever made such an identification. Alice is asked if she recalls attending a lineup at the police station and responds that she does not recall such an event.

The prosecutor calls Officer Williams and seeks to elicit from him testimony that Alice identified Donald. Does it matter whether the lineup was video and audio taped so that Officer Williams' testimony is corroborated? Does it matter whether Alice is a doddering old woman whose present memory is so poor that it appears likely that she in fact does not remember whether she made a prior identification or whether it is reasonably certain that the witness is instead refusing to implicate Donald?

13–32. Continuing the facts of Problem 13–31, in addition to identifying Donald, Alice previously told investigators that after the car ran the light and hit a pedestrian, the driver stopped and got out of the car, looking in the direction of the injured pedestrian. The driver then jumped back in the car and sped away. The testimony would help to establish that the driver was aware that his car had injured someone, which is an element of a criminal hit and run prosecution. Alice is asked about the events she witnessed in addition to her prior identification. She responds that she does not remember anything about the accident.

(A) The prosecutor seeks to introduce a statement made by Alice to an investigating officer shortly after the accident in which she relates the above information about seeing the driver get out of his car. Does it matter if Alice wrote this information out in her own handwriting and then swore that it was true before a notary public? What result if her statement was videotaped?

(B) Assume that Alice appeared before a grand jury investigating the hit and run incident and testified about observing the driver get out of the car as described above. Under those circumstances, may the prosecutor impeach Alice with her grand jury testimony about the events she stated after proper authentication? Is the judge required to determine whether the witness really does not remember or is falsely denying a lack of memory? Is a statement that the witness "doesn't recall" a prior statement always, never, or sometimes sufficient to establish that the prior statement is inconsistent with the present testimony?

13–33.   The prosecutor calls Bill who operates an auto repair shop. He testifies that on the day of the accident (*see* Problem 13–1) Donald came to his shop and asked Bill to repair a dent in the right front fender. The prosecutor asks if Donald had any special instructions concerning the bill and how it would be paid. Bill responded that Donald asked that no bill be prepared and that he wanted to pay in cash.

On cross-examination, counsel for Donald asks Bill: "Isn't it true that you have a deal with the prosecution that you will not be prosecuted for evasion of state taxes in connection with unreported repair service income if you testify against Donald in this case?" Bill responds: "Yes, that's true."

(A) On redirect, the prosecution attempts to ask Bill about three prior statements. First, the prosecution asks Bill about a statement taken under oath before a grand jury investigating allegations that Bill grossly under-reported his income by not reporting cash transactions. The testimony before the grand jury occurred two months after the accident and after he entered an agreement with the prosecutor that he would not to be prosecuted for under-reporting his income if he testified truthfully about the transaction with Donald. In the grand jury testimony, Bill provided testimony similar to his trial testimony concerning his conversation with Donald. Second, when investigators contacted him and told him that he was under suspicion for under-reporting his income and would likely be arrested but without any discussion of leniency, he made the similar statement. The prosecutor seeks to have this statement recounted. Third, the prosecution asks about statements Bill made to his wife the day of the accident recounting his conversation with Donald. Would any or all of these three prior statements be admissible for its truth under Federal Rule 801(d)(1)?

(B) Also on redirect, the prosecution offers a statement that Bill made later than all of the above statements. The defense had introduced a prior inconsistent statement of Bill that he had been harassed by the prosecution and threatened with the loss of his business and that was the only reason he was testifying. The prosecution wants to introduce Bill's assertion—made in that same statement—that he is still angry at Donald for getting him involved by insisting on giving him the cash for the repair work. The prosecution argues that the testimony is admissible to rehabilitate Bill's impeached testimony. The defense argues the timing of the statement makes it inadmissible under Federal Rule 801(d)(1)(B) no matter its purpose. How should the court rule?

13–34. Continuing the facts of Problem 13–33, Donald takes the stand in the defense case and denies that the conversation described by Bill took place. He testifies that it was Bill who told Donald that he would knock $20 off the cost of the repair if Donald paid in cash. Bill advised Donald that, on a small job like the one involved here, it would be cheaper not to report the accident to the insurance company and simply pay in cash than to file a claim and incur insurance deductibles and an increased insurance premium. On the basis of Bill's advice, Donald testifies that he agreed not to receive a receipt or pay by check. On cross-examination, the prosecution asks: "You invented your version of the conversation with Bill to make payment in cash look innocent, didn't you?" Donald responded: "That's not true at all."

On redirect, Donald is asked by his attorney: "The evening you took your car to the repair shop did you have a conversation with your wife about what Bill said to you?" The prosecution objects on the grounds that the question calls for an inadmissible prior consistent statement. If permitted to answer, Donald would testify that he told his wife about Bill's suggestion to be paid in cash on the evening that Donald asked him to do the repairs. Are Donald's answers hearsay?

13–35. Clyde is being prosecuted for selling weapons in violation of federal law. The prosecution calls Betty, whom it believes aided Clyde in the gun merchandising operation. Betty gave a statement to an F.B.I. agent shortly after Clyde's arrest. In the signed statement, which was given under penalty of perjury, she set out the whole transaction in which the two of them purchased six semi-automatic assault rifles at a Dallas gun show and resold them shortly thereafter for cash to local gang members. When called at trial, which occurred six months later, the prosecutor asked Betty about the events at the Dallas gun show and the subsequent sale. Betty responded that because of her recent extensive drug use she did not remember being at the gun show or selling any weapons and did not even recognize Clyde.

The prosecution seeks to introduce the statement to the F.B.I. agent as substantive evidence under Rule 801(d)(1)(A). The defense objects that since Betty cannot remember anything, her statement is not inconsistent with his trial testimony. Instead, the defense argues, the statement is not inconsistent or harmful to the prosecution but merely disappointing to the government's hopes. The defense also argues that the statement is not admissible because it was not given at the grand jury or other proceeding. How should the court rule?

13–36. Trial in the *civil suit* against Donald (*see* Problem 13–1) commences approximately 36 months after the accident. For the purpose of this and the following question, it is important to know Donald's physical description at the time of the accident. He is a white male, 28 years old, with blond curly hair, and wears glasses.

At trial, Ken identifies Donald as the driver of the car that struck Peter. On cross-examination, Donald's attorney asks Ken whether two months before trial he described the driver to a defense investigator as being in his 40s and having straight brown hair. Ken acknowledges that he made the statement to the investigator, explaining that he had simply given incorrect information to the investigator.

On redirect, Peter's counsel attempts to ask Ken about a statement that he gave to plaintiff's investigator one month after the accident in which he described the driver as in his early thirties and blond. Counsel for Donald objects that the statement is an inadmissible prior consistent statement under Rule 801(d)(1)(B). What ruling should the court make?

13–37. (A) In the civil suit against Donald (*see* Problem 13–1), Peter calls Joan. Joan was interviewed on the scene by a police officer. She gave a description of the car and its driver to the officer. The following colloquy occurs:

Q. Did you give a description of the car and its driver to the police shortly after the accident?

A. Yes.

Q. Do you recall now what those descriptions were?

A. Yes.

Q. Could you please tell the jury what you told the officer with regard to the appearance of the man and the car at that time?

Donald's counsel objects on hearsay grounds.

If permitted to answer, Joan would testify that she described the driver as a white male, about 30, with blond curly hair and glasses. She would testify that she described the car as a light colored foreign-made station wagon. Other evidence shows that at the time of the accident Donald owned a green Camry sedan.

Is the objection valid?

(B) In connection with the criminal case, Joan had been called to the police station for a lineup. While at the police station, she picked Donald from the lineup. She also told the person in charge of the lineup that she saw the car that hit Peter parked in the visitor's section of the police station parking lot. The car she pointed out to the police was the Camry sedan that belonged to Donald.

Peter's attorney seeks to elicit the testimony of the identification of the car and Peter from Joan. Is it hearsay?

13–38. In a criminal prosecution of Edith and Ralph, two members of an alleged conspiracy to distribute drugs, the prosecutor calls to the stand a third member of the alleged conspiracy, Dan. Earlier, Dan had testified before the grand jury that he, Edith, and Ralph has been involved in a scheme to transport drugs to Dallas and to distribute them to a series of street vendors. Even though Dan had been granted immunity under the Fifth Amendment against compulsory self-incrimination regarding any use of his testimony against him in future cases, Dan asserted his "privilege against self-incrimination" and refused to answer any questions regarding the conspiracy at the trial of Edith and Ralph.

The prosecutor asked that the judge rule Dan's grand jury testimony as inconsistent with his trial testimony and allow it to be admitted since he had taken the stand and blatantly refused to answer questions. The prosecutor argued that such a blatant and illegal refusal to testify provided a sound basis for the jury's evaluation of Dan's credibility, that Dan was legally available for cross-examination, and that the circumstances permitted admission of Dan's grand jury testimony as substantive evidence inconsistent with Dan's illegal refusal to answer questions.

Are Dan's refusal to answer questions and his earlier grand jury testimony inconsistent? Is Dan available under the federal rules? Subject to cross-examination?

13–39. Dennis was prosecuted for the armed robbery of a store. The prosecuting attorney knows that identification of Dennis will be a highly controversial matter at the trial. However, she knows that Vicky, who was in the store at the time of the robbery, can positively identify Dennis as the robber. After the robbery, Vicky had a long session with an artist whom the police hired for this occasion. The artist made a final drawing of the face of the robber based upon Vicky's description. The drawing bears a striking resemblance to Dennis. The prosecutor would like to introduce the drawing while Vicky is on the witness stand and have her testify that it was the drawing made by the artist from her description. For reasons not relevant here, the prosecutor does not wish to call the artist. In questioning Vicky, the prosecutor wants to bring out that Vicky said to a police officer, after the sketch was completed, that the sketch looked like the robber. Should the prosecutor anticipate that she can introduce the sketch and the testimony of Vicky with regard to it?

2. ADMISSIONS OF THE PARTY OPPONENT

In answering these problems, use Federal Rules of Evidence 801(d)(2).

13–40. (A) Peter has sued Donald in connection with injuries he alleges that he suffered when Donald's car ran a red light and struck Peter while Peter was walking in a crosswalk at the intersection of Franklin and Columbia Streets. As in many jurisdictions, the statute of limitations for suit against the state is much shorter than the one for suits against private individuals. The statute of limitations in Peter's jurisdiction requires that all suits against the state be filed within one year of the time that the injuries are known to have occurred. Exactly one year after the accident, Peter's attorney filed suit against the State Highway Commission alleging that the traffic light at the intersection of Franklin and Columbia Streets was not working properly at the time of the accident, thereby causing his injuries. Two years after the accident, he files suit against Donald. Before that second suit is filed he voluntarily dismisses the claim against the state. Can Donald introduce the complaint against Peter? Does it matter that the complaint was not verified; that Peter and his attorney both assert that Peter never read it; that Peter's attorney explains that he filed the suit before his investigation had been completed and did so only as a holding action to avoid the running of the statute of limitations? Assume that the Federal Rules of Civil Procedure had been copied in the jurisdiction and were governing.

(B) In addition to pain and suffering and medical expenses resulting from the trauma of the accident, Peter claims to have suffered permanent partial loss of the functioning of his right leg as a result of damage to the spinal column in the lower back caused by the impact of the car. Peter is a college student at State University, located in the town where the accident occurred. Donald denies the allegations concerning the back injury and contends that, if there were a back injury existent after the collision, it existed prior to the accident. At the trial Donald's attorney introduced evidence that Peter had suffered previous back injuries. He also wishes to introduce a form concerning Peter's health history and examination, a form that State University required as part of every admission application. The pertinent part of the form, signed by a physician, reads as follows:

	Normal	Abnormal	Details of Abnormal Findings
Skin	X		
Eyes	X		
Neck, thyroid	X		
Lymph nodes	X		
Chest	X		
Heart	X		
Lungs	X		
Abdomen	X		
Back		X	Orthopedic abnormality
Extremities	X		
Neurological (if indicated)	X		

Should Peter's attorney anticipate that this evidence will be admissible over objection?

McCormick, 6th Ed., §§ 257, 262.

13–41. Phyllis sued Dennis for personal injuries sustained by reason of a dog bite. The dog, a prize-winning show-dog allegedly belonging to

Dennis, was in the charge of a trainer, Arthur, at the time the dog allegedly bit Phyllis.

(A) One of Dennis' defenses is that he was not the owner of the dog at the time of the incident. On the issue of ownership, Phyllis' attorney wishes to introduce the testimony of Ward that about a week prior to the dog bite he was present when Dennis and Arthur had an argument concerning the dog. Ward can testify that in the argument, Arthur claimed that Dennis had sold the championship dog to him for the modest sum of $200 and that Dennis stated: "You're nuts! I never sold that dog to you. He's mine and that's all there is to it." Would Ward's testimony in this regard be admissible?

(B) Another of Dennis's defenses is that Phyllis was not bitten by the dog owned either by Dennis or Arthur but by an entirely different dog of the same breed. Dennis was not present when the dog allegedly bit Phyllis.

(i) Can Phyllis testify that the day after the dog bite she had a conversation with Dennis about the matter in which Dennis stated:

"I know the dog bit you," or

"Well, I wasn't there, but Arthur told me the dog bit you," or

"Well it was Arthur's fault. He knew the dog was vicious"?

(ii) Can Phyllis testify that the day after the dog bite Arthur told her:

"Dennis hired me to take good care of that dog and here it bit you"?

Does your answer depend upon the existence of any other evidence?

McCormick, 6th Ed., §§ 254–265.

13–42. At his separate trial on drug smuggling charges, the prosecution seeks to introduce against Sam a statement by Jimmy made in Sam's presence after their arrest. Along with several other men, Sam and Jimmy had been seen unloading boxes containing marijuana from a small boat along the Mississippi River near New Orleans. A key issue in the case is whether Sam knew that the boxes contained marijuana or was ignorant of their contents.

(A) After arrest and in the presence of Sam, the police, and the other men arrested, Jimmy said, "Why so much excitement? If we are caught, we are caught." Sam and the others made no response. Is the statement admissible against Sam?

(B) The prosecution also wants to introduce evidence that Sam was one of the men who had loaded the same boat the day before on a smaller tributary near where the marijuana was grown and packed. Marijuana was rather obvious in that area. The prosecution wants to offer evidence that before a court-ordered lineup in which witnesses from that other location were to view Sam, he shaved his beard and mustache and dyed his hair a different color. None of the witnesses at that lineup identified Sam.

McCormick, 6th Ed., §§ 261–265.

13–43. Lauren sued the Town of Mayberry Schools and the State of North Carolina Department of Education for failure to honor a promotion promised to her. She seeks to introduce a statement by Ralph, superintendent of the Mayberry Schools, that he did not intend to honor the agreement made by the principal to promote Lauren. Lauren attempted to testify to this statement that she said she was told about by Sandra, who is a Commissioner of the North Carolina Department of Education, who told her that Ralph made this statement to her when she visited the Mayberry School Board meeting. Ralph denies making the statement and Sandra denies both hearing the statement and communicating it to Lauren.

Lauren moves its introduction as an admission by her party opponents.

McCormick, 6th Ed., §§ 259, 324.1.

13–44. Stan, who was a procurement agent for the United States Defense Department, is charged with perjury in connection with his statements to the grand jury regarding the charges of conspiracy to defraud the government of honest services by a corrupt lobbyist, Adam, with whom Stan had dealings. Assume the coconspirator exclusion has been ruled unavailable in the trial of the perjury charge (although it would be available if Stan were being prosecuted for conspiracy). The government seeks to introduce against him a series of e-mails written by Adam and his associates that Stan forwarded to his subordinates as adoptive admissions.

In Exhibit A, Stan forwards the e-mail with the question: "What do you think of this request?" In Exhibit B, Stan forwards another e-mail with the statement: "Run with this." In Exhibit C, Stan states: "FYI." In Exhibit D, Stan asks: "Is this correct?" In Exhibit E, Stan states, "This is too easy." In Exhibit F, Stan writes: "He's right." Which of these should qualify as adoptive admissions?

McCormick, 6th Ed., § 261.

13–45. Over objections, could Trooper Borne testify to any of the statements of Arnold Well or Richard Roll in Appendix B, *State v. Well,* Document 3?

McCormick, 6th Ed., §§ 254–265.

13–46. Your law firm represents a small restaurant. The owner of the restaurant, Patricia, has complained that the only two local milk processors, Dairyland and Wholesome, have been fixing the prices of milk products and thus substantially increasing her cost of doing business. A decision is made to institute a civil action under the state antitrust laws, charging price-fixing. Are the following statements and/or documents admissible?

(A) Dwight, the president of Dairyland, was the speaker at a local Rotary Club meeting before this law suit was filed. Patricia was at the speaker's table with Dwight and several other people. In the course of after-dinner conversation in which four or five persons at the table were participating and just before the speaker began, Patricia said to Dwight: "You and Wholesome make sure that you both make your profit, don't you?" Dwight looked at Patricia for a moment and then stated: "The big crowd for the football game should help your business, shouldn't it, Patricia?" Dwight was then called to give his speech and no further conversation between the two occurred on that day.

(B) Up until six weeks ago, Winslow was employed as secretary to the Board of Directors of Dairyland. When it became clear that the company was under investigation by the state for price fixing, Winslow was ordered by the board to conduct an investigation of the charges. Winslow reported to the board and kept a copy of the document. After being fired by Dairyland, Winslow gave a photocopy of the report to Patricia. The document consists of reports of conversations with management personnel and statements by them to the effect that meetings to discuss prices were held between Dairyland and Wholesome.

McCormick, 6th Ed., §§ 259, 262.

13–47. Paula allegedly slipped and fell on a terrazzo floor in the lobby of the Sunrise bowling alley and suffered injuries. In a suit against Sunrise, Paula testified at the trial that after she fell she saw there were slippery and wet spots where she fell and that she found sticky, dirty spots on her clothing after she fell, which she identified as "Coke" spots from their nature. Her theory was that the wet spots came from Coke spilled on account of a fight among several teenagers that had happened a few minutes earlier.

(A) Paula testified that after she fell the man who rented bowling shoes and sold the "bowling cards" came, picked her up, and put her in a spectator's chair. During a conversation with him she noticed a janitor was mopping up the floor nearby in the lobby. At this point, could Paula's attorney over objection elicit from her that the above-mentioned employee said to the janitor, "Where have you been? You should have come when I called you, before that woman fell." There was no evidence that the above-mentioned employee of Sunrise had any authority to direct the work of janitors in the building. (Sunrise's evidence indicated there were no wet spots on the floor when Paula fell.)

(B) Suppose that in the above situation the manager of the bowling alley came and talked to Paula and that Paula would testify that the manager made the above-mentioned remark to the janitor who was mopping up the floor. Would your answer be the same?

(C) Suppose Paula would testify, if permitted, that the manager in the above situation said nothing to the janitor but said to her, "Sorry about that wet floor." Is this testimony admissible over objection?

(D) Suppose that Paula made the employee, who made the remark as related in the first paragraph, a defendant along with Sunrise on the theory that the employee was present when she fell and, having knowledge of the wet spot, failed to warn Paula of it. Could Paula testify to the remarks of the employee, as related in the first paragraph above, under these circumstances?

McCormick, 6th Ed., § 259.

13–48. A truck owned by London Manufacturing and driven by its employee, John, collided with a car driven by Esther. Esther was seriously injured in the accident. On the evening after the accident, John visited Esther in the hospital. At that time, he said to her: "It was my fault. I should not have gotten out of my lane and on your side of the road. I was in a hurry. My boss told me to take this thing and get it delivered across town right away."

In a subsequent suit against London Manufacturing for personal injuries and property damage as the result of this collision, Esther alleged that John was in the scope and course of his employment by London and that he negligently drove the truck into her causing her injuries. London denied all of the allegations of the complaint, and alleged that Esther was contributorily negligent. London will also contend that John was not an authorized driver of the truck but that he was a stock clerk who took the truck without permission and was on a frolic of his own.

Is John's testimony admissible against London? On what will your answer depend?

McCormick, 6th Ed., § 259.

13–49. Baker and Crane were indicted under a federal indictment for a conspiracy to engage in the interstate transportation of stolen automobiles, knowing the same to have been stolen. Able was named as a coconspirator but was not indicted (for reasons not pertinent to this problem). The prosecutor has much admissible evidence of the conspiracy and acts committed under it. According to the prosecutor's evidence, the conspiracy involved the transportation of stolen cars from Arizona to California, where they were sold immediately. The resulting funds were divided between Able, Baker, and Crane within a day of the sales. Also, the prosecutor can prove that the last car transported under the conspiracy charged was transported from Arizona to California by Able on April 21.

(A) A prosecution witness, Mark, will testify that on April 26 he had a conversation with Able in California, apparently about the car mentioned above. In this conversation Able said, "I want this car burned. I think that they know about me and Baker and Crane driving these stolen cars in from Arizona." Mark will state he agreed to burn the car and did burn it.

(B) The prosecutor also has another witness, Peter, who will testify that during the time of the alleged conspiracy he had stolen a few cars and delivered them to Able. He then was caught and jailed in Arizona. Able came to visit while Peter was in jail and said: "Look, I'll bail you out. Baker, Crane, and I have these hot cars we are taking to California." Peter refused the offer of bail.

(C) A third witness, Randy, will testify that on about April 15, he was drinking in a bar with Baker. Baker told him that he, Able, and Crane were getting rich doing the easiest car smuggling arrangement you could imagine. If it kept going, they would be able to retire rich and happy men.

Are the statements of Mark, Peter, and Randy admissible against Baker and Crane?

McCormick, 6th Ed., § 259.

13–50. A Company and B Company made an agreement under which they ordered the manufacture and delivery of widgets made by C Company and agreed jointly to make an advance payment of 25 percent of the agreed price and to make the remaining payment of the price upon final delivery to B, such delivery to be considered delivery to both A and B. At the same time Robert entered into a guaranty agreement by which he became surety for the payment of the remaining payment under the contract. Ultimately A and B failed to make full payment because of a dispute as to whether all the widgets had been delivered. C commenced suit against B and Robert on the theory that all the widgets had been delivered and that the full purchase price was owed. Defendants denied that the widgets had been delivered. (A was not included as a defendant for reasons not pertinent here.)

An officer of C would testify that during the dispute about the contract the officer had a conference with the president of A and that during that conference the president of A had said, "True enough, you have delivered all the widgets under the contract, but that doesn't end the matter."

Should the attorney for C anticipate that on the above facts she can elicit the above testimony over the objection by both defendants?

McCormick, 6th Ed., § 260.

SECTION C.   CONFRONTATION

In all the problems in this section, McCormick, 6th Ed., § 252 and the 2010 Supplement may prove useful.

13–51. In a criminal prosecution of Donald for hit and run (*see* Problem 13–1), the state seeks to introduce through Stan, a bystander, the statement of Charles upon seeing the car that had just struck a pedestrian drive away: "There goes Donald." Charles is available but is not called by the state. Stan testifies that Charles is well acquainted with Donald. You may assume that the statement is admissible under Rule 803(1) or 803(2). May the state introduce the statement of Charles through Stan?

13–52. On a car trip to the beach, Sam noticed that Robert, his uncle, seemed emotionally down. He asked Robert what was wrong.

Robert was hesitant at first but confided that he had gotten into some trouble. He and a friend of his, Derrick, had committed a burglary together and while inside the house, the owner returned and discovered them. They panicked and Derrick strangled the man. Robert said he thought no one would find out they were involved, but was still worried.

Some months later, Derrick was arrested and later the police arrested Robert. Sam was interviewed by the police and told them about the statement Robert made to him, thinking it made Derrick the chief culprit.

The trial court admitted the statement as against interest despite its shifting of blame. Does its admission violate the Confrontation Clause under *Crawford v. Washington*, 541 U.S. 36 (2004)? In addition, defense counsel argues that it violates the command of *Lilly v. Virginia*, 527 U.S. 116 (1999), in that it shifts blame to the other defendant which would ordinarily be simply a hearsay rule violation but *Lilly* made it a constitutional issue.

13–53. Examine the fact patterns in Problems 33–18, 14–3 and 14–4 under the Confrontation Clause. Are the statements testimonial?

13–54. Jane was the victim of apparent domestic violence. She called a friend, Wanda, and told her that her husband Dave was angry and yelling at her, and she asked Wanda to drive over and pick her up. About fifteen minutes later, Jane called Wanda back to say that she had been hurt and would be waiting outside her home. In another fifteen minutes, Wanda picked up Jane, who was indeed injured. During the ride to Wanda's home, Jane recounted that Dave had punched and kicked her, threw her against a wall, and pulled her hair. Wanda convinced Jane to get medical attention and drove her to the hospital where she spoke to the police. Jane did not testify at trial and instead Wanda testified to the statements made by her, which the trial court admitted as excited utterances. No statements made to the police were admitted.

Does Wanda's testimony violate the Confrontation Clause?

13–55. Shortly before her death, Vicky called a friend, Ken, and left a voice mail saying that she thought her husband, Dwight, was planning to kill her and asking Ken to call her back and set up a meeting. At the meeting she told Ken that she had seen disturbing writings on her husband's day planner and that he was examining troubling material on the internet. Vicky informed Ken that she had photographed part of his day planner and gave the pictures, along with a letter, to him. She told him that if she were found dead, he should know that she did not commit suicide and Dwight should be the prime suspect. In the event of her death, she wanted him to deliver the material to the authorities. The letter was addressed to the local police department, specifying two officers there. Its contents detailed Vicky's observations of the deterioration of their relationship and her various observations regarding threatening or suspicious activities by Dwight.

Within a few days after this conversation, Vicky was found dead in her home. Autopsy findings revealed that she had been poisoned. Dwight was charged with her murder based primarily upon the voice mail and conversation with Ken and the contents of the envelope. The prosecution introduced at trial the voice mail, conversation, and letter.

The defense challenged the admission based on the Confrontation Clause. The prosecution argued that the statements were not testimonial because they were made to a private individual. In addition it argues that the Confrontation Clause argument was forfeited because of the defendant's wrongdoing. Finally, the prosecution argued that the statement was admissible as a dying declaration because of Vicky's obvious and articulated belief in her imminent death.

13–56. (A) In the prosecution of Donald for hit and run (*see* Problem 13–1), counsel for the state attempts to introduce a record from Al's Wrecker and Repair Service. Assume that the prosecution satisfies the requirements of Rule 803(6), the "business record" exception. As permitted by that rule, it establishes admissibility by calling the custodian of the records and does not call the person who completed the repairs and filled out the form. Assume further that the prosecution offers the record solely to show that the fender of Donald's car was dented one day after the accident and that it was repaired at Donald's request as evidenced by his signature on the repair form authorizing the repairs. Does it matter whether Al's Wrecker and Repair Service is a large or small operation where employees are more or less likely to remember particular repairs and where it is more or less feasible to identify who would have been responsible for the repairs?

(B) When Al's Wrecker and Repair Service received the car, one of its service workers noted on the repair form that, before the car was repaired, he removed some dried red material from the surface of the fender. Assume that such a statement is admissible under Rule 803(6) as part of the business record. May the prosecution introduce it through the custodian without calling the person who made the record for the purpose of raising the inference that the red material may have been dried blood?

(C) Alternatively, the foreman at Al's Wrecker and Repair Service became suspicious of the dried red material and had a sample removed and sent to a local lab which routinely performs tests to determine the presence of human blood. The results of the test were that the dried red material was human blood of the same blood type as Peter's. Assume that all chain of custody and authentication problems have been resolved and that the report has been ruled admissible under Rule 803(6) as a business record of the lab. May the prosecution introduce the lab report without calling the technician who performed the test?

13–57. Officer Long responded to a police radio transmission reporting "shots fired" in the 1000 block of Elm Street. He parked his patrol car around the corner because he was concerned that an armed individual might still be present. As he cautiously rounded the corner, he saw an individual lying on the ground with a pool of blood gathering around his legs. The man, Williams, had apparently been shot several times.

Long asked Williams who shot him. Williams responded that it was Tony Clark, who had stolen Williams' Smith and Wesson .38 caliber pistol. The police later verified that Williams had such a pistol registered to him.

Clark was arrested and prosecuted for possession of a firearm as a felon. Williams died in an apparently unrelated shooting before trial. The prosecution introduced Williams' statement to Long to help prove Clark's possession of this weapon. The trial judge found the statement met the excited utterance hearsay exception.

Is it admissible under the Confrontation Clause?

13–58. An Atlanta, Georgia 9–1–1 operator received an emergency call. The caller, who identified herself as Frances, said that her husband was beating her. The operator asked who her husband was and Frances said Val Smith. The 9–1–1 operator asked where he was at that moment, and Frances answered she did not know.

Officer Burly responded to a radio call for an ongoing domestic assault at a specific address with a complaining witness named Frances. When he arrived at the address, he found a woman standing at the door, crying and bleeding from her nose and with a cut over her eye. He asked who did this to her. She responded, her husband, Val Smith. Burly asked where he was. She responded that he had just left. Burly asked for a description. He asked whether she needed emergency medical services, and she declined.

Burly checked the house to make sure the defendant was no longer present. He broadcast the name and description. He then returned to the scene and asked Frances for further details about the assault. She talked of Val starting to throw away some of her important papers and them arguing. Val punched her several times and then slammed her head into the wall. He also yanked out some of her hair.

Val was prosecuted for domestic battery. Despite the prosecution's efforts to secure her presence, Frances declined to participate in the prosecution. She said they had "made up" and she didn't want to put Val in jail. They needed his pay check.

The trial judge admitted all of Frances' statements under the hearsay rule as excited utterances. Are any or all of them admissible under the Confrontation Clause?

13–59. In response to a 9–1–1 call from suspicious neighbors, a police SWAT team silently surrounded a house where Ralph Fletcher, a man with a past history of violence and mental instability, was holding his aunt, Mable Forrest, at knife point. After observing the house for a period of time, the police observed Ralph walking Mable from the house while Ralph continued to hold a large knife near Mable's neck.

As Ralph turned a corner, several members of the SWAT team surprised him, throwing him to the ground, securing his knife, and separating Mable from him. The police quickly handcuffed Ralph and took him from the crime scene in a police transport vehicle. One officer took the victim to a safe location at a nearby school. A police detective had been stationed at that safe location to interview the victim when she was freed. The officer testified that she asked no questions before the victim spontaneously began describing her kidnapping, which the detective recorded in her notes.

The trial court admits the statement as a spontaneous utterance and rules that because there was no interrogation whatsoever of the victim and no formal statement produced, the statement was not testimonial. Defense counsel challenges this Confrontation Clause determination. What should the result be on appeal?

13–60. At approximately 4:00 a.m., the babysitter for four-year-old S.G. was awakened by the young girl's scream and went to her bedroom. As the babysitter approached the door, she saw a young man leave and then exit the front door of the apartment. The babysitter called S.G.'s mother, Tammy, who was working a night shift job, and asked her to come home. Tammy arrived within thirty minutes and asked the child what had happened. The child named Randy as the person who had been in her room. Tammy asked what he had done to S.G. S.G. said he touched her. Tammy asked a series of questions finding out that Randy had touched her daughter's genital area. Tammy called the police.

Officer Lewis arrived within ten minutes. He asked to talk with S.G. privately. He asked what had happened that caused her to scream. She said that a young man she knew from the neighborhood had been in her room and touched her. Lewis asked where he had touched her. S.G. said on her neck and face. Lewis then asked a series of questions to determine if Randy had touched her anywhere else and learned that he had touched her on her genital area.

Fifteen minutes later S.G. was taken to the local hospital's emergency room. Nurse Rentz interviewed her there for a history. She asked what had happened. S.G. said that Randy had touched her. Rentz asked where and learned the head and face. She asked if he had touched her anywhere else and S.G. said yes. S.G. pointed to her genital area. Rentz asked her to describe what Randy did, and S.G. described Randy's actions.

At trial, the child was not called as a witness by the prosecution, which instead offered S.G.'s hearsay statements through the three witnesses, her mother Tammy, Officer Lewis, and Nurse Rentz. With respect to the hearsay rule, the trial court admitted all three of the statements under the excited utterance exception and the statement to Nurse Rentz also under the exception for statements for medical diagnosis or treatment. Are the statements admissible under the Confrontation Clause?

13–61. Vince had a conversation at a local bar with one of his illegal drug suppliers, Arthur, inquiring when the next shipment of cocaine will arrive. Arthur promised it within two days. Vince said that was good timing because he was getting pressure for David to step up the pace of the operation. David wanted the deliveries to be larger and more dependable in their arrival time. Unknown to Vince, Arthur is a federal narcotics agent who recorded the entire conversation.

The next day Vince was arrested by uniformed police officers. Once at the station, he was told by FBI agent Ness that he had been under surveillance for several months and that the evidence against him is considerable and the prison time he is facing runs into the decades. Vince started talking about the drug operation, admitting to his participation and naming several others in the operation, including his immediate boss, David.

At his joint trial with David and others, Vince refused to testify and asserted his right not to testify. He was ruled unavailable by the trial court. The prosecution offered his recorded statement in the bar made to Authur and his statement after arrest to Ness. With regard to the hearsay rule, the first recording is admitted under the hearsay rule for coconspirator statements and the second as a statement against interest since leniency was not discussed and blame shifting was minimal.

Are either or both of the statements admissible under the Confrontation Clause?

13–62. An elderly pensioner, Ruth, was robbed and beaten in her apartment. Several hours later, neighbors, who had not seen Ruth in some time, found her in her apartment. The neighbors called the police, who arrived in about half an hour. When the police entered Ruth's apartment, two neighbors were present. The neighbors recounted finding the victim in her ransacked apartment earlier. The police then called emergency medical services. They did not know whether the perpetrator was still in the building and got information from Ruth about who did it. Ruth described the crime and the perpetrator to them, but took no formal witness statement. After receiving information from a neighbor regarding a possible suspect matching Ruth's description, the police assembled a photo array. An officer took these photographs to the hospital where the victim was being treated for her injuries and showed the photos to her. Ruth victim identified Amanda Leonard, a young woman who lived nearby.

Before trial, Ruth, the only witness to the crime, died of unrelated causes. Despite the lack of an opportunity to cross-examine, both the victim's statement to the police in her apartment describing the crime and the perpetrator and her photographic identification made to another officer were admitted at trial, the first as an excited utterance and the second under the catchall exception.

Are the statements testimonial? Both, or just one? Why?

13–63. John is being prosecuted in a separate trial for armed robbery of a convenience store and murder of the store clerk, crimes that the prosecution contends he and Ralph committed together. When interrogated by the police, Ralph admitted that he and John committed the robbery. He admitted that the murder weapon was his, that he provided it to John, and that he was in the store helping with the robbery when John got angry with the clerk and fatally shot her. At John's trial, Ralph asserts his privilege against self-incrimination and refuses to testify either for the state or the defense. The state court admits the statement against John under the state's hearsay exception for statements against interest. That exception includes statements that a reasonable person would have considered against his or her penal interest. The court determines that the statement was clearly against Ralph's penal interest in fully involving him in the murder since the act of his accomplice is attributed to him. John objects on Confrontation Clause grounds. Is admission of the use of the statement against John constitutional?

Is the result any different with respect to the use of Ralph's confession against John if both men were charged under a state statute that gives an enhanced penalty for the use of a fully automatic weapon during a crime, and in his statement to the police, Ralph acknowledged that he had altered the weapon he gave to John for use in the robbery so that it was changed from a semi-automatic into a fully automatic weapon?

13–64. Ralph is charged with armed robbery. The state calls to the stand his girlfriend Joyce and asks her whether Ralph admitted to her that he committed the robbery. She denies that he made such a statement and instead states that she told the police that Ralph had been with her at the time the robbery occurred. The prosecution then seeks to introduce a signed statement to the police in which Joyce recites that Ralph told her that he committed the armed robbery. The statement is admissible under the state's new hearsay rule that admits any prior inconsistent statement of a witness. Ralph objects on Confrontation Clause grounds arguing that the statement is not firmly rooted and that any cross-examination of Joyce's preposterous statement would be futile since she denies making the statement.

Does admitting Joyce's prior statement violate the Confrontation Clause?

13–65. Larry is being prosecuted for aggravated assault. The state has offered against him under past recollection recorded the testimony/statement of John who was a cellmate with Larry at one time. A detective and John's attorney testified that John gave each of them a handwritten statement in which he recited that Larry had recounted how he had shot the victim, describing in detail his motive, his accomplices, and the role each person played in the shooting, including the fact that Larry was the gunman. John took the stand at trial and stated that he could no longer remember anything about what Larry had told him while they were in the cell together but that he had told everything he knew to the detective and his lawyer and had written it down accurately at that time and that at that time he had remembered everything correctly.

Under cross-examination, John continues to insist that he remembers absolutely nothing about what Larry told him but that everything in the statement is correct. He can offer no explanation for why he would remember that the statement was accurate but not remember anything at all about what Larry said to him.

The defense objects on the basis of the Confrontation Clause. How should the court rule?

13–66. In a criminal prosecution of Edith and Ralph, two members of an alleged conspiracy to distribute drugs, the prosecutor calls to the stand a third member of the alleged conspiracy, Dan. Earlier, Dan had testified before the grand jury that he, Edith, and Ralph has been involved in a scheme to transport drugs to Dallas and to distribute them to a series of street vendors. Even though Dan had been granted immunity under the Fifth Amendment against compulsory self-incrimination regarding any use of his testimony against him in future cases, Dan asserted his "privilege against self-incrimination" and refused to answer any questions regarding the conspiracy at the trial of Edith and Ralph. Out of the presence of the jury, the judge ruled the privilege invalid and ordered Dan to answer, threatening him with contempt. When back in front of the jury, Dan persisted in his privilege claim. Nevertheless, the prosecutor read to him his grand jury statement and after each paragraph asked Dan whether it was true and accurate. Dan repeated his claim of privilege each time. At the request of the prosecutor, the trial judge gave defense counsel an opportunity to question Dan, which produced the same assertion of privilege and refusal to answer that had resulted from the prosecutor's questions.

The prosecutor asked that the judge rule Dan's grand jury testimony as inconsistent with his trial testimony and allow it to be admitted since he had taken the stand and was cross-examined by defense counsel. The prosecutor argued that Dan's refusal to testify provided a sound basis for the jury's evaluation of Dan's credibility and that Dan was legally available for cross-examination.

Is the grand jury testimony admissible under the Confrontation Clause because Dan was subject to cross-examination? What if instead of claiming the privilege Dan had just as consistently claimed that he had used drugs extensively since he made the statement and no longer remembered anything about the events or even his appearance before the grand jury, claims of failure of memory that the trial court determined were false?

13–67. In an effort to make hearsay broadly admissible to prosecute those who sexually abuse children, the state enacted a special hearsay provision that in sexual abuse cases admits all statements by children under the age of ten as long as the child testifies and is available for cross-examination.

Dirk is charged with abusing his stepdaughter, R.K., who was two at the time of the offense and three at the time of the trial. After R.K.'s mother noticed some irritation in her genital area, R.K. was interviewed by a forensic interview specialist for the local police department, Wilma.

According to Wilma, R.K. acted out how Dirk had fondled her and had genital contact with her.

At trial, the trial judge found R.K. competent because she knew age appropriate information and knew that it was bad to not tell the truth. R.K. took the stand in the prosecution's case but was largely unresponsive as the prosecutor asked her about what happened. The prosecutor then read Wilma's statement line by line to R.K. and received an occasional nod, but some observers thought they were little more than random movements.

On cross-examination, R.K. was virtually unresponsive.

Wilma testified to her conduct of the interview. She had a few notes that she provided to the court. She was cross-examined by the defense counsel, and insisted that R.K. acted out the sexual contact.

Does the admission of R.K.'s prior statement to Wilma violate the Confrontation Clause?

13–68. (A) The legislature in State A has enacted a new hearsay exception called the child victim hearsay exception, which provides that statements of children under the age of ten who are the alleged victims of crime may be received when the trial court finds that the child is unavailable as a witness.

In the prosecution of Robert for indecent liberties with a minor, the court examines the three-year-old victim of the sexual assault and determines that she is incompetent to testify. The prosecution then offers as evidence a statement made by the child to a social worker at a rape trauma center identifying the defendant as the perpetrator of the offense. The defendant challenges the admission of the statement under the Confrontation Clause. How should the court rule?

(B) The legislature in State B enacted a different statute that provides that where the child victim is less than ten years of age, the testimony may be admitted if the court finds the statement to be trustworthy. It also provides that the statement is admissible regardless of the availability of the child.

Richard is being prosecuted for sexual assault on his four-year-old stepdaughter Lisa. The state offers the testimony of Jane, a social worker at Lisa's day care who had a conference with Lisa several days after the alleged assault when she displayed unusual behavior in class. Lisa described the incident to the social worker and identified Richard as having committed the act. Assume the testimony has been ruled admissible under the new statute.

In response to a defense motion, the state has informed the judge that it does not intend to call Lisa as a witness because the testimony would be traumatic to her. It will rely upon the statements to Jane. The state notes that Lisa is available and subject to defense subpoena. It argues that the defendant may call the child if he wishes and under a state rule of evidence identical to Federal Rule 806 would be able to proceed as on cross-examination. Is the testimony of the social worker admissible?

(C) Assume the same facts as in Part (B) above, but this time assume the state has no special hearsay exception and instead admits the testimony under its residual exception, which is modeled on Federal Rule 807. Will it matter in deciding the issue whether Lisa's version of the event involved the use of child-like terminology, whether Jane used leading questions to elicit the story, whether it was videotaped, or whether it was corroborated both by medical testimony indicating sexual activity occurred and hair and fiber evidence linked to Richard?

13–69. In St. Louis, advocates for children have created a consolidated program for investigating and treating child abuse. In order to minimize interviews of children, a single videotaped interview is mandated in most cases. The interview is to be conducted by a trained forensic interviewer. It is conducted according to a protocol designed originally by medical personnel, but it includes as well questions that are important for the successful prosecution of perpetrators of criminal abuse. Once the interview is completed, copies are forwarded to the city's medical, social work, and prosecutorial offices if the interviewer finds evidence that would warrant concern with the health of the child, his or her custodial situation, or potential law violation.

Dwight is charged with child sexual abuse of the five-year-old daughter (W.J) of his former girlfriend. The state offers in evidence a videotape recording conducted as described above. W.J. was brought to the city's interview facility after her mother observed what she considered suspicious sexual behavior by her child and suspected her boyfriend of abusing W.J.

The videotape is introduced under the state's catchall exception. W.J. refuses to testify because of apparent trauma.

Does admission of the videotape violate Dwight's Confrontation Clause rights?

13–70. The police received a phone call from a service station attendant who stated that a wounded man who had come to his store asking for help was lying outside on the pavement. Several squad cars arrived and the officers immediately went to the man, who identified himself as Al Field, and started rendering first aid. In response to the question, "What happened?" Field responded that he had been shot about fifteen minutes earlier about six blocks away. He said he had driven himself to the service station to call for help. The police observed blood on his stomach and asked him where he had been shot. He said once in the stomach. The police had already called for an ambulance and told the man medical help was on the way. During the conversation, the man was visibly in pain and his breathing was labored.

The police continued to ask Field questions. They asked him who did the shooting, to which he responded, James Jones. They asked for and received a description of Jones. They asked Field where Jones was, and the victim said he didn't know. Field said he assumed Jones was still at Jones' home where the shooting took place and provided that address to the police. They then asked Field to explain why Jones shot him. Field said Jones hadn't returned a valuable coat that Field had left at his house and when he went to retrieve it, Jones just shot him. The police jotted the key points of this information down in their notes, but they took no witness statement from Field.

A few minutes later, the ambulance arrived, and Field was taken to the hospital. He was in the process of recovering from his serious wound, but during his convalescence, he suffered a stroke and lost all communicative ability.

Jones is on trial for the aggravated assault and attempted murder of Field. The prosecution seeks to introduce all of Field's statements to the police as non-testimonial under the Confrontation Clause because, the prosecution argues, they were made during an on-going emergency. The prosecution contends that the officers' questioning related to the need to treat a seriously injured victim and to protect him and the public by getting information to identify and apprehend a violent individual. The defense argues that the entire questioning concerned past events, starting with the question "What happened?" Further, the defense argues that since the declarant's motivation is the key and Field knew from the beginning that Jones was not nearby, the incident had clearly concluded. Moreover, almost immediately, the police learned that the crime happened some time earlier and at an entirely different location. Thus, the defense argues, whether or not Field's answer to the initial question by the police could be admitted, once that answer was heard by the police, the interview was testimonial. Are any or all of Field's statements admissible under the Confrontation Clause?

13–71. Johnson was convicted of possession of cocaine. The state offered the testimony of Ruth, a forensic analyst. The defense objected on grounds that his confrontation rights had been violated.

Ruth testified that she had not been involved in the testing of the sample and that it was no longer available to be further tested. She was not able to conduct an independent analysis. Instead, she relied upon the report of Robert, a forensic analyst and former employee at the same lab where she worked but who was no longer in the state, as the basis of her conclusion. According to his report, which was offered and received as an exhibit, the substance was cocaine. Ruth summarized the report, stating that she concurred with his conclusion. Robert reported that he had conducted a series of tests, some of which involved color tests and some of which involved instrumental analysis. Based on her examination of the work Robert reported doing and the results he recorded in his report, Ruth concluded the substance was clearly cocaine. She also stated that she would have reached the same result had she conducted the testing. On cross-examination, Ruth stated that unless Robert made mistakes or deliberately falsified the work he did or the findings he observed, the substance was cocaine.

Robert was not called as a witness by the prosecution. Was the Confrontation Clause violated by admission of Ruth's testimony and the admission of the report of the analysis conducted by Robert?

13–72. Sam was convicted of murder. He challenged two items of evidence based on the Confrontation Clause.

(A) The first was the testimony of a medical examiner, Sarah, who testified that in her expert opinion the cause of the victim's death was a knife wound and the manner of death was homicide. She testified that the autopsy upon which she relied was completed ten years before she arrived at the medical examiner's office by an examiner, Walt, who had since passed away. None of the original materials, other than a few photographs of the body, were available. She examined the photographs, which she admitted were insufficient to establish that the cause of death was a knife wound or that the manner of death was homicide, but did provide some support for those conclusions. Instead, she based her conclusions on the physical observations and the laboratory results performed by Walt. The report prepared by Walt was received in evidence, but it was offered with a limiting instruction that it was not to be received for the truth of the matter but rather only as supporting the opinion of Sarah.

(B) The second item of evidence was DNA analysis offered by forensic scientist Jennifer that showed Sam's DNA on the victim's coat. Sam's DNA was found in blood located on that coat. Jennifer had done none of the initial work in the case and none of the samples were available for independent analysis. Instead, she relied on the report of Charles and the data contained in that report. The report contained data read-outs produced by a mechanical device operated by Charles. Jennifer admitted that she had to rely upon the correctness of the procedures used by Charles, but she stated that the conclusion that Sam's DNA was present in the blood stain on the victim's coat was her own based on the read-outs produced by Charles.

Were these items of evidence and the testimony properly received?

CHAPTER 14

EXCEPTIONS TO THE HEARSAY RULE

■ ■ ■

SECTION A. PRESENT SENSE IMPRESSIONS AND EXCITED UTTERANCES

Federal Rules of Evidence 803(1) and 803(2)

14–1. A police officer on foot patrol turned the corner at the intersection of Franklin and Columbia Streets and saw Peter lying in the street with four people approaching him. The officer ran to the spot where Peter was lying and asked the four, "Did any of you see a car hit this man?" Alan said to the officer, "The car that hit him just went around the corner." A young man said, "Yeah, it was a green Camry." A middle aged woman immediately chimed in, "License number KZ 452." Dianne then said, "I didn't see the car."

The officer was examining Peter and calling on his police radio for help when these remarks were made. Meanwhile, the young man and the middle aged woman left without being identified and have never been found. Alan and Dianne stayed, but neither of them could identify the make, color, or license number of the car that struck Peter. Eventually, based upon the information related by the patrolman, Donald was identified as the runaway driver.

In a civil action against Donald, assume that Peter's attorney has sufficient evidence of the negligence of the driver of the car that struck Peter. However, the only evidence of the identity of the driver consists of the above remarks of the two unidentified bystanders (young man and middle aged woman) and the fact that the described automobile is registered in Donald's name.

Would Alan, Dianne, and the patrolman be permitted to testify over objection to the remarks of the two unidentified witnesses as related above?

McCormick, 6th Ed., §§ 271–272.

14–2. Theresa has sued the Big Rock Insurance Co. under an insurance policy covering the life of her father, James, a semi-retired chemist who died as a result of an explosion in his home chemistry laboratory. Also killed in the explosion was James' wife, Esther. Their housekeeper, Ms. Lynch, was badly burned but survived the incident. Big Rock claims that the explosion was deliberately set off by James in order to eliminate both himself and his wife and that recovery is therefore barred under the suicide clause of the policy. Plaintiff claims that the explosion was accidental. Following are excerpts from the direct examination by defense counsel of Mr. Wagoner, a close friend of the family. Be ready either to supply proper objections as plaintiff's counsel or to support the propriety of the testimony as defense counsel.

Q. Mr. Wagoner, how did you first find out about the incident in question?

A. Well, I actually found out about it before anything happened. Ms. Lynch, the housekeeper, called me about three in the afternoon and said that she had just seen James go down into the basement with a can of gasoline. She said that James had been quite depressed and had been drinking a lot recently and that she was afraid he would carry out his threat to burn the place down. I told her to call the police and that I would hurry over as fast as I could.

Q. Did Ms. Lynch sound to be very excited?

A. Actually she seemed to be surprisingly calm.

Q. What did you do then?

A. I got in my car and drove immediately to James' residence. The trip took me about 20 minutes.

Q. What did you find when you got there?

A. I found the house on fire. Ms. Lynch was standing outside. She was in great pain and parts of her clothing were still smoldering.

Q. Did she say anything?

A. Yes, she said: "He's been so depressed lately and drinking so much. He finally went and did it and now he's killed them both. I tried to stop him, but when he reached into his pocket for matches I started to run."

Q. What did you do then?

A. Well, the fire trucks were just beginning to arrive. I just stood and watched. In a few minutes, a fireman came out carrying James' wife. I went over to see if I could help. She was still alive, but just barely.

Q. Was she conscious?

A. She was semi-conscious and kept saying: "I tried to stop him, I tried to stop him. He didn't know what he was doing." She died within a few minutes.

McCormick, 6th Ed., §§ 271–272.

14–3. Alan is on trial for murdering Kelly, his girlfriend. The prosecution offers testimony from Kelly's sister Wanda, who testifies that she was in the midst of a telephone conversation with her sister when Kelly said she had to put Wanda on hold because she was getting another call. After a few minutes, Kelly returned to the conversation with Wanda. Wanda asked who called and Kelly said it had been her boyfriend, Alan. Wanda asked what he wanted. Kelly said he wanted her to give him some money and that if she didn't she would be sorry. Kelly said she had told him she wasn't giving him any more money.

The prosecutor then asked Wanda how the conversation ended. Wanda said that Kelly told her she was not going to give Alan any more money and she wasn't even going to let him into the apartment any more.

The evidence showed that the next day, Kelly was found dead in her apartment with her purse empty by her side. The door had been forced open. Alan was charged with her murder.

Defense counsel objects on hearsay grounds.

McCormick, 6th Ed., §§ 271–272. See also McCormick, 6th Ed., §§ 254, 273, 324.1.

14–4. Rick's body was found about dawn in his car along a deserted road in rural Ohio. He had been shot in the head and his wallet was missing. Autopsy results indicated he had died sometime late the previous evening.

A week later, Rick's truck was found parked outside the home of Dwight, located five miles from the scene of the murder. Found inside the truck was a notarized bill of sale dated the day before Rick's death bearing Dwight's signature. Dwight was charged with Rick's murder.

The prosecution offered at trial the testimony of Carla, Rick's girlfriend. She testified that on the evening before his body was found she received a phone call from Rick from his cell phone. She heard what sounded like road noises and asked where he was going. He said he was following a guy named Dwight who was driving his truck. He said Dwight was going to purchase his truck. He also recounted that Dwight said he knew someone who could complete the paperwork that night.

The defense objects on hearsay grounds.

McCormick, 6th Ed., §§ 271–272.

14–5. Using his flashing lights, Trooper Martin stopped John, who was weaving and apparently intoxicated. Martin asked for license and registration, asked some questions regarding alcohol consumption, made observations, and administered some field sobriety tests. He immediately returned to his patrol car and recorded on audio recording equipment the following: "Subject has equal pupil size, equal tracking, has a lack of smooth pursuit in both eyes, and has distinct eye twitching at maximum deviation in both eyes. Subject also has onset of eye twitching prior to forty-five degrees in both eyes. I observed a wine opener in subject's truck and smelled a strong odor of alcohol on subject's breath. Subject has glassy, bloodshot eyes and slurred speech."

The timing devices on Trooper Martin's patrol car showed that the recording was completed within four minutes of the time he exited his vehicle. The prosecution seeks to introduce the recording as a present sense impression.

McCormick, 6th Ed., § 271.

14–6. In a prosecution of Alex for killing two men, Roger and Steve, the prosecutor wants to call Walt as a witness to help rebut Alex's alibi that he was nowhere near the scene of the murder on the day it occurred. Walt would testify that about half an hour before the dead bodies of Roger and Steve were found in their apartment, he received a telephone call from Steve. Walt knew both Roger and Steve well and was acquainted with Alex. Walt would testify that he and Steve talked for a few minutes about nothing in particular—sports and the hot weather. Steve then said in a normal voice, "hold on a minute." It seemed that Steve had put his hand over the receiver, or at least Walt could not hear any sound for a moment. Steve then said he "would call [Walt] later but he had to go. Roger had just told him that Alex was at the front door."

The defense counsel objects that the statements are inadmissible hearsay.

McCormick, 6th Ed., §§ 271–272.

14–7. Ronald, who is unable to speak, was injured in an automobile accident when a truck driven by Darrell collided with his car at an intersection on a state highway. Ronald, who had been driving, was thrown from the automobile. His brother, Sam, had been asleep when the accident occurred and saw nothing before he was awakened by the impact.

Ronald lay where he fell for more than thirty minutes before an ambulance arrived. He was obviously in great pain. Finally, just after the ambulance arrived and while Sam and the ambulance driver, Wesley, were gathered around him, Ronald communicated for the first time. He used sign language, and his brother spoke to the ambulance driver, "Ronald says, 'That other car came into the highway without paying any attention to the stop sign. I thought he would stop first.' " Shortly thereafter in a double tragedy, Ronald lapsed into a coma and died some hours later without regaining consciousness. Sam, upon seeing his brother's dire condition, suffered a fatal heart attack.

In a wrongful death suit by Sam's heirs against Darrell, can plaintiff's attorney successfully introduce the testimony of Wesley with regard to Ronald's statement after the accident?

McCormick, 6th Ed., §§ 271–272.

14–8. Refer to Appendix A, *Hines v. National Motor Co.,* Document 5. Plaintiff calls John Young to the stand and seeks to elicit from him the statements allegedly made by Chester Hines when Hines was pulled from the car. Assume that Young's testimony would be the same as set forth in his deposition. Defendant objects. What ruling by the court? (At this point, you should only consider the admission of the statement as nonhearsay or under the present sense and excited utterance exceptions.)

McCormick, 6th Ed., §§ 269–272.

14–9. Mary, the chief prosecutor in the child sex crimes unit in Minneapolis, has received investigative files on two unrelated sexual abuse cases. Both cases involve sexual assaults on females who are ten years old. As is often the pattern, the perpetrator appears to be the live-in boyfriend of the children's mother. The prosecutor's concern is whether statements by the children will be admissible as a spontaneous statement. Both were made 18 hours after the sexual assault.

(A) In the assault against Susan, the statement, in child-like terminology, was that the named boyfriend inserted his penis in the child's vagina. The statement was made to the child's mother when the child went to the bathroom the morning following the incident. Susan yelled for her mother to come to her because of the pain of urination. Her mother asked what happened; the child said she did not want to say; the mother asked whether somebody hurt her; and then Susan told of the boyfriend coming into her room while the mother was gone the previous afternoon and committing the act. Despite repeated efforts, Susan has never again repeated the statement and appears unwilling to testify at trial about the event. The doctor's examination revealed some irritation in her vaginal area, but the cause of the irritation was inconclusive.

(B) In the assault against Debra, the child told her mother about the boyfriend committing a similar but less physically invasive act while she was sleeping the previous night. Debra made the statement when the boyfriend left the house to run an errand about an hour after her mother returned home from an overnight trip to visit a hospitalized relative. The boyfriend had been alone with the child during the previous day. Like Susan, despite repeated efforts, Debra has never again repeated the statement and appears unwilling to testify at trial about the event. In this case, the doctor's examination revealed no physical abnormalities, but as described by Debra, none would necessarily have been expected.

McCormick, 6th Ed., §§ 272–272.1.

14–10. Nelson was on a guided tour for visitors conducted at the Glen Corp. manufacturing plant. While on the tour, he fell from a steel walkway and sustained severe injuries. He sues Glen Corp., charging negligence in the construction and maintenance of the walkway. Glen Corp. takes the position that the railings on the walkway were sufficiently high and were safely constructed.

Assume that the tours are given hourly at the factory. Nelson's attorney has discovered that on the tour immediately preceding Nelson's tour, a visitor stumbled on the walkway and was only prevented from going over the railing because Jay, a fellow visitor, grabbed his arm and prevented him from falling. As this happened, the visitor said, "That railing is too low to help anyone." Jay said, "You sure proved it." Nelson's attorney would like to call Jay and have him testify to the above incident and conversation. Should he anticipate that he can do so successfully over objection?

McCormick, 6th Ed., §§ 270–271.

SECTION B. THE STATE OF MIND EXCEPTION

Federal Rule of Evidence 803(3)

14–11. Paula is suing White Manufacturing Company in connection with injuries she received on the job resulting from White's alleged negligence in maintenance of the work area. Paula contends that, as a result of a floor made slippery by an oily material used in manufacturing, she fell and injured her back, causing her continued pain that makes work and most daily activities very unpleasant and difficult.

At trial Paula has called one of her co-workers, William, who relates that since the fall Paula has on numerous occasions cried out in pain, has said to him that her back is hurting, and has told him how she has had other outbursts caused by recurring pain when doing household chores at home.

White's counsel objects that the evidence is outside Rule 803(3) and is inadmissible because it is self-serving. What ruling should the court make?

McCormick, 6th ed., §§ 273–276.

14–12. (A) Dianne claims full title and ownership of a diamond tiara which had previously belonged to her mother, Mrs. Dorothy Painter, now deceased. Pamela (Dianne's sister) claims that she is entitled to a one-half interest in the tiara under the laws of intestate succession. Pamela acknowledges that Dianne presently has possession of the tiara but claims that it was only loaned to Dianne by her mother. Roger, a family friend, can testify that three weeks after Dianne obtained the tiara, Mrs. Painter said to him, "Well, I'm glad I gave the tiara to Dianne when I did. She's a great daughter." Is this testimony admissible over objection?

(B) In the same trial, Gertrude, a cousin, takes the stand to testify on behalf of Pamela that two days before possession of the tiara was given to Dianne, Ms. Painter told her, "I am going to give the tiara to Pamela on her next birthday." Pamela's birthday occurred after Dianne obtained possession of the tiara and after her mother's death. Dianne objects to this testimony. What ruling by the court?

(C) Assume different facts regarding the tiara case. Pamela claims ownership of the tiara against Diane, her sister, who has possession of it. Pamela asserts in her civil action that it was given to her by her mother and that Diane took it from Pamela's jewelry box after her mother's death. Pamela offers testimony of a statement made by her mother, Dorothy, shortly before Pamela's most recent birthday, a birthday that occurred a few days before Dorothy's death. The statement, made to

Gertrude, is as follows: "I'm going to give my tiara to Pamela on her upcoming birthday." Except for Pamela's claim, no one saw the tiara given to her or in her jewelry box, and Diane denies the gift was made or that she took the tiara from Pamela's jewelry box. Pamela's counsel offers Gertrude's statement and argues, "The statement is admissible to show the state of mind of the declarant as evidence that the tiara was in fact given to Pamela on her birthday shortly after the statement was made." Is the statement admissible for these purposes?

McCormick, 6th Ed., §§ 273–276.

14–13. Cynthia was killed in a traffic accident as a result of the apparent negligence of a truck driver employed by CorCo, a local manufacturing company. Her husband, Ross, brought a wrongful death action against CorCo.

CorCo wishes to introduce testimony by the family's next door neighbor, Mr. Jones, that several weeks before the accident Cynthia stated that she was getting ready to leave Ross, that she could not stand his behavior, and that she had learned Ross was seeing another woman.

Ross objects to the admission of the testimony. What ruling or rulings should be made by the court?

McCormick, 6th Ed., §§ 273–276.

14–14. Stephanie was found dead in her home, killed by a single bullet to the head. The gun involved was lying by the side of the body. There were no signs of forced entry.

David, Stephanie's estranged husband, is being prosecuted for her murder. The prosecution seeks to introduce in its case-in-chief the testimony of Wanda, Stephanie's sister, that two days before the shooting, Stephanie told her: "I am deathly afraid of David. He threatened to kill me if I refuse to move back in with him."

Defense counsel objects. What ruling should the court give?

Are there any defenses that might be raised that would increase the likelihood of admission?

McCormick, 6th Ed., §§ 273–276.

14–15. Ronnie is charged with murdering his wife Cassandra. His defense is that she committed suicide. The physical evidence is that Cassandra was found inside her home which had been set on fire and that a large quantity of prescription tranquilizers were found in her system. The prosecution contends that Cassandra was involuntarily drugged and the fire was set by Ronnie. The defense theory is that Cassandra committed suicide.

The defense offers evidence of a suicide note written by Cassandra and addressed to her husband which, according to its date, had been written three months before the day of her death. The note had not been delivered but was found among Cassandra's personal papers after she died. The note said: "Ronnie, I have decided that this world is not a good place for sensitive caring people and have decided to go to a place that is not so cruel and where I will not be hurt any more. Cassandra.''

Should the statement be admitted under the state of mind exception?

McCormick, 6th Ed., §§ 273–276

14–16. Dwight and David are charged with heroin trafficking. The prosecution seeks to introduce three statements made by David to an undercover officer. On each occasion, the undercover officer asked to purchase some heroin. David said that he was about to meet with his supplier. On each occasion, shortly after the statement David either was seen with Dwight or was seen arriving at Dwight's residence.

Defense counsel objects. How should the court rule?

McCormick, 6th Ed., §§ 273–276.

14–17. Jim is charged with perjury in connection with his testimony before a grand jury. The testimony concerned an incident in which Jim had driven a van and dropped off the woman with whom he lived, Wanda, alias ''Miss R.'' The government claims that Wanda left the van, made a drug purchase and then returned to the van to be driven off by Jim. Before the grand jury, Jim admitted driving the van on the night in question but claimed that he had taken the van to visit a friend. Wanda had come along for the ride, but at some point during the ride had asked to be dropped off at the address where the drug buy allegedly took place.

At the perjury trial, the government wishes to introduce a taped telephone conversation between Wanda and Tony, the alleged drug seller. The conversation was as follows:

Wanda: Hi, Tony, what do you want at this hour?

Tony: Miss R, if you come over right away, I think we can make a deal that is advantageous for you.

Wanda: You mean the best?

Tony: Yeah, come on over; it will only take five minutes.

Wanda: O.K., I'll come right over.

The prosecution's theory is that the inference can be made from the tape, and from the fact that Jim and Wanda appeared at Tony's address shortly after the taped conversation, that Jim went on the drive because Wanda asked him to help and not for the reason given in his testimony before the grand jury. Can the prosecutor anticipate that he can successfully introduce the tape? What if Wanda said in her last remark: ''I'll have Jim drive me right over''?

Assume in both instances that Jim's testimony at the grand jury hearing was material and that there is some other evidence to support the government's charge of perjury.

McCormick, 6th Ed., § 275.

14–18. Should the prosecutor anticipate that the letter in Document 6, Appendix B, *State v. Well*, will be admissible?

McCormick, 6th Ed., §§ 273–276.

14–19. In her deposition, Appendix B, *State v. Well,* Document 12, Cary Allworth refers to statements of Mary Well concerning Arnold's threats and her fear of him. Are those portions of Allworth's deposition admissible over objection?

McCormick, 6th Ed., §§ 273–276.

14–20. (A) John is charged with the murder of Louis. Louis' body was found at the bottom of a lake a few miles from Crescent City where both John and Louis lived. The body was found wrapped in drapery and heavy chains. The state's theory is that John killed Louis in John's warehouse after Louis had failed to come up with a substantial sum of money owed to John. John told the police that he saw Louis on the evening of July 15 at about 7:30 p.m., but that there was no discussion about the money owed, that John was not in any particular hurry for the money, and that Louis had told him that he was going to Pittsburgh to see some relatives that evening. At the trial, the state has been able to connect John to the crime by showing the existence of matching drapery in John's warehouse and by hairs identified microscopically as coming from Louis's head in the trunk of John's car. State medical witnesses have fixed the time and date of Louis's death at about 8 p.m. on the evening of July 15.

The state then introduces the testimony of Louis' wife, Martha, who testifies that she did not see her husband after he left for work at about 8:30 a.m. on the morning of July 15. She adds that just as he was leaving the house, he stated: "I won't be home for dinner. I have got to go with John to New York tonight to see if Max will loan me the money I need. John has threatened to do me harm if I don't pay him."

Defense counsel objects to this testimony. What ruling by the court?

(B) Assume that instead of the testimony set forth above, Martha testifies that at about 8:30 a.m. on July 15 Louis received a telephone call. After hanging up, her husband said: "That was John. He wants the money I owe him immediately. He says he will do me in if I don't go with him to New York tonight to get the money. I am going to go." Is this testimony admissible over defense objection?

McCormick, 6th Ed., §§ 273–276.

14–21. Jack was a state area representative of the X & Y Grocery Company which owned and operated a retail chain of many grocery supermarkets, 53 of which were located in the state. In effect, he was an inspector for the 53 stores and traveled at company expense, but in an automobile which he owned, from store to store in his work.

On one of the state's highways between the cities of Cork and Qualen, Jack had an accident in which Jane, the driver of the other automobile, was killed. Jack was also killed in the accident. A wrongful death suit was brought against the X & Y Grocery Company for the death of Jane, alleging the negligence of Jack as the cause of her death and that the accident occurred while Jack was on company business.

Before the accident, Jack had been in Cork, where he lived and where his supervisor's office is located, on company business. While there he arranged a "date" with Mary for that evening in Cork. Mary would testify that about 4:30 p.m. on the day in question, however, Jack called her saying he had to drive to Qualen (about 200 miles distant) to meet two men. She responded, "Oh—No! No!", whereupon Jack replied, "Well, I've got to keep my job." As a matter of fact, X & Y has no supermarket or office or operation of any kind in Qualen. Qualen is in one corner of the state and not on any direct route from Cork to any city where an X & Y Company store is located.

Apparently just after he called Mary, Jack called his wife at their home in Cork and said he would not be home that night because he had to drive to Qualen "on company business." His wife would so testify for plaintiff. However, she has previously told plaintiff's attorney that she knew her husband had often gone to "play around" with other women after he called, claiming that he would not be home because he had to go somewhere on business.

Should plaintiff's attorney anticipate that he can successfully introduce the testimony of Mary and that of Jack's wife, repeating the above-mentioned statements of Jack, at the trial in the suit against X & Y Company?

McCormick, 6th Ed., §§ 273–276.

SECTION C.　STATEMENTS FOR MEDICAL DIAGNOSIS OR TREATMENT

Federal Rule of Evidence 803(4)

14–22. Patricia purchased a bottle of a popular soft drink. Present with her was a friend, Wendy. Patricia took a drink, and noting that the taste was bad, she looked at the contents. She saw there a partially decomposed mouse. She immediately became hysterical and cried and shook for about half an hour while Wendy attempted to calm her. Wendy and others present can substantiate these facts. The next day she consulted a physician who concluded she had suffered no physical injury or effects. But thereafter she could not sleep, or if she did sleep she had "horrible nightmares about mice." She could not drink coffee or other non-translucent liquids. She had an intense fear of mice. At the end of two weeks she consulted Dr. Hiram Curtis, a psychiatrist. Wendy, at the solicitation of Patricia and with the consent of Dr. Curtis, accompanied Patricia when Patricia consulted Dr. Curtis. Patricia related the incident described above and her subsequent symptoms to Dr. Curtis. At the consultation, Patricia could not remember what she said while she was hysterical, if anything. Wendy volunteered that Patricia had dropped the bottle and started screaming, "It bit me! It bit me!" Wendy also recounted to Dr. Curtis various other nonsensical screaming remarks about mice which Patricia made while she was hysterical. He concluded she did not need psychotherapy, and her symptoms would pass away in time. The next day Patricia retained an attorney. The attorney ascertained the various pertinent evidence and found that Dr. Curtis would testify, if necessary, that Patricia consulted him and related all of the above stated facts, from which he would conclude that the described indicia of psychological stress were caused by the episode described above. Wendy would testify that after the incident Patricia complained to her that she was unable to sleep most of the time, and that when she did she had nightmares about mice.

(A) On the basis of the above facts, would Dr. Curtis' testimony recounting any or all of the matters Patricia and Wendy told him described above be objectionable?

(B) Assume all of the above facts with the exception of the following changes. The day after the "mouse incident" Patricia retained the attorney. Her attorney arranged for her to see the physician a week later. Then her attorney directed her to go to Dr. Curtis two weeks later, as in the facts originally outlined above. Would Dr. Curtis' testimony containing any or all of the matters Patricia and Wendy told him then be objectionable?

McCormick, 6th Ed., §§ 273, 277–278.

14–23. Jean was shopping in the Super–Star Supermarket when a large wooden crate full of oranges fell on her. She was immediately taken to a hospital where she was treated by Dr. Helen Bell. Jean told Dr. Bell that the crate had apparently been set on the shelf in a precarious manner so as to lean toward the aisle. She said that she looked up in the direction of the crate when it began to fall, and that it hit her directly in the face. Jean was hospitalized for two days for treatment of the cuts and bruises she received from the fall.

A few weeks after her hospitalization, Jean went to Dr. Keith Lane, a nose and throat specialist. She told him that she had developed a cold while she was in the hospital and that she was now suffering from sinus difficulties. She described her symptoms to him.

Jean has sued Super–Star Supermarket for her injuries and claims damages not only for her injuries, but also for the subsequent sinus condition. Her attorneys would like to have Dr. Bell testify to what Jean told her when Jean first saw her at the hospital. They would also like to have Dr. Lane testify to his opinion that Jean is suffering from a permanent serious sinus condition and that this sinus condition resulted from the cold Jean suffered when she was in the hospital being treated for her injuries. Dr. Lane will testify that his opinion is based upon his physical examination of Jean and upon her account of her present and past symptoms.

(A) Would the testimony of the doctors with regard to Jean's statements be admissible? For the truth of the matters asserted?

(B) Assume that plaintiff elects to call only Dr. Lane to testify. May he relate statements that were made by Jean only to Dr. Bell as related by Dr. Bell to him? May he testify concerning the observations and conclusions of Dr. Bell?

(C) Assume alternatively that Dr. Lane was consulted by Jean at her lawyer's request solely for the purpose of providing medical testimony in her case. May he testify concerning statements made by Jean to Dr. Bell and observations made by Dr. Bell that have been related to him by Dr. Bell?

McCormick, 6th Ed., §§ 273, 277–278.

14–24. Charles died as a result of a heart attack. The administrator of his estate is suing to collect on a life insurance policy held by his employer, Dallas Oil Company, covering deaths resulting from job related activities.

Charles' job was to maintain the pumping operation for a group of the company's marginal oil wells. He worked out of his home, doing his activities on an irregular basis depending upon the needs of the well. Charles was stricken by chest pains while alone at a well site. He arrived sometime later at the office of Dr. Jones, his physician. Charles recited to Dr. Jones that at the time he left home he was feeling fine, that he was working on one of Dallas' wells when he felt pain in his chest, sweaty palms, and general nausea, and that at the time of the onset of the pain he was moving a piece of machinery weighing more than one hundred pounds.

Dr. Jones diagnosed Charles as suffering from a heart attack and hospitalized him immediately. Charles died later the same day. It is the doctor's opinion that the condition occurred at the time of the onset of the pain.

Plaintiff offers as evidence the statement made by Charles to Dr. Jones. Defense counsel objects on the basis that the statements are not admissible under Rule 803(4) because they go to fault and are not substantively admissible when offered as the basis of an expert's opinion. What ruling should the court make?

McCormick, 6th Ed., §§ 273, 277–278.

14–25. Wilson is charged with sexual molestation of his six-year-old stepdaughter, Gloria. Two days after the alleged sexual assault occurred, Gloria recounted the events to her mother, who immediately took her to the local hospital for examination and treatment. The resident in the OB–GYN unit examined Gloria and found redness and tenderness in her genital area but no injuries requiring treatment. Gloria was very sullen throughout the examination and would respond to none of the resident's questions concerning the cause of the trauma. He noted his findings, which were consistent with a sexual molestation, treated the minor physical injuries, and released her.

Gloria's mother then took Gloria to the local Rape Counseling Center. There Gloria met two volunteer counselors, Ms. Wright, a registered nurse, and Ms. Davis, a social worker. They counseled both Gloria and her mother on the psychological aspects of sexual molestation. In the process, they asked Gloria what had happened and she recounted the facts of the entire incident, identifying her stepfather as the perpetrator.

Shortly before trial, the prosecution had Gloria examined by Dr. Marshall, M.D., a physician skilled in the diagnosis of what has been termed the child sexual abuse accommodation syndrome. Gloria recited to him the circumstances of the assault, again identifying her stepfather as the perpetrator. Dr. Marshall concluded that Gloria was suffering from the syndrome.

At trial, the prosecutor calls Ms. Wright and Ms. Davis as well as Dr. Marshall. The defense objects. Should they be permitted to testify to the statements made by Gloria to them, and particularly, the statements concerning the identity of the perpetrator? Does it matter whether the expert also testifies about his diagnosis of the child as suffering from the syndrome, which is a proper subject of expert testimony under appropriate circumstances in the jurisdiction?

McCormick, 6th Ed., §§ 273, 277–278.

SECTION D.   RECORDS OF PAST RECOLLECTIONS

Federal Rule of Evidence 803(5)

14–26.   Reconsider Problems 12–15 and 12–16, above. Assume that the witnesses have no present recollection of the events referred to in the writings involved in those problems even after looking at the writings. Would the writings themselves be admissible in evidence?

McCormick, 6th Ed., §§ 279–283.

14–27.   Sam was a prominent businessman. On a certain occasion he had a conversation with Louis, the president of a corporation which had become a recent competitor of Sam's business. In summary, Louis told Sam the corporation wished to buy Sam's business and named a price which was more than Sam's business was worth. Sam refused the offer and said he would not get out of the business, whereupon Louis told him that he, Louis, would see to it that Sam "would be gotten rid of." Sam did not report this remark to the police. As a result of this remark and other circumstances, Sam became very fearful. Later, Sam was set upon, beaten, and stabbed under circumstances that made it impossible for him to identify the assailant. Sam reported the matter to the police who eventually arrested Louis for the assault. At the criminal trial, the jury brought in a verdict that Louis was not guilty. Nevertheless, Sam brought a civil suit for damages against Louis based upon the above-mentioned assault.

Before the assault, Sam suspected Louis meant what he had said. He employed Tracy, a private detective, to "tail" Louis for about four weeks before the assault and to set up a conversation with Louis during that time. At the civil trial, Sam's attorney seeks to introduce one of Tracy's reports on a conversation Tracy had with Louis (which counsel considers relevant and of some importance). The pertinent part of the examination by plaintiff's counsel is as follows:

Q. Please state your name and address.

A. Tracy. I live at 1340 S. 1st Street in the City of Antigone.

Q. What is your occupation?

A. I am a private detective.

Q. Do you have an office?

A. Yes, at 4444 4th Blvd. I have been there for twenty years.

Q. On April 23rd three years ago were you employed as a detective by Sam, the plaintiff in this case?

A. Yes.

Q. What did he employ you to do?

A. He employed me to tail Louis for four weeks.

Q. What do you mean when you say tail Louis?

A. It means to follow Louis without his knowledge 24 hours a day and to ascertain whether there was anything unusual in his movements.

Q. I see. Did you then tail Louis?

A. I did so for four weeks.

Q. Did you do anything else during this employment?

A. Yes, I did.

Q. What did you do?

A. I interviewed Louis.

Q. Will you relate the circumstances surrounding that interview?

A. Well, Sam asked me if I could talk to Louis and if I could pretend I was in the same business as Louis, that I had a lot of extra funds, and that I wanted to buy out Sam, and other matters.

Q. So you did have an interview with Louis?

A. Yes, on May 6 three years ago.

Q. This was before Sam had been assaulted?

A. Yes.

Q. Now, did you make a record of your conversation with Louis?

A. Yes.

Q. How did you do that?

A.   Well, I took along a minirecorder which has a tiny microphone and I recorded our conversation. After the conservation was over, I went back to my office and I played back the recorder, and then I asked my secretary to transcribe it. She did so immediately, and I read over the transcription.

Q.   Do you have the recorder tape?

A.   No.

Q.   Why not?

A.   It was destroyed accidentally when lightning started a fire in my office last month.

Q.   Did you keep the transcript?

A.   Yes. It was in a separate file cabinet that was not damaged by the fire.

Q.   I hand you Plaintiff's Exhibit F marked for identification. Is that the transcription your secretary made of your conversation with Louis that you have mentioned?

A.   Yes, I know because when I first read it I wrote my initials on each page. I read it as I listened to the recording.

Q.   Now, Tracy, can you relate what Louis told you in that conversation?

Defendant's attorney: We object, Your Honor. That is going to be hearsay.

The Court: Objection sustained.

Q.   Your Honor, our offer of proof is that the witness will answer that he cannot remember what Louis said.

The Court: Very well. Tracy you may answer the question.

A.   I can't remember any more just what Louis said, but I sure can remember the gist of the thing.

Q.   But can you repeat exactly what he said?

A.   No.

Q.   At this point I offer into evidence Plaintiff's Exhibit F marked for identification. Defendant's Attorney, would you care to examine it?

Defendant's Attorney: Thank you. I have seen it. Your Honor, we object to the admission of this paper because it is rank hearsay.

Plaintiff's Attorney: Your Honor, this is very important evidence. May we approach the bench?

The Court: Yes. The jury is excused for ten minutes.

Plaintiff's Counsel: This document contains several statements of Louis that it would do no good for Tracy to think about buying out Sam because Sam would not be around anyway. Either that is not hearsay, or if it is, it is within a hearsay exception. Also, Tracy has testified he cannot remember the conversation.

Defendant's Attorney: This document is not a business record. It appears to have been prepared for this lawsuit. Why is it trustworthy?

The Court: Right. Objection to the admission of Plaintiff's Exhibit F is sustained.

Was the judge's ruling correct? Why or why not?

McCormick, 6th Ed., §§ 279–283.

14–28. The police respond to an apparent domestic battering case. They take a videotaped statement from Cynthia, who is bruised and bleeding. She tells them that after drinking some beer, her husband Bob flew into a rage and beat her. She called the police and the statement was taken. In the videotaped statement, Cynthia is placed under oath. The tape is stopped, and she is also asked whether she has just seen the statement and if it is accurate. She responds that it is all correct.

At trial, Cynthia is apparently a reluctant witness. She is asked what happened the night the police were called. She says she can't recall. She is asked whether she gave a videotaped statement to the police. Assume that she responds in one of two ways. First, assume that she says she doesn't remember what she said to the police. When asked whether she would have been dishonest with the police, she says no. Second, assume she states that she remembers giving a statement and that it was all made up.

The defense objects and argues that the statement is inadmissible for multiple reasons regardless of which of the alternate facts are assumed.

McCormick, 6th Ed., §§ 279–283.

14–29. Irene, an investigator for Plymouth Car Insurance Company, is called to the stand to testify to the plaintiff's oral statement given shortly after the accident in the hospital more than two years before the trial. The agent testifies that in the conversation the plaintiff, Paul, described the events of the day of the traffic accident. Irene testifies that Paul gave a detailed account of how he drove, where he was looking, and the speed involved, narrating those events to the jury. Because of a broken arm, Paul never signed the statement. At the end of her testimony, Plymouth's attorney asks Irene if she has anything that recites what Paul said during the interview. She responds "yes"—her interview notes, and that they are an accurate statement of what Paul said. Plymouth's attorney offers Irene's notes of the conversation as her recorded recollection, arguing they are clearly more accurate than any human memory can be that long after the event. Should they be admitted? If admitted and received as an exhibit for jury use, what should be the result if the ruling is challenged on appeal?

McCormick, 6th Ed., §§ 279–283.

14–30. Andrew brought an action for personal injury resulting from an alleged slip and fall on defendant's property. Andrew is now paralyzed from the waist down. The defendant claims that the alleged fall never occurred and that plaintiff's paralysis stemmed from an occurrence antedating the claimed injury. One of the few ways in which defendant can establish its theory is by introduction of a "memorandum" made by an insurance company employee of an interview with the plaintiff after the date of the alleged fall. The "memorandum" consists of two yellow legal pad pages of scribbled notes. It was made immediately after the employee, Radcliff, interviewed Andrew in the hospital.

According to the memorandum, Andrew had mentioned the antecedent injury but had made no reference to any injury of the sort claimed in this action. Radcliff has no independent recollection of the interview with Andrew, but as a matter of regular practice prepares this kind of memorandum in connection with every interview of this nature. Prepare a direct examination of Radcliff which would lay the foundation, if one can be laid, for the introduction of Radcliff's statement.

McCormick, 6th ed., §§ 279–283.

14–31. Stephen lived in a summer lake cottage that contained a propane gas stove in the kitchen. The stove was connected to a propane gas tank outside the cottage. While Stephen was in the kitchen the stove exploded, injuring Stephen severely. Subsequently, he commenced a suit against Prop Co., the manufacturer of the stove.

Prior to trial, Stephen's attorney, Jean, obtained a copy of an expert's report which was made under the following circumstances. Stephen remained conscious for a short period after the explosion. Jean, who fortuitously is Stephen's neighbor, heard the explosion and ran to his aid. Before Stephen lost consciousness, he told Jean to do whatever was necessary to protect his rights. Jean secured a propane stove expert to examine the untouched remains of the stove. The expert examined the remains of the stove and discovered a defect in a gas valve that would permit the gas to leak. He made a written report on the matter to Jean. Just before the expiration of the pertinent statute of limitation period, Jean commenced suit on behalf of Stephen against Prop Co. Before the trial of the suit (scheduled three years after the suit was commenced) the expert told Jean that he could no longer remember anything about the stove he examined, and that all he knew was what he read in his report. The expert is willing to say that, based upon his report, his opinion is that there was a defective valve and that the defective valve caused the explosion.

Jean would like to have both the opinion of the expert and the report of the expert introduced into evidence for consideration by the jury. How should she attempt to introduce the report? Will she be successful over objection?

McCormick, 6th Ed., §§ 14, 279–283.

SECTION E.   RECORDS OF REGULARLY CONDUCTED ACTIVITY

Federal Rule of Evidence 803(6)

14–32.   Mary was injured in a two-car collision. She was driving her car, and Janis was the driver of the other car. Mary suffered a back injury and a broken leg. She was hospitalized for about a week. At the last visit of her doctor in the hospital, the doctor told her to keep a daily diary in which she should record daily her pain and discomfort, symptoms of her injuries in detail, the effect of her injuries on her daily activities, and anything at all that related to her injuries. The doctor told her the diary might help him in treating her. Following his directions very conscientiously, Mary recorded such matters every day at noon and before she went to bed at night. Two weeks later, she engaged a lawyer to represent her in her claims against Janis. Mary told the lawyer what the doctor had said about the diary. The lawyer said, "That's a good idea."

Typical of the entries in her diary during the first three weeks were the entries for April 23 (three weeks after the accident):

April 23. [In her handwriting] Noon. Could not sleep at all last night. Maybe slept fitfully two hours because my leg and back hurt so bad. Tried to get to the bathroom several times, but it was just too much. Had to have Ma's help using urinal. Both hands tingled about two hours this morning, and suddenly at 8 and 10 my neck became very painful and I could not move it at all. Staying in bed as Dr. ordered. It got worse and worse, but when I got up three times, as Doc ordered, it got a little better, but then my leg began to hurt much worse, so finally went back to bed again. I tried to straighten up my room but just could not do it. The pain when I got up was so bad I cried each time.

Before bed. I am going to try going to bed at 8:30. Felt no better and same symptoms as stated above at noon. The pain pills prescribed do not agree with me and I threw up my dinner this evening. Now I'm hungry and Ma is making milk toast for me.

8 o'clock. Ate the milk toast and could not keep it down. Tried to embroider some napkins I want to give Sally but back just hurt too much. Got knots in my neck, upper back, and shoulders. Ma has to go home tomorrow, and I don't see how I will get along.

* * *

Later entries recorded that her leg was getting better—not much pain, but her head, shoulders and upper back pains stopped her from doing any work about the house, etc.

Typical of entries about a month later was the entry for May 22.

May 22 [In her handwriting] Noon. Leg is getting better and better. No real pain there this morning. But neck, back, and upper shoulders got real bad before I got up this morning. The more I move about, the worse the pain gets. It gets so bad, I just can't accomplish a thing around the house. Am following doctor's orders, too. Can't even wash all the dishes this morning. Tried to vacuum, but it was just too much. Louise visited me and said it must be really bad.

Before bed. [More of same.]

* * *

A year later she was still keeping the diary. As a typical example, the entry for May 22, a year later, recorded details of her attempts to do housework and a couple of things outdoors, which she could not accomplish because of severe neck, shoulder and upper back pains. She also wrote, "That Janis woman ought to come here and see the suffering her stupidity caused."

The next day, May 23, she recorded in the diary she was not going to keep it any longer because it was just too much to remind herself of all her pain every day. She then gave the diary to her doctor. (While she was keeping the diary she had showed it to the doctor on her visits to him).

Mary filed suit against Janis about a year and six months after the accident. Issues raised by the pleadings concern the nature and effect of Mary's injuries and the permanency of their effect on her occupation. The evidence includes Mary's own testimony and the testimony of those who have observed her. In addition, her attorney would like to introduce the diary. Is the diary admissible over objection under Rule 803(6)? If not, would it be admissible under any other exception?

McCormick, 6th Ed., §§ 284–294.

14–33. Pearson, Inc., a large catalog order house, brought an action against Girard to collect an amount due it as a result of an alleged sale of merchandise. Pearson claims that Girard purchased $1,000 in merchandise from Pearson on his credit card and that no payment has ever been received from him. Girard defended the action, claiming that he purchased only $100 in merchandise during the period in question and that he paid that sum to the company. You represent Pearson. The company's records are entirely computerized. All records of sales and deliveries to Girard, except for those existing in the memory of the company's central computer, have been destroyed. Naturally, no individuals within the company specifically remember the sale and delivery in question. In preparation for litigation, you have the record office of the company prepare a computer printout showing the date and amount of the sale to Girard, the fact of shipment to him, and the fact that no sums have been paid to the company on his account.

What kind of a foundation will you have to lay for the admission of this printout? What difficulties would you expect to encounter with regard to the admission of the printout in evidence?

McCormick, 6th Ed., §§ 284–294.

14–34. The Delta Co. regularly purchases semi-precious stones from Rare Gems Co. by mail. Upon receipt of a shipment after an order, the number of stones are checked by Delta with an invoice which accompanies the shipment and states the number of stones in the shipment and their price. Delta then forwards payment for the shipment. The invoices received by Delta are kept for three years.

Al, an employee of Delta, was accused of taking some of the stones from two of the shipments and is being sued for conversion of the stones. The prosecutor seeks to introduce the invoices to prove the number of stones received by Delta in the two shipments. Can the prosecutor introduce the invoices through an employee of Delta, who personally inspected the shipments upon arrival and who has personal knowledge of the above procedures, after having him testify to the above routines and having him identify the invoices received with the two shipments?

McCormick, 6th Ed., §§ 284–294.

14–35. Several months ago you were consulted by a client, Michael, with regard to injuries he suffered in an automobile accident. Michael told you that he believed that he was suffering from a whiplash injury, but that his family doctor has diagnosed the pain that he was having in his neck as simply a muscle cramp.

You decided to take Michael's case against the driver of the other car, Lawrence. You advised him to see Dr. Flynn, an excellent orthopedic specialist to whom you send many of your clients. Dr. Flynn has served as an expert witness many times and is a persuasive courtroom performer. Michael took your advice. Dr. Flynn immediately caused him to be hospitalized for tests at the Flynn Clinic, a private hospital owned by the doctor. The hospitalization lasted three days.

After the hospitalization, you talked to Dr. Flynn and he told you that he definitely believed that Michael was suffering from a severe whiplash-type injury to his upper spine and that there would be permanent after-effects from the injury. You then filed suit against Lawrence. After suit was filed, Dr. Flynn died and his clinic was taken over by another doctor. Because of Flynn's death, you believe that it is essential to your case to have the records of the clinic with regard to Michael introduced into evidence. The records are typical hospital records, consisting of admission and discharge reports, doctors' notes, nurses' notes, consultation reports and reports of medical tests.

You are particularly anxious to have two portions of the records introduced. One is Dr. Flynn's opinion as to the nature and permanency of Michael's injury, which is contained in the records as part of the doctors' notes. The second is the report of Michael's statement to Dr. Flynn, which is part of the admission report, with regard to the nature of the pain he was suffering and with regard to the nature of the impact causing injury.

How would you go about getting these records into evidence and what problems would you anticipate?

McCormick, 6th Ed., §§ 284–294.

14–36. Claude is suing the prison for failure to treat his injuries properly. He alleges that he was beaten by guards at one state prison facility and then transferred to another facility for medical treatment where his injuries were largely ignored. As a consequence of the beating and the inferior treatment, he alleges that his right leg is now partially paralyzed and his left leg permanently numb.

The prison wishes to introduce a series of documents prepared at the request of the medical director of the prison hospital facility, two of which are entitled "standard cell watch" and "general observations," which were prepared by guards pursuant to directions that Claude's ability to move be observed and recorded regularly. The records note Claude moving his legs with great facility and dexterity on several occasions in addition to the more typical observations of apparent incapacity.

Should these records be admissible as business records of the prison hospital?

McCormick, 6th Ed., §§ 284–294.

14–37. Jane Brown is charged with possession of one-half kilogram of heroine with intention to distribute it. The heroine was found in the bedroom of an apartment which was leased to Ralph Smith, who other witnesses testify is Jane's boyfriend. The address of the apartment is 152 Elm Street, Apartment 24.

The prosecutor wants to introduce a sales receipt for clothing from the local K–Mart which was found in the same dresser drawer as the bag containing the heroine. The receipt has printed on it that the sale was to Jane Brown. It also lists Jane Brown's address as 152 Elm Street, Apt. 24.

Brown's attorney objects on the basis that the receipt is inadmissible hearsay. How should the court rule?

McCormick, 6th Ed., §§ 284–294.

14–38. Biggs Trucking Company is suing One–Stop Supply, its supplier of gasoline, motor oil, and replacement truck parts, for improperly over-billing. One–Stop defends on the basis that billing was accurate and proper. It offers a computer printout of the Biggs' account, which it produced from its computer files the week before trial. The custodian testifies that the printout was based on data inputted at the time of the transaction by individuals within the company working from invoices and delivery reports prepared contemporaneously with the transaction. The printout contained only data pertaining to the Biggs' account, which was obtained by coding the program to search for and sort those transactions. The custodian also testifies that keypunch errors and miscodings were corrected and several misapplications of cash payments were rectified when the printout was developed.

Is the printout admissible as a business record?

McCormick, 6th Ed., §§ 284–294.

14–39. Assuming the telephone bill in Appendix B, *State v. Well*, Document 8, is relevant, is it otherwise admissible over objection? Specify the exact steps you would take in court to attempt to introduce it.

McCormick, 6th Ed., §§ 284–294.

SECTION F. PUBLIC RECORDS AND REPORTS

Federal Rule of Evidence 803(8)

14–40. Pamela and John, who were next door neighbors, became embroiled in a dispute concerning the ownership of a small plot of land on which stood an old garage. The small plot was within the description of the deed held by Pamela, and prior deeds of her predecessors in interest, but it was not within the description of John's deed to his property and that of prior deeds of his predecessors. John claimed the small plot by virtue of adverse possession.

You have brought suit for Pamela to quiet title against John. You have discovered that the state highway department had designed and approved a freeway (four-lane highway financed primarily through federal highway funds) which would have required the condemnation of all of the properties of Pamela and John. Also, the department had initiated contact with Pamela and John preliminary to final negotiations to acquire their properties for the freeway. However, for reasons not relevant here, the highway project had then been abandoned.

In the highway department files you have found a memorandum of the highway land acquisition employee whose duty it was to attempt to acquire the land needed for the above-mentioned freeway. The memorandum states:

> [Date]. I visited John today to discuss the acquisition of his property for the [*described freeway*]. We checked the boundaries of his property and he told me that the little old garage that appears to have been used from his property near the northwest corner of his property was actually on Pamela's next door property and that it belonged to her. [*Signature of state employee*].

The land acquisition employee who wrote this report is no longer with the state highway department and cannot be located.

You would like to introduce the memorandum in evidence at the trial. What foundation would be necessary for its introduction? Is the memorandum admissible?

McCormick, 6th Ed., §§ 295–300.

14–41. Iroquois Aviation brought suit against Simon for damage to one of its planes. Simon had rented the plane in question, an Iroquois 100, a single-engine propeller plane, from Iroquois for use on a business trip from Salem to Danville. As he was approaching the Danville airport, the engine of the plane died. He made a forced landing in a field about 1,000 yards from the airport. Amazingly, he escaped injury.

On the scene shortly after the accident was Fred, a Civil Aeronautics Board inspector charged with the duty of investigating all airplane accidents in the area. Fred inspected the plane and talked to Simon and several ground witnesses. The day after the accident he conducted further interviews and again viewed the aircraft. Fred then filed a report with the C.A.B. in Washington in which he stated that on the day of the accident he observed the plane's fuel selector valve in the "off" position. The valve controls the plane's two fuel tanks. It has four positions, right tank, left tank, both tanks, and off. In his report, Fred stated that he would conclude from his investigation that Simon, in attempting to switch from right to left gas tank, had accidentally turned the selector to the "off" position.

Simon's story is that he turned the valve to the "off" position after the plane was on the ground. He states that when Fred first interviewed him after the accident he could not remember turning the valve to off while the plane was on the ground and that he had conceded to Fred that he might have turned the valve to "off" before the engine died. On the next day, however, he told Fred that he had switched the valve to "off" after the accident. Fred is currently out of the country on special assignment for the C.A.B.

Plaintiff's attorney would like to introduce the report. The defendant resists. What ruling on its admissibility? (Assume that there is no statute dealing specifically with the admissibility of this kind of report.)

McCormick, 6th Ed., §§ 295–300.

14–42. David is being prosecuted for distribution of heroin. He was arrested shortly after the police witnessed what they contend to have been a drug sale. They allege that he sold the drugs to another individual, who also was arrested. A white substance was recovered from that second individual.

The prosecution seeks to introduce three documents under Rule 803(8). The first is a copy of a police report completed by an officer who observed a drug transaction. It describes the man who sold the drugs as a black male, 6 tall, with a beard and mustache, and wearing tan pants and a maroon jacket. The second is a standard police property control form which details the officers having possession of the white substance from the time of its seizure until its production in court. The third is the chemical examination of the substance completed by the Drug Enforcement Administration chemist, which identifies the white powder as heroin.

Are these documents admissible when offered by the prosecution? If David wishes to introduce the first document (the description) under Rule 803(8), would he be permitted to do so?

McCormick, 6th Ed., §§ 295–300.

14–43. Robert brought suit in federal district court against Conner Sealines, Inc., the owner of a ship on which Robert was a merchant seaman. The charge against Conner was negligence under the Jones Act (an act which provides that seamen may sue for injuries due to negligence while on board a ship). The suit arose out of a fight between Robert and Jack on the ship. The theory of the claim was that the officers and crew of the ship (and therefore Conner) knew prior to the altercation that Jack had dangerous propensities and failed to take action to protect Robert from the attack by Jack. Jack failed to appear for several noticed depositions, and did not appear at trial. Counsel for Conner established that Jack was working on a ship docked in Calcutta, India.

Long prior to the trial, pursuant to governing regulations and statute, a Coast Guard investigator had investigated the incident and had brought charges of assault and battery against Jack based on allegations by Robert. A hearing on these charges was then held before a Coast Guard hearing officer at which both Robert and Jack testified.

The attorney for Conner has at hand a certified copy of the Decision and Order of the Coast Guard officer dismissing the charges against Jack after the hearing. The Decision and Order summarizes the evidence admitted at the hearing, points out inconsistencies in such evidence, finds that the charges "were not supported by substantial evidence," and orders the dismissal of the charges. Should the attorney for Conner anticipate that he can introduce the Decision and Order over objection?

Can the transcript of the proceedings, which include the swearing of the witnesses, their testimony, and the oral findings of fact and conclusions of law be introduced over objection as a public record?

McCormick, 6th Ed., §§ 295–300.

14–44. Floyd is being prosecuted for a conspiracy to smuggle illegal aliens across the United States–Mexican border that resulted in the death of two of the aliens from heat when they were left in the trunk of a vehicle that was abandoned when border patrol agents closed in on the smugglers. The United States attorney wishes to introduce as public records and reports under Rule 803(8) three items of evidence. First, he offers a printout of car license numbers that crossed the United States–Mexico border during a two week period before the fatal smuggling effort. The license plate registered to Floyd's car was noted to have crossed forty times during that period, including twice the day the car was found. Second, the prosecutor offers a fingerprint analysis report prepared by the Federal Bureau of Investigation that concludes that the fingerprints on the steering wheel and on the lock to the trunk belonged to Floyd. Third, the prosecutor offers the autopsy report prepared by the San Diego County Medical Examiner that shows the cause of death of the two men found in the trunk to have been dehydration and heat stroke. The defense objects on the ground that reports of this type may not be introduced against a criminal defendant. Alternatively, the prosecution seeks admission under Rule 803(6) as business records.

McCormick, 6th Ed., §§ 295–300.

14–45. Refer to Appendix A, *Hines v. National Motor Co.*, Document 6. The plaintiff seeks to offer Document 6, the police report, into evidence. The defendant objects. What ruling by the court?

McCormick, 6th Ed., §§ 295–300.

14–46. Refer to Appendix B, *State v. Well.* Assume that Arnold Well has testified consistently with his last statement, Document 4. In rebuttal, the state seeks to introduce the autopsy report, Document 5. Assume that Dr. Tarner is on vacation out of the state. Note that he is engaged in private practice of medicine and works for the state only on a case-by-case basis. How should the state proceed to attempt to introduce the report? Is it admissible?

McCormick, 6th Ed., §§ 295–300.

SECTION G. UNAVAILABILITY

14–47. David was charged with possession of marijuana in state court. He asked to present evidence to the grand jury and testified in his own behalf. He was vigorously cross-examined by the prosecutor. He was indicted despite his exculpatory testimony.

At trial, David asserted his Fifth Amendment right not to testify. Arguing that the assertion of a valid privilege made him unavailable as a witness, David sought to introduce his own grand jury testimony under Rule 804(b)(1), which testimony the prosecution concedes was vigorously cross-examined. The prosecution argues that he is not unavailable.

McCormick, 6th Ed., §§ 253, 302, 304.

14–48. Henry was charged with murder in Los Angeles. At his preliminary hearing, Kathryn who had been vacationing in the city when the crime occurred and lived in Denver, Colorado, testified. On direct examination, she testified that she had witnessed the murder as she looked out her motel window. She identified Henry as the man who shot the victim. She was cross-examined extensively by defense counsel.

Kathryn had been a fully cooperative witness, and as a result, the prosecution did not subpoena her for the upcoming trial but instead verified how to get in touch with her. When the trial was formally scheduled, an investigator contacted Kathryn, sent her a plane ticket and advanced incidental funds, and scheduled for her to arrive the morning that her testimony would be needed. Kathryn was to meet the investigator at the airport. A week before the trial, the investigator called to verify that everything was on track for the trip and was assured by Kathryn that she would be present for her testimony.

When the flight landed, Kathryn was not on the plane. The investigator called her home and a young boy, who identified himself as Kathryn's nephew, told the investigator that Kathryn had not made the trip because of a family emergency and was currently out of town attending to that emergency.

The prosecution recounted its efforts in the case to secure Kathryn and said that it had no way to find her currently and moved to have Kathryn's preliminary hearing transcript received. The defense argued that her testimony should be excluded because she was not unavailable due to inadequate pretrial arrangements and subsequent efforts to secure her presence, specifically citing the lack of a subpoena. Defense counsel concedes that the cross-examination of Kathryn at the preliminary hearing was vigorous and unrestricted but nevertheless challenges the admission of the testimony on the ground that Kathryn was not unavailable.

McCormick, 6th Ed., §§ 253, 302, 304.

SECTION H.   FORMER TESTIMONY

Federal Rule of Evidence 804(b)(1)

14–49. In the case of *State v. Day* (*see* Problem 8–13, above), the defendant, an attorney, is charged with subornation of perjury. The state alleges that he caused Larry, a motel operator, to falsify a motel registration card and to testify in court that the record was a true and accurate record of his motel. The card, if it had been a valid record, would have established an alibi for Day's client, Michael, in a robbery prosecution. Day denies that he knew the card was false.

(A) The state wishes to read into evidence Larry's testimony that was given at Michael's robbery trial when the alleged perjury occurred. Larry's testimony consists of two parts: (i) his original testimony in which he testified that the motel registration card was a true and correct record of his motel, and (ii) his testimony as a state rebuttal witness in which he stated that everything he stated as a defense witness was false and that he had been told to give that testimony by Day. Larry was recently confined to a mental institution after having been declared mentally incompetent.

(B) The state also wishes to introduce the transcript of a preliminary hearing conducted in *State v. Day*. The hearing was held before a magistrate. Under local law, the defendant had a right to cross-examination. The state called Larry, the motel operator, who testified that Day caused him to falsify the motel registration card. At the preliminary hearing, Day was represented by an attorney, Jones, who was engaged the day before the hearing. Jones made no attempt to cross-examine the motel operator. Jones died before the trial and was replaced by a second attorney, Brown.

(C) The defense would like to read two portions of the transcript of the trial at which the perjury allegedly took place into evidence at the subornation trial.

(i) One portion consists of the transcript of the sentencing hearing. Michael, Day's client, pleaded guilty to the robbery charges shortly after Larry recanted his original testimony. He then appeared before the trial judge for sentencing. When asked to speak in mitigation, Michael admitted that he had caused the motel registration card to be falsified, but added that "my lawyer didn't know nothin' about it." Michael has been indicted on the subornation charges but has not yet been tried. He is presently a resident of a federal penitentiary in another state.

(ii) The other portion of the transcript of Michael's trial desired by the defense is the testimony of Michael's wife, Lois, who testified as a surrebuttal defense witness after Larry had admitted his perjury. Lois testified that she was present at the time the fake motel registration card was made out, but that neither her husband nor Day were present. She also stated that Day's name was not even mentioned during the conversation which accompanied the filling out of the card.

Lois has been interviewed at least ten times by the state's investigators since she gave that testimony. Approximately a week before the trial, she called defense counsel and stated that she was unwilling to testify in Day's behalf and might either suffer a loss of memory or give adverse testimony if called. She sounded frightened and refused to discuss the matter further with defense counsel. The defense does not intend to call her as a witness, although she lives in the city in which the trial is being held.

Each side requests a pretrial ruling on the admissibility of the parts of the transcript which it wants to read into evidence. Be prepared to argue either side of the issue on each portion of the transcript.

McCormick, 6th Ed., §§ 301–308.

14–50. Phillip, driver of his own automobile, and his passenger, Paul, were injured in a collision of Phillip's car and a car driven by Dwight. Phillip brought suit for his injuries against Dwight. Dwight called Theresa, an eyewitness whose testimony favored Dwight, to the stand. Phillip's attorney subjected Theresa to an extended and rigorous cross-examination.

Several months later, Paul's separate suit against Dwight came to trial. Paul alleged that Dwight was liable based on the exact acts of negligence and causation asserted by Phillip. However, by the time of the trial of Paul's suit, Theresa had died.

(A) At this later trial, should Dwight have the right to show Theresa's unavailability and introduce her testimony given during the trial of Peter's claim against Dwight?

(B) Would it make any difference that Phillip had not subjected Theresa to any cross-examination? Would it make any difference that in addition to Phillip's charges of negligence, Paul charged Dwight with driving while intoxicated and with knowingly driving with defective brakes?

(C) The trial judge asks Paul's attorney to specify any deficiencies in the cross-examination of Theresa by Phillip's counsel. Does it matter whether Phillip's counsel can show substantial deficiencies or admits that all the major issues were probed?

McCormick, 6th Ed., §§ 301–308.

14–51. Oscar is charged in federal court with importation of cocaine from Columbia. He denies any involvement with the drugs that were seized from the belongings of others who were traveling on the same boat with him. This boat was intercepted by state police agents patrolling the Mississippi coast. Five passengers and two crew members were on the small boat. All were undocumented aliens. Twenty kilograms of cocaine were found in the luggage of two of the passengers, but none was found in Oscar's belongings.

Oscar seeks to introduce in his federal trial three different transcript segments under the prior testimony exception.

(A) The first came from a congressional hearing into political corruption and drug smuggling in Columbia. Karl, one of the passengers on the boat, was called to testify under a grant of immunity that made his testimony inadmissible against him in any subsequent proceeding. He testified that he had hidden the drugs in Oscar's belongings without his knowledge. He testified that all five passengers were political refugees and that the drug smuggling had been authorized by the C.I.A. as part of an effort to fight Cuban influence among insurgents fighting the pro-American regime. Counsel for both the minority and majority in the hearings vigorously cross-examined the captain. Karl was subsequently killed in a prison fire.

(B) The other member of the crew, a deck hand, testified in the federal grand jury that indicted Oscar, also under a grant of use immunity. He was called as the last witness before the grand jury and proved quite uncooperative despite the immunity agreement. When asked what he knew of the cocaine on the boat, he said "Nobody knew anything about it." The prosecutor asked him no questions on cross-examination. At the trial, the prosecutor declines to grant the deck hand immunity and the court refuses to do so on its own accord. The deck hand asserts his Fifth Amendment privilege against self-incrimination.

(C) Before his death, the captain of the boat was prosecuted on state charges related to marijuana found in the captain's compartment. He testified that he had seen the deck hand working around the bags that contained the cocaine and the compartment where the marijuana was found. He testified that after their arrest, he was in the same cell as the deck hand and confronted him about the drugs and his suspicions that the deck hand had been responsible for both the cocaine and the marijuana. According to the captain, the deck hand had admitted all the drugs belonged to him, but laughed quietly and said no one would ever believe he was the guilty party. The state prosecutor vigorously cross-examined the captain, and indeed won a conviction. The captain also asserts his Fifth Amendment privilege against self-incrimination and no immunity is made available to him.

McCormick, 6th Ed., §§ 301–308.

14–52. Frances is charged with fraud and security regulation violations in connection with an Internet company she founded and carried through a very successful initial public offering. The company's operation shortly thereafter went sour and business activity ceased. Two creditors brought a civil action against Frances and noticed a deposition of her chief operating officer, George, and personally served notice on Frances. At the deposition, Frances did not appear. The creditors examined George and he revealed that the company was entirely a sham that Frances had disguised to take advantage of the public's enchantment with Internet stocks during the late 1990s. He testified that he wished to own up to his own responsibility since he was remorseful and was terminally ill with cancer, a fact he had told Frances about only the week before. Two weeks later, Frances filed for bankruptcy for the company and personally.

George died less than a month later. The federal prosecutor wishes to introduce his prior testimony arguing that Frances, who was a party to the creditor's law suit, had an adequate opportunity to cross-examine George.

McCormick, 6th Ed., §§ 301–308.

14–53. Robert brought suit in federal district court against Conner Sealines, Inc., the owner of a ship on which Robert was a merchant seaman. (*See* Problem 14–43, above.) The charge against Conner was negligence under the Jones Act (an act which provides that seamen may sue for injuries due to negligence while on board a ship). The suit arose out of a fight between Robert and Jack on the ship. The theory of the claim was that the officers and crew of the ship (and therefore Conner) knew prior to the altercation that Jack had dangerous propensities and failed to take action to protect Robert from the attack by Jack. Jack failed to appear for several noticed depositions, and did not appear at trial. Counsel for Conner established that Jack was working on a ship docked in Calcutta, India.

The attorney for Conner knows that at the trial Robert will testify in part to the effect that he, Robert, was in the resistor house on the ship when Jack entered the house unnoticed by Robert, striking Robert on the head with an unidentified object and screaming he would kill Robert. Although Robert was seriously injured he then fought to restrain Jack's further attack upon him. During this action, in self-defense, Robert managed to pick up an iron rod and end the fight by striking Jack once with the iron rod.

Long prior to the trial and after the alleged altercation between Robert and Jack, pursuant to governing regulations and statute, a Coast Guard investigator had investigated the incident and had preferred charges of assault and battery against Jack, upon charges made by Robert. A hearing on these charges was then held before a Coast Guard hearing officer at which both Robert and Jack testified. The Coast Guard investigator and Jack had the right of cross-examination. The purpose of the charges and hearing was to determine whether Jack's mariner license should be suspended or revoked. (It would be at least suspended if the charges were considered proved.) Counsel for Conner has available the transcript of Jack's testimony at the Coast Guard hearing and wishes to introduce that part which is pertinent to the alleged altercation between Jack and Robert. Jack's testimony is diametrically opposed to Robert's claims with regard to who was at fault in the altercation between the two men.

The pertinent part of that transcript of Jack's testimony reads as follows:

Q. Now, was the ship in Yokohama on the 7th of September?

A. Yes.

Q. Would you tell us what you recall happened from the time you arrived there?

A. When I walked inside the resistor house, one of the MG sets—they have two sets in the MG house—one set was running and the other set was shut down. I saw Robert with the controller doors open looking in there, so I asked him what he was doing. You know, anytime—as I'm the electrician if they need somebody to repair something, they usually call me. I asked him what he was doing in there and that's the last thing I remember.

Q. What happened when you asked him this? Anything you can recall?

A. I don't know. He just turned around. The next thing I remember was waking up in the hospital.

Q. How long after that, do you know?

A. Oh, how long?

Q. After he turned around did you wake up in the hospital? A matter of hours or what?

A. No, it was something more or less like two or three days.

Q. Later?

A. Yes.

Q. Now, did you, in this resistor house, punch or in any way strike Robert?

A. No, sir.

Q. Did you have anything in your hands when you were speaking to him?

A. No, sir.

* * *

Q. When you woke up in the hospital, how were you feeling?

A. Terrible! I couldn't see. I had headaches. I couldn't sleep— everything—terrible. Bleeding, spitting up blood.

Q. How long did you remain in the hospital?

A. Oh, from the 7th until the 3rd. From the 7th of September until the 3rd of October.

* * *

Counsel for Conner wishes to introduce this part of the transcript at the trial in the presentation of Conner's case. Should counsel anticipate it will be admissible over objection? By what exact means should counsel attempt to introduce the above portion of the transcript?

McCormick, 6th Ed., §§ 301–308.

SECTION I. STATEMENTS UNDER BELIEF OF IMPENDING DEATH

Federal Rule of Evidence 804(b)(2)

14–54. Police were summoned to the home of Daniel and Charlotte after neighbors, having heard screams from the house about 6 p.m., became concerned when there were no sounds from the house for several hours. The police found Charlotte badly wounded and bleeding profusely from what were apparently three stab wounds in her abdomen. As the two officers approached, Charlotte, obviously in great pain, stated: "I'll get that son-of-a-bitch. Yesterday, my husband said that he'd kill me if I didn't stay away from John. Well, he really tore me apart, God damn him. I was just minding my business." She seemed unable to talk further. She remained conscious until she reached the hospital but made no other statements and appeared unable to talk. Upon arrival at the hospital she became unconscious, remained unconscious for about two weeks, and then died.

(A) The prosecuting attorney wishes to call the two police officers to testify to the above remarks at the forthcoming murder trial of Daniel for the murder of his wife and can prove the other facts stated above. He knows that it could be shown that both Daniel and Charlotte were firm and convinced atheists. Should the prosecutor anticipate difficulty in attempting to introduce the above evidence?

(B) Suppose that all of the facts are as stated in Part (A) except that Charlotte did not die from the wounds inflicted but rather died of natural causes two months later and that Daniel was prosecuted for attempted murder and assault with intent to kill. Under these circumstances, is the evidence referred to in Part (A) admissible?

(C) Assume that as stated in Part (B) Charlotte survived the immediate assault but died of unrelated causes and that Daniel was acquitted on the criminal charges. The executor of Charlotte's will then sues him in a civil case for the tort of assault and battery. May she introduce the proof set forth in Part (A)?

(D) Assume that Charlotte died of the wounds, that the prosecution is for her murder, and that John, Charlotte's alleged boyfriend, was also found in the house by the police officers. One of the officers went to Charlotte and the other went to John who was also lying bleeding with knife wounds in the abdomen and in his neck. The police officer who went to John could testify that John said to him in a whispered tone, "May God forgive me. I'll never leave this house alive. I don't think Danny would have killed us if I hadn't grabbed for my gun and Charlotte hadn't grabbed the knife." He tried to speak further, but could not be understood by the officer. The other officer did not hear the remarks. John died before he could be removed to an ambulance. At Daniel's trial, could Daniel's attorney successfully introduce the police officer's testimony to this effect?

(E) Suppose that in Part (D) above, John had made the following additional remarks to the police officer: "Danny knew I was sleeping with Charlotte. He said he didn't give a damn. This was about a bet I would not pay."

McCormick, 6th Ed., §§ 309–315.

14–55. Brian is being prosecuted for the murder of Vince. One of the chief witnesses against him is Mike, who the police initially questioned as a suspect because he was seen with Vince shortly before Vince's badly beaten body was found. Ultimately the prosecutor decided that Mike was only marginally involved in the events that led to Vince's death. Mike was granted immunity on the basis that he testify truthfully against Brian.

Mike testified that Brian provided Vince with alcohol, then when he appeared to go to sleep, took his wallet, and beat him to death when he awoke suddenly and accused Brian of robbery. During cross-examination, Brian's attorney questioned Mike sharply and suggested that he had been the one who began the beating. Trial was recessed at 5:30 p.m. during cross-examination.

That night at about 6:30 a gunshot was heard in Mike's apartment. Upon entering the room, he was found with a self-inflicted gunshot wound. He left a suicide note that stated: "I didn't kill Vince. Brian did it all. I can't take the pressure of going through this trial and having lies told about me. Tell my mom I didn't do anything wrong." The prosecutor seeks to introduce the suicide note as a dying declaration.

McCormick, 6th Ed., §§ 309–315.

14–56. Jim was charged with the murder of Adam. Adam was shot and killed just after he walked into the Horrible Bar and sat down at a table. He was accompanied by Dick who was not injured. The theory of the prosecution is that the actual assailant had been hired by Jim to kill Adam. Dick is willing to testify that just before they entered the bar Adam said to him, "I ain't been even out on the street today until now, and I'm afraid to go into this wide open public place. Jim got a contract out to get me today. Well, I might as well have a last drink." At the forthcoming trial of Jim, can the prosecutor introduce the testimony of Dick to the above remarks of Adam over objection? Would your answer to this question be any different if the last two sentences of the above remarks were as follows: "Today Jim got a contract out to get me. He told me so himself, but I might as well have a last drink."

McCormick, 6th Ed., §§ 309–315.

SECTION J. STATEMENTS AGAINST INTEREST

Federal Rule of Evidence 804(b)(3)

14–57. Henry and Mildred Thomas, husband and wife, allegedly made an oral agreement that Henry would leave Mildred all of his property if he predeceased her and that Mildred would leave all of her property to Henry if she died before him. They also agreed that if Henry died first, Mildred would leave all her property to Henry's brother, Herman. Both Mildred and Henry actually executed wills with such provisions, but neither will recited the existence of the above-mentioned alleged oral agreement.

Henry died before Mildred and she received all of his property in accordance with his will. Mildred then revoked her will and executed a new will in which she left all of her property to her close friend, Martha. Mildred then died. Herman brought suit against Mildred's estate based upon the alleged contract referred to above. Assume that if he could prove it by clear and convincing evidence, he could obtain enforcement of the original oral agreement between Henry and Mildred.

Ralph, a former friend of Henry, will testify that before his death Henry had told Ralph of the alleged oral agreement with his wife. Can Herman's counsel elicit over objection this testimony?

Would testimony of William, a friend of Mildred, be admissible that before Henry died Mildred had told William about the contract and its terms? What about similar testimony of William, except that Mildred told William the story after Henry died but before Mildred revoked her first will? After Mildred revoked her first will?

McCormick, 6th Ed., §§ 316–320.

14–58. In a wrongful death action, the amount of recovery is based, *inter alia,* on the value of the lost income resulting from the death. Pauline's executor brings a wrongful death suit against Doris based on the death of Pauline by reason of Doris' negligence. Plaintiff's attorney wishes to introduce a copy of the federal income tax return of Pauline for the year prior to Pauline's death to show that Pauline earned $70,000 a year from her business. Is the copy admissible over objection?

Suppose that Doris is attempting to show that Pauline did not earn as much from the business as claimed by plaintiff. Can Doris' attorney introduce the above-mentioned copy of Pauline's tax return?

McCormick, 6th Ed., §§ 316–320.

14–59. A large amount of money was taken from Mid–City Bank through a nighttime burglary of the bank. The bank advertised a large reward for information leading to the arrest and conviction of the robbers. Shortly thereafter, Allan called the bank's president. Allan said that he had information which could lead to the arrest of the robbers, but he wanted to be assured that he would receive the reward if his information did actually lead to their arrest and conviction. Upon affirmative assurances, he arranged to see the president at once. At the meeting, Allan told the bank's president that he guessed he was a guilty man, although he did not want to admit that, nor did he want to risk his life. Allan said he had been an employee in the architectural firm that had designed the bank building. Not long before the robbery, upon an offer of a certain sum by three persons he clearly identified, he had made copies of the firm's architectural plans of the bank and had delivered them to the three persons.

Subsequently, the above-mentioned three persons were apprehended and formally charged with the robbery. In the same case, Allan was charged as an accessory.

Before the trial, Allan was found dead, his body riddled with bullets.

At the trial of the three robbers, should the prosecutor plan that he can successfully introduce the testimony of the bank president which would relate the above matters Allan told him on the phone and at their conference?

McCormick, 6th Ed., §§ 316–320.

14–60. Howard, William, and others are charged with a double murder that local authorities believe grew out of a marijuana distribution ring operated by Howard. The victims were occasional participants in the drug operation and were found dead in their home, being shot multiple times.

In an early conversation with his defense counsel, William was asked to explain statements made by Howard that he had committed the murder. William surprised his counsel by stating that he had done the murder by himself out of anger over an insult one of the victims uttered while they were drinking together at their home. He told his defense attorney about how he traveled from the crime scene and washed his clothing. Counsel found a witness who saw William take actions consistent with his version of events, but those observations were only of the travel route and him washing his clothing, which were not unequivocally incrimination. William's gun was linked to the murder, which was consistent with both the prosecution and the defense views of the crime.

Howard and William were tried separately for the murders. William's defense counsel kept his client's statement confidential and advised him not to admit his sole guilt since that would likely result in a sentence of death. The prosecution believed that William was as an active agent in the murders but considered Howard the ringleader. Both men were convicted and sentenced to life imprisonment.

After William committed suicide in prison, his defense counsel came forward with his client's confession of sole guilt for the murders. Howard's attorney seeks to testify about William's confession of sole guilt at a hearing to set aside William's conviction, which is offered under the hearsay exception for statements against interest. The prosecution resists based on the confidential nature of the conversation and the lack of corroboration. With respect to corroboration, the prosecution points to evidence of Howard's guilty provided by two witnesses who were members of the drug ring who testified under agreements with the prosecution that Howard was involved in the planning and execution of the murders. How should the court rule?

14–61. (A) Decide whether the following statements are against the declarant's interest in terms of the rule:

(1) In a prosecution based on constructive possession of drugs found in the companion's luggage, a statement "I'm on a honeymoon trip with him" at the time of the arrest.

(2) For possession of weapons, a statement by the defendant that he was in a particular room where three weapons were found hidden.

(3) A statement of a father admitting that his adult son was a Nazi collaborator in proceedings that could lead to the forfeiture of property and criminal prosecution of collaborators.

(4) A statement by a non-resident worker that he had worked no overtime when asked the question by a labor department investigator.

(B) Decide whether the following statements regarding third parties are against the declarant's interest under the rule as construed in federal court:

(1) "My son had nothing to do with it" (referring to the processing of drugs in a home in which both the declarant and his son lived).

(2) "Jimmy and Danny and several of their friends on the west coast were in this with me. I didn't do it alone." (Referring to sale of a car by the declarant in Dallas that had been stolen in Los Angeles.) Does it matter what information the police have about the larger enterprise at the time of the statement?

McCormick, 6th Ed., §§ 316–320.

14–62. Pete was riding in an automobile driven by Ted when a collision occurred between that automobile and one driven by David. Pete sued David on the theory that David was negligent. David denied negligence, contending that Ted was at fault and that Ted's negligence was the sole cause of the collision and Pete's injuries. David testified at the trial that he does not know where Ted is, but that he has heard that he is in Montana. David's attorney then offers the testimony of a police officer that, on the day after the accident, Ted told the officer that he saw David's car approaching the intersection from the right, that he was unfamiliar with the neighborhood, that he did not see the stop sign which indicated he should have stopped before he entered the intersection, and that he entered the intersection without stopping because he did not see the sign. Is the police officer's testimony in this respect admissible?

McCormick, 6th Ed., §§ 316–320.

14–63. Consider whether any of the following testimony is within the declaration against interest exception to the hearsay rule:

(A) Blank Bonding Co. issued a bond to Giant Co. to cover the embezzlement of Giant's funds by any of its employees. Giant claims that funds were embezzled by Gary, a store manager. Blank Bonding refused to pay on the bond and suit was brought by Giant. In the suit, Giant's attorney seeks to introduce a statement made by Gary, who is presently confined to a mental institution, admitting both the embezzlement and the amount embezzled.

(B) David is on trial for the killing of Victor. The defense seeks to introduce the testimony of Roger, presently an inmate of State Prison, that shortly before Joseph, another inmate, attempted an escape from the prison he stated that David had not killed Victor but rather that he, Joseph, had committed the murder. Joseph was unfortunately killed during the escape attempt.

(C) Edward is on trial for possession of heroin. The prosecution charges that he purchased the narcotics from Sandra. Could the prosecutor call Frank to the stand to testify that Sandra had told him that she had sold the narcotics in question to Edward? Assume that Sandra could not be found before the trial as a result of an extensive search.

(D) In Problem 14–49(C)(i), above, Michael stated at the sentencing hearing after his conviction for robbery that he had falsified the motel registration card which constituted his alibi but that his lawyer Day "didn't know nothin' about it." Would a report of Michael's statement be admissible as a declaration against interest in the trial of Day for subornation of perjury? Assume that Michael is in prison in another state.

(E) Susan brought an action to collect the proceeds of a life insurance policy on the life of her husband, Kenneth. The insurance company defended the action, claiming that Kenneth took his own life. In support of its defense, the company seeks to introduce proof that shortly before his death Kenneth had told a friend that he had recently been in a mental hospital under a fictitious name. He told the friend that he had been suffering from severe depression and that he had received shock treatments in the hospital.

McCormick, 6th Ed., §§ 316–320.

14–64. Dennis was released from prison on parole. Late in the day after his release, he was arrested in a nearby community and charged with possession of heroin with the intent to distribute. He was arrested while trying to pass what turned out to be a bag of heroin to George. Just before the arrest, Dennis had stepped from a car owned and driven by Robert, a local businessman who had no criminal record. Dennis was also charged with possession of a handgun found under the front seat of Robert's car.

Dennis' defense is that he thought he was delivering a bag of valium as a favor for a prison friend Keith. Dennis claims he was asked by Keith to pick up a bag of valium from Vince, who lived near the prison, and to deliver the bag to George in a neighboring town. Dennis picked up the bag as promised and was arrested when he attempted to deliver it to George. He claims no knowledge of the handgun found under the seat of the car.

Both George and Vince will rely upon their privilege against self-incrimination at the trial. Keith was stabbed and killed in the prison prior to the trial. Robert was killed in an automobile accident. Dennis will not testify.

The defense has the following statements available to it:

(A) On the day before Dennis was released, Keith asked Adam, another inmate who was being released, to "pick up a bag of valium from Vince and deliver it to George." Adam said he could not do it because his parents would be at the prison to meet him upon his release. Then Keith said, "Oh, well, I didn't want to do it anyway. I didn't really agree." Another inmate, Leo, will testify that he overheard this conversation.

(B) Max, a cellmate of Keith, will testify that he and Keith were informed of Dennis' arrest on the day after the arrest. Upon hearing of the arrest, Keith told Max that he had arranged with Vince to have some valium delivered for Vince to George, that Vince must have made a mistake by giving Dennis a bag of heroin, and that Keith said he knew Vince had a huge supply of valium.

The prosecutor had introduced a quantity of heroin found in Vince's living quarters in a valid search conducted shortly after the arrest of Dennis. No valium or other drug was found in the search.

(C) Henry (not a prison inmate) is willing to testify that after Dennis' arrest, Vince told him, "I just made a mistake and gave Dennis a bag of heroin rather than a bag of valium. I don't think George wants any heroin—he isn't into that."

(D) Dennis' attorney seeks to introduce an affidavit made by Robert at the request of Dennis' attorney that the gun in question was owned by Robert.

(E) Ralph, who is president of a local bank, will testify that while he and Robert and others were playing poker, Robert said to him, "You know that gun they charged Dennis for; that gun was and is mine. I own it."

Are these statements admissible?

McCormick, 6th Ed., §§ 316–320.

14–65. Could the statements of Mary Well to Sally Water in Appendix B, *State v. Well,* Document 9, qualify as declarations against interest?

McCormick, 6th Ed., §§ 316–320.

SECTION K. THE EXCEPTION FOR FORFEITURE BY WRONGDOING

Federal Rule of Evidence 804(b)(6)

14–66. Syd is charge with both drug smuggling and murdering an undercover federal agent, Margaret, who had infiltrated Syd's drug-smuggling operation and was cooperating with federal agents until her murder. The charges were joined for trial.

The prosecution offers three sets of statements against Syd. The first are statements Margaret made before federal grand jury in which she testified to her observations regarding the drug-smuggling operations and statements that Syd made to her about his contacts and distribution system. She expressed no fear that Syd knew of her cooperation in these statements. These statements were taken under oath and transcribed. The second set of statements were made to F.B.I. agents who Margaret would call from time to time. A long series of these statements was offered by the prosecution. They detailed the drug operations of Syd over a period of months. The last several conversations contained Margaret's statements that she feared that Syd had discovered her cooperation and that he seemed to be maneuvering her to situations where she might be killed. The third set of statements were made to friends of Margaret in the last two days before her murder. They note her suspicions of Syd and recount various past conversations with him about his drug operations and with federal agents recounting those operations. They also include a statement that Syd had asked to meet her at a specific warehouse that night where her dead body was found.

At trial, the prosecution offered a statement from Syd's girlfriend that Syd said he had discovered that Margaret was a informant and that he planned to ''shut her up permanently.''

Syd's attorney objects on the ground that: (1) the evidence fits no exception; (2) it is not shown to be particularly trustworthy; (3) it fails to come even close to the established exceptions; (4) it is unreliable; and (5) Syd has not been previously convicted of killing Margaret or even proved by clear and convincing evidence to have eliminated her as a witness.

McCormick, 6th Ed., § 253.

14–67. Dan is charged in two cases, the sexual assault of Ruth and the murder of Whitman. Whitman was an acquaintance of Dan. He came to the attention of the police when he notified them that Dan had made statements to him while drinking heavily at a bar about getting away with the sexual assault that had been all over the papers. The sexual assault of Ruth had occupied headlines for several days in the local paper.

Sometime later Whitman contacted the police and told them that he believed Dan had tried to kill him. As he was walking into his apartment, a cement block came crashing into the sidewalk from high above, missing his head by just a few inches. He said Dan had been acting suspiciously around him since the night after the conversation in the bar and Dan knew how to get onto the roof of the apartment building.

A week after the second conversation, Whitman called the police again. He said that he received a phone call the previous night from a man who did not identify himself who said he would be dead soon if he didn't keep his mouth shut. While the voice was disguised, he recognized it as Dan's.

Shortly after that conversation, Whitman was found stabbed to death in his apartment. A knife lying near the body was identified as the murder weapon. A DNA fragment which matched Dan's was found on the knife.

At the trial of Dan for sexual assault, the prosecution seeks to introduce the first statement under Rule 804(b)(6), and at his trial for murder, it seeks to introduce the other two statements under the same exception.

McCormick, 6th Ed., § 253.

14–68. Joe Smith was charged with sexual molestation of his seven-year-old daughter J.N. while he was in the military stationed in Germany. School officials became concerned by the child's actions and called an army criminal investigator, Walter, to interview the child. The child indicated to Walter that her dad had touched her inappropriately.

Prior to trial, the government discovered J.N. was not available to testify at trial. At the government's request a German subpoena was issued to have her appear, but her mother, Ms. Smith, refused to bring her to court. Ms. Smith had consulted a German attorney, Ms. Linn, who testified that the German subpoena could not be enforced against a family member to testify against a parent. Walter had joint custody of his daughter but testified that his defense counsel advised him not to get involved with securing his daughter's presence at trial and should instead leave the decision to his wife.

The prosecution argues that the statements made to Walter are admissible under the forfeiture through wrongdoing exception and that Joe acquiesced in the wrongdoing of his wife.

McCormick, 6th Ed., § 253.

SECTION L.   THE RESIDUAL OR CATCHALL EXCEPTION

Federal Rule of Evidence 807

14–69. Davis Trucking Co. is defending two lawsuits involving claims that its trucks were defectively designed and maintained.

(A) In the first case, Peter was fatally injured when his tractor-trailer rig ran off the road, overturned, and caught fire. Peter received minor injuries as a result of the crash itself but was fatally burned by the ensuing fire. He survived for several days in the hospital, but ultimately succumbed. His executor brought suit under the state's wrongful death statute on the theory that modifications in the truck design made by Davis resulted in the fuel tank rupturing. Davis defends on the ground that the fire started independently and that the fuel tank only ruptured after the fire spread to it.

Davis offers at trial a statement made by Peter to his friend, Richard, while in the hospital that he was driving along when he saw that the cuff of his pants was on fire. That was the last thing he remembered. Assume that the court rules that the statement is inadmissible under Rule 801(d)(2), Rule 804(b)(3), and other specific exceptions. Defendant argues that it is admissible under Rule 807. How should the court rule?

(B) In a second case, Paul's executor sues Davis on the theory that it defectively maintained the truck Paul was driving, resulting in his death as a consequence of burns after a crash. Specifically, plaintiff contends that the company defectively repaired an air conditioning unit located behind the truck's cab with the result that a fuel line ruptured before the truck crashed, causing the cab to be engulfed in flames, which in turn resulted in the crash. Davis contends that the cause of the accident was driver error, that the fire resulted from the impact, and that no negligence on Davis' part was involved.

Plaintiff offers here a statement made by Paul to his wife while in the hospital after the accident. The statement was as follows: "I'm messed up for life, ain't I Honey? It's stupid. It was all their fault. I told Davis to replace those fuel lines before something awful happened." Assume here also that the court has ruled against admission under Rule 804(b)(2) and other specific exceptions. Is the statement admissible under Rule 807?

McCormick, 6th Ed., § 324.

14–70. Should the following statements, which fail to meet other hearsay exceptions, be admissible under the catchall exception?

(A) Testimony of an unavailable witness made under oath at a hearing to suppress evidence in a criminal case involving a co-defendant where the witness was called and examined by the co-defendant and cross-examined by the prosecutor;

(B) An interview by a social worker of a child who recanted her statement identifying her mother's boyfriend as committing sexual abuse against her where the interview was conducted using non-leading questions, involved events happening recently to the child, and was videotaped;

(C) A written inconsistent statement made by a witness in police custody who was available at trial for cross-examination where the facts of the statement were corroborated by physical evidence and testimony of other witnesses.

McCormick, 6th ed., § 324.

14–71. As attorney for Kale Co., you have begun a suit charging the Osborne Corp. with both patent design infringement and unfair competition by reason of manufacturing and selling ballpoint pens that are exact copies in shape and appearance of Kale's very popular and previously designed model.

Your problem is to show that when members of the public see an Osborne pen they believe it to be a Kale. You could have a large number of people who had been shown the pens testify to a confusion in identification or to misidentification in the sense that they would testify they thought the pen shown to them was a Kale, but this alternative is prohibitively expensive. It might be possible to call experts on design of industrial products who could testify to their opinion of what public confusion would be, but you want to develop and introduce more persuasive evidence.

You have retained an independent and well-known sampling and market research firm, SMR Co., to do a scientific consumer survey, and if favorable, to give the results of such survey at the trial of the case. The content of interviews, the sampling, etc., are to be worked out by SMR. Among other things, SMR proposes to conduct two separate and independent surveys. In Survey A, SMR proposes to show interviewees a Kale pen with all Kale identification marks removed and ask them what brand the pen is, and why. In Survey B, SMR proposes to show interviewees an Osborne pen with all Osborne identification marks removed and ask them what brand the pen is, and why.

You believe that SMR experts could testify at the trial to the method of making the surveys and that the method was fair, in order to establish that the surveys were objectively and scientifically conducted and thus establish their relevancy as foundation for admission of the results of the surveys by the experts.

(A) Is introduction of the results of the surveys objectionable on the basis of the hearsay rule? (The results are that 95% of the interviewees who identified the pen shown to them, whether a Kale or an Osborne, stated it was a Kale.)

(B) Assume alternatively that, after the interviewee examined the pen, the key question in both Survey A and Survey B was what brand he or she *believed* it to be and why. Is the testimony hearsay and should it be admissible?

McCormick, 6th Ed., § 324.

14–72. A local tax exemption of the Danville Community Club depended upon the Club not taking part in political elections or legislative lobbying. State authorities revoked the exemption on the ground that officials of the Club acting for and in the name of the Club had participated substantially in such activities over a period of ten years. In a suit brought by the Club for a declaratory judgment that its exemption had been wrongfully revoked, the Club attorney wished to prove that during the last ten years fewer than 2% of all Club officials had engaged in political elections or legislative lobbying in the name of the Club or acting for the Club. The Club officials included chairmen of committees and subcommittees as well as officers and members of the board of trustees. These officials changed every year. At the attorney's request, the current Club president, who is a statistician, took a poll. The poll was taken by means of the following letter, which was sent to all Club officials over the ten-year period.

> Dear _____:
>
> State authorities have revoked the state tax exemption granted to the Danville Community Club years ago on the ground that Club officials, including possibly yourself, have substantially engaged in activities in political elections and in legislative lobbying on the behalf of and in the name of the Club. State authorities are not questioning activity of our officials in political elections or legislative lobbying generally, but have revoked the exemption on the charge of such activity on behalf and in the name of our Club. The Club contends that any such activity by its officials was not on behalf and in the name of the Club and has brought a suit in court to challenge the revocation of the exemption. The purpose of this letter is to ascertain whether any political activity or lobbying activity while such persons were in office in our Club was conducted on behalf and in the name of our Club. The results of this poll will be used in our current lawsuit.
>
> As you may not know, if the Club is unsuccessful in its lawsuit, taxes of approximately $30,000.00 annually on our property are involved, which would take a large chunk of our budget. It may be that your memory is not too good as to activities quite far back, but please do your best in responding to the questionnaire which is attached.
>
> Thank you for your cooperation.

The questionnaire read as follows:

> 1. Were you a Club officer, director, committee chairman or subcommittee chairman of the Danville Community Club at any time during the past ten years? Yes___ No___

2.   If the answer to the above question is in the affirmative, did you at any time while you were such an official of the Club take part in any activity of any kind whatsoever in connection with any elections for political office of any kind? Yes___ No___

3.   If you answer the above question in the affirmative, did you engage in any such activity on behalf and in the name of the Club? Yes___ No___

Questions 4 and 5 were similar to questions 3 and 4 except that they referred to lobbying activities before specifically named legislative bodies.

The letter was sent to the 250 former officials in the ten-year time period and 102 questionnaires were returned. Eighty percent of these former officials were still members of the Club. Of these, 35 indicated political activity or lobbying, and of these 35, one indicated such activity on behalf or in the name of the Club. The president extrapolated these figures and concluded that fewer than 2% of all officials had engaged in the described activity on behalf and in the name of the Club during the ten-year period. Should plaintiff's attorney anticipate that he can introduce the results of the poll and the opinion of the statistician at the trial?

McCormick, 6th ed., § 324.

14–73.   Frank was prosecuted in federal court for receiving three new stolen tractors. He entered a plea of not guilty. The prosecutor can establish the following by evidence apart from the evidence involved in this problem. The three tractors were to be shipped from the manufacturer's plant in Michigan to a buyer in Nebraska. Transfer Trucking Co. received the tractors from the manufacturer in Michigan for hauling to Nebraska. Truckman, the driver of the truck, had authority from Transfer to make a one night stop-over in Clearview, Iowa with relatives. The tractors disappeared and were never delivered to the buyer in Nebraska.

F.B.I. agents can testify that Frank had possession of the tractors in a secluded area in Kansas. Agents also can state that Frank had equipment at this location for repainting the tractors and for changing their serial numbers and adding Kansas license plates on the tractors. Frank sold the tractors for $15,000 each, although the current manufacturer's list price was $50,000 each.

Truckman was arrested by the police in Wyoming for an alleged offense unconnected with the instant prosecution. After his arrest, he escaped and his present whereabouts have not been discovered by the police or the F.B.I.

(A)   The prosecutor wants to call F.B.I. Agent Waldo as a witness. Waldo would testify that before Truckman was arrested Waldo interviewed him. Truckman stated that while he was driving the truck loaded with the three tractors he stopped overnight in Clearview to visit a relative. He parked the truck on a vacant lot a block from where his relative lived. The next morning the three tractors were gone, although the truck was still in the vacant lot. He immediately notified the local police, the Iowa State Patrol, and his employer.

Can the prosecutor successfully introduce testimony of Waldo to this effect?

(B) The prosecutor also knows that Richard, also an F.B.I. agent, can testify that before the three tractors were discovered, a reliable informant told Richard that the F.B.I. should investigate Frank's rural place in Kansas because the three stolen tractors were there.

As a result, F.B.I. agents "staked out" Frank's place, observed Kansas license plates being attached to the three tractors, and were able to follow Frank's subsequent dealings with the tractors. Can the prosecutor successfully introduce Richard's testimony with regard to the informant's statements?

(C) Before the trial the prosecutor planned to call Anthony as a witness to testify that he worked at Frank's place in Kansas for a short time, that he saw the three tractors in question hauled into that place on a truck, and that he affixed Kansas license plates to the tractors after being ordered to do so by Frank. Anthony previously testified to the above facts before the grand jury in the case. However, the night before the trial Anthony told an F.B.I. agent that he would not testify at the trial at all. The agent asked whether he had been threatened by associates of Frank. Anthony said that he was afraid for his life and added, "You get the idea."

The next day, during the first day of the trial, the prosecutor asked that the jury be recessed so that he could have the judge determine whether he could introduce Anthony's grand jury testimony. In the absence of the jury, the prosecutor called Anthony to the stand. Anthony said he would not testify at the trial on the ground of his privilege against self-incrimination. The prosecutor then told the judge he was authorized to grant proper and appropriate immunity to the witness. Then, when asked, Anthony said that his testimony before the grand jury was true, but he persisted in saying he would not testify at the trial. The judge cited him for contempt and eventually sent him to jail. The prosecutor then introduced the conversation of the F.B.I. agent with Anthony the night before and asked for an advance ruling on the admissibility of the record of Anthony's testimony before the grand jury. The prosecutor also informed the judge that he had furnished a transcript of Anthony's grand jury testimony to Frank's attorney just before he had asked that the jury be recessed on the first day of the trial, but that he would not attempt to introduce it, if the judge permitted it to be introduced, until the third day of the trial.

What should the judge's advance ruling be? In answering this question, consider, among other matters whether the Sixth Amendment right of confrontation would be violated if the grand jury testimony mentioned were introduced against the defendant.

McCormick, 6th Ed., § 324.

14–74. Able, Baker, Cindy, and Dot were indicted for conspiracy to possess and distribute cocaine. In the same indictment Able was indicted for aiding and abetting Baker in the possession of cocaine with the intent to distribute it. Baker, Cindy, and Dot entered a guilty plea to the conspiracy charge and a judgment of conviction was entered against each of them. At the trial of Able, through the testimony of F.B.I. agents, the government showed that all four of these individuals were in an auto being driven by Baker that was under F.B.I. observation. The auto was driven into an unlighted cemetery and parked, whereupon Baker got out and passed a package (which contained cocaine) to Homer, who had suddenly come on the scene out of the darkness. As Homer was about to hand cash to Baker, the police appeared and arrested all five of them.

The government also has handwritten statements of Baker and Dot which were made to F.B.I. agents after they entered guilty pleas. Both statements waived constitutional rights that were specified in the written documents and stated that Able, Baker, Cindy, and Dot had together bought the cocaine in question to sell and that all four were in the automobile at the scene of the attempted sale to Homer so all four could see that the cocaine was delivered and, upon receipt of the money, divide the money equally. Baker's statement was in the form of an affidavit. Dot's statement was unsworn but signed by her.

With these statements in hand at the trial, the government called Cindy to the stand who testified of her own knowledge to the effect indicated in the written statements of Baker and Dot. Without objection, the defense attorney brought out that, upon her conviction, she had been given a suspended sentence.

The judge then called Baker to the stand (on the basis of a previous request of the government that he do so). In answer to questioning by the prosecution, he testified that on the above-mentioned night he and Cindy, a long-time "girlfriend," were on a "double-date" with Able and Dot, who were in the back seat of the auto. Baker stated that he and Cindy owned the cocaine and intended to deliver it that night, as they were attempting to do when they were caught. Neither Able nor Dot knew of the presence of cocaine in the front seat of the car. To his knowledge Able and Dot would not even know cocaine if they saw it. The government then questioned him about the existence of his prior statement. He admitted making it, but denied the statements in it were true. On questioning by the defense attorney, Baker stated that his prior statement was false insofar as it dealt with Able and Dot and that he had lied because he hoped to get future leniency if he gave the government "some more fall guys." Furthermore, prior to the graveyard incident, he was convinced that Able had been going out with his girlfriend, Cindy, and he was determined to get even and also stop their affair while he was "put away." He testified that as far as he knew Able had never had anything to do with drugs of any kind.

The judge then called Dot to the stand at the request of the government. Under questioning by the prosecutor, Dot testified that she never had the slightest thing to do with cocaine, that she did not know what Baker was doing when he got out of the car in the cemetery or that he was then carrying anything. When the government called her attention to her above-mentioned statement and its contents, she admitted making it but denied it was true. The defense attorney then bought out her testimony that she had lied in the statement because she was mad at Able since she had found out he had been having sexual relations with Cindy. In any event, from the time of her arrest, she knew she was innocent, but thought it hopeless to fight the government. And she had figured she would not "get much time" if she was convicted.

The government then introduced testimony of the F.B.I. agents who took statements of Baker and Dot that both had given their statements freely and voluntarily and, as to Dot, "with gusto."

Over objections of the defense attorney, the statements of Baker and Dot were introduced into evidence and read to the jury.

During the above proceedings the defense attorney made timely requests that the judge instruct the jury that they were to consider the prior written statements of Baker and Dot only for impeachment purposes. The judge denied these requests.

Were the judge's rulings in the last two paragraphs correct?

McCormick, 6th Ed., § 324.

14–75. (A) Paul is suing State University for false arrest in connection with his arrest for shoplifting a notebook at the Student Stores. The University contends that Paul hid the notebook under his sweater and was attempting to leave the store without paying. Paul, in his complaint, contends that he never put the notebook under his sweater and that the arrest was in retaliation for his refusal to go quietly when falsely accused of shoplifting. Both sides agree that Paul never left the store with the notebook and had it in his hands in full view at least after he was approached by Ralph, the clerk who witnessed the incident.

Paul wishes to introduce an affidavit of Williams, the campus ombudsman, who died before litigation began. Williams interviewed Ralph in connection with the ombudsman's efforts to mediate the dispute. According to Williams' affidavit, Ralph said that he "thought" he saw Paul stick a notebook under his sweater but that Paul probably would not have been arrested had he not used abusive language and refused to leave the store peacefully after being confronted. The affidavit was provided to Paul, Ralph and to the vice president of the University in charge of Student Stores' operations as part of the mediation effort. No resolution, however, was reached of the dispute at that level.

The University moves to exclude the affidavit generally under Rule 807. It also contends specifically that admission should be denied on the basis of a failure to give notice of an intention to offer the affidavit until the day it was proffered to the court. How should the court rule?

(B) Assume that the University's defense is that indeed it did have Campus Police arrest Paul for trespassing instead of shoplifting. It took that action based on a telephone conversation with Smith, the general counsel for the municipal police department while Paul was in the store protesting his treatment. Smith, according to the Store's manager, stated, "Sure you can have the kid arrested if he won't leave peacefully." Knowing that a suit was likely, the store manager had Smith execute an affidavit reciting that statement. Assume that if established these facts would constitute a full defense to a civil action based on false arrest.

At trial, Smith testifies that he told the manager that if the student refused to leave after being given proper notice or if he had been previously barred from the premises, then he could be arrested. His statements are thus inconsistent with the affidavit. The defendant seeks to have the affidavit admitted under Rule 807, having provided plaintiff with advance notice of that intention. Plaintiff's counsel argues against admissibility generally and, among other arguments, contends that this exception should not provide a backdoor method of introducing prior inconsistent statements substantively. How should the court rule?

McCormick, 6th Ed., § 324.

14–76. You are a state legislator. Under state case law, hearsay evidence, including prior statements of a witness offered for substantive purposes, is inadmissible unless it comes within a traditional exception to the hearsay rule. A bill is introduced in the legislature (taken from the Model Code of Evidence) which states:

> Evidence of a hearsay declaration is admissible if the judge finds that the declarant (1) is unavailable as a witness, or (2) is present and subject to cross-examination.

Would you vote for such a bill? In determining your vote, consider the constitutionality of the proposal.

McCormick, 6th Ed., §§ 325–27.

TOPIC 6

PRIVILEGE

. . .

CHAPTER 15

PROTECTING RELATIONSHIPS BY MEANS OF PRIVILEGE

■ ■ ■

SECTION A. MARITAL PRIVILEGES

15–1. James and Betty had been married but they were supposedly divorced at the time of the trial mentioned below. There was some question concerning the validity of their divorce. James was charged with larceny for allegedly stealing an automobile. According to local procedure, Betty was listed as a witness for the state. At the beginning of trial, the defense attorney requested a hearing before the judge in the absence of the jury on the question of whether James and Betty were presently married at the time of the trial. The judge denied the request, stating, "We'll take care of that if and when she is called to the stand." In the presentation of the state's case, the prosecutor called Betty to the stand and defendant immediately objected to the taking of her testimony. He was then permitted to ask her questions relating to her marital status with respect to James. These were put to her only after the judge denied his request that the jury be first temporarily excused from the courtroom. Without regard to the court's ruling on the validity of the divorce, were the judge's other rulings correct? Suppose that defendant's attorney had not requested a hearing at the beginning of the trial.

McCormick, 6th Ed., § 66; Federal Rules of Evidence 501, 601; Uniform Rule of Evidence 504.

15–2. Hal and Wanda were legally married. The couple undertook the care of a foster child, Chris, age two. Shortly thereafter, Hal told Wanda that he was leaving her to marry Tina. Wanda then began divorce proceedings. While these proceedings were still pending, Hal told Tina that his divorce was final and proposed that they be married immediately. Tina agreed and she and Hal went through a marriage ceremony that she believed to be valid but which in fact was bigamous. Wanda knew that Hal was living with Tina, and occasionally prevailed on Hal to keep Chris for short periods. When she picked up Chris on one such occasion, she remarked to Hal about severe bruises on Chris' face. Hal responded that "Tina said she had to give him a couple of whacks to shut him up."

234

The state is now prosecuting Tina for child abuse. As prosecutor, you expect Tina to testify that Chris sustained the bruising due to a fall downstairs. The jurisdiction in which the case will be tried has both forms of marital privilege. If Tina testifies as expected, how would you argue in support of your contention that neither privilege should prevent your calling Hal to impeach Tina's testimony.

Assume Hal testifies but denies Tina ever stated that Chris' injuries were caused other than by a fall. Would either marital privilege bar Wanda from testifying as to Hal's statement to her?

McCormick, 6th Ed., §§ 66, 81–84; Federal Rule of Evidence 501; Uniform Rule of Evidence 504.

15–3. Assume that a governing statute provides for certain exceptions to the statutory privilege concerning the testifying by one spouse against the other. One of these exceptions creates an exception for the situation that is described as follows, " * * * criminal actions for crimes committed by one against the other * * *."

(A) Jim was prosecuted for embezzling funds owned individually by his wife while they were married. Could he make a successful pretrial motion that the prosecutor be prohibited from calling his wife (from whom he is separated but not divorced) to the stand to testify against him? Assume that the wife will object to taking the stand.

(B) Assume that Jim embezzled his wife's funds before they were married. He and his wife were married two days before the trial. The prosecutor has some evidence that, just before the marriage, Jim paid his wife about half of the allegedly embezzled amount. The day before the trial, the defendant's attorney moves that the prosecutor be prohibited from calling his wife to the stand. Again assume that the wife will object to taking the witness stand. Should the motion be granted?

McCormick, 6th Ed., §§ 66, 84; Federal Rule of Evidence 501; Uniform Rule of Evidence 504.

15–4. The charge against James in Problem 15–1, above, was that he had stolen an automobile, altered the motor number to correspond to the motor number of a similar wrecked automobile, and had obtained transfer of title of that car to another person. The state produced a title transfer application signed, "James Briscolte, by (wife) Jane Briscolte."

After Betty was called to the stand and objection to her testifying was overruled, she testified that she was married to James but was separated from him because he had "moved out of the house permanently." She further stated that, while they were separated, (1) she went with her husband to the courthouse and applied for a license and certificate of title to an automobile and identified the application set forth in the indictment as the one she had made out and filed; (2) that Briscolte was not her name, nor her husband's name, and that she knew no such person; (3) that neither she nor her husband lived at the address given in the application for "Briscolte;" (4) that she did not know that any "Briscolte" had ever had any transaction to acquire title from the person listed as the former owner; and (5) that her husband waited in the automobile outside the courthouse while she applied for the license and transfer of title. Was any of this testimony subject to successful objection?

McCormick, 6th Ed., §§ 78–81, 84–86; Federal Rule of Evidence 501; Uniform Rule of Evidence 504.

15–5. William is charged with the murder of Phillip. As part of the state's proof, the prosecutor offers the testimony of William's wife, Mary (now divorced from him), concerning the disposition of Phillip's body. Assume alternately each of the following stories by Mary. At the time of each of these incidents William and Mary were married and living together. Could the prosecutor anticipate that at the trial she could successfully introduce the testimony of Mary as to each of the following incidents?

(A) While Mary was working on her garden plants in their fenced and very secluded back yard, William came in carrying a body and, without a word, buried it, all in Mary's presence. In the alternative, suppose the body was that of Mary's current "boyfriend." In the alternative, suppose their four-year-old child also was present.

(B) One night after William and Mary went to bed, Mary awakened and her husband was not in bed. She called him and there was no answer. She got out of bed to search for him, and heard a sound in the back yard. She went out into the yard and found William, about to lower a human body (her "boyfriend's" body) into a hole dug in the yard. When she came upon the scene, William said, "Well, I made sure you won't go out with him anymore."

McCormick, 6th Ed. §§ 79, 80; Federal Rule of Evidence 501; Uniform Rule of Evidence 504.

15–6. Alexander, John and Richard were indicted in federal court for a conspiracy to possess and sell crack cocaine. Lenore, Alexander's wife, was an unindicted co-conspirator. Before the trial, Alexander's counsel moved for a ruling that Lenore could not be called to testify against him or that, in the alternative, if she was permitted to testify, for the exclusion of any testimony on her part with regard to his oral communications to her made in confidence and within the common law rules of the privilege regarding confidential communications between husband and wife.

At the hearing on defendant's motion, the following matters were brought to the attention of the judge: Lenore would not object to testifying. Upon being confronted by F.B.I. agents about her activities, Lenore agreed to cooperate fully with the authorities in a future prosecution of Alexander concerning the alleged conspiracy. The conspiracy allegedly began a short time after her marriage to Alexander and continued for two years. Since the indictment she has not lived with Alexander, who is free on bail. She states that she intends to have nothing to do with him ever again, but that she has no plans for a divorce.

(A) How should the judge rule on the motion to keep Lenore off the witness stand?

(B) Suppose that the judge ruled that Lenore could take the stand and that at the trial, she was called by the prosecutor. She is then asked whether she had told another individual, Donald, of directions she had given Alexander during and in furtherance of the conspiracy and of some directions Alexander had given to her. Could either Alexander or Lenore object to questions put to Lenore as to what these directions were?

(C) Assume that Lenore can take the stand over objection and that Alexander and Lenore had a conversation in a motel room in furtherance of the alleged conspiracy. Danny, who was in the next motel room, heard relevant parts of the conversation because both his window and the window in the couple's room were open. Assuming the judge would decide generally that the privilege against revelation of confidential communications applies, could the prosecutor ask Danny to testify to Alexander's communications to his wife? Could the prosecutor ask Lenore to repeat those communications?

McCormick, 6th Ed., §§ 66, 78, 82–84, 86; Federal Rules of Evidence 501, 601; Uniform Rule of Evidence 504.

15–7. Don was badly injured in a multi-vehicle automobile accident. Following the accident Don was taken to a local hospital where he was treated for multiple fractures and placed in traction in a private room. The day following the accident, Don was visited at the hospital by his wife, Betty. Don indicated by gestures for Betty to approach close to his bed. When she did so he whispered to her statements strongly suggesting that the accident was caused by his [Don's] fault. Don is subsequently sued civilly for damages. Under the law of your jurisdiction, may Betty testify, over Don's objection, as to Don's statements to her? Would your answer be different if any one of the following additional facts were true?

1. Betty is willing to testify for the plaintiff because, based on Don's statements, she believes Don is morally responsible for the accident.

2. Betty brought with her the couple's five-year-old son with her when she visited Don, and was holding the son by the hand when Don whispered to her.

3. A nurse employed by the hospital was engaged in giving Don an injection at the time of Don's statement.

4. Don's statement was overheard by a police officer in the hall on his way to visit Don as part of his investigation of the accident.

McCormick, 6th Ed., §§ 80, 82–83; Federal Rule of Evidence 501; Uniform Rule of Evidence 504.

15–8. Harry meets with David to discuss the terms of a contract between businesses owned by the two of them. The negotiations are difficult and there is some animosity between the parties. During a break in the meeting, Harry steps into the hallway and calls his wife, Bea, on his cell phone simply to vent his frustration over the progress of the negotiations. Bea is herself a successful business person, although her business is entirely separate from her husband's. Nevertheless, he values her opinion and goes into some detail concerning the terms being negotiated. Unknown to either Harry or Bea, the transmission of their cell phone conversation is overheard by another cell phone user, Edward, who is using his phone in his car a couple of blocks away from Bea's office.

After the telephone conversation, Bea goes into her office coffee room for a break. She meets George, a colleague. As a matter of conversation, she relates her husband's negotiation problems to George. Although George has no personal interest in the matter, he does have some advice for Harry. Bea thinks the advice is useful and, when she returns to her office, she e-mails Harry giving him George's thoughts. She copies George on the e-mail.

During another break in the negotiations, Harry sees Bea's message on his laptop computer. He replies to her, giving more details about the contract terms. Although he intends the e-mail to go only to Bea, and not to George, he inadvertently replies to all recipients, i.e., George as well as Bea.

The contract with David was finally signed. However, a dispute occurred with regard to its terms and Harry wound up suing David for breach. The intent of the parties as to the contract terms is relevant to the law suit. Assume that David finds out about Edward's interception of the cell phone conversation, George's conversations with Bea, and Harry's reply to both Bea and George. David calls both Edward and George as witnesses. Can he examine either or both with regard to these conversations over an objection raised by Harry based on the marital communications privilege?

McCormick, 6th Ed. §§ 80, 82–83; Federal Rule of Evidence 501; Uniform Rule of Evidence 504.

SECTION B. THE CLIENT'S PRIVILEGE

15–9. (A) After various negotiations during which each was represented by his own attorney, Sam and John entered into a written contract. Alan acted only as attorney for Sam. In a subsequent suit for breach of the contract brought by John against Sam, could John's attorney successfully require Sam to produce the following documents?

1. The original copy of the contract which is in Alan's possession.

2. A preliminary draft of the contract prepared by Alan for discussion with Sam. The draft differs substantially both from the final contract and from any draft submitted to John during the negotiations.

3. A letter from Sam to Alan discussing Sam's difficulties with John in connection with the performance of the contract.

4. A letter from Sam to Alan reminding Alan to be sure to file the contract as required by the Uniform Commercial Code.

5. A witness' statement, signed by John, which Alan had obtained from John before commencement of the suit.

6. A memorandum prepared by Alan in which he recorded his own version of a conversation he had with John prior to the suit.

(B) Suppose that the witness statement obtained by Alan in Part (A)–5, above, had been obtained by Alan from John in a conversation with John, although at the time of the conversation John was represented by an attorney in the matter, that this fact was known by Alan and that, at the time of the conversation, the occurrence of the conversation was unknown to John's attorney. Would your answer as to Part (A)–5, above, be affected?

(C) In the suit for breach of contract, Sam contended that John was mentally incompetent at the time of the making of the contract. At the trial, over objection, could Alan, Sam's attorney, elicit the testimony of the attorney acting for John at the time of the making of the contract concerning peculiar actions and statements by John and the attorney's opinion that John at the time of making the contract was mentally incompetent to carry on any business? Assume that John's attorney at the time of making the contract is also John's attorney at the trial.

McCormick, 6th Ed., §§ 89–91, 96; Federal Rule of Evidence 501; Uniform Rule of Evidence 502.

15–10. Assume the same facts as in Problem 15–8, above, dealing with marital privileges. Instead of calling his wife on his cell phone, Harry calls his lawyer, Marjorie, seeking legal advice. The conversation concerns the terms of the contract and their legal implications. As in Problem 15–8, above, his cell phone conversation is overheard by Edward.

After the cell phone conversation with Harry, Marjorie confers with another lawyer in her office, Elliott, concerning the legal aspects of Harry's situation. She also consults a business advisor, Lois, on Harry's behalf, asking her for tactical, but clearly non-legal, advice in Harry's negotiation process. She communicates that advice to Harry via e-mail, sending copies of the e-mail to Lois and to Elliott. Harry responds to her e-mail, seeking additional legal and non-legal advice, with copies to both Lois and Elliott.

In the law suit referred to in Problem 15–8, above, can David call Edward, Marjorie, Elliott and/or Lois to testify with regard to the content of these communications over objections from Harry based on the attorney-client privilege?

McCormick, 6th Ed., §§ 91, 93; Federal Rule of Evidence 501; Uniform Rule of Evidence 502.

15–11. Underwood is vice-president and general counsel of Victor Shipping Co., Inc., a small trucking firm. His duties require him to act both as the company's lawyer and as a general trouble-shooter for non-legal problems. About 40 percent of Underwood's time is spent on non-legal matters.

One of the trucks owned by Victor and operated by its employee, Laughlin, was involved in an accident in which the driver of the car colliding with the truck, Craig, was badly injured. Shortly after the accident, Underwood, as part of company routine, obtained a statement from Laughlin concerning the accident. Craig has now sued both Laughlin and Victor Shipping. In the litigation, both Laughlin and Victor are represented by an attorney selected by Victor's insurance company. Laughlin's statement to Underwood is still in the company files. Craig's attorney seeks production of the statement. Victor's trial attorney objects, raising the attorney-client privilege on behalf of both Laughlin and Victor. What ruling by the judge? What ruling if Underwood had turned over the report to the trial attorney?

McCormick, 6th Ed., §§ 87–93, 96; Federal Rule of Evidence 501; Uniform Rule of Evidence 502.

15–12. Peter brings an action against Dr. David and Charity Hospital to recover damages for personal injuries sustained when Peter fell in his hospital room following surgery. Peter's complaint alleged negligence on the part of both defendants. Following Peter's fall, the hospital undertook an inquiry into the incident directed by Atlee, its Director of Risk Management. Atlee is an attorney and a salaried employee of the hospital whose duties include procuring and maintaining liability insurance for the hospital, supervising its safety programs, and procuring outside legal counsel for defending claims when necessary. Through inquiries directed to all departments of the hospital, Atlee discovered that Diane, an employee of the hospital's food service department, observed Peter's fall while engaged in distributing the daily menu to patient rooms. Atlee interviewed Diane, cautioning her at the time not to discuss the incident with others because litigation might result. Atlee stamped the written statement obtained from Diane "Confidential" and kept it in a locked file in his office until he delivered it to outside counsel employed to defend the hospital in the suit brought by Peter. Atlee did supply a copy of the statement to the attorney retained by Dr. David to represent his interests in the same suit. This action was taken before outside counsel had been retained by the hospital.

If Peter's attorney seeks production of the statement from the hospital's trial counsel before trial what arguments might he or she raise as to why the statement should not be considered to be within the attorney-client privilege?

McCormick, 6th Ed., §§ 87.1, 88, 91; Federal Rule of Evidence 501; Uniform Rule of Evidence 502.

15–13. Dairyland is under investigation for antitrust violations involving price fixing. (*See* Problem 13–46, above.) The Board of Directors orders its Vice–President and General Counsel (who is also the company's one-person in-house legal staff), Sheila, to investigate the allegations. Although she intends to hire outside counsel to represent the company in connection with any charges that might be brought, Sheila does not hire outside counsel before beginning her investigation. She decides to talk to various company employees concerning the company's activities that might have a bearing on price fixing. Because the task is too large for her to undertake by herself, she asks two staff members to help her. One of the staff members, John, works as an investigator in Sheila's office. The other, Margaret, works for the president of the corporation. Neither John nor Margaret is a lawyer.

All three of the investigators for the company, Sheila, John and Margaret, begin their conversations with the employees as follows:

The company is concerned about an ongoing investigation of its pricing activities. In particular, we are concerned that we may be sued either by the government or by private individuals for price fixing. Our legal staff and, eventually, outside counsel need to have as full a picture of our pricing activities as possible to help the company defend against these charges. I want to ask you some questions concerning the company's pricing activities. Please understand that the legal staff of the company does not represent you personally, but that we are seeking your help in defending the company against these allegations.

Two groups of employees are interviewed:

1. **The officers of the corporation—the president and five vice-presidents:** Some of the officers, including the president and vice-president for marketing, have had direct involvement in the company's pricing policies. Other officers, for example the vice-president for operations, have had no direct involvement in the pricing policies. However, they have talked to the other officers about certain pricing decisions and communications with other companies and relate the substance of those conversations to a member of the investigating team.

2. **Lower level employees, such as sales people and assistants within the marketing department:** Again, some of these employees have had direct involvement in the company's pricing policies. Others have had no such involvement but are generally aware of the policies and activities based upon conversations with other company employees.

Sheila compiles a report based upon the interviews. A copy of the report is sent to the members of the Board of Directors and to all of the officers of the corporation. After reviewing the document, copies are made for and distributed to certain lower level employees, including several assistant vice-presidents for marketing.

Dairyland is eventually sued by a private party for antitrust violations. Plaintiff seeks to discover Sheila's report. Is it protected in whole or in part by the attorney-client privilege?

McCormick, 6th Ed., §§ 87.1, 88, 91, 93; Federal Rule of Evidence 501; Uniform Rule of Evidence 502.

15–14. Dagnan is involved in a motor vehicle accident which results in extensive property damage and serious personal injuries to the occupants of the other vehicle involved. At the scene, the investigating officer informed Dagnan that he would probably be charged with operating a motor vehicle under the influence of alcohol. The following day, Dagnan retained Athos to represent him in the event criminal charges arose from the accident. Following his contact with Athos, Dagnan informed his liability insurance carrier, Insco, of the accident. Insco immediately dispatched an investigator to meet with Dagnan and take his statement. In the statement, Dagnan admitted that he had drunk three "doubles" in the half hour preceding the accident. Insco then settled all claims for personal injury and property damage arising from the accident. Dagnan was subsequently charged with operating under the influence. In preparing for trial, Athos requested and received from Insco a copy of Dagnan's statement to Insco's investigator. The prosecution has now attempted to subpoena the statement from Athos. Prepare an argument in support of an action to quash the subpoena on the ground that the statement is within the attorney-client privilege.

McCormick, 6th Ed., §§ 91, 96; Federal Rule of Evidence 501; Uniform Rule of Evidence 502.

15–15. In the situation outlined in Problem 15–11, above, Craig's attorney arranged by telephone for Dr. Susan Lirk, an orthopedic surgeon, to examine Craig, not for treatment, but to ascertain the exact nature, extent, and results of injuries Craig suffered in the accident. The attorney then telephoned Craig and requested he make a specific appointment date with Dr. Lirk for the above-stated purpose. Craig did so. After the examination, Dr. Lirk made a written report of the examination to Craig's attorney concerning the nature, extent, and results of Craig's injuries caused by the accident. Plaintiff did not list Dr. Lirk as an expert to be called at the trial under the applicable rule of civil procedure (assume a rule identical to Federal Rule of Civil Procedure 26) and plaintiff in fact has no intention of calling her as a witness. The trial court refused to issue an order that defendant's attorney be permitted to examine Dr. Lirk by deposition or any other means. Suppose that Victor's [the defendant's] attorney anticipates that the plaintiff's attorney will introduce the testimony of the plaintiff himself concerning his injuries as well as the testimony of plaintiff's treating physician. The testimony concerning plaintiff's injuries will be quite complete. However, neither Dr. Lirk nor anything concerning her examination will be mentioned at the trial. Should Victor's attorney anticipate that he can call Dr. Lirk as a witness and examine Dr. Lirk concerning the facts discovered by Dr. Lirk in her examination of plaintiff Craig and her conclusions from that examination? Would it be sensible for Victor's attorney to call Dr. Lirk on the facts recited above?

McCormick, 6th Ed., §§ 88–89, 91, 93, 96; Federal Rule of Evidence 501; Uniform Rule of Evidence 502; Federal Rule of Civil Procedure 26.

15–16. A pedestrian, John, also was involved in the accident described in Problem 15–11, above. Plaintiff's attorney would very much like to take John's deposition. He has reason to believe that John is located somewhere in the state in which the suit is brought and suspects John, for unknown reasons, is concealing his whereabouts. He has heard from a reliable source, however, that shortly after the accident John visited the office of an attorney, William. William will not tell plaintiff's attorney anything about John. He is therefore considering taking William's deposition. He anticipates that William will refuse to answer questions, based on the attorney-client privilege, about whether or not he knows John, and that even if he admitted knowing John, he would refuse to answer a question as to his whereabouts. Should plaintiff's counsel anticipate that he can successfully obtain a court order requiring William to answer such questions?

McCormick, 6th Ed., § 90; Federal Rule of Evidence 501; Uniform Rule of Evidence 502.

15–17. Daniel believed he was a suspect in connection with a bank robbery. He consulted with Alfred, an attorney, concerning the matter. However, Daniel was not charged with the robbery and did not continue to employ Alfred as his lawyer.

However, sometime later, Cal was arrested for the robbery in question and he retained Alfred as his attorney.

Alfred was subpoenaed to appear before a grand jury investigating the robbery. He was asked whether or not Daniel had consulted with him at any time after the robbery. He was asked if Daniel had retained him to act for Daniel in connection with the grand jury investigation of the robbery. He was asked if anyone had paid him a fee or promised him a fee to represent Daniel in connection with the grand jury investigation of the robbery. Alfred refused to reply to all of these questions on the basis of the attorney-client privilege.

In addition, Alfred was asked, "Who retained you to represent Cal after he was arrested?" "Did Daniel employ you to represent Cal?" "Did Daniel give you the funds which you deposited as bail for Cal?" Alfred also refused to answer each of these questions on the ground of the attorney-client privilege.

Can the prosecutor successfully obtain a court order that Alfred answer all of the above questions? Assuming that such a court order is obtained, and that Alfred continues to refuse to answer, can Alfred be punished for contempt? As a related question, if the court orders Alfred to answer, should he answer, or should he refuse to do so and suffer the citation for contempt?

McCormick, 6th Ed., §§ 90, 92; Federal Rule of Evidence 501; Uniform Rule of Evidence 502.

15–18. In the contract situation involved in Problem 15–9, above, during the negotiations for the contract between Sam and John, Alan had a conference with his client, Sam, concerning the proposed contract. Sam brought his uncle, Addie, to be present as his business adviser. However, Addie was not paid or employed in any formal way by Sam in this matter or in any other business matter of Sam's. John's attorney knows that at the trial of the suit he will have to depend for success upon the interpretation of a very ambiguous clause in the contract and that oral evidence concerning the pertinent intention of the parties will be admissible under the parol evidence rule. He has talked with Addie who had a "falling out" with Sam after the above-mentioned conference between Alan and Sam. Addie has expressed a willingness to testify that Sam expressed an intention at the conference relevant to the ambiguous contract clause. The intention would be very favorable to John's case at a forthcoming trial. Can John's attorney successfully obtain Addie's testimony at the trial concerning the conference with Alan? Although he probably would not wish to do so, could he call Alan, who represents Sam at the trial, to testify to these statements made by Sam to Alan?

Alternatively, assume that Sam brought his wife, Jean, to the conference with Alan instead of his uncle. Sam indicated to Alan at the time that Jean often advised him as to business matters. Sam and Jean have now separated and Jean is willing to testify for John as to what transpired at the conference with Alan. Any different result?

McCormick, 6th Ed., §§ 91–92; Federal Rule of Evidence 501; Uniform Rule of Evidence 502.

15–19. After the trial of the contract suit between Sam and John (*see* Problems 15–9 and 15–18, above) ended in a judgment for John, Alan, Sam's attorney, retired from the practice of law. His law office, equipment, and files were taken over by George. By arrangement with many of Alan's clients, his practice was continued by George. Alan died shortly after giving up his practice. Later, Sam became involved in another breach of contract suit, this time against Robert. After the suit against Robert was commenced, Sam died and the executor of his estate was substituted as plaintiff. Sam, and now Sam's estate, are represented by Lois. George has had nothing to do with this action or with its subject matter. The contract with Robert incorporates, by specific reference to the Sam–John contract, the ambiguous clause mentioned in Problem 15–18, above. The attorney for Robert, Beverly, has learned that Alan's file with respect to the Sam–John contract matter, which is now in George's office, contains a letter from Sam to Alan with respect to Sam's intent as to the pertinent ambiguous clause in the Sam–John contract. Can Robert's attorney successfully secure the production of this letter in George's file for inspection prior to trial?

McCormick, 6th Ed., § 94; Federal Rule of Evidence 501; Uniform Rule of Evidence 502.

15–20. Duce, a wealthy man, died testate, bequeathing the bulk of his fortune to charity. Wilda, who was once married to Duce but divorced from him several years before Duce's death, brings suit against the estate. Wilda alleges that at the time of the divorce she was induced to accept a modest property settlement because Duce promised to bequeath her the sum of $1,000,000 on his death. After filing her suit, Wilda sought to depose Atticus, the attorney who had represented Duce in the divorce, concerning his discussions with Duce at the time of the divorce. Wilda also seeks production by Atticus of any wills or codicils prepared for Duce by Atticus between the date of the divorce and Duce's death. If counsel for the estate objects to such testimony and production by Atticus, how should the court rule? Would your answer be different if Wilda's attorney should produce either:

(a) An affidavit from Stella, Atticus' former secretary, that she typed several of Duce's earlier wills and is familiar with their contents.

(b) Affidavits from three individuals who had served as witnesses to earlier wills of Duce to the effect that Duce insisted on reading the text of the will aloud in the presence of the witnesses before executing it.

McCormick, 6th Ed., §§ 91, 93–94; Federal Rule of Evidence 501; Uniform Rule of Evidence 502.

15–21. Megaworks Corporation is an enormous, publicly held corporation. Steven, owner of 100 shares, has brought a shareholders derivative action on behalf of Megaworks against the principal officers and the members of the Board of Directors of the corporation. Steven charges that the officers and directors manipulated the price of the stock of the corporation by various means, including the fraudulent alteration of financial reports. His complaint has survived a motion to dismiss for failure to state a claim. The parties are now in the discovery stage. Although they were originally represented by the same law firm, Harrison & Hall, the individual officers and directors now have their own lawyers and a separate firm has been hired to represent the corporation itself.

(A) Steven seeks to discover copies of various memoranda passing between the defendants and in-house counsel for the corporation concerning the financial reports in question. These memoranda were written at about the time that the financial reports were prepared. He also seeks to discover communications passing between the defendants and lawyers from Harrison & Hall, the outside law firm originally hired to represent both the officers and directors and the corporation itself. These communications were made after Steven had written to the defendants making his charges, but before he had brought suit. Can he obtain copies of the memoranda and communications against a claim by the defendants of attorney-client privilege?

(B) One of the vice-presidents of the corporation, Marie, has filed a cross-claim against the other defendants seeking contribution in the event that she is held liable to the plaintiff. Marie, together with all of the other officers and directors, had been represented by Harrison & Hall. She now has her own counsel. In discovery, she seeks copies of communications from lawyers at Harrison & Hall to other defendants. She had not originally been copied on such correspondence because it dealt solely with the activities of those other defendants. The other defendants object to her request for discovery based on the attorney-client privilege. In the alternative, the other defendants ask that an order be issued preventing Marie from sharing the contents of the correspondence with the plaintiff.

McCormick, 6th Ed., §§ 87.1, 91.1; Federal Rule of Evidence 501; Uniform Rule of Evidence 502.

15–22. Assume that the following facts occurred in the situation outlined in Problem 15–11, above. After the accident mentioned in that problem, Craig went to an attorney, Brenda. Craig told her that Victor's employee had turned left in front of him while driving in a heavy rain without operative windshield wipers. Brenda later had a conference with Craig and informed him she had investigated the matter sufficiently to come to the conclusion that the defendant's windshield wipers were operating at the time of the alleged left turn and that the left turn was made when Craig was far enough away so he easily could have avoided running into the Victor vehicle. Without denying these statements, Craig said he had qualms about Brenda's representation of him. By amicable agreement, it was decided between them that Brenda would no longer act as attorney for Craig.

Thereafter, Craig contacted another attorney, Rebecca. In his initial interview with her, he again stated that the defendant's employee made a left turn in front of his oncoming auto without warning and when he was so close to defendant's vehicle that he could not avoid a collision. Rebecca had no time to do an independent investigation of Craig's version of the accident but simply took his word for it. She agreed to act as Craig's attorney and brought the suit for Craig. Prior to trial, the attorney for the defendant discovered that Craig consulted first with Brenda. He wishes to take Brenda's deposition about her conversations with Craig. Can he obtain a court order requiring her to answer his questions as to such conversations despite her claims of both attorney-client and work-product privilege?

McCormick, 6th Ed., §§ 95–96; Federal Rule of Evidence 501; Uniform Rule of Evidence 502; Federal Rule of Civil Procedure 26.

15–23. If the prosecutor calls Lester Caren to testify to the matters Lester stated in Appendix B, *State v. Well*, Document 7, should Lester's anticipated claim of the attorney-client privilege be sustained?

McCormick, 6th Ed., §§ 94–95; Federal Rule of Evidence 501; Uniform Rule of Evidence 502.

15–24. During the course of a robbery, a bank employee is killed by the robbers. F.B.I. agents suspect that Madison is one of the robbers and the killer. Madison is frightened and he visits Bill, an attorney, at his law office. Madison tells Bill that he believes he is suspected of participation in the bank robbery, but he did not participate in it. Bill tells Madison to hold on a minute, and that if he is a suspect, he had better tell him the truth. Madison repeats that he did not participate in the robbery and states that he had been recently interviewed by F.B.I. agents concerning the matter and gave them $348 in dollar bills which he had on his person for their examination in an attempt to prove it. Bill told Madison he was not sure what Madison's course of action should be, but he would decide and that Madison should come back in two days. Madison left and then Bill talked to the F.B.I., ascertaining that the money stolen from the bank could be identified. When Madison came back two days later, Bill informed him that he didn't think Madison had told him the truth, whereupon Madison said he did not participate in the robbery—that was the truth. However, the day after the robbery a man (whom Madison would not identify) had given him a large package which the man said contained money and had requested Madison to put the package in a safety deposit box in Madison's name. The man had told Madison that he should ask no questions and that if Madison touched the money, or if the money was traced to Madison, Madison would be "dead"—"dead" as of that moment. Bill then professed disbelief in this account, whereupon Madison said, "Here, take this key, go to the First State Bank (not the bank which had been robbed) and see what is in there for yourself." When Bill asked Madison to bring it, Madison protested that he was taking a terrible risk of death if he went near that bank. So Bill took the key, went to the bank, opened the safety deposit box, found the package, opened it, and found it contained currency bills in large denominations. In addition to the package in the safety deposit box, he found a revolver which apparently had been fired and was loaded except for two cartridges.

What should Bill do after his discovery of the money and the revolver? McCormick, 6th Ed., §§ 89–90, 95; Federal Rule of Evidence 501; Uniform Rule of Evidence 502.

15–25. Ann is a first year associate in a large law firm. The firm represents XYZ Co. against ABC Co. in a breach of contract action in federal court. As part of the exchange of documents in discovery, Ann was put in charge of reviewing all documents that were to be sent to opposing counsel. There were approximately 1000 documents reviewed. Her principal task was to make sure that privileged documents were excluded from disclosure.

For the most part, Ann did a thorough job, carefully reading all of the documents. However, in the course of her review, she failed to notice an internal memorandum written by an XYZ vice-president to an in-house lawyer. The memorandum was directed to a lawyer who was employed by XYZ for only a few months. The memorandum did not indicate that the recipient was part of the legal staff. The memorandum read as follows:

From: Harold Dunn, Vice–President for Purchasing
To: Alice Fisher
Date: June 14, 2010.

Please look at the ABC contract, previously sent to you. Does it fully provide for all of our concerns? Get back to me by tomorrow, June 15.

A memorandum from Alice Fisher to Harold Dunn, dated June 15, 2010, referring to the contract, was withheld by Ann from the production based upon privilege.

Ann's failure to exclude the above memorandum was not noticed by the partner in charge of the litigation until two weeks after it had been sent to opposing counsel. The partner immediately communicated with opposing counsel and asked her to return the memorandum. ABC has refused to return the document and has indicated that it will offer the memorandum in evidence at the trial. In addition, ABC has moved for the production of all other correspondence and memoranda related to the draft contract on the grounds the disclosure of the June 14 memorandum operated as a waiver of the attorney-client privilege with regard to all communications relating to drafts of the contract in question.

How should the trial court rule on ABC's motion with regard to waiver of the privilege both with regard to the disclosed memorandum and all other documents relating to the draft contract? Consider both the common law rules and Federal Rule of Evidence 502.

McCormick, 6th Ed., § 93; Federal Rule of Evidence 502.

SECTION C. ADDITIONAL PRIVILEGES

15–26. Thomas is divorced from his ex-wife, Jane, but has visitation rights with their five-year-old daughter, Mary, every other weekend. He has filed a motion with the court seeking sole custody of Mary based upon his claim that Jane and the man with whom she lives have neglected her. Visitation has continued as before while the motion is pending.

One Monday, after Mary had spent the weekend with Thomas, Jane brought her to a clinical social worker, Wayne. Wayne subsequently prepared a report in which he stated that Mary had reported sexual abuse of her by Thomas. The report has been filed with the court considering the custody question and a copy has been sent to the local prosecutor, who is investigating the charges.

Thomas vehemently denies any misconduct. He strongly suspects that Jane has planted the sexual abuse story in order to retain custody of Mary. Thomas has learned that Wayne was the second social worker to whom Jane brought Mary on that day. Mary was also seen by Marianne, a social worker at another office. Given the fact that no report was issued by Marianne, Thomas believes that Marianne would not have made the same report as Wayne and that she may have evidence that Jane had planted the story. He seeks to subpoena Marianne in order both to obtain her records of her session with Mary and to take her deposition. Marianne resists the subpoena, claiming that her conversation with Mary was within the psychotherapist-patient privilege. Should the court recognize the privilege under these circumstances?

McCormick, 6th Ed., §§ 98, 103; Federal Rule of Evidence 501; Uniform Rule of Evidence 503.

15–27. Refer to Appendix A, *Hines v. National Motor Co.*, Document 10. During the trial of this case, the defendant calls Dr. Robert Hadler to the witness stand. Plaintiff's counsel asks leave to approach the bench and objects to Hadler's testimony, asserting the physician-patient privilege on behalf of his client. What ruling by the trial judge with regard to the privilege?

McCormick, 6th Ed., §§ 98–100, 102–105; Federal Rule of Evidence 501; Uniform Rule of Evidence 503.

15–28. John received various injuries in an automobile accident and subsequently brought suit against Quincy, the driver of the automobile involved in the accident. After the accident, John was treated by a physician, Stephen, for his injuries. After John arrived home from the physician's office, he thought he did not understand what had been said to him about the nature of his injuries and could not understand the directions given to him. Many questions occurred to him and he began to worry about the injuries. He was not married, so he called up a fellow worker and friend in his office, Mary, and told her that he did not understand a word that the physician had said and that he "simply can't communicate with that guy." She agreed to go back with John to the physician the next day to see what she could do. On this visit, Stephen described to John and Mary precisely the nature of the injury, the indicated treatment for the injury, the exact actions John should take in the treatment of the injury, etc. He responded primarily to questioning by Mary. After they left Stephen's office, John said he now understood what it was all about.

Later, a suit was commenced by John against Quincy. Because John's physical state was gradually becoming critical, John's attorney decided to take John's deposition and included questioning of John about his physical injuries. Quincy's attorney, without objection, cross-examined John about the time and place of his visits to the physician, discovering that he made the above-mentioned visit to Stephen with Mary. Then, in answer to the questions of Quincy's attorney, John told exactly what Stephen had said about his injuries, etc., at that appointment.

At the trial, over objection that the physician-patient privilege applied, may Quincy's attorney ask Mary what Stephen told Mary and John? Assume John's attorney called John to describe his injuries and a "forensic" physician to testify to John's injuries, but did not call Stephen.

McCormick, 6th Ed., §§ 100–101, 103; Federal Rule of Evidence 501; Uniform Rule of Evidence 503.

15–29. John and Virginia were involved in an automobile collision. John suffered severe injuries and was treated by McCotter, a physician and surgeon, for his injuries.

John brought a personal injury suit against Virginia in connection with the collision. Virginia's attorney submitted written interrogatories to John, which John answered, and took the oral deposition of John. Some of the questions in the interrogatories and at the deposition concerned John's alleged physical injuries. John also voluntarily sent to Virginia's attorney medical reports of two doctors who had examined him for purposes of the law suit. John also voluntarily produced copies of all of his hospital records in connection with his injuries. At this juncture of the suit, Virginia's attorney wishes to take the oral deposition of McCotter concerning his examination and treatment of John in connection with John's injuries allegedly due from the collision. Should Virginia's attorney anticipate that he can do so over John's objection?

Suppose that in the above situation, John had not voluntarily sent to Virginia's attorney the medical reports of the two "non-treating" doctors who had examined him, and that these doctors had been originally employed by John's attorney to examine John. John's attorney does not plan to call these doctors as witnesses at the trial. Can Virginia's attorney take the oral depositions of these doctors? If they are not called by John at the trial, can Virginia's attorney call them and examine them concerning the information which they derived from their examination of John? Could Rule 35, Federal Rules of Civil Procedure, afford defendant's attorney some tactic by which he might have some hope of obtaining McCotter's written reports, prepared in the course of treating John?

McCormick, 6th Ed., §§ 98, 100, 103, 105; Federal Rule of Evidence 501; Uniform Rules of Evidence 502–503; Federal Rule of Civil Procedure 35.

15–30. Keller is under indictment for the murder of Wolf. Wolf's death occurred in a isolated warehouse close to the United States–Mexico border. The prosecution's theory is that Wolf, who is known to have been engaged in smuggling illegal aliens into the United States, was ambushed and killed by Keller and robbed of a large sum of money Wolf was then carrying. Keller insists that Wolf was killed during a struggle that ensued when Keller found Wolf using the warehouse to hide a group of aliens.

Before trial, Keller's attorney learns of a recent television newscast prepared by Jolly, a television newsperson specializing in in-depth reports on news topics of current interest. Jolly recently prepared and broadcast a special report on the smuggling of illegal aliens into the U.S. One segment of the report consisted of a videotaped interview with an individual who recounted his own experience in entering the U.S. illegally. This individual, who was interviewed wearing a bag over his head to preserve his anonymity, recounted how he and others paid $1,500 apiece to a man known as Wolf to be brought into the country. He also described how, while he and his companions were being hidden in a warehouse on the U.S. side of the border, he witnessed an altercation between Wolf and another man. The interviewee then told how he and his companions became terrified and fled when Wolf drew a revolver.

Keller seeks to subpoena Jolly for the purpose of having him testify as to the identity of the person interviewed on television.

Would Jolly have any basis for claiming a privilege with respect to the information?

McCormick, 6th Ed., § 76.2; Federal Rule of Evidence 501.

15–31. Paul, a policeman, was struck in the head and severely injured by a brick thrown during a demonstration by animal rights activists. Paul sues Devon for damages, alleging that Devon was the person who threw the brick. Devon denies the allegation. Paul has some evidence tending to show that Devon is, in fact the responsible party, but the sufficiency of the evidence will present a close question. During his investigation, Paul's attorney learns that Devon is a member of a small sectarian church known as the Church of the Elect. The tenets of this church include the belief that confession of wrongdoing to one's fellow church members, all of whom are considered ministers of the church, is essential to salvation. A portion of each worship service is devoted to such confessions. Paul's attorney proposes to depose several members of Devon's congregation and to ask them whether Devon ever admitted injuring Paul by throwing a brick.

Is there any basis for an argument by Devon that any such communications by him would be privileged? What do the statutes of your jurisdiction provide? If the statute in effect does not cover this situation, are there any grounds on which the statute might be argued to be unconstitutional?

McCormick, 6th Ed., § 76.2; Federal Rule of Evidence 501; Uniform Rule of Evidence 505.

15–32. As a member of the state legislature, you have been asked to consider the following piece of legislation:

"Parent–Child Privilege"

(a) *Definitions.* As used in this statute:

    1. A "child" is a person who has not reached the age of majority.

    2. A "parent" is a birth, adoptive or step-parent or legal guardian.

    3. A "confidential communication" is a communication effected by any means which is made privately and not intended for further disclosure except to those persons present in furtherance of the purpose of the communication.

(b) *General Rule of Privilege.* Each party to a confidential communication between parent and child has a privilege to refuse to disclose and to prevent another from disclosing the confidential communication.

(c) *Exceptions.* There is no confidential communications privilege in any proceeding in which:

    1. A parent or the parent's child is a party in any criminal or juvenile proceeding if the basis of the proceeding is alleged acts committed against the person or property of a family member;

    2. A parent and the parent's child are opposing parties;

3. A child's parents are opposing parties.

How would you vote on the proposed legislation? Why?

McCormick, 6th Ed., §§ 72–77.

15–33. (A) Should a privilege statute similar to that cited in Problem 15–31, above, be enacted to protect confidential communications between teachers and students? Between academic or scientific researchers and their sources? Between marriage counselors and their clients?

(B) Make a list of all types of confidential communications between any types of persons which you believe should be protected in a manner similar to the manner of protection generally given to confidential communications between attorneys and clients. Be prepared to support your list and defend the omission of groups to which you would not extend such protection but which occur to you as possible candidates for such a privilege.

McCormick, 6th Ed., §§ 72–77.

CHAPTER 16

PRIVILEGES DESIGNED TO SAFEGUARD GOVERNMENTAL OPERATIONS

■ ■ ■

16–1. Walter is being prosecuted for possession of marijuana. He challenges, under the Fourth Amendment to the Constitution, the legality of his arrest and search on the ground that the police lacked probable cause.

At the suppression hearing, Officer James testifies that on the evening of January 10 at approximately 8:00 p.m. he was making observations with the aid of binoculars from an observation post located near the intersection of Reno Street and Cambridge Avenue. He describes the area as mixed business and residential, with a number of businesses, office buildings, and apartment buildings ranging in height from two to five stories. He states that the area is also well known for marijuana trafficking.

Officer James testifies on direct examination by the prosecutor that he observed Walter standing on the street corner wearing a long trench coat. He states that he saw a car pull to the curb in the vicinity of Walter and stop. At that point, Walter motioned for the driver to pull into a nearby lot. Once in the lot, Walter approached the window and appeared to engage in conversation with someone in the car. Walter reached into a paper bag he was carrying and removed from it a clear plastic "baggie" containing some dark colored material. He handed the "baggie" to a passenger, and received in return some small paper items the size of paper money.

The car then drove away and Walter returned to the corner, carrying his paper bag. James radioed his information to officers in a nearby patrol car, giving them the description of Walter, and telling them to arrest him. The officers drove to the corner, arrested Walter, and seized the paper bag, which contained a number of "baggies" containing marijuana.

Officer James testifies that, from his experience and the nature of the locality, the exchange of items he saw led him to believe that he had witnessed the sale of marijuana, the marijuana coming from the paper bag in Walter's possession. Assume that if these observations are not successfully challenged that they, together with the nature of the location and the officer's experience, constitute probable cause sufficient to render the arrest, search, and seizure legal.

On cross-examination, defense counsel establishes that a number of walls, posts, signs, cars, and trucks that could block vision from some locations are in the vicinity of the intersection of Reno and Cambridge. Officer James, however, claims to have witnessed the initial conversation and the exchange of items without obstruction. When asked to provide his location, which defense counsel argues is essential to permit a successful challenge of James' observations, the prosecutor objects, contending that the information is privileged.

How should the court rule? Must it grant or deny the claim of privilege on the basis of the information supplied or does it have alternative methods of proceeding? If so, what are the alternatives, and are they warranted in this case?

McCormick, 6th Ed., § 111; Federal Rule of Evidence 501, and Rule 510 issued by Supreme Court but rejected by Congress.

16–2. Sam was arrested and charged with the unlawful possession and sale of heroin on three different dates in one month. The sales were made to Otis, a government narcotics agent. In his direct testimony, Otis merely testified that on all three occasions he went to Sam's apartment and purchased heroin in a package each time. Each time he asked Sam, "Do you have the heroin here to sell me now?," and each time Sam answered that he did. Upon payment of a specified sum, Sam delivered the package of heroin to the agent. The packages, properly identified and also identified as containing heroin, were introduced into evidence. The dates of the alleged sales were July 10, July 21, and July 28.

After direct, the following cross-examination of Otis by Sam's defense counsel occurred:

Q. Now, when you first met Sam in the Oak Apartments, was he a friend of yours?

A. No, sir.

Q. Who introduced you to him?

PROSECUTOR: Objection, Your Honor.

THE COURT: Sustained.

DEFENSE COUNSEL: Well, that is a preliminary question, Your Honor.

THE COURT: Sustained.

Q. Didn't someone introduce you to Sam before you went to his apartment on July 10?

A. Yes, sir.

Q. Didn't you go to see Sam after having had a conversation with that person?

A.   No, sir.

Q.   Didn't you have a conversation with somebody aside from police officers before you went to Sam's apartment?

A.   Yes.

PROSECUTOR: Objection.

THE COURT: Sustained.

Q.   Who do you know who also knows Sam?

PROSECUTOR: I will object, Your Honor, to this line of questioning. I think it is improper, and I think counsel knows it.

DEFENSE COUNSEL: Well, it may be improper, Your Honor, but I sure don't know it.

THE COURT: I know what you're trying to get at is whether an informer told him.

DEFENSE COUNSEL: No, Your Honor.

THE COURT: I am going to rule that the informer is protected. This man had a transaction. Where he got his information is immaterial.

Q.   Well, hasn't anyone you know who knows Sam been arrested for a narcotics offense?

PROSECUTOR: I will object, Your Honor.

THE COURT: Sustained.

PROSECUTOR: I don't think this is material.

DEFENSE COUNSEL: Well, Your Honor, I am seeking to show that there wasn't a purchase from Sam, but that it was from some other party.

THE COURT: Well, then, why don't you ask that? Did you purchase Exhibit 1 from someone else? Did you purchase Exhibit 3 from somebody else than this defendant?

Q.   Well, Mr. Witness, now didn't you make arrangements to purchase something from someone other than Sam?

PROSECUTOR: I will object, Your Honor.

THE COURT: Sustained. Not what arrangements he made, it is what he did.

Q.   Who was supposed to get the money that you gave Sam on July 10th?

PROSECUTOR: Objection.

THE COURT: Sustained.

DEFENSE COUNSEL: If Your Honor please, it seems like I ought to be able to finish the question.

THE COURT: All right ask it. You finished it, I thought. Go ahead and ask it again. We're not trying any higher-up here, we're trying Sam.

DEFENSE COUNSEL: Your Honor, the witness has testified in regard to the alleged transaction on this particular date. I think I'm entitled to go into the circumstances surrounding that transaction.

THE COURT: Ask him if there was anybody else in the room. Ask him whoever else was in the room, as to this transaction. Who told him or what else, I think is immaterial, particularly in this type of a case.

DEFENSE COUNSEL: Well, Your Honor, I think I would make an offer of proof that—

THE COURT: All right. Let the jury go out. Not in front of the jury. Go on out, please. (The following proceedings took place in the absence of the jury.)

THE COURT: What is your offer of proof?

DEFENSE COUNSEL: Well, I offer to prove by this witness if permitted, with regard to this transaction of July 10, that this witness, Otis, had met with somebody who knew Sam and that the witness, Otis, came in and said to Sam, "Did someone leave me a package?", and that Sam said, "Yes," and that the transaction was had. Also that there was a blond fellow present and that the transaction was really with him—a decoy-informer.

THE COURT: What is your name?

WITNESS: Otis.

THE COURT: Well, I might let you ask if such a conversation took place.

DEFENSE COUNSEL: Well—

THE COURT: But I am not going to let you try somebody else. This witness, as it stands now, at least at this point, his testimony is that he purchased these articles from this man. What the man had in mind in doing it, if he was doing it for somebody else, still wouldn't get him out from under the law. That is a part of his defense. But I might let you ask what did the defendant say. Give the conversation.

DEFENSE COUNSEL: All right. Fine.

THE COURT: Bring in the jury. (The following proceedings took place in the presence of the jury).

THE COURT: Counsel, as to each exhibit, I will allow you to ask him what conversation he had with the defendant when he met him on each occasion, but let's limit it to specific occasions.

Q. On July 10, Mr. Otis, when you went to see Sam, what did you say? You knocked on the door, did you?

A. Yes, sir.

Q.   And did he open the door?

A.   Yes, sir.

Q.   What did you say?

A.   "Hello."

Q.   Okay. What did he say?

A.   We went on into the room, and Sam and I had a general conversation regarding heroin, the price, the quantity, the amounts.

Q.   Did you tell him who you were?

A.   Yes, sir.

Q.   Who did you tell him you were?

A.   I told him, "I am Benny."

Q.   And then what else did you say to him? Did you say, "I'm Benny"?

A.   Yes.

Q.   Then what?

A.   I said, "I understand maybe you've got a little merchandise for sale?"

Q.   And what did he say?

A.   He said, "Yes."

Q.   Then what?

A.   He reached under the stove in the cabinet and took out the brown paper bag.

Q.   And this is the first time you had ever seen him before.

A.   Yes, sir.

Q.   You didn't have to persuade him to do anything?

A.   No, sir.

Q.   He was ready, willing, and so forth?

A.   Yes, sir.

Q.   Did you tell him you were a tavern owner?

A.   I didn't tell him that; no sir.

Q.   Was there any other party present on this July 10th?

A.   Yes, sir.

Q.   Oh, there was?

A.   Yes, sir.

Q.   Who was present?

PROSECUTOR: Objection.

DEFENSE COUNSEL: Objection?

THE COURT: Well, that is proper. Go ahead and ask him who was there.

Q. Who was there?

A. A blond headed fellow.

Q. And what did he say?

A. Nothing.

Q. Now, wasn't this transaction really with this second fellow rather than with the defendant?

A. No, sir.

Q. What is this blond haired fellow's name?

PROSECUTOR: I will object, Your Honor. I don't think this is appropriate and I think the state has a privilege in these regards.

THE COURT: Sustained.

DEFENSE COUNSEL: Well, if Your Honor please, this blond haired fellow was in the room. I might have a reason to subpoena him if I can find out who he is and where he is.

THE COURT: Sustained.

DEFENSE COUNSEL: Exception, if Your Honor please.

THE COURT: Sure.

Were the court's rulings correct? How would you improve the questioning and the statements of defense counsel to obtain his apparent goal?

McCormick, 6th Ed. § 111; Federal Rule of Evidence 501, and Rule 510 issued by Supreme Court but rejected by Congress.

16–3. Rose, a thirteen-year-old female, was discovered by police in the act of sexual intercourse with an adult male. Both were taken into custody. In due course, Rose was charged with a variety of acts amounting to juvenile delinquency under pertinent state law, and a hearing was held in juvenile court under that law. As authorized by an applicable statute, the hearing was closed to the public at Rose's request. An attorney had been appointed for Rose, but at the hearing, she admitted various petty crimes and acts of sexual intercourse with various adult males, some for pay and some not. She named George as a man with whom she had sexual intercourse on at least a dozen occasions, but later in the course of the hearing changed her story and denied that she had ever had any sexual intercourse with George.

Circumstantial evidence, and direct evidence of other witnesses, indicated that her initial charges as to George were true, and finally he was charged with having carnal knowledge of a female thirteen years of age. He pleaded not guilty. His attorney anticipates that Rose will be called by the prosecution as a witness, and he is informed that, although at her juvenile court hearing she made the above-mentioned accusations as to George, she recanted at that same hearing. If Rose is called at the forthcoming trial and testifies to the sexual acts with George, he would like to call the judge who presided at the juvenile hearing to testify to her later changed story at the hearing. He also would like to introduce the transcript of the hearing to show the same retraction.

In addition, George's attorney believes that Professor Data of Intrastate University School of Law and two of her law students know the contents of the record of Rose's juvenile hearing. The professor had obtained a trial court order for the examination by herself and the two law students of the records of female juveniles charged in the instant juvenile court with delinquency concerning sex matters, in the conduct of statistical research. The order contained a provision that she and the students were to keep all information learned about individuals anonymous and confidential. The order was obtained by *ex parte* motion. No one appeared in opposition to her motion for the order, and it was not appealed by anyone. She had examined the file of Rose's hearing in her research.

There are two pertinent statutes. The first statute merely states, "A public officer shall not be examined as a witness to communications made to him in official confidence when public interest would suffer by the disclosure." A second statute provides that probation records considered at a juvenile hearing and any transcripts of such a hearing should not be subject to public scrutiny without the permission of the juvenile, his or her parent, or guardian except as ordered by the court in the public interest. It also provides juvenile hearings should be closed to the public at the request of the juvenile.

Assuming that the prosecution objects and that Rose refuses to give her permission, should George's attorney be able to introduce the testimony of the judge, the transcript of Rose's juvenile hearing, and the testimony of Professor Data, concerning Rose's retraction of her charges against George?

McCormick, 6th Ed., §§ 107–108; Federal Rule of Evidence 501, and Rule 509 issued by the Supreme Court but rejected by Congress.

16–4. Joyce, who is African American, was the Director of the Parks and Recreation Division, sues the City of Garden Grove for wrongful discharge under Title VII and Section 1983 alleging wrongful discharge based on racial discrimination. At the time her contract came up for review, she was notified that she would not be renewed in the position.

She asserts that the discriminatory decision was taken during a closedoor executive session meeting between the city council and the mayor. The City resists, citing the deliberative process privilege that is designed to protect the internal decision-making processes of the executive branch of government in order to protect the quality of decisions and to facilitate candor.

How should the court rule?

16–5. Cyrl sues Johnson Air Carrier for its part in the extraordinary rendition program. Cyrl alleges that Johnson provided flight planning and logistical support services to the aircraft and crew on the flights that carried him to Morocco where he was tortured. He alleges Johnson is directly liable in damages for actively participating in his forcible and arbitrary abduction and for conspiring in his torture. In the alternative, Cyrl asserts that Johnson is liable for aiding and abetting agents of the United States and Morocco in subjecting him to torture because Johnson knew or should have known that the passengers of each flight for which it provided logistical support services were being subjected to such treatment by agents at the termination of the trip. Finally, he alleges in the alternative that Johnson demonstrated reckless disregard as to whether the passengers of each flight for which it provided logistical support services were being subjected to torture.

The Director of the CIA asserted the state secrets privilege and moved for dismissal. It stated in its public filing that disclosure of the information covered by this privilege assertion reasonably could be expected to cause serious and in some instances exceptionally grave damage to the national security of the United States and therefore that the information should be excluded from any use in this case. The Director argues that at the core of plaintiff's case against Johnson are allegations of covert U.S. military or CIA operations in foreign countries against foreign nationals and this is clearly a subject matter which is a state secret. The Director contends that the very subject matter of this case is a state secret and that as a result the case must be dismissed.

How should the court rule on a motion to sustain the privilege and dismiss Cyrl's lawsuit?

16–6. (A) The United States was engaged in an unpopular "non-war" involving armed conflict by the armed forces of the United States, with battle casualties, etc. Allegedly, Lieutenant Lambert had been "fragged" by a Private Benjamin, that is, Benjamin had deliberately thrown a hand grenade at Lambert, during a battle with the enemy of the United States. There allegedly were several witnesses. An official investigation was made by the appropriate army authorities who took the statements of the alleged witnesses and who set forth the exact details of the scene of the incident as viewed by the investigators. These documents were classified "Top Secret." No court-martial or other criminal proceedings were brought against Benjamin. However, in due time, Lambert's widow was told of the incident by a witness and also discovered that Benjamin had a fairly large personal fortune, whereupon she engaged an attorney. Ultimately, a suit was brought against Benjamin for wrongful death in a federal court after Benjamin had been discharged from the United States Army (a good conduct discharge). Federal jurisdiction is based upon diversity of citizenship. Prior to trial, production was demanded from the appropriate officials of the United States Army of the records resulting from the above-mentioned investigation. Production was refused, finally, by the Secretary of the Army. How should the attorney for the widow attempt to obtain these documents? What do you anticipate will happen with regard to the production of these records?

(B) Assume that Mrs. Lambert's efforts to obtain a copy of the records were unsuccessful, but that she was nevertheless successful in her wrongful death action against Benjamin. Assume also that the United States government now seeks to prosecute Benjamin for murder and that such an action in the United States District Court would be proper at this time. Benjamin's attorney would now like to obtain a copy of the records of the military. The government refuses his request. How should Benjamin's attorney attempt to obtain these documents? What do you anticipate will happen with regard to the production of these records?

McCormick, 6th Ed., §§ 106–110; Federal Rule of Evidence 501, and Rule 509 issued by the Supreme Court but rejected by Congress.

16–7. John, who is a prisoner at the state's maximum security prison, is minister of an obscure radical religious sect. He claims that his recent transfer from a prison near his home to one in a distant part of the state, as well as the loss of privileges and his extended stay in solitary confinement have occurred because of his religious beliefs and practices, and the bigotry of prison authorities and their opposition to his ministry. He has brought suit in federal court under 42 U.S.C. § 1983, alleging that his First Amendment rights have been violated.

The state responds by denying that the actions were taken in retaliation for religious beliefs or religious activities. Instead, it contends that John is involved in illegal activities within the prison in which the religious organization is a front. It contends that he was transferred after he began plotting the taking of hostages and that each of the actions that John complains about were taken in good faith on the basis of reliable information obtained by the prison authorities.

In order to substantiate his claim, John moves for discovery of the facts supporting the prison actions and the internal administrative prison documents setting out the deliberations regarding the punitive actions taken by prison authorities.

The state objects to production of the documents under common law governmental privileges. It provides the documents requested by John to the judge for *in camera* inspection. The state also moves for summary judgment, suggesting that the judge will see from the documents submitted that each of the actions was fully supported by reports from prisoners concerning John's threats to do violence, which the prison was entitled to act upon regardless of their truth. Therefore, the state contends there are no issue of material fact outstanding and no basis for John's claim.

How should the court rule? What types of privileges might be cited in support of protecting the documents? Is summary judgment appropriate assuming the documents submitted contain the facts alleged by the state?

McCormick, 6th Ed., § 108; Federal Rule of Evidence 501, and Rule 509 issued by the Supreme Court but rejected by Congress.

16–8. (A) Earle brought an action in federal court under 42 U.S.C. § 1983 against three election officials charging that the officials, acting under color of state law, had deprived him of his right to vote. There was an investigation of the incident by the Federal Bureau of Investigation. Earle's attorney would like to have access to the reports giving the results of that investigation in order better to prepare his case. He requested the reports from the F.B.I. but was refused. A deposition subpoena duces tecum was answered by a statement from the local F.B.I. director stating that the production of the reports of the investigation would be contrary to the public interest. Earle's attorney now seeks a court order requiring production of the investigation reports. As trial judge, what should you do?

(B) Assume that the action against the election officials was not brought in federal court, but rather in the courts of the state in which your law school is located. Under your state statutes and rules, would you, as trial judge, reach any different result with regard to Earle's request for an order requiring the F.B.I. to produce the reports of the investigation?

(C) Assume not only that the action is brought in your state court, but also that the reports of the investigation are in the hands of a state investigatory body such as the state police or State Bureau of Investigation, rather than the F.B.I. Under your state statutes and rules, would you, as trial judge, reach any different result with regard to Earle's request for an order requiring production of the reports of the investigation?

McCormick, 6th Ed., §§ 107–108, 110; Federal Rule of Evidence 501, and Rule 509 issued by Supreme Court but rejected by Congress.

16–9. The Equal Employment Opportunity Commission brought suit against the Fiddelout Co. in a federal district court under the Fair Labor Standards Act (29 U.S.C. §§ 201 *et seq.*) charging the defendant with employing some of its employees at rates of pay less than the minimum wages prescribed by the Act and with employing other employees for overtime work (and for selling goods manufactured under such conditions in interstate commerce). The defendant answered the allegations of violations of the pay provisions of the Act by stating it was without knowledge or information sufficient to form a belief as to the truth of such allegations and therefore denied the allegations. Then, by interrogatories pursuant to Federal Rule of Civil Procedure 33, defendant asked the plaintiff to state "the identity and locations of persons having any knowledge of payment of less than minimum wages and minimum overtime pay as alleged in the complaint, pursuant to Rule 26(b)(1) of the Federal Rules of Civil Procedure." Plaintiff objected to answering the above interrogatory on the ground that the information was privileged official information and that in order to protect present and former employees of the defendant, it need not reveal its "informers." On motion of the defendant under Rule 37(a), should the court order the plaintiff to answer the above-mentioned interrogatory?

McCormick, 6th Ed., §§ 106–110; Federal Rule of Evidence 501, and Rule 509 issued by Supreme Court but rejected by Congress.

16–10. (A) The *News–Paper*, a daily newspaper in Calley, State of Gordon, a state of the United States, carried a news article that a "deli" (a food store) was a "front" for a "bookie" operation by its owner, Gamble. The article was accompanied by a photo of the front of the store, under which was the phrase, "And you thought it was a deli." Subsequently Gamble brought a suit in a local state court against the owners of the *News–Paper* for libel. Under the law of the particular jurisdiction (and the pleadings) the truth of the above-mentioned article was one of the issues in Gamble's suit. During the pretrial stage of the suit, defendant's attorney sent a request to plaintiff to produce for inspection plaintiff's copies of plaintiff's federal income tax returns for the year during which the above-mentioned article was published and also such copies for the previous year. In the particular state jurisdiction, Federal Rules of Civil Procedure 34 and 37 have been copied verbatim. Pursuant to Rule 34, the plaintiff served an objection to the production of such copies. Defendant's attorney, pursuant to Rule 37, then made a motion that the plaintiff be required to produce the above-mentioned copies in response to its request. Should the trial judge grant this motion?

(B) Prior to the commencement of the instant suit a grand jury investigation concerning gambling operations in Calley had been conducted. Gamble was not named in any indictments, but the attorney for the *News–Paper* learned from Dan that Dan had testified before the grand jury to the effect that he knew that Gamble conducted a "bookie operation" at his deli. Dan had also testified to details of the "bookie operation."

The attorney for the *News–Paper* took the deposition of Dan, in which Dan related the above matters. The attorney then asked Dan whether he had recited these matters as a witness before the grand jury. Dan (at the advice of his own lawyer) refused to recount what he had stated to the grand jury on the ground that the grand jury proceedings were secret. The examination was completed, and thereafter the attorney for the *News–Paper* moved under Rule 37(a)(2) for an order of the appropriate court that Dan be required to answer the questions concerning his grand jury testimony. Should the judge order that Dan answer such questions?

McCormick, 6th Ed., §§ 112–113; Federal Rule of Evidence 501, and Rules 502 and 509 issued by Supreme Court but rejected by Congress.

16–11. To attack a verdict, the defendant who has been convicted wishes to introduce testimony from a juror as to the following:

(A) Juror Mildred Smith, in violation of explicit instructions by the trial judge, took notes during lunch and overnight of the events of each day. She read those notes to the other jurors during deliberation. Her use of the notes was very persuasive; she was elected foreperson as a result of their use and was the clear opinion leader on the jury.

(B) Juror James Jones, who sat closest to the witness stand, stated that he noticed impressions of the nose pieces of eye glasses on each side of the star defense witness' nose, indicating that she wore glasses. He also noted that she squinted often which, he knew as a glasses wearer, was the reaction that one has when one's eyesight is very poor and one is straining to see without glasses. The jury agreed in its deliberations that the witness was not wearing her glasses at the time of the observations critical to the case and therefore was not a credible or able witness.

The witness in question was critical to the defense case in that she was the only one who claimed to have seen the decedent pull a knife before the defendant shot him. The truth is that the witness has no such nose-piece impressions on her nose and that she squints because of a nervous condition.

(C) While inspecting the jacket of the defendant, the jurors found in one of the pockets a small yellow pill labeled B–I–62, which they assume (correctly) is an illegal drug.

(D) After three days of deliberating, the jury remained divided. All members agreed to be bound by a flip of a coin, which came out tails for guilty. The jurors returned that verdict.

(E) Juror Charles Wright during deliberations discussed a crime similar to that on trial in which his sister was killed. He broke into tears when talking about it, and he had been a persuasive spokesman for the need to convict the defendant because he posed a threat to society. All jurors had been asked during voir dire if they or any member of their family had been the victim of a serious crime or if any member of their family or any close friend had been a victim of a homicide. Wright had not responded when the general question was asked to all prospective members of the jury. The jury returned a guilty verdict.

(F) Juror Jane Smith, who is black, was berated with racist insults, cursed, and physically threatened by another female juror, who appeared to the witness juror to be a total bigot, each time Smith argued during deliberations in favor of the innocence of the defendant, who also is black. Smith changed her initial vote of not guilty after several days of deliberations and joined the unanimous guilty verdict.

McCormick, 6th Ed., § 68; Federal Rule of Evidence 606.

16–12. Dr. Ruth Jones is a nuclear physicist who possessed government security clearances and worked on military-related projects for various government defense contractors. In February, Dr. Jones lectured at the Far–Eastern Institute of Technology. The government alleges that, sometime during her visit, a Chinese mathematician asked her intrusive and suspicious questions. Dr. Jones reported this encounter to the United States Consulate, allegedly resulting in numerous meetings with embassy personnel.

In July, after her return to the United States, Jones alleges that she met with an individual under an alias who identified himself as a C.I.A. employee and who questioned Jones about her contact with the Chinese national. In August, Jones was informed that her security clearance had been revoked due to "inactivity."

Jones claims that, beginning in September, she became the focus of a campaign of harassment and psychological attacks. She alleges that unknown individuals entered her house and rearranged things, that she began to receive strange telephone calls, some indicating that her telephone was bugged, and that someone broke into her car. She also alleges that she was drugged with a substance which caused "terrifying hallucinations."

She brought suit in federal court charging the United States, the C.I.A., the F.B.I., the Department of Defense, the Department of State, and ten John and Jane Does (alleged to be employees of the C.I.A., the F.B.I., the Department of Justice, and the Department of Defense) with violations of her Fourth Amendment rights. Jones also alleged a right to recover under the Federal Tort Claims Act for negligence (breach of a duty to obtain informed consent before using her as an informant or a subject of experimental research, for assault and battery, and for intentional infliction of emotional distress).

Included in the information Dr. Jones sought during discovery were the identities of government personnel with whom she came into contact, the nature and purpose of those contacts, and the locations of the contacts. She also sought all documents concerning the reasons for the revocation of her security clearance and the data upon which this revocation was based. The Director of the C.I.A. submitted an affidavit to the court asserting that the information sought by Jones was privileged and exempt from disclosure.

(A) Which governmental privileges might attach to the information sought by Jones?

(B) Assume that you are the district court judge. Would you require the government to disclose any of the information? Which information would you hold privileged? Why? How would you make that determination?

(C) Assume you are the attorney representing Jones. What arguments would you make to gain access to the information? How do you anticipate that the court will respond to these arguments?

McCormick, 6th Ed., §§ 107–108; Federal Rule of Evidence 501, and Rule 509 issued by the Supreme Court but rejected by Congress.

APPENDIX A*

HINES v. NATIONAL MOTOR CO.

■ ■ ■

Table of Contents

Document 1

DESCRIPTION OF CASE

Linda Hines brings an action against the National Motor Car Co. for the wrongful death of her husband, Chester. Mrs. Hines charges that Chester died as a result of injuries sustained when his new Cheetah automobile, manufactured by National, went off the road and hit a tree. Plaintiff alleges that the accident was caused by a defect in the steering mechanism of the car.

Defendant claims that the car had no defect and that the collision must have been caused by a driving error on Chester's part.

The following documents are taken from the files of the attorneys for both parties, except as indicated.

---

* Appendix A is used in Problems 7–9, 8–1, 8–9, 8–10, 8–11, 8–34, 9–3, 10–4, 10–6, 10–7, 12–31, 12–62, 14–8, 14–45, and 15–27.

Document 2

COMPLAINT

Filed July 23, 2010

11:00 A.M.

UNITED STATES DISTRICT COURT FOR THE
MIDDLE DISTRICT OF CALLICE

Civil Action, File number 2010–C–715

LINDA HINES,
as Administrator of the
Estate of Chester Hines

v.   COMPLAINT

NATIONAL MOTOR
COMPANY

Plaintiff, Linda Hines, as administrator of the Estate of Chester Hines, alleges:

1. Plaintiff is a citizen of the State of Callice and defendant is a corporation incorporated under the laws of the State of Delaware and has its principal place of business in a state other than the State of Callice. The matter in controversy exceeds, exclusive of interest and costs, the sum of seventy-five thousand dollars.

2. On April 17, 2010, plaintiff was duly appointed administrator of the Estate of Chester Hines, deceased (hereinafter "decedent"), by the Superior Court of Clay County, Callice, and duly qualified for said office and ever since has been and now is the administrator of said estate and brings this action as such administrator pursuant to Chapter 70 of the Callice Revised Statutes.

3. Defendant designs, manufactures and is in the business of selling, through franchised dealers, passenger automobiles including a 2010 model known as the Cheetah.

4. On February 3, 2010, decedent purchased a new 2010 model Cheetah automobile from Clay Cheetah Company, a dealer franchised by defendant.

5. The automobile purchased was designed and manufactured by defendant and sold to Clay Cheetah for the purpose of resale to consumers. There was no substantial change in the condition of the automobile from the time it left defendant's factory until it was sold to decedent.

6. Defendant designed and manufactured this automobile with a defective steering mechanism.

7. The automobile was in a defective condition in this regard so as to be unreasonably dangerous to any person driving or riding in it in violation of Callice Revised Statutes, § 80–402A.

8. Decedent was driving this automobile on or about March 16, 2010, in a northerly direction on a road in Clay County, Callice, near the city of Island.

9. At that place and time, as a direct and proximate result of the aforesaid defect in the steering mechanism of the automobile, the automobile failed to recover from a turn in the highway and crashed into a tree.

10. As a direct and proximate result of the collision referred to in Paragraph 9, decedent sustained severe injuries resulting in his hospitalization and finally in his death on March 17, 2010.

11. Decedent left surviving him, his wife, plaintiff Linda Hines, as his only heir at law and next of kin.

12. By reason of the above, the decedent incurred expenses for his care, treatment and hospitalization in the amount of $10,000, and suffered great pain of body and mind.

13. By reason of the death of the decedent, Linda Hines has incurred funeral expenses for the decedent and has lost the income, support, services, protection, care, assistance, society, companionship, comfort, guidance, kindly offices, and advice of the decedent.

WHEREFORE, plaintiff demands judgment against defendant in the amount of two million dollars and costs.

JURY DEMAND

Plaintiff demands a trial by jury in this action.

/S/ Samuel A. Thomas
Samuel A. Thomas
Attorney for Plaintiff
Thomas and Reed
517 High Street
Island, Callice

Document 3
ANSWER

Filed August 8, 2010

4 P.M.

UNITED STATES DISTRICT COURT FOR THE
MIDDLE DISTRICT OF CALLICE

Civil Action, File number 2010–C–715

LINDA HINES,
as Administrator of the
Estate of Chester Hines

v.

NATIONAL MOTOR
COMPANY

Defendant, National Motor Company, answers the complaint as follows:

1.   Defendant admits the allegations of paragraph 1, except that it denies that the matter in controversy exceeds the sum of seventy-five thousand dollars.

2.   Defendant admits the allegations of paragraph 2.

3.   Defendant admits the allegations of paragraph 3.

4.   Defendant admits the allegations of paragraph 4.

5.   Defendant admits the allegations of paragraph 5.

6.   Defendant denies the allegations of paragraph 6.

7.   Defendant denies the allegations of paragraph 7.

8.   Defendant admits the allegations of paragraph 8.

9.   Defendant denies the allegations of paragraph 9, except that it admits that decedent's automobile crashed into a tree at that place and time.

10.   Defendant admits the allegations of paragraph 10.

11.   Defendant admits the allegations of paragraph 11.

12.   Defendant denies the allegations of paragraph 12.

13.   Defendant denies the allegations of paragraph 13.

First Defense

14.   Plaintiff's complaint fails to state a claim upon which relief can be granted.

Second Defense

15. Decedent misused the automobile involved in this action by driving at an unsafe speed and by improper steering of the automobile on a turn.

WHEREFORE, Defendant demands that the Complaint be dismissed and judgment entered in favor of the Defendant with the costs and disbursement of this action.

FLYNN, WEST & GODFREY

By /S/ Jovita Flynn
Attorneys for Defendants
Suite 1603, City Park Building
Island, Callice

Document 4

APPLICABLE CALLICE STATUTES

Chapter 70, Section 1

Whenever the death of a person shall be caused by wrongful act, neglect or default, and the act, neglect or default is such as would, if death had not ensued, have entitled the party injured to maintain an action and recover damages in respect thereof, then and in every such case the person who or company or corporation which would have been liable if death had not ensued, shall be liable to an action for damages, notwithstanding the death of the person injured, and although the death shall have been caused under such circumstances as amount in law for felony.

Chapter 70, Section 2

A. Damages recoverable for death by wrongful act include:

(1) Expenses for care, treatment and hospitalization incident to the injury resulting in death;

(2) Compensation for pain and suffering of the decedent;

(3) The reasonable funeral expenses of the decedent;

(4) The present monetary value of the decedent to the persons entitled to receive the damages recovered, including but not limited to compensation for the loss of the reasonable expected:

(a) Net income of the decedent.

(b) Services, protection, care and assistance of the decedent, whether voluntary or obligatory, to the persons entitled to the damages recovered.

(c) Society, companionship, comfort, guidance, kindly offices and advice of the decedent to the persons entitled to the damages recovered;

(5) such punitive damages as the decedent could have recovered had he survived, the punitive damages for wrongfully causing the death of the decedent through maliciousness, willful or wanton injury, or gross negligence;

(6) Nominal damages when the jury so finds.

B. All evidence which reasonably tends to establish any of the elements of damages included in subsection (A), or otherwise reasonably tends to establish the present monetary value of the decedent to the persons entitled to receive the damages recovered, is admissible in an action for damages for death by wrongful act.

* * *

Chapter 80, Section 402A

(1) One who sells any product in a defective condition unreasonably dangerous to the user or consumer, or to his property, is subject to liability for physical harm thereby caused to the ultimate user or consumer, or to his property, if

(a) The seller is engaged in the business of selling such a product, and

(b) It is expected to and does reach the user or consumer without substantial changes in the condition in which it is sold.

(2) The rule stated in Subsection (1) applies although

(a) The seller has exercised all possible care in the preparation and sale of his product, and

(b) The user or consumer has not bought the product from or entered into any contractual relation with the seller.

[The above statute was adopted from the Restatement of Torts 2d, and the legislative history was incorporated in the accompanying advisory notes.]

Chapter 80, Section 402B

(1) Contributory negligence shall not be a bar to liability for physical harm under Section 402A.

(2) Misuse of the product is a defense to liability for physical harm under Section 402A.

(3) Assumption of the risk is a defense to liability for physical harm under Section 402A.

Document 5

DISCOVERY DEPOSITION OF JOHN YOUNG

* * *

Examination by Mr. Godfrey (Attorney for National Motor Car Company.)

Q. Would you state your name, please, for the record?

A. John Quincy Young.

Q. And your address?

A. 518 Guilford Lane, this city.

Q. What is your occupation?

A. I drive an ambulance for the South Clay County Rescue Squad.

Q. And how long have you been so employed?

A. Six years.

Q. Have you any medical training?

A. I have no formal medical training. I have an Associate certificate from Community College in Health Administration. I have taken numerous first-aid courses since being employed by the company. I am planning to go back to school next year to study nursing.

Q. Turning your attention to March 16 of this year, were you on duty on that day?

A. Yes, sir. I came on at 7 A.M.

Q. What were your duties on that day?

A. The same as they are everyday; to respond to emergency calls that may come in.

Q. Can you describe for us the circumstances of the call involving Mr. Hines?

A. That call came in around 8:30.

Q. In the morning?

A. Yes.

Q. Go on.

A. I was sitting around the office drinking a cup of coffee. A passing motorist called and said that some guy had hit a tree out on old highway 86. We got directions and went out in the ambulance. When we reached the scene, we found this new Cheetah slammed against the tree. My partner and I saw this guy inside and started to work on getting him out.

Q. Who was your partner?

A. That day it was Ralph Gibson.

Q. Did you talk to the man while you were pulling him out?

A.   Yeah, we did some. He kept on screaming for us to hurry, that he was hurt real bad and stuff like that.

Q.   Did you have trouble getting him out?

A.   Well, we couldn't open the door right away. The door was jammed in tight and the steering wheel was pressed against the guy. But we were finally able to pry the door open with a crow-bar. We thought we were going to have to use blow torches, but the crow-bar finally did the trick.

Q.   What happened then?

A.   Well, we got the guy out and put him on a stretcher.

Q.   What was his condition at that time?

A.   Well, he was in a lot of pain. He was really hurt. There was a lot of blood, both on his head and in his midsection. We could see part of his rib sticking out of his body.

Q.   Did he say anything to you at that time?

A.   Yeah, mainly about how bad he hurt.

Q.   Anything else?

A.   He kept talking about the accident. He kept saying that the steering wheel just seemed to lock into place. He said he took that turn in the road at about 40, but that he couldn't bring the car out of the turn.

Q.   What were the specific words that he used?

A.   Well, I don't remember exactly, but I believe they were: "I was just turning the curve, just about forty. The god-damn wheel locked. I can't believe a new car would do that." Then he kept saying "Could you believe that, could you believe a new car would do that?" I told him I would believe anything about a new car.

Q.   Did you notice anything else about the man?

A.   Nothing in particular, what do you mean?

Q.   Any evidence of alcohol* either in the car or on his breath?

A.   Yeah, there was broken bottles of beer on the floor near the front seat. I figure they broke on impact.

Q.   How about the odor of alcohol on his breath?

A.   I just don't remember. I know there was an odor of alcohol in the car, but I can't remember about the man. We put an oxygen mask on him right away, so I couldn't get much of a smell of his breath once he was out of the car.

Q.   Did you notice anything else?

---

* Due to the accidental destruction of tissue and blood samples by the hospital and the cremation of Mr. Hines body several days after his death, no scientific evidence exists as to whether he had consumed alcohol.

A. No, we were pretty anxious to get him to the hospital.

Q. What did you do after you got him to the stretcher?

A. We put him in the ambulance.

Q. What happened then?

A. We drove as quick as we could to the hospital. We brought him into the emergency room and turned him over to Dr. Foster. We then went back to the office.

Q. Did you have any further contact with the man?

A. No, I later found out his name was Chester Hines.

Q. Did the police arrive before you left the accident scene?

A. Yeah, a state trooper arrived just as we were pulling him from the car, Officer Bob Schwartz.

Q. Did you have a conversation with Officer Schwartz at that time?

A. He just asked if we needed help. We told him we could manage. I also told him what the guy had said about the steering wheel locking.

Q. How long did it take you to reach the accident scene after you received the call from the passing motorist?

A. Five to ten minutes.

Q. Anything further about the accident you would care to relate?

A. That's it.

Q. I have no further questions.

Mr. Thomas (attorney for plaintiff): I have nothing.

* * *

Document 6

POLICE REPORT

Date of Collision: 1 16 10 | Day of Collision: T | Time (use 2400 hours): 8:42 | County: Clay

[DOCUMENT 6]

4 Miles N of North Street ON Old State 86

Non Intersection — Between: See above

Distance & Direction from Reference: 4 Miles W of North Street

Collision Involved: Total No. of Vehicles [1] | No. Killed 1 | No. Injured

Object Struck: Tree on side of Old State 86 | Est. Damage $

UNIT NO. 1 — DRIVER

Field	Unit No. 1	Unit No. 2
Driver's Name (Last, First, Middle)	Hines Chester	No other unit
Street Address	601 Glenwood Lane	
City	Island	
Driver's License No. / State / Sex / Date of Birth	7342JL CAL / CAL / M / 6 23 79	
Codes: 3 Injury Class	A	
Nature of Injuries	Died 3-17-10	
Removed from Scene by	Ambulance	
Veh. Year	2010	
Make	Cheetah	
Style	2 Dr.	
Veh. Color	Grey	
License Plate No. / State	CL 4451 / CAL	
Vehicle Identification No.	5 2 J 7 1 5 B 3 2	
Registered Owner	Same as driver	
Est. Damage	$ Total	
Towed Away By	Johnson's Garage	

DIAGRAM OF COLLISION

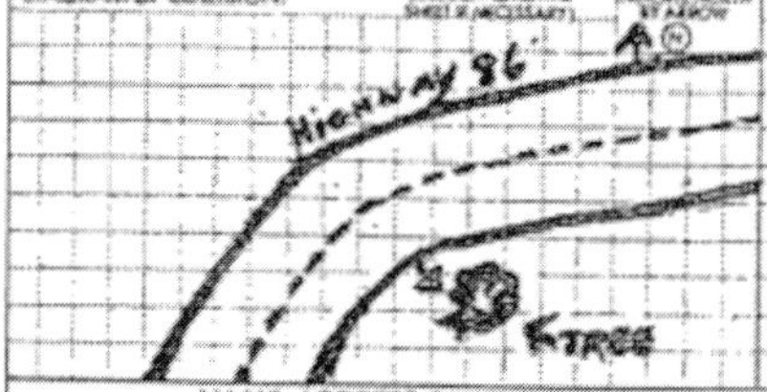

DESCRIPTION OF COLLISION

Car failed to come out of turn. Hit tree. Being taken from car by Rescue Squad when we arrived. No skid marks. Ambulance driver said driver complained of steering problems. Absence of skid marks confirms mechanical problems. Alcohol (Beer) present in front seat. Smell present, all bottles broke on impact.

NAME, ADDRESS & INJURIES OF PERSONS INVOLVED — OCCUPANTS / WITNESSES

Name	Address	Nature of Injuries	Sex	Age	Status	Seat Posit.	Inj. Class	Removed from Scene by
Chester Hines	601 Glenwood Lane, Island, CA	Died 3-17-10	M	41	1	Dr.	A	Amb.
No witnesses								

Investigating Officer's Name & Rank: X Robert S. Schwartz | Badge or I.D. No.: 12-11-41 | Date of Report: 3-16-10

Document 7

SUPPLEMENTAL POLICE REPORT

Supplemental Accident Report—Report #841. March 16, 2010

Island Police Department

March 17, 2010

When I arrived at accident scene, I looked into window in front seat of vehicle. Noticed beer bottles. All but one bottle was broken. Unbroken bottle was upright in carton. Lid was off and looked like it was half-full. Continued investigation outside of vehicle. Followed ambulance to hospital. Returned to accident scene at 9:30 a.m. Several persons loitering in area of vehicle. Asked them to leave and reached into the vehicle for the bottles. Verified original opinion that five of the bottles were broken and one unbroken with lid off. Bottle was less than one-half full. Assume bottle opened, and drunk from, prior to accident. Took bottle (12–oz. Budweiser) and brought to station. Locked in evidence locker, evidence No. MVA 6795. Bottle remains in locker pending disposition.

/s/ Robert Schwartz
Off. No. 12–1141

Document 8

JOHNSON STATEMENT

JOHNSON'S GARAGE FIRST AND MOUNTAIN
ROAD ISLAND, CALLICE

Statement of Edward G. Johnson

I am the owner of Johnson's Garage, First and Mountain Road in Island.

On March 16, our wrecker brought in a 2010 Cheetah that belonged to Chester Hines. Mr. Thomas, a lawyer, asked me to check the steering on the car. I found the steering locked in place. I took the car apart and looked at the mechanism. The mechanism had been damaged by the wreck so it was a little hard to tell whether the lock occurred before or after the collision. However, I don't think the collision really hurt the steering enough to lock it in place. I'd say there was better than a 75% chance that the lock occurred before impact.

I have been a mechanic for twenty-three years. I have worked on the steering of many cars including all models of Cheetah.

/s/ Edward G. Johnson

Witnessed:
/s/ Samuel Gray
[Investigator hired by attorneys for plaintiff]
4–3–2010

Document 9

DAVIS STATEMENT

September 16, 2010

My name is Francine Davis. I used to live at 603 Glenwood Lane, right next door to the Hines. We moved about a year ago. While living next door to the Hines, we noticed lots of times when there would be loud noises coming from the Hines house. They were yelling and screaming at each other. I'd say these fights would occur about once a week for the three years we lived there. One time, shortly before we moved, Linda Hines came to our back door and asked us to protect her. Her clothes were in disorder and she had several bruises on her face. She said her husband was drunk and was beating her up. She stayed with us that night. The next morning she had two blackeyes. They apparently made up because she went back home the next day without so much as a thank you to us. I saw Chester Hines staggering down the street drunk several times while I was living on Glenwood. He had a reputation in the neighborhood as a drunk.

I have read the above statement. It accurately sets forth what I told Mr. Ronald Watson and is in my own words.

/s/ Francine Davis
Francine Davis

Witnessed: /s/ Ronald Watson
Ronald Watson

Document 10

DEFENSE COUNSEL MEMORANDUM

Confidential Memorandum

(Defense counsel file only)

FROM: Edward Godfrey
TO: Jovita Flynn
RE: Hines v. National Motor Car—our file 2010–63

I have found out some interesting information, although I am not sure how we can use it. I spoke to Dr. Robert Hadler, a neurologist from Slant. Chester Hines had been seeing Hadler for several months prior to the accident. Hadler was reluctant to talk to me saying that the information he had was probably private. However, I kept pushing him and he finally agreed to talk. He is not too happy with Lindaia Hines because she apparently has not paid any of Chester's back bills.

Hadler says that Hines had been seeing him about instances in which he would black-out momentarily. Hines would apparently lose consciousness for a few seconds at a time. On one such occasion, he was driving a car. Fortunately, that time he wound up on the shoulder of the road without having a wreck. Hadler had Hines undergo numerous neurological tests, but found no abnormalities. Hadler knows that Hines had a drinking problem and believes that the incidents occurred when Hines was drunk. He does not believe there was anything wrong with Hines neurologically. Hines apparently saw no other doctor about his condition. The only records of Hines' medical history in this regard are in Hadler's office.

Hadler says that, if the court lets him, he would be more than glad to testify and bring his records into court.

EG
10/9/2010

Document 11

ANSWERS TO INTERROGATORIES

UNITED STATES DISTRICT COURT FOR THE
MIDDLE DISTRICT OF CALLICE

Civil Action, File Number 2010–C–715

LINDA HINES
as Administrator of the
Estate of Chester Hines   ANSWERS TO PLAINTIFF'S
v.   INTERROGATORIES
NATIONAL MOTOR COMPANY

Herman Ingram, as President of National Motor Company, on oath, responds to the interrogatories propounded by plaintiff as follows:

* * *

Interrogatory 16: Describe any changes in design with regard to the steering system or mechanism of the Cheetah which have occurred during the model years 2008, 2009, and 2010.

Answer: The steering system and mechanism have remained the same for 2008, 2009, and 2010 model Cheetahs.

* * *

Interrogatory 26: Set forth any instances in which National Motor Company has received information with regard to problems with the steering mechanism of the 2008, 2009 and 2010 model Cheetah automobiles.

Answer: Two complaints have been received by National with regard to the steering on Cheetahs. Both concerned the 2008 model Cheetah. They are as follows:

A. Mr. Irving Tannenbaum, 1578 Yellowstone Drive, New Orleans, Louisiana, wrote a letter dated October 15, 2009, complaining to us that his steering locked in place momentarily while he was driving his car on an interstate highway near his home. He stated that he was able to recover in time to avoid an accident. Our local dealer checked out the car, but found no problems. No further incidents have been reported by Mr. Tannenbaum.

B. Miss Theresa Rudolph, of Miami, Florida, the owner of a 2008 model Cheetah, was involved in a two car accident in February, 2009. She claims that the steering on her car locked in place. Miss Rudolph has filed an action in Florida against National based upon this incident, Dade County Court File 2009–C–6734.

* * *

Interrogatory 30: State whether the 2008, 2009, or 2010 model Cheetahs have ever been recalled from their owners for the purposes of correcting any problems in those automobiles.

Answer: All 2010 model Cheetahs were recalled, beginning May 7, 2010, for the purposes of checking and modifying their steering mechanisms.

* * *

APPENDIX B*

STATE V. WELL

■ ■ ■

Table of Contents

Document 1
DESCRIPTION OF CASE
STATE v. WELL

Following is the partial case file of the County Prosecutor of Clay County, State of Callice, in the case of State v. Well, a prosecution of Arnold Well for the murder in the first degree of his wife Mary Well on June 30, 2010.

The theory of the state is that the defendant forcibly drowned his wife in about two feet of water in a ditch alongside a country road. The state's case depends upon a variety of circumstantial evidence. The theory of the defense is that Mary was hit by a hit-and-run driver and thrown into the ditch. The defendant and others were unable to use emergency measures to prevent her death from drowning.

The defendant was not arrested until about two weeks after the death of his wife. The police officers involved had accepted his version of the

---

* Appendix B is used in Problems 7–4, 8–15, 8–16, 9–4, 10–8, 12–41, 12–57, 13–45, 14–18, 14–19, 14–39, 14–46, 14–65, and 15–23.

incident until they received the autopsy report. The alleged hit-and-run driver was never found.

Island, Red Lake, and Bendon are small cities in Clay County and Slant is a very large city which is the county seat of Clay County. All dates in the documents are during the same year unless otherwise indicated.

Document 2

STATEMENT OF ARNOLD WELL, JUNE 30, 2010

CLAY COUNTY DEPARTMENT OF PUBLIC SAFETY

STATEMENT

Case No. 10–46421   Date   June 30, 2010   Hours   2130

Taken at: Camel Hospital, Bendon

Statement of ARNOLD WELL, age 27, 442–7541

Address _____ Phone _____

Date of Birth _____ At _____

Occupation _____ Employer _____ Phone _____

Status _____

EXPLANATION OF MY CONSTITUTIONAL RIGHTS

Before questioning and making of any statement, I, ARNOLD WELL, have been advised by Trooper Sten Borne of the following rights:

1. I have the right to remain silent.

2. Any statement that I do make can and will be used as evidence against me in a court of law.

3. I have the right at this time to an attorney of my own choosing and to have him present before and during questioning and the making of any statement.

4. If I cannot afford an attorney, I am entitled to have an attorney appointed for me by a court without cost to me and to have him present before and during questioning and the making of any statement.

5. I further understand that I have the right to exercise any of the above rights at any time before or during any questioning and the making of any statement.

/s/ ARNOLD WELL

WAIVER OF CONSTITUTIONAL RIGHTS

I have read the above explanation of my constitutional rights, and I understand them. I have decided not to exercise these rights at this time.

The following statement is made by me freely and voluntarily and without threats or promises of any kind.

/s/ ARNOLD WELL

SIGNATURE

Witnesses: /s/ W.S. Yam, Trooper

I was driving s/b on the Island–Red Lake county road towards Red Lake with my wife, Mary, from our house in Island. We were going to look for blackberries along the road and I parked on the right side of the road just before a curve in the road with my car partly on the road because of the narrow shoulder. Mary and I got out. She walked along the same side of the road out ahead of the car and I walked along the same side of the road backwards from the car to find blackberry bushes. A car came past— a small grey two-door foreign car—the same direction in which my car was parked. I paid no attention to it when I heard a bang noise and my wife screamed. I ran up around the curve. Around the curve a ways she was lying in the ditch. I went and tried to pull her out of the ditch. She was face down in the water. I got her head out of the water and then ran back to a house I had seen back down the road to get help. A woman there said she would call the police and I ran back to where Mary was to give her first aid. When I got back to Mary I pulled her onto the roadway. I felt 2 pulses on her left wrist. I started to give her mouth to mouth. About that time this person (white male) grabbed me and started to wrestle with me. I told him I knew what I was doing and he said, "I've been a policeman and don't touch her." I didn't pay any attention and he started punching me in the face. About that time the State Patrol arrived. Q: What time did this accident happen? A: I don't wear a watch so I'm not sure, maybe 7:30. Q: How fast was the foreign car going? A: It was really speeding. When I got around the curve it was out of sight around another curve down the road. She must have been in the roadway as it came around the curve and grazed her. I tried to get her out of the ditch initially but I couldn't get her out. The only thing I could do was get her head out of the water. Earlier before we started I had 3 beers. That was around 6:30 or so. I didn't have anything after that. I wasn't taking drugs or smoking marijuana. The cigarette in the ashtray isn't my cigarette. It's probably been there 4 or 5 days. I don't smoke cigarettes. I do smoke pot but I wasn't smoking it tonight. The last time I smoked pot was May 1st. I never attempted to put Mary into the rear of my pickup. Why would I do that. I couldn't have gotten her in there anyway. I didn't pay no attention to the foreign car. It was a small grey two-door, maybe a Japanese car. I didn't notice the license number—had no reason to.

/s/ ARNOLD WELL

Document 3

REPORT OF TROOPER STEN BORNE

C.C. Case No. 10–46421

<u>Detective William Worn</u>   <u>Page 1</u> of 1   <u>July 5, 2010</u>
           To   Page   Date

Bill, this is a continuation of information for you.

I need to mention that when I first arrived at the scene I spoke to a bystander who was quite distraught. He was a heavy-set fellow, balding with a army unit tattoo on his right arm. He told me that he had come on the scene and observed "the husband wrestling with the lady." When the bystander asked him what he was doing, the husband replied that he was trying to give her artificial respiration. He said that the husband was doing it all wrong and that his method would "more likely choke the lady than revive her." When the husband wouldn't stop, an altercation occurred and the bystander said that he hit the husband on the jaw. He said he was about to administer CPR when the ambulance arrived. I arrived within about two minutes of the ambulance. I left the bystander after this brief conversation. When I looked for him about ten minutes later, I couldn't find him. Other bystanders told me that he and the lady he was with left. No one knew the individual. I have had no luck in tracing him. We may have lost this lead for good.

On Friday, June 30, 2010, while at Camel Hospital in Bendon with Arnold Well I took a statement from him. You presently have a copy of this statement. Immediately after completion of the statement Well all of a sudden stated, "Ok get it over with, take me in and book me or what ever it is you're going to do." I thought it a bit odd for him to blurt this out so I asked him if that could be part of his statement; he said, "Yes," and then I asked him directly then and there, why he would make a statement like that. I asked him if he had something more to tell me that he hadn't previously stated. He hesitated for a moment and then stated "no, I've told you all there is to tell." Anyway, I did not add this to the written statement.

On Saturday, July 1, 2010, while at my residence, between Noon and 1300, I received a telephone call from Arnold Well while at my residence. He was concerned about the accident and asked me if he should go and talk to the parents of Mary. I advised him I didn't think this was the proper thing for him to do at this time. I told him I wouldn't do it if I were him but he could do what he wanted to. In the course of our conversation at least twice he wanted to know if he was going to be charged with anything or if he was in trouble. I assured him that if the accident had occurred as he had earlier stated that there was slim chance of his being charged with anything. I asked Well if they had gone blackberry picking before while they were married and he said yes.

On Monday evening, July 3, 2010, I had a telephone conversation with an attorney named Richard Roll, telephone 911–1212, Red Lake. Mr. Roll indicated he was representing Arnold Well and asked me some questions as to what my investigation revealed. I advised him that due to my activities of investigating other accidents, etc., that I had not arrived at any conclusions in my investigation of Well's case.

In answer to your question on the phone this morning, when I arrived at the scene where Mrs. Well was hurt, the demeanor of Mr. Well was unusual. He did not show the slightest interest in or concern for his wife, Mary.

Document 4

STATEMENT OF ARNOLD WELL, JULY 7

CLAY COUNTY DEPARTMENT OF PUBLIC SAFETY

STATEMENT

Case No.   10–46421   Date   July 7, 2010   Hours   1410 hrs.

Taken by   DELLAND WHITE

Statement of   ARNOLD WELL   Age: 27

Address   7224 S.W. 20th, Island   Phone: 442–7541

Date of Birth   July 7, 1983   At:

Occupation   STUDENT   Employer   NONE   Phone

Status MARRIED, MARY COINSTRA WELL

EXPLANATION OF MY CONSTITUTIONAL RIGHTS

Before questioning and making of any statement, I, ARNOLD WELL, have been advised by DET. WILLIAM WORN of the following rights:

1.   I have the right to remain silent.

2.   Any statement that I do make can and will be used as evidence against me in a court of law.

3.   I have the right at this time to an attorney of my own choosing and to have him present before and during questioning and the making of any statement.

4.   If I cannot afford an attorney, I am entitled to have an attorney appointed for me by a court without cost to me and to have him present before and during questioning and the making of any statement.

5.   I further understand that I have the right to exercise any of the above rights at any time before or during any questioning and the making of any statement.

/s/ ARNOLD WELL
SIGNATURE

WAIVER OF CONSTITUTIONAL RIGHTS

I have read the above explanation of my constitutional rights, and I understand them. I have decided not to exercise these rights at this time. The following statement is made by me freely and voluntarily and without threats or promises of any kind.

/s/ ARNOLD WELL
SIGNATURE

Witnesses: /s/Richard Roll

[This statement is similar to the first statement of Arnold Well dated June 30, 2010, except the remainder of the statement below which begins when Arnold saw Mary in the ditch.]

I saw Mary in the ditch face down and facing towards Island and she was panicking; she was kicking her legs and flapping her arms. I heard her take two big gasps of fluid, I jumped in the ditch to help her. I grabbed her by the back of her jeans and tried to pull her up the embankment, I was in the muck up to above my knees. I then pulled her by her arm and her hair. I kept trying to pull her out, she seemed waterlogged and I took a pulse reading on her and could feel a pulse and turned her head towards the road so that she would not get any more water. I could not get her out. So I ran back towards Island to the house I had seen and I saw a woman in the front yard and I yelled out that my wife was hit by a car and call the police. She said OK. I then left and ran back. After I got back I got down on my knees and tried to drag Mary out of the ditch, this was towards the road; I wanted to try to revive her. I leaned over her and picked her up by placing my arms around her stomach and duck-walking her up till my knees hit asphalt. I took a croatic pulse and got a small mimic; I then picked her up while standing up and took her to the back of the truck. My intentions, since nobody was there, were to get the water out of her. I did not know if the police had been called. I used the truck as a support by placing her back against the truck. At this time a car drove up, I saw it coming, I laid Mary down and put out my right arm and the individual stopped, the guy jumped out, this guy was a burly short type, with his wife. I told them I needed some help, he ran over and took her pulse; he said that she had slight pulse. He then told me to leave; I said no I'm an ex-medic; he said I'm an ex-trooper; I said well I am not going to leave. His wife walked up, was looking at the girl; he told her to get back to her car; for no cause at all the guy turned and smashed me and decked me a good one, he did not knock me out. At this time Mary's legs were out in the road and her head was towards the ditch. At the time that this guy said that she had a minimal pulse. The guy held me down by setting on my stomach and holding my hands. I was on the ground between my car and this guy's car, my head was towards Island. He was setting on me when the aid car arrived. They parked in front of my truck and brought a stretcher around to the back of my truck. When he let me up, I threatened him; I told him I was going to kill him, I then went to my truck to get a gun, the gun was not there. I was upset with him because he would not let me help with Mary. I had no intentions of assaulting him. I was upset with this guy because he did not give Mary any assistance. Just his wife tried. A patrol car arrived from Island. One of the officers from that car took me to Camel Hospital in Bendon. They took skull and mandible x-rays—they told me to return when the swelling went down for fracture x-rays. I was questioned by Officer Borne and another officer. I was given my rights and I told them I didn't want to talk without an attorney. I then changed my mind and gave them a statement; they showed me a hat that they said Mary was wearing and I told them that I didn't remember she had it. I do not remember her having the hat on at the time of the accident. On Tuesday my sister-in-law answered our phone and Trooper Borne left a message for me to call—I returned his call and he asked me if I intended to put Mary in the truck, I told him no. He then asked me about the assault between myself and the other person at the accident scene. He asked me if I was trying to assault the other person and I said no. He said something about the person having broken knuckles. On Wednesday I contacted my attorney, RICHARD ROLL.

I have read this statement that consists of ten pages and I find it to be true and correct to the best of my knowledge.

Signed: ARNOLD WELL

/s/RICHARD ROLL

Document 5
AUTOPSY REPORT, MARY COINSTRA WELL
OFFICE OF CLAY COUNTY MEDICAL EXAMINER

AUTOPSY REPORT*

M.E. Case #6332

DATE OF EXAMINATION:

1 July 2010, 1410h

IDENTIFICATION:

Tags accompanying the body.

CLOTHING:

1.   Wet brown pair of leather boots.
2.   Blue jeans.

---

* Prepared by and used with the permission of Dr. Donald T. Reay, M.D., King County Medical Examiner, King County, Washington.

3.   Two red socks.

4.   Multicolored bikini type panties.

5.   A blue windbreaker type jacket.

6.   Green sweater type shirt.

7.   Tan sweater type shirt.

Also on the body is adhesive tape around the wrist and tape and gauze over the left antecubital fossa.

BODY MARKS:

A small wart is noted on the right forearm; otherwise there are no scars or tattoos present. A pierced ear is present on the left while no piercing of the ear is noted on the right. There is a 1/2 x 1/4 inch brown hairy nevus on the right lower thigh, anterior in location 6 inches above the patella, and a 1–inch nevus of the left axilla.

EXTERNAL EXAMINATION:

A general description of the body is that of a normally developed average white female appearing of the recorded age of 27 years. The body measures 5 feet 8 inches in length and weighs 143 pounds in the clothed state. The preservation is good and there is no evidence of embalming. The lividity is developed over the posterior aspect of the body and is purple in color. Rigidity is likewise developed in all extremities. The body is of room temperature and has not been refrigerated. The hairline is normal and long brown hair is present. The eyebrows are brown and the body hair is normally distributed in an average female distribution. The scalp and ears are intact. The eyes are brown with bilateral conjunctival petechia. The nose contains mucous and the teeth are natural and in good repair. Otherwise the mouth contains scanty amounts of mucous. The breasts are symmetrical and unremarkable. The hands and feet likewise are unremarkable except for a few injuries to be described. The back demonstrates no areas of injury. The genitalia are those of a normal appearing female.

EXTERNAL EVIDENCE OF INJURY:

1.   Three 1 inch circular abrasions located over the left forehead.

2.   A one 1/2 inch oblique abrasion of the tip of the nose over the left nostril.

3.   A vertical linear abrasion of the left abdomen occupying an area 3 x 6 inches and on the average measuring 3 inches in length.

4.   Two 1/4 inch abrasions of the dorsum of the right hand.

5.   A circular abrasion over the right upper and lower chest wall (CRP).

6.   A faint 1 inch contusion over the xiphoid process.

7. Faint contusions 3/4 inch in maximal diameter just at the left of the midline, in the scalp and hair and located 41/2 inches above the left eye.

8. The left arm shows 3 needle puncture wounds in a cluster in the left antecubital fossa. A single puncture wound is noted over the antecubital fossa of the right arm.

9. Bilateral petechia of the conjunctiva are noted and these occur primarily on the lower aspects of the eyelids.

INTERNAL EXAMINATION:

The body is opened with the usual incision and the cavities are examined. Both the right and left pleural cavity contain the usual amount of fluid with no abnormalities noted. The remaining pericardial and peritoneal surfaces are smooth and glistening. The mediastinum and the retroperitoneum demonstrate no abnormalities.

INTERNAL EVIDENCE OF INJURY:

1. Two areas of contusion visible upon reflection of the scalp:

   a. A 1 inch in diameter contusion located 11/2 inches to the left of the midline and 2 inches above the left eye.

   b. A 1–1/2 inch in diameter and slightly irregular contusion of the left frontal scalp approximately 5 inches above the left eye. In addition a few petechia are noted within the galeal scalp. No further internal injuries are demonstrated.

ORGAN SYSTEMS

CARDIOVASCULAR SYSTEM:

The HEART weight is estimated at 180 grams. The coronary arteries are normally disposed without abnormalities. The myocardium is smooth and glistening with the usual appearance. The origins of the great vessels are unremarkable and the aorta throughout its course likewise demonstrates no lesions. The blood present in the vennela is mainly fluid.

RESPIRATORY SYSTEM:

The LARYNX, TRACHEA and BRONCHI contain rather thick mucous but no appreciable dirt is noted. The LUNGS are both heavy with the right lung weighing an estimated 700 grams and the left weighing an estimated 600 grams. The cut surface shows a rather prominent frothy congestion which is present in all lobes. The smaller bronchi likewise contain thick mucous. The vessels supplying the lungs are unremarkable and no emboli are demonstrated.

HEPATO–BILIARY SYSTEM:

The LIVER weight is an estimated 1200 grams and has a normal cut surface. The GALL BLADDER contains a small amount of green bile with no stones present.

LYMPHO–RETICULAR SYSTEM:

The SPLEEN has an estimated weight of 100 grams with no notable lesions. The THYMUS is atrophic and no notable changes are present in the lymph nodes.

URINARY SYSTEM:

The right and left KIDNEYS each has an estimated weight of 125 grams with the normal cut surface. The PELVIS, URETERS and VESSELS supplying the kidneys are unremarkable. The urinary BLADDER is empty.

GENITALIA:

The VAGINA is examined with a speculum and no abnormalities are identified. A nonparous cervix is present with a slight cervicitis. The endometrium is mildly hemorraghic. The tubes are unremarkable. The right ovary likewise demonstrates a normal appearance while a small pedunculated one cm. fibroma is present over the left ovary. Otherwise the cut surface of this ovary is unremarkable.

GASTO INTESTINAL TRACT:

The PHARYNX contains a small amount of mucous and in the ESOPHAGUS regurgitated food is noted. The STOMACH likewise contains 300 cc. of grey-brown fluid which is mushy with what appears to be identifiable mushrooms. The SMALL INTESTINE and LARGE INTESTINE are unremarkable and the APPENDIX is present.

ENDOCRINE:

The PITUITARY, THYROID and ADRENALS are demonstrated to have an unremarkable appearance as does the PANCREAS.

MUSCULO–SKELETAL SYSTEM:

No fractures are demonstrated and the bone marrow is unremarkable.

MISCELLANEOUS:

No other abnormalities are identified.

CENTRAL NERVOUS SYSTEM:

The injuries to the SCALP have been described. The calvarium is removed and examined in the usual fashion and no abnormalities are present. The dura is intact and the cerebrospinal fluid is clear. Both middle ears show no evidence of hemorrhage. The BRAIN has an estimated weight of 1350 grams and there is a general overall impression of edema. No hemorrhage is likewise noted. Likewise no contusions are demonstrated. The meninges are slightly congested but otherwise unremarkable. The vessels at the base of the brain are normally disposed. The portion of the SPINAL CORD examined in situ shows no lesions and there is abnormal mobility of the A–O joint. Serial sections of the brain show the cerebrum, mid-brain, pons, medulla, cerebellum demonstrate the usual anatomical landmarks without abnormalities.

MICROSCOPIC EXAMINATION:

1. Sections of the lungs show a hemorrhagic type pulmonary edema with many of the small bronchi containing foreign debris in which diatoms are identified. In addition some of the bronchi likewise show focal aspirated skeletal muscle fibers.

2. Kidneys: congestion.

3. Heart: normal.

4. Endometrium: proliferative type.

5. Ovary: small leiomyoma otherwise unremarkable.

6. Adrenals: congestion.

7. Pancreas: congestion.

8. Brain: congestion.

9. Liver: congestion.

PATHOLOGICAL DIAGNOSES:

1. Asphyxia due to drowning with

     a. aspirated foreign material containing diatoms:

     b. petechia of the conjunctiva and galea;

     c. generalized visceral congestion with hemorrhagic pulmonary edema.

2. Numerous abrasions and faint contusions of the head and trunk.

3. Needle puncture wounds bilaterally of the arms and circular abrasions of the precordium (cardio-respiratory resuscitation).

4. Small leiomyoma of the left ovary.

OPINION:

This twenty-seven-year-old, white female came to her death as a result of asphyxia due to drowning. No evidence that subject was struck or grazed by an automobile.

TOXICOLOGY REPORT:

Blood alcohol: 60 mgs. %

Blood barbiturate (Phenobarbital): .96 mgs. %

Blood group: A

/s/ James Tarner, M.D.
James Tarner, M.D.
Medical Examiner
Clay County

Document 6
LETTER OF MAY 22

May 22, 2010

Dear Arnie:

I've been thinking. Instead of fighting like we usually do when I get back from this visit to my sister we ought to sit down and work out all our problems. Lets do that. I was reading an article and it tells how to do it. Lots of people worse off then us have done it, it said. When you get back you can read it. We just don't have to be horrible to each other all the time.

Mary

[Letter obtained in legal search of Arnold Well's home after his arrest.]

Document 7

CLAY COUNTY PROSECUTOR'S OFFICE
INTEROFFICE MEMORANDUM

To: Donald Q. Lem, Senior Deputy
From: Len M. Carmikel Case No. 10–46421
Date: July 16, 2010

Lester Caren, a local attorney with offices at 2142–45 in the Slant First National Bank Building, called me today, saying he had read in the paper about the arrest of Arnold Well on a homicide charge. He said after much thought and consultation with three prominent criminal defense attorneys and an ex-judge of the local Circuit Court he thought he should call me and tell me that on May 15, 2010, Arnold had consulted him, saying he had an interest in a business operated by another person and that he had not reported his income from that business (for the last tax year) in his federal income tax return which was filed April 15 and that he did not intend to report such income for the last tax year (ever). Arnold wanted to know what would happen to him if the IRS found out about such failure to report, saying in addition that he made a mistake and told his wife about his intention and she was insisting that he report the above-mentioned income. Arnold also consulted him about getting a divorce from Mary but at the end of such consultation Arnold said he thought the financial difficulties of getting a divorce would brunt his financial situation too much. However, Lester also stated that if he were asked to make any written statement or testify in any proceeding he would feel compelled to refuse to testify on the ground of the attorney client privilege.

Len M. Carmikel
Deputy County Attorney

Document 8

CLAY COUNTY PROSECUTOR'S OFFICE
INTEROFFICE MEMORANDUM

To: Memo for file Case No. 10–46421
From: _____
Date: July 18, 2010

     Attached is telephone bill of Arnold Well, seized in a search of the home of Arnold Well under a search warrant dated July 17, 2010, which is in the file. The telephone bill shows over $2,000 in long distance calls placed to a number in Guam. The telephone company house counsel has indicated by phone that the telephone company can procure a witness to testify how these bills are prepared and who can identify the bill as one of his company's bills. That witness could explain how computer printout is made and used for the bill. The house counsel, Jeffrey L. Journal, 987–2345, stated the local office would not have the name of the subscriber called in Guam as a special part of its local records, but just in case that was important, an employee could call the number listed in the attached bill and ask the person who answered who that person was. He has since informed me that was done and that the person who answered identified himself as Dick Dave. The employee could also identify a Guam telephone book which is kept in the local office as the telephone company's Guam telephone book, and which contains the number mentioned in the attached bill, and lists Richard R. Dave as the subscriber for that number.

/S/ Len M. Carmikel, Deputy County Attorney

TACONIC TELEPHONE CO.	Business Office Number 911 777–8402l	Date of Bill June 1, 2010	Total Due 2005.60	
			DATE PAYMENT DUE	
ARNOLD WELL	(911) 934–9876	881	June 15, 2010	
AMOUNT PREVIOUSLY BILLED			54.20	
CREDITS APPLIED SINCE LAST BILL 04/1/2010				
PAYMENT—THANK YOU			54.20	CR
BALANCE FROM PREVIOUS TWO MONTHS				.00
CURRENT TWO MONTHS' CHARGES				
TELEPHONE SERVICE AND EQUIPMENT				
FROM 03/21 to 05/21			12.50	
LONG DISTANCE CALLS—SEE DETAIL			2005.60	
EFFECT OF CITY TAX AT 4.8 PERCENT			.06	
U.S. TAX AT 2 PERCENT			40.34	
PLEASE PAY THIS AMOUNT BY JUNE 15		TOTAL DUE		2058.50

[Detail of long distance calls, all to number in Guam.]

Document 9

STATEMENT OF SALLY WATER, August 11

CLAY COUNTY DEPARTMENT OF PUBLIC SAFETY
ADDITIONAL INFORMATION SHEET

Case No.
10   46421

To _____   Via _____   Date   Time
8/11/10

From   Subject: Continuation of Officer's Report Regarding

DETECTIVE WILLIAM WORN STATEMENT OF SALLY WATER

Item:

My name is Sally Water. My age is 29 years. My residence is at 13940 E. Salt Street, Island, Callice 44054. I have lived there for about five years. I have lived in Slant all the rest of my life. I am a computer programmer for Stellar Corporation in Slant and have had that job for about five years, a little over five years.

Since I started my job at Stellar Corporation I have known another programmer in my department there, Mary Well. She lived in Island all that time. About six weeks ago she was killed in an automobile accident. She was then 27 years old.

Up until about three months before her death, Mary had a friend, Dick Dave. I know he was a friend because almost every Thursday for about four months, I drove her to Dick Dave's house from work and usually stopped for a short time for a coffee with her and Dick. Dick was always there when we came in. He usually kissed her when we came in. On these occasions I usually stayed from a half an hour to an hour and then left. Dick was always still there when I left.

About three months before Mary's death, Dick was transferred by his company to Guam. He was involved in some kind of government construction contract. Shortly after he left, Mary told me that each time I had taken her there she had stayed most of the night and maybe all night with him after I left. She said she was married and she might get hurt but she didn't care because maybe she would get a divorce. That is all she said about her husband. I do not know anything else about her relations with Dick because she never talked about it and except when she made the remark that she stayed overnight with him when I had taken her to Dick's on Thursdays, she was very close-mouthed about it all. I rarely saw her otherwise, other than on work hours, during the months I drove her to Dick's or for the three months before she died.

/s/Sally Water

Document 10

REPORT CONCERNING POLYGRAPH EXAMINATION

CLAY COUNTY DEPARTMENT OF PUBLIC SAFETY
ADDITIONAL INFORMATION SHEET

Case No.
10   46421

To
DETECTIVE WILLIAM WORN   Via _____   Date   Time
                                          8/11/10   _____

From   Subject: Continuation of Officer's
                                      Report Regarding
TROOPER STEN BORNE   POLYGRAPH EXAMINATION
                                      GIVEN TO ARNOLD WELL

Item:

On Monday, July 7, 2010, commencing at 1:27 PM, ARNOLD WELL was present in the Clay County Polygraph Examination Room with Clay County Polygraphist TELL ALLEN. WELL'S attorney, RICHARD ROLL, and I were in an adjacent room looking into and listening to what was taking place. We were looking through a two way mirror. Mr. ALLEN and WELL were unable to observe us. However, we could see and hear them. In the pre-polygraph interview, Mr. ALLEN talked in casual conversation to ARNOLD WELL. After several minutes of casual conversation, Mr. ALLEN advised WELL of his Constitutional rights. They went through the statement that WELL had given to Detective WILLIAM WORN on July 7. They then discussed the statement that WELL gave to me at Camel Hospital on June 30. During their conversation about this statement, WELL stated, "The statement I gave to BORNE had some lies." When asked why he lied, WELL stated, "Because I was scared." Also in the course of their conversation, WELL indicated to Mr. ALLEN another story as to what actually occurred. WELL indicated several times (not responding to questions) that when he saw Mary in the ditch, face down in the water in the ditch, he did nothing, but first ran back to the house where he asked the woman to call the police and then ran back to try to get her out of the ditch and revive her. Later, Polygraphist TELL ALLEN told me that the polygraph test of ARNOLD WELL was inconclusive. He was not a subject who could be tested.

Document 11

CLAY COUNTY PROSECUTOR'S OFFICE
INTEROFFICE MEMORANDUM

To: _____
Memo for file   Case No. 10–46421

From: _____
Date: July 18, 2010

After interviewing Cal Coleman on August 12, 2010, he told me that Richard Roll, the attorney for defendant Well, wanted to talk to him. Cal asked me whether he should talk to Roll. He said he was afraid to have anything to do with Arnold Well or his attorney, even if Arnold was in jail. I told him I surely would not do so, but he could talk to Richard Roll if he wanted to. On August 13, 2010, Richard Roll called me and said he had tried to interview Cal, but that Cal had refused to talk to him, saying I had told Cal not to talk to him. I told Roll that I had said to Cal that when he asked if he should talk to Roll that I surely would not do so but that he (Cal) could do so if he wished. I told Roll I would telephone Cal that day and give him that message again. Roll protested that I should just tell Cal to talk to him (Roll). That day I called Cal Coleman and told him exactly what I said at the end of our interview as recounted above, after telling him that Roll had called me about Cal's refusal to talk to Roll. On August 15, 2010, Richard Roll called me again and said Cal still refused to talk to him (Roll). I told Roll exactly what I had told Cal in the above-mentioned telephone call and I told Roll I thought that was all I should do.

Donald Q. Lem
Senior Deputy Prosecuting Attorney

Document 12

DEPOSITION OF CARY ALLWORTH

CIRCUIT COURT OF THE STATE OF CALLICE
IN AND FOR CLAY COUNTY

State of Callice   )
     v.   )   Deposition of Cary Allworth
Arnold Well   )

State of Callice   )
)   ss.
County of Clay   )

Deposition of Cary Allworth, a witness, taken before me in my office at 3030 4th Avenue in the City of Slant in said county on the 18th day of

August 2010, pursuant to the annexed order of court, the annexed notice on the part of the State of Callice and the annexed subpoena in the above-entitled action now pending in the Circuit Court of the State of Callice in and for Clay County, in which Arnold Well is charged with the murder in the first degree of Mary Well.

The witness being first duly sworn by me to testify to the truth, the whole truth and nothing but the truth relative to the above-entitled action in answer to oral interrogatories propounded by Len M. Carmikel, Deputy Prosecutor for the State of Callice, County of Clay, who appeared for the State of Callice, Richard Roll appearing as attorney for Arnold Well, deposed and made answer as follows:

Question: Please state your name, age and residence.

Answer: My name is Cary Allworth, my age is 28 years, and my residence is at 7171 E. 4th Street, Slant, Callice 44058.

Question: What is your occupation?

Answer: I am an assistant traffic manager at the Eastside Slant office of the Taconic Telephone Co.

Question: Very shortly, what does that mean?

Answer: I am in charge of 25 telephone operators and handle any problems that arise in their work. That is on the day shift.

Question: Do you fully understand that you are testifying under oath and are obligated to tell the truth in answer to my questions and any questions that Mr. Roll here, the attorney for the defendant in the instant case, may ask you later?

Answer: Yes, I do.

Question: Have you been acquainted with Mary Well, that is, Mrs. Arnold Well, in the past?

Answer: Yes, for a long time.

Question: And you know she is now deceased?

Answer: Yes.

Question: What has been your general relation with her?

Answer: We have been friends for about ten years.

> [Questions and answers describing the relation between the witness and Mary Well, knowledge on her part of Mary's marriage to Arnold Well and incidents in their married life of which she had knowledge are omitted at this point.]

Question: When did you see her last before she died?

Answer: On June 28, 2010 at about 7 p.m. at my house.

Question: That was about two days before she died?

Answer: Yes.

Question: How long was she at your house?

Answer: About 10 minutes.

Question: Why was she there?

Answer: She said she just had to tell somebody something, and wanted to stop by.

Question: After she came into your home did she tell you anything?

Answer: Yes.

Question: What was it about? MR. ROLL: Now she is going to repeat a hearsay statement. I object.

Answer: About Arnold Well, her husband.

Question: What did she say about him? MR. ROLL: That question clearly calls for hearsay and I object. This is nothing to take on a deposition. It should not be allowed.

Answer: She said she had a terrible argument with Arnold the night before and he told her he was really going to hurt her if she opened her mouth for a whole week. She started to say something, and he then yelled at her he was going to kill her in the next day or two anyway if he didn't get to feeling better about her. She said she believed him this time, that she was real scared and that she didn't know what to do. She started to shake. MR. ROLL: Taking this on deposition should not be allowed. It's all irrelevant too. It can never be used. I am going to take it to court and have it stricken as soon as this is over. MR. CARMIKEL: You can make all your objections later.

Question: Did she say anything more along those lines?

Answer: No she did not.

Question: Did you say anything to her about that matter?

Answer: No.

Question: Why not?

Answer: She then said she had to rush off to get home before Arnold got there, and she left.

Question: Did you have any further contact with her before she died?

Answer: No.

Answer MR. CARMIKEL: Your witness, Mr. Roll. MR. ROLL: No questions, none of this can be used. The remarks are all hearsay and none of it is relevant.

Signed: _____
Cary Allworth

[Proper certificate of notary public before whom the deposition was taken; and notation that copy signed by the witness had been filed with the court clerk.]

[Annexed order of court, annexed notice and annexed subpoena omitted.]

[Criminal rules of procedure of the state of Callice provide for the taking of depositions authorized by court order and provide for the use of depositions taken and for objections to admissibility as follows: (The federal rules of civil procedure were copied in the state)

"(d) Use. At the trial or upon any hearing, a part or all of a deposition so far as otherwise admissible under the rules of evidence may be used if it appears: that the witness is dead; or that the witness is unavailable, unless it appears that his unavailability was procured by the party offering the deposition; or that the witness is unable to attend or testify because of sickness or infirmity; or that the party offering the deposition has been unable to procure the attendance of the witness by subpoena. Any deposition may also be used by any party for the purpose of contradicting or impeaching the testimony of the deponent as a witness."

"(e) Objections to Admissibility. Objections to receiving in evidence a deposition or part thereof may be made as provided in civil actions."]

[A death certificate for Cary Allworth, dated after the date of the above transcript is attached to the above transcript.]

Document 13

STATEMENT OF CAL COLEMAN

CLAY COUNTY DEPARTMENT OF PUBLIC SAFETY
ADDITIONAL INFORMATION SHEET

Case No.
10   46421

DETECTIVE WILLIAM WORN STATEMENT OF CAL COLEMAN
Item:

I, CAL COLEMAN, have known ARNOLD WELL for a long time and we have been good friends off and on. Because of things for a while, he isn't a friend now as far as I am concerned. Around May, 15, 2010, we were down at the Illegit Tavern drinking beer. He knew my wife and me don't get along too well. He got to talking about his fights with his wife, Mary, how he knew she was running out on him, and a bunch of stuff like that. Then he had the guts to make me a proposition. He said he was desperate about it so he said he would like to work out a plan with me that if I would do away with his wife, Mary, he would if I wanted him to do away with my wife as a return favor to me. So I asked him just how would we ever do that. He said well I have couple of ideas about how that can be done out in the country, but first I had to agree to do it. I said I did not want to hear another thing about it. I said maybe I didn't like Helen so well, but after all I could just leave her. Divorce was good enough for me. About 15 minutes later he repeated the same idea, and I told him he must be crazy and drop it. We talked some more about basketball teams and stuff like that and suddenly he said he must be crazy because two years before he had robbed the Imperial Bank in town and never got caught, that he was crazy like a fox. I told him he didn't have the guts. He says where do you think I got the money to buy my BMW two years ago? I said he better shut up about it now and forever, that I never heard him say any such thing. Anyway I can't stand the guy for a long time now. I don't want anything to do with stuff like that. In answer to your question I would be willing to testify about these here things, you bet I would.

In answer to your question whether I have seen ARNOLD WELL since Monday, June 30, 2010, yes I have, in the Illegit Tavern on Tuesday, the day afterward. I wandered in there and he was drinking a glass of beer with Howard Hales, so I sat down there. Anyways Howard told Arnie he had heard about Mary's accident and how did Arnie feel alone now? He said great but maybe the police was interested in him, but they didn't really seem to be. Howard says why should they be? Then he said, well I want to make sure so I guess maybe I will think of a way to do away with Dorothy Phillips, who lives down the block and hangs around the tavern a lot. You know that dizzy dame. Then the cops will think there is a crazy loose. I told him why do you keep up with these crazy put-ons and he said they were not put-ons. He said he knew a way. I do not know what Howard would say but he was there and you can check it all if you want.

/s/ CAL COLEMAN

Document 14

LETTER AND CRIMINAL HISTORY OF CAL COLEMAN

City of Slant

DEPARTMENT OF PUBLIC SAFETY

Records Division

Date: _____

Detective William Worn

Clay County Department of Public Safety

Clay County Court House

Slant, Callice 44755

Dear Detective William Worn:

By this hand delivered letter I am forwarding the attached Criminal History of COLEMAN, CAL, of 455 Callo St., Island, Callice, dated August 1, 2010, as it appears in our files.

Bora Colin
Chief Clerk
Records Division

City of Slant, Department of Public Safety
Criminal History of COLEMAN, CAL

Date   August 1, 2010
Date of Birth   September 2, 1981

Name and Address	C.B.No.	Date of Arrest	Arr.Off.	Charge	Disposition
Cal Coleman	2802241	Sept. 8, 1997	Janis, 4th Dist. Theft † 2 years (on Oct. 8, 2007) Probation, Judge Jarn		
Cal Coleman	2977329	May 3, 2007	Molrad, 5th Dist. DWL–suspended 6 mos. ‡ (on June 21, 2007) Probation, Judge Alen		

Document 15

JUDGMENT AND SENTENCE, IN THE CIRCUIT COURT OF THE STATE OF CALLICE

For the County of Clay

THE STATE OF CALLICE   )
         Plaintiff   )   No. 04732
       v.   )   JUDGMENT AND SENTENCE
ARNOLD WELL   )
         Defendant   )

    The Prosecuting Attorney, the above-named defendant and counsel DENICE DELLEN came into court. The defendant was duly informed by the Court of the nature of the _____ information found against him for the crime(s) of obscuring the identity of a machine by knowingly possessing a vehicle held for sale knowing that the serial number or other identification number or mark has been obscured contrary to Callice Code § 7.432.541§ of his arraignment and plea of "not guilty of the offense charged in the _____ information," of his trial and the verdict of the jury/finding of the court on the 4th day of November, 1996, "guilty of obscuring the identity of a machine by knowingly possessing a vehicle held for sale knowing that the serial number or other identification number or mark has been obscured."

    The Court having determined that no legal cause exists to show why judgment should not be pronounced, it is therefore ORDERED, ADJUDGED and DECREED that the said Defendant is guilty of the crime(s) of obscuring the identity of a machine by knowingly possessing a vehicle held for sale knowing that the serial number or other identification

---

† Shoplifting

‡ Driving without a license while license had been suspended, punishable by a fine or imprisonment for less than one year.

§ The state crime is a misdemeanor punishable by imprisonment for less than one year.

number or mark has been obscured contrary to Callice Code § 7.432.541 and that the defendant be sentenced to imprisonment in the Clay County Jail for a maximum of six months.

This sentence is hereby SUSPENDED pursuant to the provision of Callice Code § 7.493.231 upon the following terms and conditions:

(1) The Defendant shall be under the charge of a Clay County probation and Parole Officer employed by the Department of Social and Health Services, and follow implicitly the instructions of said Department, and the rules and regulations promulgated by said Department for the conduct of the Defendant during the term of his probation hereunder.

(2) The termination date of probation shall be set at 6 months from date of this order.

(3) The defendant shall not commit any law violations.

(4) The Defendant shall pay all costs, within 60 days from date of this order.

(5) The Defendant shall serve a term of 6 months in Clay County Jail if the defendant shall violate the above terms and conditions.

DONE IN OPEN COURT this 4th day of November, 2006.

/s/JOHN HANTA
Judge

Presented by:
Deputy Prosecuting Attorney

†